828.1 MCL

STRELSY, AND THE
OMANTIC POETRY

This is a new history and theory of British poetry between 1760 and 1830, focusing on the relationship between Romantic poetry and the production, circulation, and textuality of ballads. By discussing the ways in which eighteenth-century cultural and literary researches flowed into and shaped key canonical works, Maureen McLane argues that Romantic poetry's influences went far beyond the merely literary. Breathing new life into the work of eighteenth-century balladeers and antiquarians, she addresses the revival of the ballad, the figure of the minstrel, and the prevalence of a "minstrelsy complex" in Romanticism. Furthermore, she envisages a new way of engaging with Romantic poetics, encompassing both "oral" and "literary" modes of poetic construction, and anticipates the role that technology might play in a media-driven twenty-first century. The study will be of great interest to scholars and students of Romantic poetry, literature, and culture.

MAUREEN N. McLANE is Associate Professor of English at New York University. She is the author of *Romanticism and the Human Sciences: Poetry, Population, and the Discourse of the Species* (Cambridge, 2000), and co-editor, with James Chandler, of *The Cambridge Companion to British Romantic Poetry* (Cambridge, 2008). She is also the author of *Same Life: Poems* (2008).

WITHDRAWN FROM LIBRARY STOCK

CAMBRIDGE STUDIES IN ROMANTICISM

Founding editor
Professor Marilyn Butler, *University of Oxford*

General editor
Professor James Chandler, *University of Chicago*

Editorial board
John Barrell, *University of York*
Paul Hamilton, *University of London*
Mary Jacobus, *University of Cambridge*
Kenneth Johnston, *Indiana University*
Alan Liu, *University of California, Santa Barbara*
Jerome McGann, *University of Virginia*
David Simpson, *University of California, Davis*

This series aims to foster the best new work in one of the most challenging fields within English literary studies. From the early 1780s to the early 1830s a formidable array of talented men and women took to literary composition, not just in poetry, which some of them famously transformed, but in many modes of writing. The expansion of publishing created new opportunities for writers, and the political stakes of what they wrote were raised again by what Wordsworth called those "great national events" that were "almost daily taking place": the French Revolution, the Napoleonic and American wars, urbanization, industrialization, religious revival, an expanded empire abroad and the reform movemement at home. This was an enormous ambition, even when it pretended otherwise. The relations between science, philosophy, religion and literature were reworked in texts such as *Frankenstein* and *Biographia Literaria*: gender relations in *A Vindication of the Rights of Woman* and *Don Juan*: journalism by Cobbett and Hazlitt: poetic form, content and style by the Lake School and the Cockney School. Outside Shakespeare studies, probably no body of writing has produced such a wealth of response or done so much to shape the responses of modern criticism. This indeed is the period that saw the emergence of those nations of "literature" and of literary history, especially national literary history, on which modern scholarship in English has been founded.

The categories produced by Romanticism have also been challenged by recent historicist arguments. The task of the series is to engage both with a challenging corpus of Romantic writings and with the changing field of criticism they have helped to shape. As with other literary series published by Cambridge, this one will represent the work of both younger and more established scholars, on either side of the Atlantic and elsewhere.

[For a complete list of titles published, see end of book.]

BALLADEERING, MINSTRELSY, AND THE MAKING OF BRITISH ROMANTIC POETRY

MAUREEN N. McLANE

CAMBRIDGE
UNIVERSITY PRESS

CAMBRIDGE UNIVERSITY PRESS
Cambridge, New York, Melbourne, Madrid, Cape Town,
Singapore, São Paulo, Delhi, Tokyo, Mexico City

Cambridge University Press
The Edinburgh Building, Cambridge CB2 8RU, UK

Published in the United States of America by Cambridge University Press, New York

www.cambridge.org
Information on this title: www.cambridge.org/9780521349505

© Maureen N. McLane 2008

This publication is in copyright. Subject to statutory exception
and to the provisions of relevant collective licensing agreements,
no reproduction of any part may take place without the written
permission of Cambridge University Press.

First published 2008
First paperback edition 2011

A catalogue record for this publication is available from the British Library

Library of Congress Cataloguing in Publication data
McLane, Maureen N.
Balladeering, minstrelsy, and the making of British
romantic poetry / Maureen N. McLane.
p.   cm.
(Cambridge studies in romanticism)
Includes bibliographical references and index.
ISBN 978-0-521-89576-7
1. English poetry – 18th century – History and criticism.   2. English poetry – 19th century – History
and criticism.   3. Romanticism – Great Britain.   4. Ballads, English – Great Britain – History
and criticism.   5. Ballads in literature.   6. Minstrels in literature.   1. Title.
PR590.M42   2008
821′.709145–dc22
2008037117

ISBN 978-0-521-89576-7 Hardback
ISBN 978-0-521-34950-5 Paperback

Cambridge University Press has no responsibility for the persistence or
accuracy of URLs for external or third-party internet websites referred to in
this publication, and does not guarantee that any content on such websites is,
or will remain, accurate or appropriate.

... Fled is that music ...?
                  – John Keats, "Ode to a Nightingale"

... inside the constant repatterning of a thing ...
                  – Jorie Graham, "The Dream of the Unified Field"

Contents

Illustrations

Acknowledgments

This book has been long and sometimes arduous in the thinking and writing but thankfully often pleasurable in the discussing, thanks to the wonderful company it encouraged me to seek and keep. Penny Fielding, Kevis Goodman, Celeste Langan, Susan Manning, Ruth Perry, and Ann Wierda Rowland have been for years the most engaging and stimulating interlocutors one could wish for: as will become clear, this book is indebted to their work. Every page they saw is better for their having read it, and their friendship has sustained me as well as this project. Ian Duncan, Theresa Kelley, and Michael Macovski offered me timely, generous opportunities to present work-in-progress; I am grateful as well to James Chandler for his energizing conversation and his scrupulous reading of the completed manuscript. The Society of Fellows at Harvard provided the ways and means for the launch of this project; MIT's Committee on Media Studies supported its development, as did the University of Edinburgh's Institute for Advanced Studies in the Humanities; and the companionable crew of the Committee on History and Literature at Harvard witnessed its completion. I am grateful to the colleagues and students I had throughout this sojourn: their conversation and work informed this book in ways that may surprise them.

Throughout the writing of this book I had the benefit of the historical expertise, as well as the dear friendship, of Durba Ghosh and T. Robert Travers. So too Erika Naginski brought her profound knowledge of eighteenth- and nineteenth-century European culture to our ongoing conversations, and godson Sebastien Naginski in his bilingual excellence has encouraged me to pursue French balladry in the future. Amanda Gable, Ross Halbert, Margaret Harrison, and Chitra Ramalingam helped me haunt the stacks and archives; Molly Hester explored ballad scholarship with me. Poet Tom Pickard gave hope that the book might not be headed for the antiquarian dustbin – at least not yet. At a crucial moment, Peter Sacks offered thoughtful encouragement, as did Susan Stewart and Katie

Trumpener. Jorie Graham graciously gave me permission to quote from "The Dream of a Unified Field" for one of my epigraphs.

While preparing this book for publication, I have had once again the benefit of editor Linda Bree's counsel: she has shepherded this book through every stage, for which I am grateful, as I am for Elizabeth Noden's expert attention and extraordinary support, Rosina Di Marzo's crucial assistance in production, Penny Wheeler's scrupulous copy-editing, and Maartje Scheltens' care. The two anonymous readers for Cambridge University Press wrote incisive, enormously helpful reports on the manuscript: perhaps only they and I can know how much their responses transformed this book (albeit perhaps not in every instance as they would have liked!). I owe thanks as well to the tireless efforts of those librarians, curators, and archivists who provided vital assistance en route: especial thanks to Josie Lister and The Bodleian Library, Oxford; Robin McElheny and the Harvard University Archives; Ashley Reed and The William Blake Archive; and Kevin LaVine and the Library of Congress, Music Division. Early versions of Chapters 1 and 4 appeared in, respectively, *The Eighteenth Century: Theory and Interpretation* 47:2/3 (Summer/Fall 2006) and *Critical Inquiry* 29.3 (Spring 2003); I am grateful to the editors there and to the editors of *European Romantic Review, Modern Philology*, and *Oral Tradition* for publishing material which flowed into the broader currents of this book.

This book is in part a long meditation on the situation of poetry, and of poets; my own situation was incalculably enriched by the conviviality and conversation of those already mentioned, and by that of Daniel Aaron, Shahab Ahmed, Danielle Allen, Ed Barrett, Sara Bershtel, Jonathan Bolton, Celia Brickman, Mary Ellen Brown, Robin Brown, Claire Connolly, Beverly Corbett, William Corbett, Marcia Dambry, Leith Davis, Fiona Doetsch, Jeff Dolven, Dianne Dugaw, Jonathan Elmer, Mary Favret, Noah Feldman, Susannah French, Michael Gordin, Robert von Hallberg, Sonia Hofkosh, Fanny Howe, Amy Johnson, Robert Kaufman, Bruce King, August Kleinzahler, Emily Lyle, Peter Manning, Barry Mazur, Gretchen Mazur, Askold Melnyczuk, Diana Morse, Brighde Mullins, Gregory Nagy, Victoria Olwell, Katie Peterson, Leah Price, Howard Purdie, Emma Rothschild, William St. Clair, Elaine Scarry, Julia Targ, Elizabeth Taylor, William Todd, Mirka Zusi, and Peter Zusi. My unwritten chapter on drinking songs is dedicated to them and to the buoying spirit of their fellowship: their company has offered, as Burns put it, a "darling walk for my mind." Carole Slatkin's support throughout has been a mainstay and a gift. I would also like to thank my parents, Michael and Beth McLane, and my siblings and their partners – Michael and Meredith McLane, Colleen and Micheal Mullen – for their steadfast interest in this work and where it's led me; Darcy and Bridget McLane and Liam Mullen have reminded me of the pleasures of absorption and transmission, poetic and otherwise. On another front, the complete lack of interest in this project shown by my cats Bopr and Biscuit offered its own peculiar solace: they continually reminded me that there are other ways to vocalize than speech or song.

No one knows better than Laura Slatkin where this book comes from and how it has developed. Given her profound engagement with this project, I have had occasion to worry that she, even more than I, "suffered what I wrote, or viler pain!," in the words of Shelley's Rousseau. Small and perhaps perverse recompense then to write that this book is for her.

Introduction: Poetry Bound

> An edge of song that never clears.
>   – Wallace Stevens, "Country Words"[1]
>
> A single text, granite monotony
>   – Wallace Stevens, "Notes Toward a Supreme Fiction"[2]
>
> As if her song could have no ending.
>   – William Wordsworth, "The Solitary Reaper"[3]
>
> A mountainous music always seemed
> To be falling and to be passing away.
>   – Wallace Stevens, "The Man with the Blue Guitar"[4]
>
> The song goes on longer than we expect
> because it is from another culture: collected,
> as it were.
>   – Rebecca Wolff, "Good enough for folk music"[5]

This book stations itself, sometimes uneasily, between Stevens' "edge of song" and a poem's possible "single text, granite monotony" – between a poetics of evanescence and one of artifactualization, between words and tones ever "passing away" and those that get "collected, as it were," in Rebecca Wolff's wry phrase. This book thus reflects a complex haunting by "romantic intonings," in Stevens' words, by the ongoing marks, tracks, and sounds of poems, their dispersal and their collection, their composition, transmission, and theorization.

---

[1] Wallace Stevens, "Country Words," l.8, in *The Collected Poems of Wallace Stevens* (New York: Vintage, 1982), 207.
[2] Stevens, from "It Must Change" (VI), in "Notes toward A Supreme Fiction," *Collected Poems*, 394.
[3] William Wordsworth, "The Solitary Reaper," l. 26, *Poems, in Two Volumes, and Other Poems, 1800–1807, by William Wordsworth*, ed. Jared Curtis (Ithaca: Cornell University Press, 1983), 185.
[4] Stevens, "The Man With the Blue Guitar" (XXVI, ll. 11–12), *Collected Poems*, 179.
[5] Rebecca Wolff, *Figment* (New York: W. W. Norton, 2004), 86.

This project has given me ample opportunity to ponder the relation of poetry to the production of cultural goods, not least scholarship. Its questions arise out of my previous work on Romantic and contemporary poetry, ongoing discussion with friends and colleagues about the interface of history and literature, and a desire to explore further the many workings of *poiesis*: the relation of literary poetry to phantasized or "collected" orality, for example, or the use of poetry as evidence in cultural or historical argument. Late twentieth-century North American poetry and poetics offer many examples of such poetic–cultural work (see, for example, the Black Arts Movement; the rise of "ethno-poetics"; the efflorescence of poetry slams and spoken word art); so too, in another key, do British poetries and discourse on poetry in the late eighteenth and early nineteenth centuries.[6]

Some years ago while I was staying in London, the proprietor of the guest house, Miss St. Clair, asked me what the book I was then writing was about.[7] When I told her the book contained essays on British Romantic poetry, she looked askance, though indulgent: how curious, she made plain, that I should devote myself to a foreign poetry. Miss St. Clair offered me a clarifying estrangement: for truly, though I often read Wordsworth, Blake, Shelley et al. as "my" poets, or as offering a "natural and inalienable inheritance" (as Wordsworth put it),[8] one could also rightly say with Rebecca Wolff that part of the force of British Romanticism for a twenty-first-century American is that "it is from another culture." Or perhaps it is better to say that working on late eighteenth- and early nineteenth-century British poetries involves a constant calibration of proximity and distance: what looks like "familiar matter of today," as Wordsworth put it in "The Solitary Reaper," may from another angle reveal itself to be quite strange, even ultimately inaccessible – whether for temporal, linguistic, cultural, epistemological, or other reasons. Such strangeness sometimes lodges itself within the heart of *poiesis*, for example in Homer's incorporation of words whose sense had long been obscure even by the time of Homeric composition; or in

---

[6] For a recent effort to place historically and culturally disparate oral poetries and performance traditions in conversation, see John Miles Foley, *How to Read an Oral Poem* (Urbana: University of Illinois Press, 2002), which offers four case studies for recurrent, comparative analysis: a Nuyorican Slam poet, a Serbian epic singer, Homer, and the Beowulf-poet. See too Ruth Finnegan's comparative survey, *Oral Poetry: Its Nature, Significance, and Social Context* (Bloomington and Indianapolis: Indiana University Press, 1992), with its discussion of British and American balladry alongside other oral poetries, and Ch. 5 for her theorization of performance styles and modes of transmission.

[7] That book became *Romanticism and the Human Sciences: Poetry, Population, and the Discourse of the Species* (Cambridge University Press, 2000; paperback edn. 2006).

[8] William Wordsworth, Preface to the *Lyrical Ballads*, Additions of 1802, in Wordsworth and Coleridge, *Lyrical Ballads*, ed. R. L. Brett and A. R. Jones, 2nd edn. (London and New York: Routledge, 1991), 259.

Wordsworth's question, regarding the Highland reaper whose Gaelic song enthralls but also mystifies him: "Will no one tell me what she sings?"; or in Wolff's mordant observation about the duration of song, which "goes on longer than we expect/because it is from another culture."

So the past, along with the poetry of the past, is another country, and so is Britain for the American, and Scotland for the English, and the Scottish Highlands for the Borderers, and so on. It is striking that these matters of historical and cultural difference not only conditioned late eighteenth- and early nineteenth-century writing: such problematics lodged themselves within the heart of *poiesis*, as this book aims to demonstrate.

When working on this project, I experienced another pointed and diagnostic moment of cultural estrangement. In a certain archival institution, I spent several days reading through transcriptions of ballads, the notes accompanying which were fascinating, featuring a kind of coded commentary about various recitations and singers. Eager as always to explore just how such collections got made and assessed, particularly by their first mediators, I asked the librarian to clarify these notes. I couldn't have asked a ruder question. I was immediately advised to close my notebook and leave the archive, and I was warned not to publish any such notes; my few scribbles narrowly escaped confiscation. I was made to re-sign release forms, to prove my academic affiliations, to produce once again a host of identity cards, and only then was I allowed to skulk out of the freezing small rooms down a narrow staircase into the harsh light of a midsummer day. My question had violated protocol: most people visited the archive, I was told, to confirm a verse or a stanza from this or that ballad; typically they knew such material from their families. No one went snooping around asking meta-questions about methods of notation, compilation, annotation, and so on. I was asking the *wrong questions* of this material. I had revealed myself to be distinctly *not* a native, nor in tune with native sensibilities and local practices. The librarian understood this archive to be a repository of long-standing community ties, fondly remembered singers, old relatives and shared history; it was decidedly not a trove of materials to be subjected to any kind of discourse analysis or methodological critique. I had understood myself to be a benign researcher; I was understood to be a plunderer and spy.

As I slunk out of the archive, I thought again, as I would often have occasion to do, of Walter Scott: his expropriations of popular, oral poetry; his use of such poetic *materia* for historical ruminations; his elaborate antiquarian annotations in *Minstrelsy of the Scottish Border* (1802–3) and woven through his romances; his constant traffic in oral poetries for literate, commercial ends; and the ambivalence and even hostility this provoked and continues to provoke among Scots. I was at best a lesser Scott, a "border-raider" plundering not the "living miscellany" Mrs. Hogg (one of his oral informants) but a manuscript archive for my own inscrutable but undoubtedly alien, infernal ends.[9]

This uncomfortable encounter brought home – and proved on the pulse, as Keats might have said – the problematics I'd been tracing in eighteenth-century *poiesis*: the contended territories that poetries both inhabit and map. The impasse in the archive points to ongoing questions about the use and abuse of poetry: who, as well as what, is poetry for?

In 1830, Walter Scott provided one horizon for answering this question. In his "Introductory Remarks on Popular Poetry" (1830), prefacing the "magnum opus" edition of his influential collection, *Minstrelsy of the Scottish Border* (1802–3), Scott reminded his readers that he and several friends had made it their business when young to walk and ride through the Scottish countryside in search of ballads. Indeed, Scott wrote, he himself was once able "to recollect as many of these old songs as would have occupied several days in the recitation."[10] In this brief aside, a highly literary, professionalized, critically and commercially successful poet presents to us another face: that of the poet as self-editing native-informant, a latter-day "minstrel" (to use his term), a receiver, transmitter and enactor of an oral tradition. Reading Scott's self-representations as an allegory of the situation of poetry, we begin to see how permeable, at least in one direction, was the boundary between what we now call high and low culture, between literate elites and semi-literate rural folk, between memory and ethno-poetics, between individually produced well-wrought urns and collectively remembered folksong, between a notionally oral transmission of tradition and its multi-media, commercialized "invention" for literature.

Following the trail laid down by Scott and his eighteenth-century balladeering predecessors, this book proposes an account of poetry and the figure of the poet in Britain circa 1800, and hopes to suggest some ongoing resonances into our own moment. These chapters put oral tradition, literary poetry, and theories of both in direct conversation, just as they were in the work of Burns, Scott, Wordsworth, Hogg, Byron, and numerous other collectors,

---

[9] For Mrs. Hogg as a "living miscellany," see her son James Hogg's letter to Walter Scott, June 30 [1802]: "My mother is actually a living miscellany of old songs I never believe that she had half so many until a came to a trial: there are none in your collection of which she hath not a part…" *The Collected Letters of James Hogg*, Vol. I, 1800–1819, ed. Gillian Hughes (Edinburgh University Press, 2004), 15.

[10] Walter Scott, "On Popular Poetry," in *The Poetical Works of Walter Scott, Bart. together with the Minstrelsy of the Scottish Border. With the Author's Introductions and Notes* [1830 edition] (New York: Leavitt and Allen, n.d.), 9.

editors, and poets; just as they are (however differently inflected) in the work of such contemporary poets and theorists as Jerome Rothenberg, Amiri Baraka, Anne Waldman, Christian Bök, Saul Williams, and Harryette Mullen. This book proposes to offer a re-mapping of what we conventionally call "pre-Romantic" and "Romantic" poetry and poetics in light of emergent disciplines and discourses: literary history, cultural theory, and what we would now call ethno-poetics and media theory. Balladeering and minstrelsy, launched in the eighteenth century and continued by various means since, together offer one crucial genealogy for contemporary debates about orality, literariness, disciplinarity, and the so-called "death of poetry": it was precisely through their vexed engagement with the multiply-mediated, historical situation of poetry that eighteenth-century antiquarians, poets, and historians formulated crucial arguments about cultural nationalism, the status of vernaculars, and emergent British historiography. It was through poetry, that is, that the eighteenth century discovered and argued about "the predicament of culture."[11]

Indeed, ballad scholars Tom Cheesman and Sigrid Rieuwerts have made the following suggestive claim: "The modern study of culture begins with the study of ballads."[12] This study takes the broader (or perhaps looser) rubric of *poiesis* to be its remit, though I will often have occasion to discuss balladry and ballad scholarship, as well as the phenomenon of minstrelsy – that trope of poetic inheritance, transmission, and imminent obsolescence: in these aspects a signal trope for "culture," as well as for "poetry." Indebted to the work of, and aiming to speak to, ballad scholars, folklorists, romanticists, media theorists, literary historians, and ethno-musicologists, this book also aspires to put the case of poetry – "literary" and "traditionary" and hybrids thereof – smack in the center of current discussions about "the location of culture," in Homi Bhabha's phrase.[13]

---

[11] See James Clifford, *The Predicament of Culture: Twentieth-Century Ethnography, Literature, and Art* (Cambridge, MA: Harvard University Press, 1988). Clifford Siskin also identifies this period as crucial for the invention of the culture-concept and modern disciplinicism; he locates these cruces, however, in Jacobitism, not in *poiesis* per se. See Siskin, "Scottish Philosophy and English Literature," in *The Work of Writing: Literature and Social Change in Britain 1700–1830* (Baltimore, MD: Johns Hopkins University Press, 1998), 79–99.

[12] *Ballads into Books: The Legacies of Francis James Child*, ed. Tom Cheesman and Sigrid Rieuwerts (Bern: Peter Lang, 1997), 5. The editors elaborate thus: "The eighteenth-century 'discovery' of ballads in popular tradition (that is, the putting of ballads into scholarly books) began an enduring debate which was crucial in defining what came to be called Romanticism. All modern theories of culture and poetics trace their ancestry to this debate, especially as it developed in dialogue between the English- and the German-speaking worlds."

[13] For this phrase, see Homi Bhabha, *The Location of Culture* (London, New York: Routledge, 1994). Here and elsewhere I follow eighteenth-century balladeers and later scholars of balladry in using the term "traditionary" as virtually interchangeable with "traditional" – "traditionary" perhaps flagging more clearly the status of such poetry as both *traditional* but also *oral-traditionarily mediated*.

"Poetry" is after all a strikingly elastic category, spanning everything from oral-traditionary ballads to seventeenth-century broadsides to highly wrought romantic odes to twentieth-century spoken word art: this project analyzes that multiplicity and the theoretical conundrums it suggests. My discussion focuses on the emergence of poetry as an object of medial and cultural theory – from eighteenth-century antiquarians working their way toward preliminary "oral theories" in the wake of the Ossian controversy and the ballad revival, to the complex "romance of orality" characteristic of Romanticism, to late twentieth-century American inquiries into ethno-poetics, performance, and the medial condition of poetry. This work is committed to re-opening, for both the long eighteenth century and our own moment, the questions that both Wordsworth and Coleridge posed: "What is poetry?" and "What is the poet?"

To think of British Romantic poetry, for example, is for many people to recall specific poets and poems: Wordsworth's "Tintern Abbey" and his *Prelude*, Shelley's "Adonais," Blake's "The Tyger," Keats' "Ode to a Nightingale," Burns' "To a Mouse." Certain terms and phrases may come to mind: negative capability, romantic imagination, the child is father of the man, poets are the unacknowledged legislators of the world. It is less likely that one would invoke, as specimens of Romantic poetry, the ballad of Johnny Armstrong, the ballad "Chevy Chase," or the ballad "Barbara Allen." Yet these ballads and songs, vitally sung, transmitted, and recreated long before – and long after – what some have called "the Age of Wordsworth," are equally constitutive of poetry in the Romantic era.

This book argues that the situation of British poetry, 1760–1830, offers us a window onto the transhistorical condition of poetic "mediality" – the condition of existing in media, whether oral, manuscript, print, or digital.[14]

---

[14] On "mediality" as "the general condition within with, under certain circumstances, something like 'poetry' or 'literature' can take shape," see David E. Wellbery's Foreword to Friedrich A. Kittler, *Discourse Networks, 1800/1900*, trans. Micheal Metteer, with Chris Cullens (Stanford University Press, 1900), xiii. To Wellbery's "poetry" and "literature," we might add "balladeer-ing," or "literary history," or "cultural nationalism": all of which took shape within, and were determined in the last medial instance by, the circumstances of late-eighteenth-century print. "Whatever historical field we are dealing with, in Kittler's view, we are dealing with media as determined by the technological possibilities of the epoch in question." One need not subscribe to Kittler's emphatic techno-determinism to find his bracing diagnoses of Romanticism, modernism, and the horizons of the regime of print, now closing, to be conceptually useful. For further discussion of British Romantic mediality, see Celeste Langan and Maureen N. McLane, "The Medium of Romantic Poetry," in *The Cambridge Companion to British Romantic Poetry* (Cambridge University Press, 2008), 239–62.

To consider how poetry mediates itself – whether through the poet's body and voice, composition-in-performance, a transcription, or a printed text – is to examine, in the broadest sense, the means through and historical conditions under which human imagination materializes itself. 1760 stands as my launch date because it was then that James Macpherson's Ossianic *Fragments* first appeared, poems which purported to be the work of a third-century Highland bard, but which skeptics believed were forged. The Ossian controversy – and its complex relations to theories of orality, cultural authenticity, translation, and historicity – is one inaugural test-case for the problematics of *poiesis* elaborated in this period. And 1830 stands as a provisional terminus to this project not least because it was then that Walter Scott penned his essay "On Popular Poetry," which offers a rapid-fire literary history of the period as well as an anticipatory summation of some of this book's concerns. In his emphasis on revived balladry, antiquarian predecessors, and a minstrelling *poiesis* distributed across Great Britain and Ireland, Scott sets out a horizon of poetic production that has often been obscured in critical discussions oriented to cultural nationalism on the one hand or individual authors on the other.

Poets in the late eighteenth and early nineteenth centuries found themselves re-thinking poetry along several newly emergent (and in some regards still obtaining) cultural, historical, and aesthetic axes. In late eighteenth-century Britain, poets became conscious of themselves as undertaking a project that straddled and ambiguated several borders: the imperial/national/regional borders constituted by the 1707 Act of Union that created Great Britain; the border between orality and literacy; between the "popular" and the "refined"; speech and writing; improvization and fixed transcription; common language and "poetic diction." We might consider the poetry in this period in its broadest sense as a field of cultural making and negotiation: in this light, *poiesis* – the making of poems, poetics, poetic apparatus, historical essays and ethnographic reveries on poetry – reveals its profound engagement with discourses and practices more typically associated with the antiquarian, the historian, the folklorist, the linguist, and the ethnographer. The case of Walter Scott is not idiosyncratic: the complex situation of poetry in this period – a situation recognized by the poets themselves – allows us to re-consider what we talk about when we talk about poetry.

As must be clear, my discussion throughout is shadowed by contemporary discussions within and without the academy regarding the status of poetry and its relation to the presumed condition of culture. This book emerges from years of thinking, teaching, reading, writing, reviewing, and talking about poems and the condition of poetry, both in the contemporary US and during the British Romantic period. Laments (or huzzahs) for the death of poetry have been a conspicuous feature of US cultural politics since the 1980s: from Joseph Epstein's 1988 *Commentary* article "Who Killed Poetry?" to Dana Gioia's *Can Poetry Matter?* (1992) to his recent *Disappearing Ink: Poetry at the End of Print Culture* (2005) to Camille Paglia's and Harold Bloom's latest ventures into the public sphere, poetry becomes the occasional means through which public intellectuals, media dons, and the chattering classes talk earnestly about the fate of democracy, the sanctity of literature, the threat to literate elites and their presumed values, skills in reading, and habits of contemplation.[15] Poetry would seem to be beset by all manner of foes: slam poets, rap, declining attention spans, plummeting literacy rates, bad teaching, multiculturalism, the ascendancy of new media. It is of course typical that these notional foes can, in some accounts, also serve as friends to a renewed engagement with poetry: worried about your students' attention spans? Teach a lyric poem – it's short and has a quicker payoff than a Victorian novel! Afraid that today's students won't respond to dead white poets? Turn to one of the many anthologies featuring fine poets of every nation, gender, color, and sexuality! Disturbed by hiphop? Re-think: it's the hottest oral *poiesis* around, the liveliest zone of metered rhyme in contemporary America and beyond. Oppressed by the proliferation of DVDs, gameboys, iPods, and cellphones? Seize the means of mediation and produce new kinds of poems! Indeed I found when running a weekly poetry seminar for 8–11-year-old children that newer media – the video camera in particular – proved indispensable in getting the more resistant children to connect: imagining themselves as performers, as recordable, viewable, and audible creative subjects, allowed some children to enter into a communal experiment in *poiesis*.

The uncertainty of my tone in the preceding paragraph underlines an ongoing ambivalence regarding this discourse about poetry: for usually "poetry" is a blank counter in such discussions, something to be used, brandished, idealized, desecrated, and all too rarely explored, much less

---

[15] See Dana Gioia's *Can Poetry Matter?: Essays on Poetry and American Culture* [10th anniversary edn.] (St. Paul, MN: Graywolf Press, 2002) and *Disappearing Ink: Poetry at the End of Print Culture* (St. Paul, MN: Graywolf Press, 2004). Camille Paglia's *Break, Blow, Burn: Camille Paglia Reads Forty-Three of the World's Best Poems* (New York: Pantheon, 2005) represents the latest taming of the self-styled outlaw humanist by the middlebrow. Gioia writes thoughtfully about the resurgence of oral forms and traditional meters, and the new medial condition of poetry in the electronic era; praising cowboy poets and rappers as well as the phenomenon of the poetry reading – now the primary form of publication, as he notes – Gioia nicely avoids the clichéd laments for the death of print culture more usually found in such books.

read, heard, made, or enjoyed. I turned some years ago to a study of British Romantic poets precisely because I felt that signal poets, Wordsworth and Shelley most prominently, intuited and diagnosed certain aspects of the modern condition of *poiesis*: what "poetry" is almost always remains to be seen, and heard. Poetry needs to be re-thought again and again, for poetry, unlike for example the novel, pre-existed print and writing and will undoubtedly outlast them. Poetry thus offers especially rich territory for transhistorical, transmedial reflections.

The book argues that literary and cultural history as well as poetics look quite different when we consider "traditionary" poetry alongside "literary" poetry (as writers like Scott and Wordsworth certainly did, as the Norton Anthology still, in limited ways, does). Pursuing this medial interface – these "oral–literate conjunctions," we might call them – I argue that the situation of poetry circa 1800 may be read more broadly as an index of "mediality" (to use the term proposed by Friedrich Kittler and amplified by David Wellbery).[16] Analyzing the problem of "dating orality" – which preoccupied signal poets as much as it did the stadial historians of the Scottish Enlightenment – I trace the means by which late eighteenth-century Anglo-Scottish balladeering (along with its attendant discourses, "minstrelsy," "national song," etc.) and its modes of poetic research and production (e.g. collecting, surveying, transcribing, forging, annotating, editing) helped to shape practices and discourses constitutive of emergent disciplines – proto-ethnography, philology, and historiography as well as folklore and literary history.

In recent years scholars have re-animated the eighteenth-century "scandals of the ballad" (viz. Susan Stewart) and the literary-historical stakes of cultural nationalism in this period (see Katie Trumpener, Ina Ferris, and numerous other scholars); and more scholars are recognizing that we need a broader frame in which to consider literary production, vernacular literatures, and oral traditions together.[17] What has been too little noted (with

---

[16] See note 14.

[17] See for example Steve Newman, *Ballad Collection, Lyric, and the Canon: The Call of the Popular from the Restoration to the New Criticism* (Philadelphia: University of Pennsylvania Press, 2007) – a book whose concerns are kindred in several respects to this one: "the popular" rather than *poiesis* provides Newman's angle of entry into a "long eighteenth-century" phenomenon and its ongoing repercussions. Like Newman, but with a broader comparative remit, Thomas A. DuBois questions the partitioning of "ballad" and "lyric" – the former supposedly communal and oral, the latter singly produced and typically glossed as literary: see his *Lyric, Meaning, and Audience in the Oral Tradition of Northern Europe* (University of Notre Dame Press, 2006). The convergence of theoretical, historical, and medial concerns in these and other recent books (including this one) – in part animated by a rethinking of the ballad, the oral, and the literary – suggests that the critical spirit of the age is increasingly sponsoring a newly mediatized analysis of the literary as well as of the oral.

some striking recent exceptions) is the way these controversies consistently forced a definition of the objects in view. In other words: what was (or is) a ballad?[18] And what was (or is) "oral tradition"? (These questions bear, obviously, on my previously stated, overarching question: What is Poetry?) Despite the remarkable proliferation of ballad collections in the eighteenth century, it was by no means obvious what a ballad was. And then too, polite editors strove to excise or ignore large swaths of a vital, ongoing ballad tradition – not least street ballads, those broadsides topical and political and sometimes bawdy. The "hybrid textual and oral" status of ballads (as Paula McDowell puts it[19]) offers us a throughline into the heart of a transmedial as well as transhistorical poetics.

This project assumes as well that the partitions between eighteenth-century studies and Romanticism will not stand, and that the eighteenth-century discovery of the medial condition of poetry is of particular interest for twenty-first-century readers and writers, conscious as we are of profound techno-material changes in communications. When read through ballad-eering, moreover, our "high/low" debates (however moribund) start to look more like "literate vs. oral" debates. This is not to overlook the occasionally supercharged class and cultural–national valences of balladeering, but rather to point to the medial-theoretical terms in which balladeering debates were also conducted. Eighteenth- and early nineteenth-century ballad collections are very peculiar composite objects – coordinating everything from broadsides to manuscripts to oral recitations, such that their editors (such as Thomas Percy, Joseph Ritson, Walter Scott, William Motherwell) felt the need to theorize these heterogeneous materials and their medial condition. Such collections are thus full of poems but also of footnotes and headnotes and anecdotes and historical dissertations and glossaries – objects as if

---

[18] For a trenchant analysis of the problem of defining a "ballad" – one constituted in part because several disciplines continue to take ballads as their objects of study – see Dianne Dugaw, "On the 'Darling Songs' of Poets, Scholars, and Singers: An Introduction," *The Eighteenth Century: Theory and Interpretation* 47:2/3 (Summer/Fall 2006): 97–113. Dugaw notes that most scholars adopt a fairly standard distinction between "traditional" and "broadside" ballads, the former connoting greater antiquity and oral origin or transmission, the latter denoting a print-era product, often topical and political. Yet these distinctions will not always hold and were themselves artifacts of eighteenth-century balladeers' polemical classifications, as Paula McDowell argues in "'The Manufacture and Lingua-Franca of *Ballad-Making*': Broadside Ballads in Long Eighteenth-Century Discourse," *The Eighteenth Century: Theory and Interpretation* 47:2/3 (Summer/Fall 2006): 149–76. Ballad collectors set forth their "ancient" and "popular" ballads and polite collections precisely in contradistinction to the unruly, topical, politicized, and often bawdy broadsides flying off the eighteenth-century presses; they also developed a "new confrontational model of balladry" (150) by which print/street ballads were imagined to displace "traditional" ballads beginning in the Elizabethan era: a displacement lamented by polite editors hostile to the broadside/street tradition of print.
[19] McDowell, "The Manufacture," 158.

designed for a cultural studies and historical media analysis. These books served as well as the crucial manuals for the eventually more famous "original" poets like Wordsworth, Blake and Byron (and Scott as "original" poet). The whole problem of representing something like a ballad in print, moreover – its tune as well as its words, its variants, its ellipses – is one that eighteenth-century editors identified and grappled with in revealing ways. Equally telling, the late eighteenth-century problem of representing ballad informants – indeed, whether to represent them at all – forecasts the kinds of debates scholars like Johannes Fabian, Edward Said, James Clifford, and others have animated regarding twentieth-century ethnography and more broadly the representation of "others." If we have worried about whether the subaltern might speak, we may also consider the ways in which the subaltern (or more properly, the tenant farmer, the dairymaid, the genteel housewife, the aristocratic lady) *sang*.

Rethinking the situation of poetries in English via balladeering and minstrelsy, this project aims to re-open, and to keep open, questions in several domains. The construction of poetic authority in Romanticism, the status of literary ballads, the meaning of eighteenth-century and twentieth-century "oral turns" – these all look different when considered in light of a long history of poetic mediality and theories about it. As the foregoing description of questions and topics suggests, the book sits at the intersection of historical, theoretical, and poetic issues and also hopes to offer, via balladeering and cultural poetics, one archaeology of the humanities and some of its impasses. One story tracked here is the transformation of antiquarianism by Enlightenment historiography; another is the relation of poetic practice to proto-ethnography and to narratives of cultural formation and nationalism; a third is a meditation on the place of poetries in the UK, 1760–1830; and a fourth is a historical inquiry into poetry, mediality, and media studies – the situation of poetry, and of humanists, in the present.

To re-enter the world of antiquarian debate – as some of the following chapters do – is to encounter a peculiar and not always flattering mirror-image of the work of humanist scholarship. The endless footnotes, the petty squabbles, the obsolete pursuits, the territoriality, the leaden in-jokes, the anxious dependence on patrons and other luminaries, the contempt for less well-established scholars: one finds all these in ballad collections, essays on minstrels, and antiquarian correspondence, as well as in the contemporary academy. Yet amidst such wrangling, forging, flattering, denouncing, and proclaiming, one also finds (both then and now) a constant thread of impassioned rigor, an ideal of dispassionate commitment, a devotion to materials, to standards of authentication, to conversation and lively argument, to a sociable, engaged community of fellow researchers and devotees. If at times I have felt myself to be a latter-day antiquarian, this project riddled with antiquarians' vices and none of their virtues, I have found great solace amidst the web of scholars, from the eighteenth century till now, whose work everywhere informs this project. And when it has seemed an act of typically American chutzpah to venture into Scottish and English territory others know so much more deeply in their bones, I have thought hopefully of the Englishman Ritson's forays into Scottish balladry and Alan Lomax's later journeys into same, and of Cecil Sharp's three ventures into Appalachia: while there are enormous benefits to studying this material as a native, perhaps it is not completely myopic to try to re-enter this zone of *poiesis* as a relative outsider – an outsider both by birth but also by training. It will become obvious that I write primarily as one trained in literary-historical and not ethnographic, ethno-musicological, or folklore studies, though I have learned much from work in the latter fields: each of these disciplines has its own history of debates about nationalism, cultural property, transactions with materials (textual, musical, and human), standards of evidence, modes of argument. And then too when confronted with the sobering or tart comments of singers[20] – those embodied transmitters and recreators of tradition who often look askance at academic transmutations of their materials – I have understood myself again to be a participant in a long, vexed history of poetic appropriation, transmutation, and exploration.

This book aims to analyze and theorize that history. It moves roughly in chronological fashion, though throughout there will be occasion to return to prior moments and poems (e.g. the Ossian controversy, Scott's *Lay of the Last Minstrel*) as well as to forecast later historical and poetic outcomes (e.g. the fortunes of minstrelsy in Francis James Child, or in Wallace Stevens). The first chapter lays out the late eighteenth-century effort to periodize and theorize "orality" in Britain; it further establishes the terms and terrain for my investigation of *poiesis* as historical, historicizable, and transmedial. James Beattie's *The Minstrel* (1771, 1774) and an antiquarian citation of a milkmaid's song offer two initial cases for exploring the era's heightened consciousness of oral-literate interactions; the representation of such interactions, both within poetry and in discourse around it, becomes the focus of

---

[20] As in the great balladeer and activist Jean Ritchie's pointed exclamations regarding Dave Marsh's take on "Barbara Allen" in the opening essay of Greil Marcus and Sean Wilentz, eds., *The Rose and The Briar: Death, Love, and Liberty in the American Ballad* (New York: W. W. Norton, 2005): "I read that essay; it's just crazy!" Comments in Concert sponsored by The Folk Song Society of Greater Boston, St. John's Methodist Church, Watertown, MA, April 30, 2005.

subsequent chapters. Chapter 2, "How to do things with ballads," offers an extensive, detailed history and theory of late eighteenth-century balladeering. Balladeering emerges as a discourse with an attendant set of practices (collecting, transcribing, editing, etc.) and protocols of authentication that continue to structure contemporary anthologies, whether in print or on CD or the web: antiquarian headnotes might be construed as liner notes *avant la lettre*. This chapter tracks the transformation of antiquarian balladeering, as its protocols adjust to accommodate the newly (albeit ambiguously) sanctioned oral informant. Oral tradition enters the printed ballad collection as an editor's competitive bid for authority over sources (and other editors) as well as an index of Scottish and ultimately British cultural capital. One sign of this broader transformation is the 1805 *Report on Ossian*, for which native informants in the Highlands were solicited to provide their memories of Ossianic material but also, when possible, their memories of encounters with James Macpherson, the poet-researcher who had first published Ossianic *Fragments* in 1760. What had been considered a deficit in the cultural politics of the 1760s and 1770s – perceived reliance on merely oral tradition, merely living reciters – had become by the early nineteenth century a criterion of ethno-poetic authority. From antiquarianism through Romantic cultural poetics, then, we find poetry and discourse about poetry inseparable from the development of what we would now call historiographic and ethnographic discourse.

This second chapter establishes the historical and theoretical groundwork for the rest of the book. In the next chapter, "Tuning the multi-media nation," I take up what antiquarians all too often neglected, the mediation of ballad musics as well as texts: here again, we find balladeers deeply engaged in problems of mediation, cultural and technical, not least because the printing of musics before the invention of lithography required decisions about the merits of typesetting versus engraving. In subsequent chapters I turn to the phenomenon of "minstrelsy," proposed as a discursive movement within and around poems – ultimately the figure of *poiesis* itself. Chapter 4, "How to do things with minstrels," focuses on minstrelsy as the place where poetry and history meet: minstrelsy becomes the means by which *poiesis* reckons with its historical situation. Showing how mid-nineteenth-century US minstrelsy drew on British antiquarian balladeering for its major cultural tropes, the chapter then offers several diagnostic readings, returning to Beattie's *Minstrel*, Scott's *Minstrelsy of the Scottish Border*, and his *Lay of the Last Minstrel* to illuminate the ways poetry internalized the many modes of historical discourse emergent in the late eighteenth century. Francis James Child here appears as a minstrel-curator in a long line thereof.

"Minstrelsy, or, Romantic Poetry" (Chapter 5) explores minstrelsy further as an *intra-poetic* discourse, a set of tropes about the imminent obsolescence and perpetual revivability of poetry. Here we move decisively from antiquarianism into the more familiar precincts of Romanticism. After exploring antiquarian debates about the status of minstrels, I offer several theoretical propositions about the work "minstrelsy" does, both in the late eighteenth and early nineteenth centuries and now. I then read Scott's *Lay of the Last Minstrel* (1805), Wordsworth's "Song, at the Feast of Brougham Castle" (1807) and "Hart-leap Well" (1800), and John Clare's several minstrelling works, as critical meditations on the project of reviving minstrels and more broadly on their own poetries. Wallace Stevens' *Notes toward a Supreme Fiction* offers a brilliant variation on the minstrelsy problematic, his "idiot minstrelsy" the very name for a decayed yet potentially revivable Romanticism.

"Seven types of poetic authority circa 1800" (Chapter 6) aims to distill and further the theoretical implications of the previous discussions of balladeering, minstrelsy, and ethno-poetic authority. I provide a brief sketch of these seven types, ranging from bardic to anonymous to editorial to ethnographic to experiential authority, showing how testimonial discourse and oral authentication pervade both poems and their attendant commentaries. In its broadest scope, this chapter proposes two functions as structuring *poiesis* circa 1800: the authority of extended subjectivity (internalization) and the authority of editorial objectivity (externalization). Scott's editorial commentary in the *Minstrelsy* and his self-representations in his metrical romance *Marmion* (1808) demonstrate the reciprocity of these functions, as do Wordsworth's *Lyrical Ballads* and *The Prelude*.

Throughout the book, I aim to offer a model of reading as well as alternate genealogies, cross-disciplinary constellations, and areas for further study. Chapter 7 extends this case-study approach, reading specimen poems and passages through the book's theoretical and historical concerns about oral-literate conjunctions and romantic mediality. Blake's *Songs of Innocence and Experience*, Byron's *Childe Harold*, Wordsworth's *Lyrical Ballads*, "Lines, written on a blank leaf of Macpherson's Ossian," and his "Solitary Reaper" stand as diagnostic Romantic investigations of *poiesis*. Within such poems, as within late eighteenth-century theory, poetry emerges as a historically situated medium of culture, its workings trans- and inter-medial – moving across oral, writerly, and print modalities – and thus potentially unbindable. A brief turn to late twentieth-century poetics suggests the ongoing romance of orality in a new intermedial configuration. Finally, the Conclusion, "Thirteen (or more) ways of looking at a blackbird," offers in miniature a tour of the preoccupations of this book: tracking the fortunes of Child Ballad No. 26 (counterparts known as "The Three Ravens" and "The Twa Corbies"), this essay follows a ballad as it moves from a 1611 songbook through antiquarian balladeering into the twentieth century – the multiply-mediated elegy of a black bird ballad become simultaneously a requiem for and a celebration of *poiesis* itself.

This is, then, a long book, and a varied book, mixing modes of writing, objects of analysis, as well as angles of approach: technical historical argument segues into essay, case study into theorization, argument into close-reading, literary-historical analysis into media study. I lay out these chapters here as a kind of tuning-up; so too I provide an extended table of contents, to enable the reader to zoom in on those sections he or she might wish to.

Given the long history of ballad scholarship emerging from within several disciplines, and given the recent efflorescence of work on the ballad revival, cultural nationalism, the fortunes of historicism and the cultural meanings of orality, one sometimes feels that there is little more to be said on such matters, or certainly little that must needs be said. Perhaps this is merely the ghost of a fantasized desire for originality – a desire that may haunt humanist inquiry but is rarely consummated within it: unsurprisingly so. For balladry and minstrelsy, not to mention the wonderfully engaged scholarship around it, give the lie to the romantic fetish of originality: perhaps it is enough to aspire to do what the medieval minstrels and troubadours did, that is, to *move*, if not *make*, the song.[21]

---

[21] On the troubadours and *mouvance*, and the problematics of "authority" and "authorship" in a culture of performance, see Gregory Nagy, *Poetry as Performance: Homer and Beyond* (Cambridge University Press, 1996): "To perform the song, however, is to recompose it, to change it, that is, to *move* it. In this light, *mouvance* is the same thing as recomposition-in-performance" (17). Despite the pitfalls of adopting an oral-traditional analogy for a project almost wholly enmeshed in a discourse network of print, I hope the reader may find in this a useful image of the collaborative re-making encoded in this book and in any academic monograph.

CHAPTER I

Dating orality, thinking balladry: of minstrels and milkmaids in 1771

"Say that a ballad / wrapped in a ballad // a play of force and play // of
forces ... Dark ballad and dark crossing / old woman prowling //
Genial telling her story ... "
   – Susan Howe, "Speeches at the Barriers," 1983[1]

"There are two things that are interesting history and grammar.
History is historical."
   – Gertrude Stein, *History or Messages from History*[2]

"There is no history without dates."
   – Claude Lévi-Strauss, *The Savage Mind*[3]

These epigraphs from Howe, Stein, and Lévi-Strauss point to the central
concerns of this book. Howe's lines evoke the mobility of ballads – their
many dark crossings – and point to the ways a ballad might be "wrapped in a
ballad," or in other forms and media: a progress poem, an antiquarian's
notebook, a collector's headnote, a novel, a film, a singer's voice, a CD.
Ballads may be seen as a mode of "speech at the barrier," in Howe's words,
but also as a mode of crossing beyond, or at least confounding, barriers:
between classes, genders, generations, nations, but also between historical
period (say, fourteenth- vs. eighteenth- vs. twenty-first-century poetries)
and medial realizations ("orality" vs., say, "print"). It is also true that ballads
and balladeering have long served to install rather than surmount barriers:
barriers between, for example, "oral tradition" and "literary culture,"
between illiterate "old women" singers and male literati, between notionally
primitive pasts and polemically progressive presents. Balladeering – a broad
term encompassing everything from the singing, making, inventing, forging, collecting, editing, printing, and digital recording of ballads – offers us

[1] Susan Howe, "Speeches at the Barriers," 1983, *Postmodern American Poetry*, ed. Paul Hoover (New York: Norton, 1994), 347.
[2] Gertrude Stein, *History or Messages from History* (Copenhagen: Green Integer, 1997), 22.
[3] Claude Lévi-Strauss, *The Savage Mind*, "History and Dialectic" (University of Chicago Press, 1966), 258.

a striking trans-historical test case: in Anglo-Scottish and American ballad-eering we witness the persistence and transmutation of a poetic and musical phenomenon as it encounters new media and new historical situations. In this chapter, and indeed often throughout this book, I will be talking not so much about ballads *per se* as about the way ballads could be put to work – to do a new kind of cultural work, a new kind of historical, intellectual and poetic work, beginning in the late eighteenth century in Britain.

And thus, to turn to the second epigraph: regarding Stein's two interesting things, "history and grammar," we might add: poetry is historical. Poetry is interesting. How British poetries in the late eighteenth century found themselves to be historical, how they participated in the location of culture, how balladeering in particular created a space for such cultural inquiry, invention, and mediation: these are the questions this chapter hopes to open.

As Stein's own work suggests, poetry might pivot us between History and Grammar, between the discourse of the past and the structure of language. History is historical, Stein tells us, in typically gnomic fashion. But how is history historical? Lévi-Strauss would remind us that history depends on a "chronological code." As he declared in "History and Dialectic," the ninth chapter of *The Savage Mind*: "There is no history without dates."

So let us begin with a date: a specific kind of date: a year, 1771. In 1771 innumerable things happened in Britain, more specifically in Scotland: in 1771 Walter Scott was born. In 1771 the professor of Moral Philosophy at Aberdeen, James Beattie, published the first installment of his poem, *The Minstrel, or, the Progress of Genius*. This poem appeared simultaneously in England and Scotland, published both in London and in Edinburgh[4]; and excerpts from the poem appeared in that dated compendium of British record, *The Annual Register* of 1771. And also in 1771, a ballad collector identified only as W. L. transcribed a milkmaid's rendition of the ballad, "The Bonny Hynd."

Beattie's minstrel and W. L.'s milkmaid both enter the historical record in Britain in 1771; they are preoccupied in different yet related ways with the problematics of dating cultures, of periodizing poetry as well as notional cultural epochs. These test cases allow us to explore how poetry in Britain partook of and contributed to new ways of modeling the historicity of

---

[4] See James Beattie, *The Minstrel; or, The Progress of Genius: A Poem. Book the First* (London and Edinburgh, 1771).

culture. In other words, we may begin to consider how poetry, and the ballad in particular, was made to think its own date.[5]

If there is no history without dates, as Lévi-Strauss announced, it is also true that dates presuppose their own hermeneutic. There are hot dates and cold dates, we have been told; and indeed 1771 – and more broadly the decade of the 1770s – is arguably a rather cool one in Britain when considered exclusively from a high-cultural literary perspective. More profoundly, we know that the heat of one historical code cools rapidly when relativized against another – 1776 perhaps not so hot a date for the Senegalese as for the American; 1789 arguably hotter for the French than for the Japanese; D-Day hotter for US veterans of World War II than for today's skater bois. To say 1776, or 1789, or 1968, or 1989, or September 11th is to place us immediately within a semantic field – the ideologics of dates. So if there is no history without dates, it is also true that, as Lévi-Strauss observed in *The Savage Mind*: "History is therefore never history, but history-for."[6] History is always a history-for – a history for someone, some community, some cultural or ideological project. So too *poiesis* may be regarded as poetry-for, serving a host of possible ends.

It is no accident that my two poetic test cases are Scottish: for the Scots were exceptionally attuned to the problem of thinking historical and cultural difference, and their poetry as much as their historiography reflected that attunement.[7] Legislatively harnessed to England since the 1707 Act of Union created Great Britain, divided within itself between increasingly industrializing or commercially thriving towns with the most literate population in Europe and the harsher, denuded regions of the Highlands, between speakers of Scottish English and of Gaelic, Scotland provided its intellectuals with a powerful incentive to theorize the problem of what some now call uneven development.[8]

---

[5] For a discussion of the problems of dating ballads, manifested in particular in their uncomfortable placement in successive *Norton* anthologies of poetry, see Mary Ellen Brown, "Placed, Replaced, or Misplaced? The Ballads' Progress," *The Eighteenth Century: Theory and Interpretation* 47:2/3 (Summer/Fall 2006): 115–29.

[6] Lévi-Strauss, *Savage Mind*, 257.

[7] Over the past decade several important works in British literary historiography have appeared which explicitly address not only the problem of dating or otherwise historicizing culture but the very invention of the problem – the invention of the historical situation, as James Chandler puts it in *England in 1819: The Politics of Literary Culture and the Case of Romantic Historicism* (University of Chicago Press, 1998). Chandler recovers in Scottish Enlightenment thinking an alternative to Hegelian historicism, such that we might track not the dialectical unfolding of *Geist* but the critical formations of historicizeable structures in time. See especially Ch. 4, "Altering the Case: The Invention of the Historical Situation," 203–64.

[8] On the crucially re-animated case of eighteenth- and nineteenth-century Scotland, and its intellectuals' acute consciousness of the problematics of modernity, there is a burgeoning historical and

Poetry in all its mediations offered British intellectuals many opportunities to confront the problem of dating cultures, of periodizing development and historicizing cultural and medial productions. The most famous case of dubiously dated poetry was, of course, the Ossian poems, introduced to the literary public sphere by James Macpherson in his *Fragments of Ancient Poetry, Collected in the Highlands of Scotland* (1760), and continued in epic installments through the 1760s.[9] Were these fragments and epics

critical scholarship. Informing this and other observations are Katie Trumpener on cultural nationalism, oral tradition, and Ossian in *Bardic Nationalism: The Romantic Novel and the British Empire* (Princeton University Press, 1997); Penny Fielding, *Writing and Orality: Nationality, Culture, and Nineteenth-Century Scottish Fiction* (Oxford University Press, 1996); Cairns Craig, *Out of History: Narrative Paradigms in Scottish and English Culture* (Edinburgh: Polygon, 1996); Robert Crawford, *Devolving English Literature* (2nd edn. Edinburgh University Press, 2000); Chandler's *England in 1819* (an England which seems to have required an eighteenth-century Scotland to think itself and its own historicity); the several essays and books by Fiona Stafford, including *The Last of the Race: The Growth of a Myth from Milton to Darwin* (Clarendon Press, 1994); Ian Duncan's work, including "Authenticity Effects: The Work of Fiction in Romantic Scotland," *The South Atlantic Quarterly* 102:1 (Winter 2003): 93–116; "The Upright Corpse: Hogg, National Literature, and the Uncanny," *Studies in Hogg and his World* 5, (1994): 29–54; *Modern Romance and Transformations of the Novel: The Gothic, Scott, Dickens* (Cambridge University Press, 1992); Susan Manning's important essays on disciplinarity and antiquarianism, including "Notes from the Margin: Antiquarianism, the Scottish Science of Man, and the Emergence of Disciplinarity," *Scotland and The Borders of Romanticism*, ed. Leith Davis, Ian Duncan, and Janet Sorensen (Cambridge University Press, 2004), 57–76; Mary Poovey's differently oriented yet complementary analysis of the epistemologic of Scottish conjectural history in *A History of the Modern Fact: Problems of Knowledge in the Sciences of Wealth and Society* (University of Chicago Press, 1998), 214–63; and Clifford Siskin on "culture" and "Jacobitism" in Ch. 3, "Scottish Philosophy and English Literature," *The Work of Writing: Literature and Social Change in Britain 1700–1830* (Baltimore, MD: Johns Hopkins University Press, 1998), 79–99. Murray Pittock's work addresses cultural nationalism and identity in Ireland as well as Britain: see in particular *Inventing and Resisting Britain: Cultural Identities in Britain and Ireland, 1685–1789* (New York: Houndmills, 1997). Among historians, Colin Kidd offers perhaps the most trenchant and influential account of the creation of "Anglo-British identity" and the various impediments of older historiographies to a Unionist narrative: see *Subverting Scotland's Past: Scottish Whig Historians and the Creation of an Anglo-British Identity, 1689–c. 1830* (Cambridge University Press, 2003) and the earlier *British Identities before Nationalism: Ethnicity and Nationhood in the Atlantic World, 1600–1800* (Cambridge University Press, 1999). On Scottish Enlightenment thinkers and their contribution to socio-cultural as well as economic theory (or rather, the inseparability of the two), one might consider Emma Rothschild's important critical rescuing of Adam Smith from neo- (and paleo-) conservative economists in *Economic Sentiments: Adam Smith, Condorcet, and the Enlightenment* (Cambridge, MA: Harvard University Press, 2001).

9   After the success of the *Fragments*, Macpherson set forth "equipped with a clear agenda: the recovery of Scotland's ancient epic," as Fiona Stafford puts it in her Introduction to *The Poems of Ossian and Related Works*, ed. Howard Gaskill (Edinburgh University Press, 1996), xiii. These researches yielded *Fingal: An Ancient Epic Poem in Six Books. Together with Several Other Poems Composed by Ossian the Son of Fingal* (1761) and *Temora: An Ancient Epic Poem in Eight Books. Together with Several Other Poems Composed by Ossian the Song of Fingal* (1763) and published together as one volume, *The Works of Ossian*, in 1765. Macpherson's/Ossian's strongest contemporary defense came from Hugh Blair, Professor of Rhetoric and Belles Lettres at Edinburgh University, whose "Critical Dissertation on the Poems of Ossian" and authenticating "Appendix" appeared with the 1765 *Works of Ossian* (and are reprinted in Gaskill's edition of the *Poems of Ossian*) and laid the ground for a friendly reception throughout much of Europe (see Notes, *Poems of Ossian*, 542–3).

truly the translations of third-century Scottish Gaelic epic, sustained by oral and manuscript transmission, as Macpherson and his defenders claimed; or were these poems, as Samuel Johnson and others later insisted, wholly the mid-eighteenth-century concoctions of Macpherson, the work of sentimental print culture channeling itself through the ingenious "impositions" of Macpherson and his defenders?[10]

    The Ossian controversy pointed more broadly to the problem of representing national culture, its poetries, its pasts and its present. The problem of dating cultures here was strongly inflected by cultural nationalism – Scottish literati were more favorably disposed to Macpherson (though the English poet Thomas Gray was impressed, if a doubter), while Samuel Johnson in high John Bull mode later derided them; and Irish cultural nationalists complained that Ossianic lore was in fact Irish.[11] The Ossian

---

[10] One can't help but give short shrift here to the full nuances, historical, inter/national, and theoretical, of Ossian, debates over Ossian, and "Ossianism" as an eighteenth-/nineteenth-century cultural phenomenon, but regarding the state of current scholarly discussion, it is perhaps most economical to quote Fiona Stafford: "*The Poems of Ossian* look less and less like the quaint hoax of a few decades ago" (Intro., *Poems of Ossian*, xviii). For an excellent, brief account of the genesis and impact of Ossian poems, and a survey of their reception, see Stafford, "Introduction," v–xxi. As Stafford observes, the Ossianic corpus has received renewed and respectful scholarly attention since the 1980s, though there still persists an older, prematurely simplifying view that the work is an outright fabrication. For a high-water mark of twentieth-century contempt for Ossian, one might consult Hugh Trevor-Roper's "The Invention of Tradition: The Highland Tradition of Scotland," in *The Invention of Tradition*, ed. Eric Hobsbawm and Terence Ranger (Cambridge University Press, 1984), 15–41: "Indeed, the whole concept of a distinct Highland culture and tradition is a retrospective innovation" (15). Recent scholars have strongly disagreed. As an index of the revitalized discussion about Macpherson and the Ossian debate, particularly in light of the history of folklore, work with traditionary material, and ethnopoetic research, see the special issue of *The Journal of American Folklore* 114: 454 (2001), particularly James Porter, "'Bring Me the Head of James Macpherson': The Execution of Ossian and the Wellsprings of Folkloristic Discourse" (396–435) and Thomas A. McKean, "The Fieldwork Legacy of James Macpherson" (447–63). For recent literary-historical considerations, see Matthew Wickman, "The Allure of the Improbable: *Fingal*, Evidence, and the Testimony of the 'Echoing Heath,'" *PMLA* 155:2 (March 2000): 181–94, which offers a reading of the Ossianic corpus as reflective of shifts in eighteenth-century "evidential thought"; see also Corinna Laughlin on the ramifications of Ossianic language, "The Lawless Language of Macpherson's *Ossian*," *Studies in English Literature* 40:3 (Summer 2000): 511–37. For an illuminating consideration of Macpherson and the Ossianic debates in light of Scottish Enlightenment discourse, correspondence, and modes of inquiry, see Susan Manning, "Ossianic Testimonies: Mackenzie's Highland Society Report and the Nature of Literary Evidence," Lecture, May 7, 2003, Foundational Lecture Series 2002–3, "Ossian and the Making of Modernity," Research Institute for the Culture, History, and Ethnology of Scotland (private communication). For another tactical survey of the scholarship, one may also consult the *Selected Bibliography: James Macpherson and Ossian* by Richard B. Sher with Dafydd Moore (New Jersey Institute of Technology), www.andromeda.rutgers.edu/~jlynch/C18/biblio/macpherson.html, last revised 13 March 2004, accessed 3 April 2007.

[11] For analysis of the stakes of the Ossian controversy in light of cultural nationalism, see Trumpener, "The End of an Auld Sang: Oral Tradition and Literary History," Ch. 2 in *Bardic Nationalism*, 67–127; see also the collection of essays, *From Gaelic to Romantic: Ossianic Translations*, eds. Fiona Stafford and Howard Gaskill (Amsterdam and Atlanta, GA: Rodopi, 1998), in particular Luke

controversy was also, crucially, a problem of dating and historicizing media – of theorizing oral poetries vs. manuscript evidence vs. print cultural artifacts. For critics with a writerly bias, like Johnson, the Ossian poems could only be authenticated by manuscript; for those critics more friendly to oral tradition – and the Scots were in general friendlier to theorizing and recognizing oral tradition – manuscript evidence was simply one kind of evidence among others.

The controversy over Ossian, and other related "scandals of the ballad," pointed to a new interest in the status of oral tradition, oral culture, oral composition and performance, and literary simulations thereof. For poets, antiquarians, and collectors, the complex situation of orality turned out to be in some ways a boon, particularly in post-Culloden Scotland (that is, after the 1745 Jacobite rebellion had been violently quashed), when the volatility of political Jacobitism gave way to a milder cultural nationalism: an illustrious Scottish national past – an oral past – could be celebrated without necessarily challenging British hegemony. Thus Walter Scott in his *Minstrelsy of the Scottish Border* (1802–3) could celebrate medieval Border minstrels and contemporary street criers in Aberdeen like "Mussel mou'd" Charlie (as well as their passionate antipathy to England), while also supporting British military maneuvers against Napoleonic France. Yet more rebellious and revolutionary spirits like Burns aimed to keep alive the subversive force of Scottish identity, conducted through representations of orality; and James Hogg in his 1819 collection of Jacobite songs later allied himself with popular resistance channeled through popular song.[12]

As was true in so many zones of late eighteenth-century cultural enquiry, British antiquarians made enormous contributions to the preservation and theorization of oral poetry; their work in turn stimulated the most original

Gibbons, "From Ossian to O'Carolan: The Bard as Separatist Symbol," 226–51, for eighteenth-century Irish responses. See Joseph Falaky Nagy, "Observations on the Ossianesque in Medieval Irish Literature and Modern Irish Folklore," *Journal of American Folklore* 114: 454 (2001): 436–46, for another scholar's Irish turning (or re-turning) of Ossianic matters. For Ossian explored in light of emerging, contentious discourse about "polite" language, nation, and empire, see Janet Sorensen, *The Grammar of Empire in Eighteenth-Century British Writing* (Cambridge University Press, 2000), especially her chapter, "The Figure of the Nation: Polite Language and its Imaginary Other," 138–52.

[12] See *The Jacobite Relics of Scotland, being the Songs, Airs, and Legends of the Adherents to the House of Stuart, collected and illustrated by James Hogg* (Edinburgh: Blackwood; London: Cadell, 1819), which features such lively numbers as "The Curses" (a diatribe occasioned by the 1707 Act of Union: "Curs'd be the parliament, that day,/Who gave their confirmation;/And curs'd be every whining Whig,/And damned be the whole nation") and "Perfidious Britain" ("Perfidious Britain, plung'd in guilt,/ Rebellious sons of loyal race,/How long, how long will ye insult/Your banish'd monarch suing peace?"), 104–5. For analysis of Hogg's (and others') sustaining of the Jacobite cause, see Murray Pittock, "Scottish Song and the Jacobite Cause," in *The Edinburgh History of Scottish Literature*, Vol. II: *Enlightenment, Britain, and Empire (1707–1918)*, ed. Susan Manning et al. (Edinburgh University Press, 2007), 105–9.

poets of the age – Robert Burns, for example, saluting the English antiquarian Joseph Ritson's 1783 *Select Collection of English Songs* as his *vade
mecum.* Scott and Wordsworth acknowledged their debt to Thomas Percy's
Reliques of Ancient English Poetry (1765), and indeed no poet seems to have
been untouched by Ossianism.[13] For eighteenth-century Scots, the introduction of orality into print form often functioned as a form of cultural
resistance to the dominance of English and a London-based Britain; it also
offered an opportunity for striking entrances into a newly thriving *British*
print culture, as attested by the success of (for example) Allan Ramsay,
songster, editor, and bookseller. While the majority of the Scottish literati
embraced English for speaking and writing prose from 1603 onwards, the
1707 Act of Union provided a catalyst for a reconsideration of Scots as a
viable and creative language for poetry. From Allan Ramsay through Robert
Fergusson and Robert Burns, eighteenth-century Scottish poetry under-
went several striking, many-hued efflorescences, as these poets boldly
claimed the authority to write equally brilliantly in vernacular Scots –
with its notional proximity to oral culture – and in standard English, or
in hybrids thereof. It was not of course "orality" *per se* but rather a variety of
orality-effects that Scottish poets strove to attain. What we see more broadly
in eighteenth-century British poetry is the emergence of a new, multivalent
literary orality.[14]

By the late eighteenth century, poets had developed sophisticated techniques for exploiting the aura of orality in print; and literary antiquarians,
scholars, and critics had kept pace by developing equally refined commentaries on and theories of the oral, oral poetry, and oral transmission.
Eighteenth-century Scots were especially alive to the many cultural
meanings of "orality": indeed, one could argue that eighteenth-century
Scots were the first to theorize orality.[15] It was a Scottish antiquarian,

---

[13] As Scott observed in the *Edinburgh Review*, writing on Malcolm Laing's edition of Ossian in 1805, the
Ossian poems gave "a new tone to poetry throughout all Europe" (quoted in Fielding, *Writing and
Orality*, 48).

[14] For further reflections on this topic, see Leith Davis and Maureen N. McLane, "Orality and Public
Poetry," in *The Edinburgh History of Scottish Literature*, 125–32.

[15] A number of scholars have found in eighteenth-century Scotland intriguing precursors for the
development of twentieth-century oral theory most famously formulated, regarding Homeric verse,
by Milman Parry and his colleague and furtherer Albert Lord (viz. Albert Lord, *The Singer of Tales*,
2nd edn., eds. Gregory Nagy and Stephen Mitchell [Harvard University Press, 2000]). See, for
example, Nicholas Hudson, "Oral Tradition: The Evolution of an Eighteenth-Century Concept," in
Tradition in Transition: Women Writers, Marginal Texts, and the Eighteenth-Century Canon, ed. Alvara
Ribeiro, SJ and James G. Basker (Oxford: Clarendon Press, 1996), 161–76; and his more recent
"Constructing Oral Tradition: The Origins of a Concept in Enlightenment Intellectual Culture," in
The Spoken Word: Oral Culture in Britain, 1500–1850, ed. Adam Fox and Daniel Woolf (Manchester

John Pinkerton, who wrote one of the earliest essays on oral poetry, "On the Oral Tradition of Poetry," prefixed to his 1781 *Scotish Tragic Ballads*; and it was a later collector and editor, William Motherwell of Paisley, who may be credited with developing the first rigorous theory of oral composition, articulated in his Introduction to *Minstrelsy: Ancient and Modern* (1827).[16]

"Orality" is of course a very broad term, evoking everything from "peoples without writing" (viz. Lévi-Strauss) to lore and legend to traditionary cultural practices to bodily consumption to popular expressive forms persisting into the age of print media (e.g. ballads, folktales, songs). Orality makes sense as a term only when we clarify, historically and theoretically, its implicit counters: literacy, the literary, writing, print, elite culture. Penny Fielding, in *Writing and Orality: Nationality, Culture, and Nineteenth-Century Scottish Fiction* (1996), acutely distinguishes between the orality savored and that decried by Scottish intellectuals: actual il- or pre-literate Scots, or those who spoke Scots, or English with a rich array of "Scotticisms" (all these of course contentious socio-linguistic descriptions) were long felt by forward-looking men to be an embarrassment, whereas the cultural riches and romantic aura of orality could be mined for all manner of improving and aesthetic projects. Thus the importance of such works as Hugh Blair's *Lectures on Belles Lettres* and Adam Smith's *Essay on Language*: if it was Scottish intellectuals who "invented 'English Literature,'" as Robert Crawford has argued, they did

University Press, 2002), 240–55. Hudson takes a longer and broader European perspective since the Renaiassance but flags the prominence of eighteenth-century Scottish thinkers. In "Oral Tradition," Hudson notes the early appearance of the concept of oral tradition within Catholic theological discourse, particularly refined within Counter-Reformation polemics as a defense against Protestant scripturalism; he cites Joseph Francois Lafitau's *Moeurs des sauvages amériquains* (1764) as a crucial text for "the development of this new ethnographic idea of 'oral tradition'" (165). The other significant works Hudson cites in this development are Scottish: Thomas Blackwell's influential *Enquiry into the Life and Writings of Homer* (1735) and Macpherson's *Poems of Ossian*, which Hudson calls "a landmark in the developing concept of oral tradition": as many scholars have observed, Macpherson was a student at Aberdeen's Marischal College, where Blackwell was principal. Hudson further notes, in "Constructing Oral Tradition," the appearance of Robert Wood's *An Essay on the Original Genius and Writings of Homer* (1769, 1775), as an important event. The Scottish nexus is here quite striking; so too the emergence of the concept via ethnographic researches, whether Lafitau's among Mohawk, Blackwell's and Wood's in archaic Greece, or Macpherson's among the Highlanders. After this book was largely finished, I had the benefit of hearing Paula McDowell present work from her book-in-progress, *Print Culture and the Idea of Oral Tradition in Eighteenth-Century Britain*, parts of whose argument align with the movements laid out here: she similarly locates the emergence of concepts of orality and oral tradition in the eighteenth century and acutely analyzes these developments as a reckoning with print commerce.

[16] See Pinkerton, *Scotish Tragic Ballads, with A Dissertation on the Oral Tradition in Poetry* (London: J. Nichols, 1781). On Motherwell's significant contribution, see Mary Ellen Brown, "The Mechanism of the Ancient Ballad: William Motherwell's Explanation," *Oral Tradition* 11 (1996): 175–89.

so in part by accepting the peripheral status of Scottish literature, language, and orality.[17]

For many ambitious Scots, "the oral" – and Scotland figured as "oral" – connoted a residual phase of cultural development, and was thus best left behind, or confined to friendly local communities. That paragon of Standard Englishness, Samuel Johnson, grounded his blasts against James Macpherson's Ossian poems in his contempt for merely oral tradition (and for Scotland: orality and Scotland tellingly equivalent). It is striking that for many years, Macpherson and his defenders implicitly endorsed Johnson's dismissal of the oral as a legitimate basis for poetic production: when Johnson challenged the source-bases of the Ossian poems and thundered, show us the manuscripts!, Macpherson did not, in the first instance, launch a defense of oral-traditional poetry and transmission; he rather referred to his earlier displaying of his manuscript sources in a bookseller's window. Well into the 1760s and 70s, then, "orality" bore the taint of illegitimacy, and Scottish orality within the Scottish as well as British cultural imaginary remained a much-vexed domain.[18]

Yet as the Ossian poems themselves stunningly demonstrated, the conjuring of Scottish and a notionally British orality and traditionary culture in print would have a great success in the later eighteenth century. If the Ossian poems' authenticity was doubted, their great appeal for print publics – in Scotland, England, North America, and across Europe – could not be.[19] The Ossianic bard, as he appeared on the literary scene, emerged out of Macpherson's cultural researches, and in the ensuing decades throughout

---

[17] See Fielding, *Writing and Orality*, 5; and Robert Crawford, *Devolving English Literature* (1992, 2000), and Crawford, ed., *The Scottish Invention of English Literature* (Cambridge University Press, 1998), Crawford, Sorensen, Fielding, and Trumpener make plain from different angles how central Lowland Scots were, as engaged and ambitious "peripherals," in developing "disinterested" notions of polite English. See, for example, Sorensen, "Figure of the Nation," *Grammar of Empire*, 138–52.

[18] According to Paul deGategno, one can identity at least "three phases" of its historical unfolding in the late eighteenth and early nineteenth centuries (see Paul J. deGategno, *James Macpherson*, Twayne's English Authors Series [Boston: G.K. Hall, 1989], 99). It is perhaps best to consider phases of the Ossian controversy as a kind of discursive phenomenon through which theoretical, as well as cultural–national, issues got played out. As Nicholas Hudson sagely observes, "Johnson and Macpherson, despite their intense antagonism, were in fact partners in defining the difference between 'oral' and 'literate' language. Macpherson delineated the possibility of a poetic tradition passing down through a whole culture, where every individual was an agent in that tradition, and where the basic content of the poetry was preserved by the mnemonic resources of verse. Johnson described the ways in which writing releases language from the particular 'occasion' of its utterance, facilitating its refinement in literate culture" (172). As we shall see regarding antiquarian debates, the Ossian controversy ended up refining issues *precisely* through its antagonistic charge.

[19] See, for example, the illuminating essays in Howard Gaskill, ed., *The Reception of Ossian in Europe* (London and New York: Thoemmes/Continuum, 2004).

Britain other culture-workers (editors, poets, antiquarians) took note.[20] An appreciation of Macpherson's success, and a more general fascination with ancient poets and poetry, fueled other related but differently inflected works on both sides of the border, from Thomas Percy's *Reliques of Ancient English Poetry* (1765), the influential anthology of supposedly ancient English (but in fact quite heterogeneous) poetry,[21] to such "original" works as James Beattie's "Minstrel."

BEATTIE'S *MINSTREL*: REPRESENTING THE REMEDIATION OF THE ORAL

Beattie's *Minstrel* was one of the many minstrelling works that appeared in the second half of the eighteenth century. Usually cited for its pre- and proto-romantic mapping of poetic sensibility, "The Minstrel" is also important for its attempt to date culture – or more precisely, for its aspiration to periodize cultural development as a succession of medial, as well as socio-economic, phases.[22] A Progress Poem, of a genre flourishing in the progress-minded eighteenth century, Beattie's *Minstrel* follows the progress of the arts and sciences from antiquity onward (the typical trajectory of the progress poem). In an influential innovation, he encodes this trajectory via the development of a young minstrel-in-training, one shepherd Edwin, who after a childhood spent listening to a Beldame's ballads and tales comes

---

[20] Philip Connell offers a bracing corrective to scholarship too ready to see in the Ossian controversy, in Percy's *Reliques*, and other ventures into "ancient poetry," the signs of fixed and clear cultural oppositions, e.g. Celtic Nationalism v. English Gothicism. In "British Identities and the Politics of Ancient Poetry in Later Eighteenth-Century England," *The Historical Journal* 49:1 (2006): 161–92, Connell tracks a much more complex, and more specifically politicized, career of the "Gothicism" touted in Percy's and other English collections: such Gothicism was sufficiently elastic as to include Scotch song, Scottish correspondents, and indeed, in Percy, ancient French as well as ancient English minstrels. The radical Wilkeite politics of the 1770s, moreover, made a belligerent Scoto-phobia increasingly untenable for genteel editors such as Percy: not a libertarian English patriotism but a softened British Gothicism was the preferred option for meliorist conservative types. The work of Percy and many others involved in collecting and editing ancient poetry was precisely to de-politicize, or rather, to de-radicalize, the force of cultural nationalism.

[21] The definitive work on Percy's *Reliques* is Nick Groom, *The Making of Percy's "Reliques"* (Oxford University Press, 1999). Groom reconstructs the actual composition of the work, its several stages, imagined contents, and rubrics, and discusses the inclusion of "Scotch songs" as well as Shakespearean lyrics alongside, and under the rubric of, "ancient English relics." This heterogeneity was typical of eighteenth-century collections – the actual contents of ballad-and-song collections often resisted and sometimes escaped the national, regional, historic, generic, thematic, and linguistic taxonomies and typologies imposed on them.

[22] Though Kathryn Sutherland offered in 1982 a terrific account of the figure of the Minstrel as an image of both cultural and autobiographical development, from Beattie to Wordsworth. See her "The Native Poet: The Influence of Percy's Minstrel from Beattie to Wordsworth," *Review of English Studies* New Series 33 (132) (November 1982): 414–33.

under the tutelage of a hermit-historian. Inspired in part by Percy's *Reliques* and his theory of "ancient minstrels," *The Minstrel* ushers its hero from a "rude age" – in which Edwin imbibes "tradition hoar" from the Beldame – to Enlightenment, presided over by the hermit-historian and the "historic muse." Just as the hermit supplants the Beldame as pedagogue, so too the hermit's discourse, History, supersedes the Beldame's discourse, Tradition. Said hermit and his helpmeet, the "historic Muse," instruct Edwin in the logic of history, its unfolding in time and place, culminating in the triumph of arts and sciences in "Albion," a phantasmal Britain. Edwin is encouraged to renounce his hazy fanciful ways and take up the valorous role of modern minstrel, to partake of the "philosophic spirit," as Beattie put it in a footnote, "in banishing superstition; in promoting navigation, agriculture, medicine, and moral and political science."[23]

Beattie's vision of poetic and cultural progress, incarnated through minstrel *Bildung*, invites us to reflect on the schemes available in the 1770s for periodizing poetry, from its oral through its print realizations. Beattie presents his minstrel as passing through a "rude age" but also through what we might call an "oral stage" of culture. In his concern to present oral tradition in action, in the person of the Beldame, Beattie shows how cultural theories of poetry and its historicity were making room for the oral. Among the more striking passages in the poem is Beattie's rendition of the Beldame's oral repertoire. In the first book, we learn that young Edwin and his fellows gather within a snug cottage while the snow pours down; there they listen enthralled as the Beldame weaves her oral spell (key words and phrases in bold)

> Then, as instructed by tradition hoar,
> Her **legend** when the Beldame 'gan impart,
> Or chant the **old heroic ditty** o'er,
> **Wonder** and **joy** ran thrilling to his heart;
> Much he the tale admired, but more the tuneful art. (I. 43)

[23] James Beattie, "The Minstrel; or, The Progress of Genius," in *The Minstrel; or, The Progress of Genius: and Other Poems* (1771; New York: Barstow, 1821), 63. Further quotations from the poem will be cited by book and stanza in text. Thanks to Ruth Perry for encouraging me to return to the matter of the Beldame and her repertoire in *The Minstrel*. For a magisterial account of Beldames, nurses, and old women as crucial agents for transmitting oral tradition (fairy lore, witchery, tales, legends, ballads – the very stuff of Beattie's Beldame's repertoire) in the preceding period in England, see Adam Fox, Ch. 3, "Old Wives' Tales and Nursery Lore," *Oral and Literate Culture in England: 1500–1700* (Oxford University Press, 2000). On the prominent yet ambiguous status of nurses and children in Scottish balladry, see Ann Wierda Rowland's suggestive, "'The Fause Nourice Sang': Childhood, Child Murder, and the Formalism of the Scottish Ballad Revival," in *Scotland and the Borders of Romanticism*, 225–44.

Various and strange was **the long winded tale**;
And halls, and knights, and feats of arms displayed;
Or merry swains, who quaff the nut-brown ale,
And sing, enamoured of the **nut brown maid;**
The moonlight revel of the fairy glade;
Or hags, that suckle an infernal brood,
And ply in caves the unutterable trade,
'midst fiends and spectres, quench the moon in blood,
Yell in the midnight storm, or ride the infuriate flood. (I. 44)

But when to horror his amazement rose,
A gentler strain the Beldame would rehearse
A tale of rural life, a tale of woes,
The orphan-babes, and guardian uncle fierce.
O cruel! Will no pang of pity pierce
That heart by lust of lucre seared to stone?
For sure, if aught of virtue last, or verse,
To latest times shall tender souls bemoan
Those helpless orphan-babes by thy fell arts undone. (I. 45)

In this passage, Beattie takes great care to represent oral poetry in its many modes as a crucial part of minstrel *Bildung*. What we have here is an intensely detailed imaging of oral tradition in action – songs sung, legends recited, emotions aroused ("wonder," "joy," "horror"). The Beldame's repertoire includes, as we see above, legend, heroic ditty, chivalric tale, faery lore, frightful witchery, and two specific ballads whose contents were well known to Beattie's audience and indeed to those in Britain who could not read Beattie – the "Ballad of the Nut-Brown Maid," published in Percy's *Reliques*, and the ballad "Babes in the Wood" (cf. "a tale of rural life" and "the orphan-babes" above), more commonly known as "The Children in the Wood" – a ballad first registered with the Stationers' Company in London on October 15, 1595 as "The Norfolk Gentleman, his Will and Testament, and howe he committed the keeping of his children to his own brother whoe delte most wickedly with them, and how God plagued him for it."[24] (See Fig. 1 for a broadside version of "The Children in

---

[24] William Chapell and J. Woodfall Ebsworth, eds., *The Roxburghe Ballads*, 8 vols. (Hertford: Stephen Austin and Songs, 1895), Vol. II, 214. For this information and for a deeply researched account of this ballad's career into twentieth-century North America, see Susan L. Porter, "'Children in the Wood': The Odyssey of an Anglo-American Ballad," in *Vistas of American Music: Essays and Compositions in Honor of William K. Kearns*, ed. Susan L. Porter and John Graziano (Warren, MI: Harmonie Park Press, 1999), 77–96. Porter offers richly detailed musicological comparisons of tunes as well as a close historical tracking of texts; here, as elsewhere, I focus on the ballad as "covered" in high cultural print poetry, its music perhaps hallucinatorily imported by readers over and against the metrical pulse of the poem.

THE CHILDREN IN THE WOOD,

Or the Norfolk Gentleman's last Will and Testament,

A TRUE STORY.

NOW ponder well ye parents dear,
  These words which now I write,
A doleful story you shall hear,
  In time brought forth to light.—
A gentleman of good account,
  In Norfolk dwelt of late,
Who did in honour for farmours,
  Most all men of great estate.
Sure sick he was, and like to die,
  No help his life could save;
And both his children dead did lie,
  Which lay by him sick did lie.
No love between these two was lost,
  Each was to other kind,
In love they lived, in love they died,
  And left two babes behind.
The one a fine and pretty boy,
  Not passing five years old,
The other a girl more young than he,
  And fram'd in beauty's mould.
The father left his only son,
  As plainly doth appear,
When he to perfect age should come,
  Three hundred pounds a year.
And to his little daughter Jane,
  Six hundred pounds in gold,
To be paid on the marriage day,
  Which might not be controul'd.

But if these children chanc'd to die,
  Ere they to age should come,
Their uncle should possess their wealth,
  For so the will did run.
Now brother, said the dying man,
  Look to my children dear,
Be kind unto my boy and girl,
  No friends else have they here.
To God and you I recommend,
  My children dear, this day,
But little time we have, 'tis true,
  Which in this world to stay.
You must be father and mother both,
  And uncle all in one,
God knows what will become of them,
  When I am dead and gone.
And then bespoke the mother dear,
  Oh! brother kind, quoth she,
You are the man must bring our babes
  To wealth or misery;
And if you keep them carefully,
  Then God will you reward,
But if you otherwise should deal,
  God will your deeds record.
With lips as cold as any stone,
  They kis'd their children small,
God bless you both our children dear,
  Then down the tears did fall.

These speeches then the brother spake,
  To this sick couple there,
The keeping of your children dear,
  Dear sister, do not fear,
God never prosper me nor mine,
  Nor aught else that I have,
If I do wrong your children dear,
  When you are laid in the grave.
The parents being dead and gone,
  The children home he take,
And bring them straight unto his house
  Where much of them he makes.
He had not kept these pretty babes,
  A twelvemonth and a day,
But for their wealth he did devise,
  To take them both away.
He bargain'd with two ruffians strong,
  Who were of curious mood,
That they should take these children,
  And slay them in a wood.
Then told his wife and all he had,
  He did the children send,
To be brought up in fair London,
  By one that was their friend.
Away these went these pretty babes,
  Rejoicing at that ride;
Rejoicing with a merry mood,
  They should on horseback ride,
They prate and prattle pleasantly,
  As they ride on the way,
To those that should their butchers be,
  And work their lives decay;
So that the pretty speech they made,
  Made the murderers heart relent,
And they, who undertook the deed,
  Full sorely did repent.
Yet one of them more hard of heart,
  Did vow to do his charge,
Because the wretch who hired him,
  Had paid him very much,
The other won't agree thereto,
  So here they fall to strife,
And for the other did fight,
  About the children's life,
And he that was of mildest mind,
  Did slay the other there,
Within an unfrequented wood,
  While babes did quake for fear.
He took the children by the hand,
  While tears stood in their eyes,
And bid them straightway follow him,
  And made they did not cry.

And two long miles he led them then
  While they for bread complain.
The keeping of your children dear,
Stay here, quoth he, I'll bring you bread
  When I come back again.
These pretty babes went hand in hand,
  And wander'd up and down,
But never more did see the man
  Approaching from the town.
Their pretty lips with blackberries,
  Were all besmear'd and dy'd,
And when they saw the darksome night,
  They fat them down and cry'd.
Thus wander'd these two pretty babes,
  Till death did end their grief,
In one another arms they died,
  As babes wanting relief.
No burial these two pretty babes,
  Of any man receiv'd,
Till Robin Redbreast painfully,
  Did cover them with leaves.
And now the heavy wrath of God
  Upon their uncle fell;
Yea, frightful fiends did haunt his house
  His conscience felt a hell;
His barns were fir'd, his house consum'd
  His lands were barren made,
His cattle died within a field,
  And nothing with him staid.
And in a voyage to Portugal,
  Two of his sons did die,
And to conclude, himself was brought,
  To want and misery.
He pawn'd and mortgag'd all his land,
  Ere seven years were out,
So, now at length this wicked deed,
  By this means came about.
The fellow that did take in hand,
  The children for to kill,
Was for a murder judg'd to die,
  As was God's blessed will.
He did confess the very truth,
  O what is here expect'd,
The uncle died, who e'er for debt,
  Did long in prison rot
You that executors be made,
  And overseers eke,
Of children that be fatherless,
  And infants mild and meek,
Take you example by this thing,
  And yield to each his right,
Lest God for such like cruelty,
  Your wicked minds requit,

the Wood, or The Norfolk Gentleman.") "The Children in the Wood" appeared as a black-letter broadside ballad through the seventeenth century and had a long afterlife: Joseph Addison praised it as "one of the Darling Songs of the Common People" in *Spectator* essay no. 85 in 1711, Thomas Percy published it in his *Reliques*, Samuel Johnson ridiculed it, and Wordsworth later defended it, when defending his own *Lyrical Ballads* in his 1800 "Preface." (And in fact – regarding the afterlives of this ballad – one soon discovers that Ruth Rendell has written a mystery entitled *The Babes in the Wood*,[25] and also that, perhaps inevitably, one can find an "adult film" in DVD format called *Babes in the Woods*. There is also a children's store on the web called "Babes in the Wood" – a curious choice, given that "Babes in the Wood" is a child-murder ballad, a Hansel-and-Gretel-type story in which the children are abandoned and eventually die.)

Beattie was not the only eighteenth-century poet to offer a minstrelling "cover" of "The Children in the Wood": John Gay's brilliant pastoral, *The Shepherd's Calendar* (1714) features a rustic minstrel, "Bowzybeus" (a cheerfully drunken lesser Meliboeus), the comic hero of the final eclogue "Saturday: or, the Flights." In Bowzybeus' repertory Gay deftly incorporates a wide variety of folk sayings, proverbs, street ballads, and popular songs – "Ballads and Roundelays and Catches sung" (l. 28) – and among the songs he sings is "The Children in the Wood":

> Then sad he sung *the Children in the Wood*.
> Ah barb'rous Uncle, stain'd with infant Blood!
> How Blackberrys they pluck'd in Desarts wild,
> And fearless at the glittering Fauchion smil'd;
> Their little Corps the Robin-red-breasts found,
> And strow'd with pious Bill the Leaves around. (ll. 91–6)[26]

Bowzybeus goes on to sing, among other things, "Chevy-Chace" (another ballad Addison had singled out for special praise), "Lilly-burlero" (the great anti-Stuart anti-Papist seventeenth-century song) and other well-known ballads and tunes.

Gay's rustic minstrel has a strikingly broad repertoire, yet like Beattie, Gay gives special prominence to "The Children in the Wood," offering in the lines above a mini-résumé of its plot – a distillation that anticipates the

[25] Ruth Rendell, *The Babes in the Wood* (London: Hutchinson, 2002).
[26] See "Saturday; or, The Flights," *The Shepherd's Week*, 122, in *The Poetry and Prose of John Gay*, ed. Vinton A. Dearing with Charles E. Beckwith (Oxford: Clarendon Press, 1974), Vol. I of II. See the editors' illuminating notes on Gay's sources and his engagement with Virgil and with song, hymn, and balladry, Vol. II, 535–40.

ultimate compression of the ballad into three pathetical stanzas, which
feature the dying children, blackberries eaten, the covering robins, and
expressions of woe (in this version, now the current one in US, the back-
story about wills, uncles, ruffians, etc. is largely abandoned, as it has been for
some time). Notably, while Gay gives us a rustic minstrel in action, singing
his repertoire for an engaged, flirtatious audience, he does not foreground
this scene as one of transmission, nor as one crucial to minstrel self-fashioning, as does Beattie. If in Gay, the ballad is part of a male rustic minstrel's
repertoire, in Beattie, such a ballad becomes the province of Beldames
bound to hearths. We move from Gay's represented scene, of casual out-
door seasonal encounters among rustics, to Beattie's – the developmentally
crucial pedagogical scene of young children sitting indoors before an old
woman. From Gay to Beattie we move as well, of course, from Augustan
pastoral to a progress-poem inflected by the Spenserian revival: ballad
repertory is now gendered female, its audiences infantilized.[27]

Beyond Beattie's representation of oral-tradition and -transmission at the
level of content, we are also – and this is most significant – in the presence of
a *remediation* of the oral.[28] This remediation is most conspicuous in the one
line Beattie actually purports to quote from the traditional Babes in the
Wood, in the course of the Beldame's redaction of it. The traditional
ballad reaches its pathetic climax in the following lines, already much
quoted by Beattie's era:

---

[27] The crucial study of romantic Spenserianism is Greg Kucich, *Keats, Shelley, and Romantic
Spenserianism* (University Park, PA: Pennsylvania State University Press, 1991), a book which in its
attention to eighteenth-century predecessors shows both the flexible persistence of the Spenserian
stanza and mode and also the impossibility of rigorously isolating what would seem pre-Romantic
ventures (e.g. Beattie's poem) from Romantic ones.

[28] On "remediation" as a concept within media studies, see, for example, Jay David Bolter and Richard
Grusin, eds., *Remediation: Understanding New Media* (Cambridge, MA: MIT Press, 1999), especially
"Introduction: the Double Logic of Remediation," 2–15, and Ch. 1, "Immediacy, Hypermediacy, and
Remediation," 20–50; *Rethinking Media Change: The Aesthetics of Transition*, ed. David Thorburn
and Henry Jenkins (Cambridge, MA: MIT Press, 2003), Introduction, 1–16; N. Katherine Hayles,
Writing Machines (Cambridge, MA: MIT Press, 2002). This wave of work invokes even as it often
critiques the mid-twentieth-century efflorescence of media studies by (among others) Marshall
McLuhan, Eric Havelock, Raymond Williams, and Walter J. Ong. This work might be explored
in conjunction with other scholarship explicitly immersed in the Romantic period (as Williams' and
Ong's certainly were), which suggests extensive oral-literate interactions and occasional feedback
loops: such as Dianne Dugaw's work on balladry, Mary Ellen Brown's and Carol McGuirk's work on
Burns, Kevis Goodman on Wordsworth, and Celeste Langan's reflections on mediality in Walter
Scott's *Lay of the Last Minstrel*, Friedrich Kittler's several books: scholarship to be more specifically
addressed later in this chapter and subsequently. Media studies announced as such often exhibits,
perhaps understandably, a remarkably presentist bias, fixating on twentieth-century technological
innovations; the work cited here is more subtle and supple in its handling of historical media
formations and in its resistance to progressivist (or decadent) narratives.

> These pretty Babes with hand in hand
> went wandring up and down,
> But never more they saw the man
> approaching from the Town.
> Their pretty lips with black-berries
> Were all besmear'd and dy'd
> And when they saw the darksom night
> They sat them down and cri'd.[29]

Beattie's Beldame comes to a similar climax in her rendition of the ballad.
As she says:

> Behold with berries smeared, with brambles torn,
> The babes now famished lay them down to die
> Amidst the howl of darksome woods forlorn,
> Folded in one another's arms they lie;
> Nor friend, nor stranger, hears their dying cry:
> **"For from the town the man returns no more."**
> But thou, who heaven's just vengeance dar'st defy,
> This deed with fruitless tears shalt soon deplore,
> When death lays waste thy house, and flames consume thy store.
>
> (Book I, st. 46, emphasis added)

These lines, containing one conspicuously marked as a quotation, offer a
reworking of the matter versified in ballad quatrains quoted directly above.
A number of things are happening, then, in Beattie's brief "cover" of the
traditional ballad: first, Beattie creates the illusion of oral mimesis. He does
this at the level of content through the simulation of a traditional hearth-
scene of ballad-singing and tale-telling and, at the level of print mediation,
through the typographical convention of quotation. But we see that Beattie
is not so much "quoting" the oral as staging its remediation. We note the

---

[29] From "The Norfolk Gentleman, his last Will and Testament," (a broadside version of "The Children
in the Wood"), no. 255 (and companion versions 254 and 256), in *The Euing Collection of English
Broadside Ballads in the Library of the University of Glasgow*, intro. John Holloway (University of
Glasgow, 1971), 415–16. For other broadside versions of "Babes in the Woods," one might consult the
Bodleian Library *allegro* Catalogue of Ballads online: www.bodley.ox.ac.uk/ballads/ballads.htm; the
broadside as found in the Pepys collection may be found on the excellent UCSB Early Modern
Center Ballad Archive, 1500–1800, directed by Patricia Fumerton: www.english.ucsb.edu/emc/
ballad_project/ballad_image.asp?id=20246. The first of the two stanzas quoted here is the one
Johnson parodied and Wordsworth approvingly quoted in his *Preface*. I draw here on the broadside
tradition, an earlier print remediation of the oral, to get at the notionally oral *materia* of the Beldame;
no one of my acquaintance was able to sing "The Babes in the Woods," though Dianne Dugaw
reports that Shannon Applegate of Oregon has made a recent recording of the ballad, and you can
hear it sung, full-length, at the UCSB site, which is dedicated to offering plausible reconstructions of
the broadside singing as well as textual tradition. That this ballad seems to have been circulating in
several medial forms for several centuries only begins to suggest how complex the media situation of
balladry was and is: print did not kill orality, at least in this case.

conservation of key rhyme words (forms of "die" and "cry" in both the broadside and Beattie); we observe the preservation of plot and key elements ("the Man," "the town," the "berries" in each) and the maintaining of striking diction in both (the woods "darksome," the children berry-"smeared"); yet we find in Beattie a significant expansion of lofty editorializing (viz. "But thou..."). In this passage we are experiencing not so much the oral as what Friedrich Kittler calls a "transposition of media."[30] A medium "cannot be translated" (265), Kittler argues, but a medium, and a medial channel, can certainly be represented and indeed evoked: to wit, the Beldame-as-medium and the Beldame's orality – both her matter (traditionary poetry and lore) and means (oral performance). We recall that the notionally oral *materia* invoked here would have been cast into a ballad stanza, as it is in the broadsides: that is, in a quatrain with lines alternating 4/3 beats, rhyming abab (or abcb); whereas Beattie stretches his quotation of the notionally oral to fill out the iambic five-beat requirements of the line in his Spenserian stanza. Or, from another angle, we could say that Beattie actually compresses traditionary material into his lines: the ballad's "But never more they saw the man/approaching from the Town" is distilled into Beattie's "For from the town the man returns no more." (The actual complexities of the transformation of the material exceed, of course, a comparison of these few lines: the re-shaping is metrical, attitudinal, narratological, as well as typographical, as you see comparing the stanzas quoted above or if you study a black-letter broadside version of the ballad.) The point here is this: the very attempt to stage the oral, to incorporate it into this minstrel fiction, has required a metrical remediation as well as an allegorical transubstantiation into writing and print. What is being represented here then is not the oral *per se* but rather print culture's solicitation and transmediation of oral materials. The metrical adjustments – the move from ballad to Spenserian stanza – demonstrate at the level of grammar, rhythm, and prosody the gap between the fantasized orality of a "rude age" and the neo-Spenserianisms of 1771.

One would never guess from Beattie's *Minstrel* that the broadside circulation of "The Children in the Wood" was still active throughout the eighteenth and into the nineteenth centuries (in England if not as widely

---

[30] See Kittler, *Discourse Networks, 1800/1900*, in particular the section "Untranslatability and the Transposition of Media," in "Rebus," 265–73. Kittler is describing the media transpositions possible ca. 1900 (e.g. the transposition of images and sounds into letters, the interest of such for Freud), but his analysis opens up as well the intermedial transpositions possible and of interest ca. 1800: the conversion of the oral, for example, into a typographically set quotation.

in Scotland)[31]; not only was the ballad still circulating in late-eighteenth-century oral tradition – it was flourishing in some parts of the UK in an alternate print modality! But Beattie was not concerned with broadsides or with the vitality and multi-media messiness of actual ballad transmission. He re-animates the Beldame's notional repertoire precisely to dramatize its supercession. The broader point here is this: in Beattie, the representing of balladry as orality has required the theorizing and historicizing of both balladry and orality. Beattie's allegorical representation of oral poetry gives us a drama of planned obsolescence, one particularly relevant to late-eighteenth-century Scotland; oral tradition and its poetries are imagined as sustained by unlettered women, to be superseded by male pedagogues and by writing technologies – here figured as the Muse of History who "unrolls her page" before the minstrel. The gendered oral imaginary emerges here as an essential feature of the broader Scottish cultural imaginary, negotiating its status within Great Britain – Beattie's phantasmal "Albion." And it is important to recognize that the cultural theory encoded here did not confine itself to high-cultural poetries in Scotland – for indeed, the broader romance with orality so characteristic of cultural inquiry in the eighteenth century fueled other, more ethnographic, modes of poetic research. To wit: the researches and transcriptions of the man, W. L. who transcribed "The Bonny Hynd" in 1771, and sent his copy to the antiquarian David Herd.

THE MOUTH OF A MILKMAID: CITING AND DATING THE ORAL

This transcription in question made its way into David Herd's manuscripts in the 1770s, yet despite publishing his important collection of ballads in

---

[31] The Bodleian archives (www.bodley.ox.ac.uk/ballads/ballads.htm) attest to multiple versions from the seventeenth through nineteenth centuries, broadsides printed for example between 1658–64 (Wood 401(109v, 110r)); 1736–63 (Harding B 4(30)); 1780–1812 (Harding B 4(34)); 1790–1813 (Harding B 4(36)). It is true, however, that the broadside ballad trade did not flourish in north-eastern Scotland until a boom in the mid-1770s (contemporary with the second book of Beattie's "Minstrel," 1774): in and around Beattie's Aberdeen, then, it is possible that "The Children in the Wood" traveled in a mode of oral circulation less pressured by, and indebted to, the broadside modality. See David Buchan on "The Regional Tradition" in balladry (particularly in north-east Scotland), and the crucial differences in the "trade in printed balladry" in England and Scotland, in *The Ballad and the Folk* (East Linton: Tuckwell Press, 1997 [1st edn. London: Routledge & Kegan Paul, 1972]), esp. the Introduction and Ch. 16; 4, 215. Speaking of an earlier moment, Dave Harker notes, "Scotland had only one broadside-song printer in the later seventeenth-century while England had forty": this meant not that Scotland had no broadside tradition but rather that the English trade could penetrate unobstructed into north-east Scotland, thereby imposing pseudo-"Scotch songs" on a Scottish populace. See Harker, *Fakesong: The Manufacture of British 'Folksong' 1700 to the Present Day* (Milton Keynes and Philadelphia: Open University Press, 1985), 7.

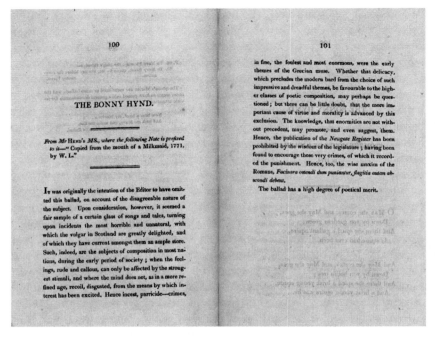

2 "The Bonny Hynd," headnote from Walter Scott, *Minstrelsy of the Scottish Border*

1776, and revising it in 1791, he did not include this ballad specimen.[32] The first time this ballad appears in print is in fact in the 1802–3 first edition of Walter Scott's *Minstrelsy of the Scottish Border*, when the poem appears with a subtitle above the headnote (see Fig. 2):

From Mr. Herd's MS, *where the following Note is prefixed to it* – "Copied from the mouth of a milkmaid, 1771, by W.L."[33]

What precisely has been dated here? Dated here, I'd suggest, is the first stage of what Michel de Certeau has called "the ethnographic operation," that epistemological-technical process through which the speech or song of "primitive" others is textualized, brought into writing and later print by

[32] See David Herd, *Ancient and Modern Scots Songs* (Edinburgh, 1769; 2 vols., 1776; rev. 1791; Edinburgh and London: Scottish Academic Press, 1973).

[33] Walter Scott, *Minstrelsy of the Scottish Border*, in *The Poetical Works*, 173. Further references to the *Minstrelsy* will be cited by page in text.

literate, transcribing cultural researchers.[34] What is dated here, then, is not the ballad, nor even the recitation, but the conjunction of milkmaid and man under the sign of cultural collecting. The date refers precisely to a media operation, a medial translation: this copy here is no copy, in the sense of a replication or recreation – it is a remediation into writing, further remediated into print. Marshall McLuhan's axiom, by which the content of one medium is always another medium, is rather baldly demonstrated here. Both the ballad proper and its authenticating note are differentially remediated into print. In terms of the rhetoric of authentication and of cultural location, the note renders this ballad another kind of object than it would be without such a frame. It is important to recognize that this note, this ethnographic lab-note, as it were, is not simply an empirical trace but is rather deeply figural and rhetorical – it collapses the space between the milkmaid's vocalization and the man's transcription, as if one could truly copy from the mouth, as if this were, as Lacan might say, an encounter with "The Real." It's worth noting here that the authenticating phrase, "from the mouth," and "out of the mouths," becomes formulaic in balladeering citation, in Herder and Goethe as well as in British collections.[35] Despite this somewhat alarming proliferation of mouths in balladeering, we observe here that the actual process of singing or reciting is elided, such that we do not know whether the milkmaid sang, spoke, recited, chanted, or droned the ballad. These aspects of vocalization have not yet been conceptualized as significant cultural facts – *that* she vocalized, not *how* she vocalized, is the relevant cultural datum.

The date here, moreover, appears in Scott not only as an index of a historical or ethnographic operation: the date here has become a media datum – a print fact. Unprinted, the date resides in Herd's manuscript,[36]

---

[34] In his essay, "Ethno-Graphy: Speech, or the Space of the Other: Jean de Lery" included in *The Writing of History*, trans. Tom Conley (New York: Columbia University Press, 1988), 209–43.

[35] See, for example, the headnote to the first song in Herder's *Stimmen der völker in liedern [Voices of the People in Songs]* (Leipzig, 1778–9): "Das Lied vom jungen Grafen; Deutsch"; "Aus dem Munde des Volks in Elsaß": Out of the mouths of the people of Alsace. Herder here orients us to a folk-community, not to individuals as indices of a folk or a nation – this being one distinguishing feature of German vs. British balladeering. The European source-base of Herder's collections stands in striking contrast to the largely Scottish and English provenance of late-eighteenth-century British collections. On the German trajectory of balladeering as it intersected with English and Scottish projects, one might consult Tom Cheesman's and Sigrid Rieuwerts' introduction to *Ballads into Books*.

[36] See the Herd MSS in the British Library, where on a page pencil-numbered 224 one finds "The Bonny Heyn – copied from the mouth of a Milk Maid in 1771, by W. L." Also pencilled in the body of the text, by another hand, is the first line of the fourth stanza that Herd himself, and Scott following him, declined to write or print out – the sex-stanza: "He has ta'en her by the milkwhite hand,/And saftly laid her down; /And when he lifted her up again,/He gae her a silver kaim" Lockhart helpfully restored this stanza in a note to the ballad, included in the "collective edition" of Walter Scott's works, 1830–3; and Child printed it in his second volume, 1884.

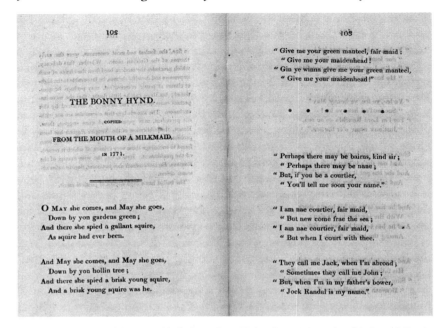

3a "The Bonny Hynd," note and ballad text from Walter Scott, *Minstrelsy of the Scottish Border*

evidentiary *materia* held privately by a zealous collector corresponding with other song-collectors and antiquarians, known to each other by initial and by club nicknames (Herd's was "Graysteil"). But printed in Scott, and indeed in later compendiums including Francis James Child's (Fig. 3b)[37] the dated note and the dated ballad become another kind of evidence, a print fact.

By 1803, then, the dated transcription event has passed what Foucault would call a "threshold of epistemologization," such that it may become part of the evidentiary discourse of that singular mode of cultural inquiry, balladeering.[38] Here we are bordering on an inquiry into historical episte-mology – an investigation into what Lorraine Daston calls "the history of

---

[37] See "The Bonny Hynd," No. 50, *The English and Scottish Popular Ballads*, ed. Francis James Child (Boston: Houghton, Mifflin, 1882–98), in Vol. II of X, 444–7.

[38] See Michel Foucault, *The Archaeology of Knowledge and the Discourse on Language*, trans. A. M. Sheridan Smith (New York: Pantheon, 1972), in particular Ch. 6, "Science and Knowledge," with its elucidation of several thresholds of emergence of a "discursive formation": the thresholds of positivity, epistemologization, scientificity, and formalization (186–7). Foucault observes in "The Discourse on Language" that discourse analysis (unlike, say, the "history of ideas") orients us to "the power of constituting domains of objects": the production of ballads as eighteenth-century objects of inquiry obviously fall within this analytic purview.

Herd's MSS, II, fol. 65. "Copied from the mouth of a
nilkmaid, by W. L , in 1771."

1 O MAY she comes, and may she goes,
  Down by yon gardens green,
And there she spied a gallant squire
  As squire had ever been.

2 And may she comes, and may she goes,
  Down by yon hollin tree,
And there she spied a brisk young squire,
  And a brisk young squire was he.

3 'Give me your green manteel, fair maid,
  Give me your maidenhead ;
Gif ye winna gie me your green manteel,
  Gi me your maidenhead.'

4 He has taen her by the milk-white hand,
  And softly laid her down,
And when he 's lifted her up again
  Given her a silver kaim.

5 'Perhaps there may be bairns, kind sir,
  Perhaps there may be nane ;
But if you be a courtier,
  You 'll tell to me your name.'

6 'I am nae courtier, fair maid,
  But new come frae the sea ;
I am nae courtier, fair maid,
  But when I court 'ith thee.

7 'They call me Jack when I 'm abroad,
  Sometimes they call me John ;
But when I 'm in my father's bower
  Jock Randal is my name.'

8 'Ye lee, ye lee, ye bonny lad,
  Sae loud 's I hear ye lee !
Ffor I 'm Lord Randal's yae daughter,
  He has nae mair nor me.'

9 'Ye lee, ye lee, ye bonny may,
  Sae loud 's I hear ye lee !

For I 'm Lord Randal's yae yae son,
  Just now come oer the sea.'

10 She 's putten her hand down by her spare,
  And out she 's taen a knife,
And she has putn 't in her heart's bluid,
  And taen away her life.

11 And he 's taen up his bonny sister,
  With the big tear in his een,
And he has buried his bonny sister
  Amang the hollins green.

12 And syne he 's hyed him oer the dale,
  His father dear to see :
'Sing O and O for my bonny hind,
  Beneath yon hollin tree !'

13 'What needs you care for your bonny hyn ?
  For it you needna care ;
There 's aught score hyns in yonder park,
  And five score hyns to spare.

14 'Four score of them are siller-shod,
  Of thae ye may get three ; '
'But O and O for my bonny hyn,
  Beneath yon hollin tree ! '

15 'What needs you care for your bonny hyn ?
  For it you need na care;
Take you the best, gi me the warst,
  Since plenty is to spare.'

16 'I care na for your hyns, my lord,
  I care na for your fee;
But O and O for my bonny hyn,
  Beneath the hollin tree ! '

17 'O were ye at your sister's bower,
  Your sister fair to see,
Ye 'll think na mair o your bonny hyn
  Beneath the hollin tree.'

*   *   *   *   *

'The Bonny Heyn,' I, 224.
3². *Should be* It 's not for you a weed. *Motherwell.*
4¹. *The third copy omits* when.
4³˙⁴. he lifted, He gae her. *Motherwell.*
5¹˙². *The second copy has* they.
6⁴. *All have* courteth. *Scott prints* wi' thee, with thee.

7⁸. *The third copy has* tower.

10³˙⁴. She 's soakt it in her red heart's blood,
  And twin'd herself of life. *Motherwell.*

13, 14. *The first copy omits these stanzas.*

3b "The Bonny Hynd," ballad text and note from Child No. 50, *The English
and Scottish Popular Ballads*

competing forms of facticity"[39]: such an inquiry, preliminarily undertaken here, would in its fullest reach explore how "ballad facts" become formalized as objects of knowledge, and how they make their differential way into media. Broader implications soon emerge: as I hope to show in subsequent chapters, taking antiquarian balladeering seriously also sheds light on the conditions of producing (and obscuring) knowledge within and about what we now call the humanities. Lisa Gitelman invokes Lorraine Daston's observations about the uneven distribution of scholarly attention: we have histories of instruments and objectivity for science, but "far more rare are considerations of how knowledge in the humanities comes about: How have literary critics learned to criticize?"[40] Here too the antiquarians have much to offer.

Encoded in Herd's note is a communication and evaluation network, one in which antiquarians and collectors cite themselves, date their transcriptions, remark their informants' occupations but not their names. Such a note partakes of a larger discourse of citation emergent in late-eighteenth-century ballad collections – headnotes and footnotes through which ballad collectors and editors authenticate their sources and burnish their bona fides. These citation protocols began as a mechanism for citing antiquarian correspondents – the circle of men who shared manuscripts and textual finds and less frequently oral "copies" and "communications," as they called them. Mid-eighteenth-century collectors typically cited their antiquarian correspondents, not their oral informants, if they were even willing to use them, and certainly not the date of recitation and transcription. Percy in his *Reliques*, for example, printed several Scottish Songs sent to him by Sir David Dalrymple (later Lord Hailes), some of which he had copied from various Scottish informants (most aristocratic): while Percy elaborately acknowledged the Scottish lawyer's communication of songs to him, never did he print the date of the recitation or the transcription thereof, nor did he or, apparently, Dalrymple, find it important to name the actual singer. What was documented in such notes, in other words, was chains of antiquarian transmission, not performance occasions. Yet as Herd's note suggests, an increasing awareness of the value of oral tradition and oral informants caused a shift in the citation paradigm: by Scott's *Minstrelsy*, a manuscript note such as Herd's was balladeering news fit to print.

[39] See Lorraine Daston, "Historical Epistemology": 282–9, in *Questions of Evidence: Proof, Practice, and Persuasion across the Disciplines*, ed. James Chandler, Arnold I. Davidson, Harry Harootunian (University of Chicago Press, 1994); and also her "Marvelous Facts and Miraculous Evidence in Early Modern Europe": 243–74.

[40] See Lisa Gitelman, *Always Already New* (Cambridge, MA: MIT Press, 2006), 40; and quoting Daston in her epilogue, "Doing Media History," 153.

On the internal structure of the note itself: let us recall that, according to Gertrude Stein, there are two things that are interesting, history and grammar. The grammar of this note will help us to historicize it. "Copied from the mouth of a milkmaid, 1771, by W. L." We note the passive construction of this note, its verb shifted into the passive voice, the agent, the transcriber, submerged into a prepositional phrase: copied by W. L. We note the indefinite article: *a* milkmaid, a member of a class of anonymous female farm workers. We note the successive levels of mediation, the receding horizon of the informant's body: the ballad is copied FROM the mouth OF a milkmaid.

A milkmaid and her mouth stand grammatically as indirect objects of the implied subject, W. L., whose object was the ballad: in other words, if syntactically transformed, the note would read, "W. L. copied 'The Bonny Hynd' from the mouth of a milkmaid." The milkmaid's mouth emerges notionally as a transparent vessel, an frictionless orifice of the real. The Milkmaid does not matter as a nameable individual: she is significant as a member of a class of persons: rural laborers in possession of oral tradition. In such a note we see that the milkmaid is not in fact the medium of the ballad message, if we understand medium, technically, to be a determining conduit. She is rather an authenticating ground, the signifier of living tradition; she introduces no cultural or historical noise; she does not re-create her song, as contemporary oral-theory might describe such a performance; she merely, passively, channels it.

Grammar thus helps us to construe this sentence as an instance in the history and ideology of mediation: the ballad as musical and verbal process and event becomes ballad as textualized object. Dating renders the ballad ready for history – for cultural history, for literary history, for a history of anthropological salvage operations.

And indeed, the ballad itself functions for Scott as evidence in a larger cultural argument, for "The Bonny Hynd" pushed Scott to the limits of his editorial composure (see Fig. 2):

It was originally my intention to have omitted this ballad, on account of the disagreeable nature of the subject. Upon consideration, however, it seemed a fair sample of a certain class of songs and tales, turning upon incidents the most horrible and unnatural, with which the vulgar in Scotland are greatly delighted, and of which they have current among them in ample store. Such, indeed, are the subjects of composition in most nations, during the early period of society … Hence incest, parricide – crimes, in fine, the foulest and most enormous, were the early themes of the Grecian muse. (Headnote to "The Bonny Hynd," 173)

As an incest ballad full of taboo sex and suicide, "The Bonny Hynd" threatens to break out of the decorous culturally nationalistic project

Scott had set for himself – and indeed, Scott, following Herd's omission in his manuscript, chose not to print the crucial sex-stanza which he quite likely knew: that stanza seems to have appeared in canonical print only when Francis James Child restored it some eighty years later (see Fig. 3– asterisks in Scott denote the omitted stanza). Scott's headnote both cements his cultural authority and installs him as censor: he has printed this thing with some disgust, he makes plain, but his printing of this lurid thing is different, he insists, from other print accounts of crime – for example those in the Newgate Register.[41] Scott's headnote both recognizes the ballad's sensationalism and decriminalizes the ballad such that it may stand as a cultural curiosity, a bit of evidence about what "the vulgar" now enjoy; ballad contents are, moreover, displaced in the headnote such that "The Bonny Hynd" can in Scott's hands signify "culture" itself, more precisely, a stage of culture: "the early period of society."

That the "early period of society" is discoverable in the most literate European nation in 1771 offers us much food for historical and medial thought.

Dating your evidence prepares it for history. The date in this case has the peculiar effect of historicizing the contemporary. The emergent collecting procedures in Britain in the later eighteenth century thus anticipate a displacement and repression that Johannes Fabian analyzed some years ago in *Time and the Other*, his critique of ethnographic writing. If Fabian's book explored "how anthropology makes its object," as his subtitle put it, we might explore further how balladeering, minstrelsy, and other ethno-poetic projects made their objects: ballads, of course, but also informants, cited correspondents, and the very concepts of "culture" and "society" informing such *poiesis*. A balladeering open to the oral, to ethnographic collecting, as Scott's guardedly was, tends to require and produce what Fabian calls "a denial of coevalness." Fabian observed that what is truly required for ethnographic (and by extension, ethnopoetic) fieldwork is co-existence, a synchronicity, a time and space provisionally shared by fieldworker and informant.[42] Yet in the representation of such encounters in ethnographic writing, we typically find a denial of that co-existence, a

---

[41] Toward the end of his headnote, Scott approvingly notes that "the publication of the *Newgate Register* has been prohibited by the wisdom of the legislature, having been found to encourage those very crimes of which it recorded the punishment." Properly censured, however, "The Bonny Hynd" may be published, not least because it "has a high degree of poetical merit." (Headnote to "The Bonny Hynd," *Minstrelsy*, 173). Here I am indebted to Ann Wierda Rowland's remarks on this ballad, and to her work on the logic of distinction and the bid for cultural capital manifest in Scott.

[42] Johannes Fabian, *Time and the Other: How Anthropology Makes its Object* (Columbia University Press, 1983).

rendering of the informant[s] as somehow "other"; a conversion of the ethnographic present and intersubjectivity essential to fieldwork into a distantiating objectifying ethnographic discourse about others: and indeed, the milkmaid's utterance is ultimately taken by Scott to specify "an early period of society," not an interaction characteristic of the human sciences and cultural research circa 1771. The milkmaid stands not as a late-eighteenth-century singer but rather as a living relic, a living fossil, a body or more precisely a mouth bearing the archaic into Scottish and more broadly British modernity.

Scott's Herd's W. L.'s milkmaid thus enters history, even as Beattie's eponymous Minstrel enters history: yet we recall that Beattie's minstrel is imagined to enter as a subject of history, not as a mere supplier of its evidence base. If Beattie's minstrel leaves orality behind in his march toward Enlightenment, Scottish ballad collectors were increasingly turning to the oral, in practice as well as theory. What was theorized as archaic, "rude," and primitive was seen to persist into the modern, particularly in the Scottish cultural imaginary. By this cultural logic, milkmaids and their songs existed *in* 1771 but were not *of* 1771. When Scott published "The Bonny Hynd" in 1803, he characterized it as a ballad "from the early period of society," not as a song of 1771. To date orality was already to historicize it, to render it archaic, or, in Raymond Williams' terms, *residual*.[43] The collecting procedures of W.L. and the Spenserian stanzas of Beattie's progress poem thus share a common cultural logic, however different their modes and aims: for both the antiquarian transcriber and the poet-philosopher, the oral is always already *dated*, always behind us.

The romance of fled music: that is what orality offered literate poets.

The prospect of deep, thick, yet notionally audible pasts: this is what orality offered antiquarians and conjectural historians interested in "the early period of society."

The primitive within: this is what the oral offered cultural theory.[44] The persistence of ballads like "The Bonny Hynd" or the gruesome infanticide

---

[43] For a discussion of the "residual," and more broadly of Williams' tri-partite model of cultural formation, see Raymond Williams, *Marxism and Literature* (Oxford University Press, 1977), esp. Chapter 8, "Dominant, Residual, and Emergent," 121–7. For a subtle elaboration of Williams' "structures of feeling" as they make themselves felt in history, particularly in this era, see Kevis Goodman, *Georgic Modernity and British Romanticism: Poetry and the Mediation of History* (Cambridge University Press, 2004). Goodman is especially astute on the way "history" makes itself felt as an "absent cause" (viz. Althusser) through Georgic, and thus offers a salutary critique of some versions of Romantic historicism.

[44] That this recourse to "the primitive within" has long informed other disciplines and discourses might almost go without saying. For one recent, trenchant study of the racialized anthropo-logic of the

ballad "Lamkin," which Scott decided not to publish, were indices of a Scotland, and more broadly a Britain, existing in several historical time-zones: the scandalous or recalcitrant ballad appears, when allowed to appear, as an ethnographic datum, ostensibly purged of sensation, an object of cultural curiosity and proper, classed delectation – obviously it is not milkmaids but antiquarians and literati whom Scott envisions reading his *Minstrelsy*.[45] In this light the oral informant is the means of production claimed and owned in print by the entrepreneurial Editor.[46] A milkmaid is important because she authenticates not only the ballad's contents but its media status as oral evidence, and thus she offers circa 1800 (i.e. the time of the *Minstrelsy*'s publication) evidence of the persistence of an earlier stratum of cultural development in Scotland, as recently as 1771.

Whether the dating of cultures can ever push us to imagine futures as well as pasts – this is still our question inasmuch as we are willing to reflect on our own historicizations and prospects. The cultural logic by which the oral is virtually co-extensive with the primitive, the prior, and the archaic is still with us, despite the many theoretical critiques (not to mention rap songs and DVDs) that strive to liberate us from the presumption that print culture is the *telos* of world history. When thinking culture, Fredric Jameson advised us years ago to "always historicize"; Dipesh Chakrabarty has more recently asked that we provincialize Europe, that we relativize our archives, that we scrutinize our impulse to date cultures along a uniform grid.[47] With US leaders threatening not long ago to bomb Afghanistan back to the Stone Age – a peculiar boast, given that country's already devastated condition – it is worth thinking about the procedures, concepts, and motives we and our representatives continue to invoke when dating any

"primitive within" structuring psychoanalytic discourse, and Freud's metapsychology in particular, see Celia Brickman, *Aboriginal Populations in the Mind: Race and Primitivity in Psychoanalysis* (Columbia University Press, 2003).

[45] Yet the avid participation of James Hogg, shepherd and poet and eventual novelist, writer of tales, and man-of-letters, and of his mother, the redoubtable informant Mrs. Hogg, puts pressure on this presumption of a monolithic elite audience: Scott was being read by, as well as helped by, people across the spectrum of class and literacy: viz. Mrs. Hogg's much-reported chastising of Scott for having "ruined" her ballads by printing them. That Mrs. Hogg criticized Scott's text and spelling reveals that she most likely had *read* the *Minstrelsy*, as well as recited for it. Scott's notes and apparatus do seem expressly designed, however, to participate in antiquarian and otherwise specialist conversations.

[46] Such an assessment chimes in some respects with Dave Harker's rather severe but lucid and informative Marxian analysis of British balladeering as a venture dependent on the expropriation of workers' song-culture; see his *Fakesong*.

[47] See Fredric Jameson, *The Political Unconscious: Narrative as a Socially Symbolic Act* (Ithaca, NY: Cornell University Press, 1981), 9; Dipesh Chakrabarty, *Provincializing Europe: Postcolonial Thought and Historical Difference* (Princeton University Press, 2000). Chakrabarty takes his title from Gadamer.

Table 1

	"Name"/ Medium	Site	Dates of media realizations
RECITER	"A milkmaid"	?? – Scotland	1771: transcription event: oral production
TRANSCRIBER	W. L.	?? – Scotland	1771: transcription event: written recording
MS. COLLECTOR	David Herd	Edinburgh, Scotland	Post-1771: collecting, correspondence
COMPILER, EDITOR	Walter Scott	Kelso, Edinburgh Scotland	1802–3 print publication
COMPILER, EDITOR	F. J. Child	Boston USA	1884: print publication
SINGER	June Tabor	S. Carolina and CA	1991: digital recording
D. J.	M. McLane	Essex, NY	8.2.07: CD played

culture. The Stone Age may be a name for our human future as much as for our imagined past.

In terms of the futurities of the dated cultural works discussed in this chapter, it is a fact that while Beattie's *Minstrel* has largely receded into the genteel dustbin of literary scholarship on sensibility, "The Bonny Hynd" has outmaneuvered its consignment to "an early period of society" in 1803. "The Bonny Hynd" probably had a long life before print, and it may well have a life after it: the ballad has resurfaced in media neither the milkmaid nor Walter Scott could have foreseen, the CD[48]– the appearance of which reminds us again that, to invoke Susan Howe, a ballad may yet undertake unforeseen "dark crossings" (see Table 1).

---

[48] For example, June Tabor's CD, *Abyssinians*, 1983 (Topic TSCD 432), which features on its penultimate track a terrific rendition of the ballad in Tabor's powerful contralto.

CHAPTER 2

How to do things with ballads: Fieldwork and the archive in late-eighteenth-century Britain

"Copied from the mouth of a Milkmaid, 1771, by W. L."
– note to the ballad "The Bonny Hynd," in David Herd's manuscript

"Who is actually the author of fieldnotes?"
– James Clifford, "On Ethnographic Authority"

"Today the establishment of sources requires also a founding gesture,
signified, as in former times, by the combination of a place, an
'apparatus,' and techniques."
– Michel de Certeau, "The Historiographical Operation"

Sometime in the latter half of the eighteenth century, ballads changed –
sometime between, say, the publication of Thomas Percy's Reliques of
Ancient English Poetry (1765) and Walter Scott's Minstrelsy of the Scottish
Border (1802–3). Or more precisely, the protocols for representing ballads in
print changed. This chapter proposes to track that shift, and proposes as
well to show how fieldwork entered balladeering books, most specifically
through the transformation of antiquarian ballad citation.

This chapter moves through several sections, first describing the antiquarian discourse community that undertook ballad research, outlining as
well the protocols for citing sources that developed within that community.
As competition between collectors and editors sharpened antiquarians'
standards, there emerged newly sophisticated ways of handling and authenticating source material in several media. One sees as well a new, careful
privileging of the oral, particularly in the work of Scottish editors, who
claimed a special, native access to the oral tradition they and their English
fellows were so energetically remediating into print. Thus we find editors
mobilizing the discourse of ethnographic authority alongside, indeed as part
of, their editorial authority. This new-found respect for fieldwork, oral
informants, oral tradition, and representations thereof, finds its ratification
in the enquiries of the Highland Committee of Scotland, which in the
late 1790s sought out native informants as possible verifiers of James

Macpherson's poetic researches – some forty years after his Ossian poems began to appear before print publics.

This chapter argues, then, that in its conjunction of practices and discursive domains, in its coordination of fieldwork and archives, late-eighteenth-century balladeering should be seen as a laboratory for the human sciences as well as a formative moment in the history of the production of British literature and the consolidation of cultural nationalisms. I will further suggest that the balladeers, forced to handle and theorize relations among different media (oral, manuscript, print), began a methodological inquiry into the condition and historicity of mediality – an inquiry that still has much to teach us.[1]

Several scholars have re-acquainted us with the extensive and often mind-numbing *apparatus criticus* of eighteenth-century ballad collections, especially those with scholarly, taste-making, or patron-seeking ambitions. The novel has long been discussed in terms of its heteroglossia and its theoretically open form; its ungainly cousin, the eighteenth-century ballad collection, is equally notable for its mustering, display, and attempted disciplining of heterogeneous materials and its formidable textual apparatus: introductions, headnotes, footnotes, appendices, dissertations, commentaries. Such apparatus, offering historical, topographical, linguistic, political, and customary information, has the peculiar effect of distracting us (as it did perhaps its first readers) from the often sensational contents of the ballads – tales of incest, bloodfeud, childmurder, supernatural abduction, parricide, and so on.[2] As Ann Rowland acutely observes, "The impressive scholarly apparatus that the ballad revival bequeaths to British literature is, in fact, a way of *not* reading or responding to the contents of ballad literature."[3] This chapter will collude, perhaps unfortunately, with the swerve that balladeering apparatus generally makes from ballad contents.

Such authenticating, explanatory discourse was symptomatic of a crisis in the handling of source materials and more broadly of the problematic of authenticity created by the scandalous ballad revival. However labored, rebarbative, or *recherché* such apparatus may now seem (and in fact often seemed to the balladeers' contemporaries), this discourse was not

---

[1] On "mediality," see Introduction, n. 14. Friedrich Kittler's work, in conjunction with scholars of eighteenth-century oral theory (e.g. Nicholas Hudson), illuminates eighteenth-century balladeers as media theorists in their own right.

[2] On the constitutive disjunction between framing apparatus and ballad contents proper, see Ann Rowland, "Fause Nourice," 227: "most frequently, the grisly, scandalous contents of the ballads go unnoticed altogether." Nick Groom offers an extended meditation on Percy's preoccupation with dismemberment, textual and corporeal, in *Percy's "Reliques,"* 52–60.

[3] Rowland, "Fause Nourice," 227.

extraneous to but rather constitutive of the emergent genre of the ballad collection, a genre that was clearly recognized as such by its practitioners.[4] The consolidation of this genre required the collaborative work of numerous collectors, transcribers, annotators, correspondents, editors, printers, and publishers; it also required, at the level of representation, the formalization of various rhetorical and discursive protocols.

One might instructively contrast antiquarian ballad citation – and its predilection for the headnote – with the development of the historical footnote, as illuminated in Anthony Grafton's *The Footnote: A Curious History* (1997). If the footnote becomes the major technique through which historians present their second story – that of their research and critical comparison of sources – the headnote becomes the space through which antiquarians do the same but also frame and authenticate their documents *as documents*. Antiquarians represent themselves, then, as establishing, as well as gathering, documentary collections (though their appendices, "dissertations," and introductory essays offer pointed historical narratives in their own right); historians present themselves as narrators of a past critically worked up out of primary sources. Grafton concludes: "A full literary analysis of modern historical writing would have to include a rhetoric of annotation as well as some version of the existing rhetorics of narration."[5] I suggest that we regard antiquarian balladeering as a repository of such annotative "modern historical writing" as well as a form of literary-cultural spelunking.

In the following pages I will explore how the rhetoric of ballad documentation and citation – the headnote in particular – had to adjust to accommodate the appearance of a new subject: the ballad informant, the living reciter, the medium of oral tradition. The native informant, the oral source, was not so much a subject as an object of ballad discourse. In this he or she – most usually she – became a discourse-object alongside her equally documented transcriber–transmitter and song-mediator, the antiquarian and later the romantic collector and balladeer.[6]

---

[4] On source-mediation, see Groom, *Percy's "Reliques,"* for example, Introduction, 7, and 191: "Percy's very arrangements [of his ballads] were commentaries on the media of his sources." On the problematic of authenticity, see Stewart, "Scandals of the Ballad"; on emergent genres, including ballad collections and the national tale, see Trumpener, Preface, *Bardic Nationalism*, xi.

[5] Anthony Grafton, *The Footnote: A Curious History* (Cambridge, MA: Harvard University Press; London: Faber and Faber, 1997; paperback edn. 2003), 233. Chapter 4 addresses more extensively the complex relationship between antiquarian and historical discourse in Britain in this period.

[6] I adopt the term "song-mediator" from Dave Harker, whose detailed and tart *Fakesong* provides lucid biographies of all major balladeers (including Percy, Ritson, Pinkerton, Scott, and Burns) and traces the historical arc of what Harker sees as the systematic expropriation of workers' song-culture by some aspirationally and some successfully petty-bourgeois and bourgeois balladeers in the eighteenth and

Eighteenth-century ballad collections were typically made out of variable stuff, their contents drawn from private collections of broadsides and manuscripts, re-discovered manuscripts like Percy's famed Folio Manuscript, previously printed and sometimes published garlands and miscellanies, transcriptions of this or that recitation, and occasionally trash – not to mention plenty of familiar, authored, literary poems (by Suckling, Dryden, Shakespeare, and so on) as well as new poems – "imitations" acknowledged and unacknowledged – by the Editor and his associates.[7] Over the course of the eighteenth century, spurred in part by Joseph Addison's appreciative essays on old ballads ("Chevy Chase" and "The Children of the Wood") in *The Spectator* (1711), antiquarian ballad-eering amassed and produced first an archive, the proliferating mass of ballad *documenta* in various mediums (e.g. manuscript, black-letter broadsides, chapbooks, multivolume compendiums), and ultimately a canon, consisting of the published ballad collections themselves, culminating in Francis James Child's monument, *The English and Scottish Popular Ballads* (1882–98).

A Collection of Old Ballads: Corrected from the Best and Most Ancient Copies Extant. With Introductions Historical, Critical, and Humorous (1723, 1725) was, in ballad scholar Sigrid Hustvedt's account, the first of its kind.[8] A three-volume, literary compendium accompanied by copperplate illustrations, its editor to this day still unknown, *A Collection of Old Ballads* had no real predecessors to acknowledge.[9] Its lengthy headnotes were genial

nineteeth centuries. His salutary focus on the bourgeois book market and the class stakes of ballad collecting, publishing, and circulating offers an incisive Marxian alternative to, or foreground for, my argument here. The problem and discourse of authentication is clearly the discursive symptom of the alienation, in all senses, of ballads – their alienation from oral tradition, fantasized or actual; from workers and singers and women; from specified locales and first singing and printing into a British, Anglo-American, and ultimately global print imaginary; their alienation into commodities. That "alienation" need not be a pejorative term or deleterious process I will leave to argue for another time.

[7] On Percy's retrieval of a ragged manuscript from the fire at his friend Humphrey Pitt, see Groom, *Percy's "Reliques,"* 6. The Pepys ballads is a collection of 277 broadsides, their sheets often cut in half; 110 of these ballads appear in the Roxburghe collection. See *The Pepys Ballads, 1535–1625*, vol. I of VIII, nos. 1–45, ed. Hyder Edward Rollins (Cambridge, MA: Harvard University Press, 1929), vii. For the diagnostic heterogeneity of ballad collection contents – their conjunction of anonymous and authored works, oral-traditional and literary stuff under the sign of an emergent national literature – consider Percy's inclusion of Shakespeare's songs alongside Chevy Chase and the Battle of Otterbourne and his section of "Mad songs"; Scott's enlarging roster of "modern" contributors with each edition of the *Minstrelsy*; and the mix of anonymous and authored, undated and dated works, in collections by Ramsay, Pinkerton, and Ritson.

[8] Hustvedt, *Ballad Criticism in Scandinavia and Great Britain during the Eighteenth Century* (London: Oxford University Press, 1916), 98.

[9] See *A Collection of Old Ballads. Corrected from the Best and Most Ancient Copies Extant. With Introductions Historical, Critical, and Humorous*, Illustrated with Copper Plates, 3 vols. (London, 1723, 1725). Groom notes that its editor, once thought to be Ambrose Phillips, is still in question.

disquisitions on the historical background informing the ballads, most of which the editor drew from broadside archives.[10] Cheerfully mixing drinking songs with historical ballads, combining Robin Hood ballads (the "Greenwood" ballads) with "Scotch songs,"[11] this was an ambitious but neither overly serious nor vociferously nationalistic collection; nor was its editor conscious of participating in a literary history of the genre, the ballad collection. Within fifty years, however, any editor of a ballad collection worth his stuff would formally rehearse in his introduction, itself now a more or less obligatory part of the genre, a long and by then standard (if growing) list of previous ballad collections (including *A Collection of Old Ballads*) along with the manuscripts, garlands, orts and fragments he had been privileged to consult.[12]

A brief glance at some titles on the title-pages of some later ballad collections confirms that their editors were increasingly concerned to display and lay claim to their sources:

Reliques of Ancient English Poetry, consisting of old heroic ballads, songs, and other pieces of our earlier poets, (chiefly of the lyric kind.) Together with some few of later date (ed. Thomas Percy, London, J. Dodsley, 1765, 3 vols.)

Ancient Scotish Poems, never before in print. But now published from the Ms. Collections of Sir Richard Maitland, of Lethington, Knight, Lord Privy Seal of Scotland, and a senator of the college of justice. Comprising pieces written from about

---

[10] The broadside basis of this collection is evident both in the titles, which duplicate those in Pepys' and Euings' collections, but also in the subheadings below most: "The Children of the Wood ....To the tune of, *Rogero*" (221); "An Unhappy Memorable Song of the Hunting in *Chevy-Chace* between Earl *Piercy* of *England*, and Earl *Douglas of Scotland*. To the Tune of *Flying Fame*" (108). On the significance of this anthology for establishing headnote protocols, and for the diffusion of interest in balladry across the class spectrum, see Dianne Dugaw's important essay, "The Popular Marketing of 'Old Ballads': The Ballad Revival and Eighteenth-century Antiquarianism Reconsidered," *Eighteenth-Century Studies* 21 (1987): 71–90.

[11] For Scots songs and ballads, in theme if not provenance, see "Bonny Dundee," "The Scotch Lass's Complaint" in vol. I; "The Bonny Scott," "The Scotch Lovers," and "The Scotch Wedding" in vol. II; "The Lass of Peatie's Mill" and "The bonny Scot" in vol. III, *Old Ballads*. The editor bundled Scotch songs, as he called them, toward the end of each volume.

[12] For an example of Joseph Ritson's zealous bibliographic research and other source-cataloguing, see his Preface to *Scotish Song in Two Volumes* (London: J. Johnson, 1794), in which he lists among his sources his own previous ballad collections, Allan Ramsay's *Tea-Table Miscellany* and his *Evergreen*; the *Edinburgh Magazine*, "manuscript copies transmitted by Mr. Tytler" (a Scottish authority on song and poetry) (iv); Herd's *Ancient and Modern Scots Song*; Percy's *Reliques*; T. Evans' *Old Ballads*; and Napier's collection. Ritson also notes that he obtained song-music from Oswald's *Caledonian pocket companion* (vi); Thompson's *Orpheus Caledonius*; Ramsay's collections; Johnson's *Scots Musical Museum*, and that he consulted the manuscripts of Scotish Tunes in the library of the Society of the Antiquaries of Scotland made for the laird of Macfarlane, which unfortunately only "afforded one single air" (xi). In his "Remarks on Popular Poetry" and "Essay on Imitations of the Ancient Ballad" (1830) Scott included a similarly exacting and comprehensive catalogue, the specifics of which I will spare the reader.

1420 till 1586. With Large Notes, and a Glossary. Prefixed are An Essay on the origin of Scotish Poetry. A List of All the Scotish Poets, with brief remarks. And an appendix is added, containing, among other articles, an account of the contents of the Maitland and Bannatyne Mss. (John Pinkerton, London: C. Dilley, 1786, 2 vols.)

Minstrelsy of the Scottish Border: consisting of Historical and Romantic Ballads, collected in the Southern Counties of Scotland. (Walter Scott, Kelso: Ballantyne/ Cadell and London: Davies, 1802, 2 vols.; by 1810, expanded title: ... *with a few of Modern Date, founded upon Local Tradition.*)

Popular Ballads and Songs, from tradition, manuscripts, and scarce editions; with translations of similar pieces from the ancient Danish language, and a few originals by the Editor. By Robert Jamieson. 2 vols. (Edinburgh: Constable; London: John Murray, 1806; working title in 1801: *Reliques of Ancient Scotish Poetry*)

If Thomas Percy antiqued, nationalized, and sanctified his ballads as "English relics," Scott simultaneously localized and nationalized his, while also remarking the distinctive ethnographic *praxis* of his collecting on the border. We see that Pinkerton announces privileged access to manuscripts and aristocrats; we observe that Jamieson – after abandoning his working Perceian title (viz. "*Reliques*") – foregrounds the heterogeneous source-base and mediality of his collection, which coordinates oral tradition, manuscripts, and print "editions." We may observe in these title pages, with their elaborate subtitles, a variegated exploration and coordination of axes of editorial distinction in balladeering: antiquity and novelty (Pinkerton's "never before in print," echoed throughout Scott's headnotes), popularity and refinement (Jamieson's "popular song" versus Pinkerton's display of aristocratic title and position), common property (in all senses of "common") and scarcity (Jamieson's "scarce editions"), tradition and innovation (Jamieson's "few originals by the author"). It is also clear that balladeering created a peculiar retro-neo chronotope,[13] conjoining as it did supposedly "ancient" and thus potentially historicizable poetry with what Scott called work "of modern date."

Title pages and prefaces produced a general source-frame for a whole collection; yet the sources of individual ballads were increasingly specified as well. As part of their ostentatious editorial displays of source mediation, ambitious ballad editors often followed Percy in documenting in their head-

---

[13] On "the chronotope" as the space–time configuration generated both within narratives and between a work and its compositional contexts, see "Forms of Time and of the Chronotope in the Novel: Notes toward a Historical Poetics," included in *The Dialogic Imagination: Four Essays by M. M Bakhtin*, ed. Michael Holquist, trans. Caryl Emerson and Michael Holquist (Austin: University of Texas Press, 1981), 84–258. Bakhtin observes that "it is precisely the chronotope that defines genre and generic distinctions, for in literature the primary category in the chronotope is time" (85).

and foot-notes the provenance of each ballad – the sources from which a ballad was collated, and the people and places from which the editor had obtained his copies, his raw materials, to collate. Here what we might call the antiquarian discourse network becomes important.[14]

FROM ANTIQUARIAN CORRESPONDENTS TO CITED INFORMANTS: BALLADEERING CIRCUITRY AND THE RHETORIC OF ANNOTATION

Eighteenth-century balladeering was typically the pursuit of gentlemen, clergymen, lawyers, and some quirky bachelors with antiquarian interests and leisure time; it was also profoundly advanced by the labors of those Marilyn Butler calls "anti-establishment scholars" – men unaffiliated with Oxbridge, often from provincial cities and towns in the north of England and the Scottish Lowlands, often marginal to the cosmopolitan discourse and literary production of London. Considered as a subset of "popular antiquarianism," antiquarian balladeering undertook "a study of British national culture: of English, Welsh, Gaelic, and Irish as vernacular languages, and of their oral as well as their written traditions – not merely literary forms and art, but beliefs, customs, festivities."[15] This was also a social, collaborative activity, sustained through correspondence and, for the privileged, summer meetings at country houses and appointments at private libraries. Percy, for example, did not edit his *Reliques* in isolation: William Shenstone claimed to have given Percy the idea of editing his Folio Manuscript and advised Percy quite intensively, as did, to a lesser extent, Samuel Johnson and Thomas Warton, Professor of Poetry at Oxford. The later Scottish balladeers were if anything even more collaborative, if often and simultaneously competitive: David Herd, an important collector and publisher of Scottish song and ballad, was helped by George Paton, who was also a correspondent of the English antiquarian Joseph Ritson, who himself corresponded with Walter Scott, who in turn seems to have corresponded

---

[14] See Kittler, *Discourse Networks, 1800/1900*. The title is the translation of the original German *Aufschreibesysteme 1800/1900*. Throughout *Discourse Networks* and the more recent *Gramophone, Film, Typewriter* (Stanford University Press, 1999), Kittler deploys a metaphorics and sometimes a materialistics of circuitry and networks, through which he conjoins practices and technologies (writing, alphabetization), cultural–ideological orders (the Imaginary, the Symbolic), and discursive spaces ("poetry"). Although Kittler's cases are primarily German, his methodological and metaphorical disposition should help us to rethink British literary antiquarianism, and its Romantic transformation, both as a discursive system *and* a media network.

[15] Marilyn Butler, "Antiquarianism (Popular)," Essay 35, *An Oxford Companion to the Romantic Age: British Culture 1776–1832*, ed. Iain McCalman et al. (Oxford University Press, 1999), 333, 328.

with and masterfully commandeered the efforts of every ballad antiquary, living and dead, in England, Scotland, Wales, and Ireland.[16]

The antiquarian traffic in balladry rested, then, on an extensive network of antiquarian correspondence, acquaintance, and exchange; this was truly a traffic among men, a homosocial activity, as Susan Manning has observed, which required complex negotiations and often surprisingly flexible crossings of class, nation, region, party, and religion, as part of the collation and mediation of sources.[17] Balladeering afforded opportunities for many kinds of collaboration: offering financial assistance, granting access to archives, giving editorial advice, providing linguistic glosses, offering annotations from custom, procuring historical documentation, as well as sending along ballads themselves, whether from one's own collection or from another's.

Yet for all the gentlemanly aspirations of Percy, a grocer's son who eventually became Bishop of Dromore in Ireland, and the later moderate tones of Scott, antiquarians continued, in a lesser key, the strain of vituperation so prominent in earlier eighteenth-century literary-cultural controversy – viz. the Ancients vs. Moderns, Pope's endless salvos, Swift's devastations.[18] Joseph Ritson, a London conveyancer originally from Newcastle, was the most infamous calumniator of his fellow balladeers and scholars, even meriting a caricature by Gillray in 1803.[19] Ritson's animadversions on Percy's touching up of ballads, and his derisive remarks on Percy's theory of ancient English minstrels, became a *locus classicus* of

---

[16] On "the corporate effort" required to make Percy's *Reliques*, see Groom: "Percy was as much the mastermind behind a gang of textual bibliographers as he was the editor of a parcel of old ballads" (174). For "the clan of Scott," the balladeering deputies Scott sponsored and to some extent exploited, see Hustvedt and John Sutherland, *The Life of Walter Scott: A Critical Biography* (Blackwell, 1995), 79. Sutherland believes that "Scott's great trick as a ballad collector was his ability to foster collaboration – something that came very hard to the antiquarians" (76).

[17] Susan Manning, "Antiquarianism, Balladry, and the Rehabilitation of Romance," in *The Cambridge History of English Romantic Literature*, ed. James Chandler (Cambridge University Press, 2008), for the "homosocial" nature of balladeering; see her essay as well for the unsettled valences of antiquarianism, its status as a target of ridicule, its resistance to systematization, its love of proliferating data, its facilitation of cross-class collaboration. For song-mediators' backgrounds and their class valences, see Harker, *Fakesong*. Prominent among recent positive revaluations of these antiquarians is Rosemary Sweet's work, which strongly challenges older, still lingering satirical views. Sweet emphasizes their development of complex, pluralistic ethno-historical narratives and restores antiquarians to the "republic of letters." See Rosemary Sweet, *Antiquaries: The Discovery of The Past in Eighteenth-Century Britain* (London and New York: Hambledon and London, 2004); and "Antiquaries and Antiquities," *Eighteenth-Century Studies* 34:2 (2001): 181–206.

[18] For the literary genealogy of historical footnotes in eighteenth-century English satire, see Grafton, *The Footnote*, 111–18.

[19] For Ritson's career in the context of popular antiquarianism, see Butler, "Antiquarianism," 332, and for Gillray's caricature, see Butler, "Antiquarianism," 333. For a sympathetic account of the life and work, see Bertrand H. Bronson, *Joseph Ritson: Scholar-at-arms* (Berkeley: University of California Press, 1938).

ballad controversy alongside the scandal of the Ossian poems, those disputed "translations" of Scottish Gaelic fragments and epics produced by James Macpherson. Eighteenth-century balladeering was thus always already polemical, however much Scott later tried to pacify it by historicizing its practice and productions under the teleological sign of the Union and British Empire.[20]

In his "Essay on Imitations of the Ancient Ballad" (1830), Scott pointedly described antiquarianism as a discourse-community, its polemics understandable only within the context of community standards regarding address and the treatment of evidence: "It must be owned, that such freedoms [in editing, as Percy practiced], when assumed by *a professed antiquary, addressing himself to antiquaries, and for the sake of illustrating literary antiquities,* are subject to great and licentious abuse; and herein the severity of Ritson was to a certain extent justified" (emphasis added; *MSB*, 181). Ballad competition and collaboration should be seen as two sides of the same discursive coin, and antiquarian exchange, both cooperative and competitive, should be seen as a communication circuit, a discourse network materially sustained by the mails and improved roads, through which ballads and ballad *documenta* both flowed and slowed.[21] And if the antiquarian communication network became a major channel for ballad transmission, it also became an object of ballad citation.

Alongside notices of manuscripts, garlands, and previously published books, traces of antiquarian correspondence entered the ballad collection as part of its authenticating apparatus – for example, when Percy observes in his headnote to "Edom O'Gordon, a Scottish Ballad," "We are indebted for its publication (with many other valuable things in these volumes) to Sir David Dalrymple, Bart., who gave it as it was preserved in the memory of a lady that is now dead."[22] Or when he silently salutes Sir David Dalrymple (later Lord Hailes of Edinburgh) again in "Lord Thomas and Fair Annet":

---

[20] For Scott's relation to the prior balladeering tradition, in particular to Percy and Ritson, see Susan Oliver, *Scott, Byron, and the Poetics of Cultural Encounter* (New York: Palgrave Macmillan, 2005), 19–68.

[21] On the specifics of the improvement of roads in the early eighteenth century, and its impact on antiquarian fieldwork, see Stuart Piggott, "Ruins in a Landscape: Aspects of Seventeenth and Eighteenth Century Antiquarianism," *Ruins in a Landscape: Essays in Antiquarianism* (Edinburgh University Press, 1976), 115. Piggott notes that the first turnpikes officially date from 1663, and that signposts were required as of 1697. On the mails as a media channel, and on Habermas' failure to assess them as such, see Kittler, *Gramophone, Film, Typewriter*, 37.

[22] Percy, "Edom O'Gordon," Ballad 12, Vol. I, book 1 (final ballad in this book); in Thomas Percy, *Reliques of Ancient English Poetry, Consisting of Old Heroic Ballads, Songs, and Other Pieces of our Earlier Poets, Together with Some Few of Later Date*, ed. with intro. etc. Henry B. Wheatley, 3 vols. (New York: Dover, 1996; repr. of London: Swan Sonnenschein, 1886), 140.

"from a MS. copy transmitted from Scotland." Or, for a later example, when Scott in his *Minstrelsy* announces that "fourteen verses [of "the Cruel Sister" were] *transmitted to the editor by J.C. Walker, Esq.*, the ingenious historian of the Irish bards"; or when he hails another antiquarian correspondent in his note to "The Queen's Marie": "that [copy] principally used *was communicated to me*, in the most polite manner, by Mr. Kirkpatrick Sharpe, of Hoddom, to whom I am indebted for many similar favours."[23] The point I wish to stress here is that, not only does antiquarian correspondence function as a mediating circuit for balladry, a transmission channel: ballad editors made the citation of such correspondence a constitutive generic element of the ballad collection.

In the citations above, antiquarian transmitters are placed and located along axes of class, region, and if appropriate, profession: Lord Hailes of Edinburgh, the polite Sharpe of Hoddom, J. C. Walker Esq., the Irish historian, and so on. It is important to observe that citation tracks and documents the fact of antiquarian exchange, the correspondence-event, not necessarily the content of the correspondence. What is cited are the chains of transmission, the nodes on the circuit, the junctures of antiquarian mediation, not necessarily its message. When correspondents send a "copy" or a "communication," they offer to the recipients raw material for the compiler/editor to collate, process, transform, and selectively cite.

Citing and localizing the antiquarian informant was one thing; handling an oral informant was another. One of the very few times Percy acknowledged, albeit indirectly and only implicitly, an oral informant – a reciter – was in the above-mentioned headnote to "Edom O'Gordon": Percy writes that his correspondent Sir David "gave it as it was preserved in the memory of a lady that is now dead."[24] Percy's headnote specifies axes of authority, discourses of authentication, and problems of editorial mediation that continued to preoccupy balladeers right through the nineteenth and twentieth centuries. We see that Percy's rhetoric of citation traces a series of mediations, from an origin in the deceased lady's "memory," its preserving power a kind of archival space, through the mediating transcriber-correspondent Sir David Dalrymple, whose name as well as his aristocratic status are remarked, to the correspondent–addressee–editor Percy, who

---

[23] Walter Scott, "The Cruel Sister" (170), "The Queen's Marie" (171), in *The Poetical Works*. Further references to the *Minstrelsy of the Scottish Border* (*MSB*) will be cited in text by page.

[24] Percy, "Edom O'Gordon," 140.

proceeds to collate this traditionary Scottish oral material, now textualized, with his own fragmentary English manuscript text.[25]

What we do not know, what does not enter the field of representation – the discursive space of the note – is how the lady acquired the contents of her memory, the ballad itself. Also unspecified: the mode of mediating that memory. Lord Hailes "gave it as it was preserved in [her] memory," but how was that memory mediated? I have been assuming that she recited or sang the ballad to Lord Hailes, but she might well have written it down at his request: such was the prerogative of a noble and presumably literate "lady." The fact of her memory, however, insured by her elevated pedigree, offers Percy a picturesque, pleasing source, as well as a discursive basis for source-authentication.

If it was important for a scholarly editor in 1765 to represent the mediations of the ballads he presented, it was also true, as we have seen, that all mediations did not require the same level of elaboration and attention. Thus "the lady" above rests comfortably and unproblematically in genteel anonymity, whereas the Scottish correspondent – Percy's co-collector – is named and specified. Ballads needed not authors but authenticators: bona fide sources and bona fide transmitters. A source, as Percy's note suggests, need not have a name; he or she did need, however, a pedigree and a locale – in other words, a provenance. Antiquarian trans-mitters, on the other hand, especially if they were "polite" correspondents, did indeed enter ballad discourse as named, acknowledged contributors. In the course of remediation and artifactualization into printed books, the multiple collaborations that made balladeering possible thus entered spe-cific discursive spaces and submitted to specific protocols for representing and differentiating (and, as one often discovers, suppressing or finessing) the kinds and degrees of collaboration involved.

ORAL TRADITION AND THE INDIVIDUAL TALENT: MEDIUMS, MESSAGES, AND THE TRANSFORMATION OF CITATION

However complex it was to handle textually fixed, artifactual materials, the ballad informant presented editors with an even greater methodological challenge, even for those friendlier to oral tradition than Percy. Should one solicit recitations? If one obtained them, by design or inadvertently, should

---

[25] "The reader will here find it improved and enlarged with several fine stanzas, recovered from a fragment of the same ballad, in the Editor's Folio MS." Percy, note to "Edom O'Gordon," 140.

one use them as sources?[26] And if one did make use of an oral source, should one cite it, and how? What status should one accord a recently transcribed recitation versus a centuries-old manuscript copy or a previous printing of a ballad? And further, how should one evaluate "oral communications" of any kind, and the routes of their transmission?

As previously suggested, one crucible for posing and addressing such questions was the Ossian controversy and the various ballad scandals which brought to the fore of debates in the British literary public sphere the problem of the oral source – the medium of much disputed oral tradition.[27] Although James Macpherson proffered fragments and epics, not ballads, the linguistic, cultural, and historical theorization surrounding his work inevitably informed the balladeering *poiesis* of his peers and successors. Among them was Thomas Percy, who invented his own theory of ancient English minstrels in part to provide for his English ballad "relics" a cultural provenance as compelling as the Ossianic bardic tradition was for Scottish Gaelic poetry. Percy had little interest in handling the stuff of contemporary oral traditions; he saw how dangerous it was to embark on the project of "editing" oral tradition.[28] It was, moreover, his providential discovery and retrieval from the flames of a seventeenth-century manuscript and not, as in Macpherson's case, a privileged relation to Scottish Gaelic culture, which launched his balladeering. Unlike Macpherson or Robert Burns or Walter Scott, Percy did not ground his project in his childhood and adolescent memories of absorbing ballads, whether heard or read.

We will have occasion to return, if not to the Ossian poems, to the Ossian problematic: for Macpherson's tussle with the literary establishment forecast an ongoing crisis of the source – oral and literary – as well as of authenticity,

---

[26] Groom notes that Percy was sent several unsolicited ballads taken from recitation south of the Tyne, about which he was ambivalent, including none in successive editions of the *Reliques*; and which have since been claimed as almost the sole example of living oral tradition collected in England in the eighteenth century. See Groom, *Percy's "Reliques"*, 29.

[27] For specifics, see Groom, "Macpherson and Percy," in *Percy's "Reliques"*, 61–105; Trumpener, "The End of an Old Song: Oral Tradition and Literary History," *Bardic Nationalism*, 67–127. Groom believes that Macpherson and his defenders could have carried the day, or at least defended themselves more effectively, had they stuck with their original conception: that the Ossian poems were an exemplarily oral poetry, handed down orally though also committed to writing; that the bardic oral tradition offered its own mechanism of transmission wholly other than and independent of manuscript or print culture. It is striking that, whereas older scholarship often paired Macpherson and Chatterton as fellow forgers, more recent scholarship tends to pair Macpherson and Percy, their projects and fates handily diagnosing the oral-literate problematic of the period and the national/imperial inflections thereof.

[28] On Macpherson's challenge to Percy, see Groom: "Percy had to construct a cultural provenance," "Macpherson and Percy," *Percy's "Reliques,"* 97. Groom notes that Macpherson's case may have strengthened "Percy's lack of interest in collecting the living tradition," 29.

cultural and poetic property, and theories of cultural transmission. Groom observes, "The rival claims of Percy and Macpherson on the literary establishment reveal that the handling of the source was crucial to the antiquarian reception of literature and its incorporation into the canon."[29] Samuel Johnson had contemptuously dismissed the very notion of oral tradition, of a rich culture-hoard sustained among illiterate, barefoot, Erse-speaking people; yet if the Johnsonians seemed to have won – at least in London – the revivified battle over Macpherson's poems in the 1770s, they lost the theoretical war. For oral tradition, humble though it was, came to acquire – especially in the work of Scottish balladeers – a new and unembarrassed status both as an authenticating source and as an archival domain. More particularly, the oral-source-medium, the living transmitter, acquired a special status, since he or she could serve as both an authentic medium of the ballad message and also as a putative documentary link in a chain of oral transmission.

One might call this transformation, "how oral tradition became respectable and sometimes got a name." Under the cover of "tradition," it is true, balladeers could smuggle in dubious ballad goods: John Pinkerton, an authority on Scottish antiquities but also a ballad-hoaxer, wrote an essay "On the Oral Tradition in Poetry" to accompany his *Scotish Tragic Ballads* (1781).[30] In that same volume he also included several poems "now first published from tradition" – most of which he had to admit five years later were his own productions.[31] That "tradition" as a source was still somewhat disreputable in the 1790s, at least for English antiquarians, is indicated by Joseph Ritson, who observed in his "Historical Essay on Scotish Song" (1794) "how poetry is preserved for a succession of ages by mere tradition"[32] Yet Ritson's "mere tradition" was losing its self-evidence as a sneer. Invoked and theorized almost exclusively in the context of Scottish traditionary poetry (even though Herder and Goethe were busily pursuing their own

---

[29] Ibid., 62.

[30] Of this essay Hustvedt observed that it was "the first connected discussion of ballad technique" – refrain, internal rhyme, alliteration, and the nature of the ballad stanza. See Hustvedt, *Ballad Criticism*, 248.

[31] See Pinkerton, *Scotish Tragic Ballads* (London: J. Nichols, 1781), with two dissertations prefixed: "On the Oral Tradition of Poetry" and "On the Tragic Ballad," 37. Poems authenticated as "from tradition" included "Binnorie" and "I wish I were where Helen lies," as well as a "complete" version of "Hardyknute." For his confession and retraction, see his *Ancient Scotish Poems, never before in print ...* (London and Edinburgh, 1786], two volumes: "Of the second part of Hardyknute, written in 1776 but not published until 1781, the editor must now confess himself guilty" (cxxviii); he also notes that his version of "Binnorie" was "half-tradition" and half his; that the "Death of Menteith" was "wholly by the editor," as was "I wish I were where Helen lyes" (cxxxi).

[32] Ritson, "Historical Essay on Scotish Song," *Scotish Song*, lxxxi.

balladeering in Germany³³), "tradition" persisted as a citable source and an axis of authentication, as when Scott later wrote in his note to "Jellon Grame": "this ballad is published from tradition, with some conjectural emendations. It is corrected from a copy in Mrs. Brown's MS, from which it differs in the concluding stanza" (*MSB*, 150).

Scott's note, coordinating "tradition" with Mrs. Brown's Manuscript (itself supposedly a textualization of tradition, preserved by Mrs. Brown's memory³⁴) suggests the multi-layered absorption and deployment of oral tradition. We might also ponder the following headnote to the "Sang of the Outlaw Murray" in the *Border Minstrelsy*:

In publishing the following ballad, the copy principally resorted to is one, apparently of considerable antiquity, which was found among the papers of the late Mrs. Cockburn of Edinburgh, a lady whose memory will long be honoured by all who knew her. Another copy, much more imperfect, is to be found in Glenriddell's MSS. The names are in this last miserably mangled, as is always the case when ballads are taken down from the recitation of persons living at a distance from the scenes in which they are laid. Mr. Plummer also gave the Editor a few additional verses, not contained in either copy, which are thrown into what seemed their proper place. There is yet another copy in Mr. Herd's MSS., which has been occasionally made use of. Two verses are restored in the present edition, from the recitation of Mr. Mungo Park, whose toils during his patient and intrepid travels in Africa, have not eradicated from his recollection the legendary lore of his native country. (*MSB*, 57–8)

Such a note, with its ostentatious and virtuosic display of his editorial mediations among various manuscript and oral sources, is typical in Scott, in form and protocol if not specific content. Reveling in his magisterial command of sources, his immersion in border lore, his correspondence with three ballad-antiquaries (Glenriddell, Plummer, and Herd), his association with deceased balladeering ladies, and his ties to Mungo Park, Scott perfects the discursive function of the note as simultaneously a site of authentication

---

³³ In *Ballads into Books*, editors Tom Cheesman and Sigrid Rieuwerts identify Percy's as "the first ballad book premised on the notion that ballads must now go into books, to be preserved from an extinction brought about by bookculture: Percy's *Reliques of Ancient English Poetry*. It was Herder who put the first international selection of ballads into books (1778–9)," 10. Scott's and Coleridge's interest in German balladry is well-known; Scott's first published poems were translations of German ballads; but what is extremely striking are the almost exclusively internal preoccupations of eighteenth-century British balladeering: the English, Scottish, Welsh, and Irish antiquaries primarily oriented to and citing each another.

³⁴ On Mrs. Brown, a famous "polite" informant for Scott, Jamieson, and indirectly for later compilers like Child, see Scott, 1802 Introduction to *MSB*, 37: he quotes Alexander Frazer Tytler's letter describing her childhood absorption of ballads and how they were first taken down; Scott emphasizes her genteel status.

and an opportunity for the display of cultural capital. Percy had documented with equal verve his many antiquarian correspondents and his
privileged relation to sources; what is new in Scott's note – what had been
slowly emerging since Percy and partially in competition with him – is the
appearance of documented "recitation" as still another collatable, citable,
and indeed theorizable source. (On theorization, consider how Scott
accounts for the mangling of names in Glenriddell's Manuscripts with his
theory of remote reciters – itself a geographically inflected subset of the
prevailing theory that oral transmission inevitably mangled oral-traditionary goods.) Most important for my argument here is that Scott's note lays
out an oral axis of authentication almost completely eschewed in Percy's
Reliques. Living recollection had entered the archive, and ballad citation had
found ways to bring it into the printed ballad collection.

Mungo Park is, of course, an intriguingly anomalous if not anonymous
oral source. But the *Minstrelsy* is chock full of named and unnamed reciters,
their copies collated, whenever possible, with other versions – recited,
written, or printed. In the *Minstrelsy* Scott specifically invokes the concept
of the "collated edition"[35]: he did not seek to publish a single recited version
of a ballad; he believed in the comparative scrutiny of copies, when possible,
and exercised a rather free, if informed, editorial hand. In this aspect of his
editorial practice, Scott followed Percy, much to the consternation of later
ballad collectors and compilers (e.g. Child and the editor of the 1969 *Oxford
Book of Ballads*[36]). An exhaustive analysis of ballad-citation rhetoric could
pursue the differentiations Scott developed to distinguish among anonymous, undated recitations, usually going by the name, "Tradition," and
named and/or dated informants. That Scott typically named his polite,
genteel informants (as he did his antiquarian correspondents) as opposed
to the many unnamed workers (blacksmiths, dairymaids, gardeners, etc.)
in the *Minstrelsy* should not surprise us – his notes specialize in a genial
condescension, and his project was imagined as conservative in all senses.
Suffice it to say, however, that, whether named or unnamed, the native
informant emerges as a privileged source in Scottish ballad collections. The

---

[35] See his note to "Dowie Dens of Yarrow": "I found it easy to collect a variety of copies; but very
difficult to select from them such a collated edition, as might, in any degree, suit the taste of these
more light and giddy-paced times" (147). Scott's editing under the sign of "taste" is notable, as is his
sense of its historicity.

[36] See James Kinsley's Introduction to *The Oxford Book of Ballads* (Oxford University Press, 1969),
vi. Kinsley notes with satisfaction that Scott in 1825 spoke of his editorial regrets; he goes on to censure
his predecessor, Quiller-Couch – editor of the 1910 *Oxford Ballads* – for his use of composite texts.
Kinsley adheres in his anthology to a single-source-text principle, whether that text was obtained from
recitation, print, or manuscript.

native reciter or singer or raconteur thus takes his and her place alongside that of dog-eared manuscripts, black-letter ballads, garlands, and miscellanies.

Why did this happen? Oral tradition and representations of recitation entered ballad collections in the late eighteenth century for several reasons, under a conjunction of conditions, including the resurgence of Scottish cultural nationalism; developments in the human sciences, especially in conjectural history, historiography, and political economy, which promoted what we might call, anachronistically, an eighteenth-century zone of cultural studies interested in oral tradition and oral culture; and last, and perhaps most important in terms of the internal development of the genre, competition among balladeers.[37] Ritson had ridiculed Percy as an armchair editor; his Scottish colleagues and successors were even more assiduous than he in tromping over dales and swales, tracking through the fields, barns, and farms for living reciters, in "getting their boots muddy," as Scott's recent biographer John Sutherland puts it[38] – partly as cultural conservators, and partly to gather materials for collections distinguishable from Percy's *Reliques*, and later from Scott's *Minstrelsy*. Ballad collections, like all commodities in the literary public sphere, strove to distinguish themselves in the marketplace, and their editors took pains to differentiate their collections, editions, or compilations from those prior or in the works.

Late-eighteenth-century ballad editors had the delicate task of navigating between ballads as old news and ballads as new finds. Despite, or alongside of, the prestige of antiquity, ballads were also and simultaneously novelties – "finds," "discoveries," retrievals from the ruin of history, now in print, "never before published." As museum curators tell us, an artifact re-captioned is not the same object: so too with ballads, which could, when re-introduced, sometimes rewritten, and always differentially re-authenticated via recitation, appear in a ballad collection as both a new thing (not that same old thing) and the more authentic thing. Each editor strove to emphasize the singularity of his collection. A serendipitously and, best of all, exclusively acquired recitation helped the editor to ensure the distinction, as well as the cultural authenticity, of his ballad.

---

[37] For situating this competition in the literary bookmarket and in terms of embourgeoisement, see Harker, *Fakesong*, 15–42.

[38] Sutherland emphasizes Scott's commitment to collecting in the field: "The real ballad collector, Scott implied, needed to get his boots muddy," *Life of Walter Scott*, 81. On Percy as an armchair editor, see ibid., 81. David Hewitt also believes that we should consider Scott a fieldworker, see his entry on Scott, Sir Walter (1771–1832) in the *Oxford Dictionary of National Biography* (Oxford University Press, 2004).

The gold standard for ballad collections remained, of course, Percy's *Reliques*, and Scottish editors devoted themselves with fervor to the project of revising and criticizing Percy.[39] Percy had, as we have seen, effectively established the protocols for citing antiquarians. As a discursive recognition of the background mediations balladeering required, such citation was perfectly poised to accommodate the mediations of the oral, which were increasingly acknowledged, indeed boasted about, by Scottish balladeers. From the perspective of the history of media, moreover, we might speculate that this emphasis on documenting recitation, on citing your access to native informants, was an attempt to restore to ballads – or bestow upon them – the aura of oral immediacy and bodily presence that mechanical mass-reproduction and remediation in books threatened to strip from them.

Under these conditions ballad collections became capable not only of alluding hazily to "oral tradition" but indeed of processing and privileging it, although only in certain highly regulated directions. Collecting and transcribing practices increasingly made their way into print – even if editors like Herd and Scott did not do much transcribing themselves.[40] By the time of Scott's *Minstrelsy* (1802–3) we see a theoretically informed, methodologically savvy handling of sources, with a strong emphasis on documenting oral-transmission and ethnographic transcription, such that Scott and his contemporary Robert Jamieson frequently cited recitations and communications of recitations as the sources used to "correct" or supersede manuscript and previously published versions of ballads.

Robert Jamieson's headnote to "Lord Thomas and Fair Annet" exemplifies the Scottish critique of Percy by means of privileged access to the oral. Jamieson notes that Percy had published this ballad in the first volume of his *Reliques*, where it was "given with some corrections 'from a MS. copy transmitted from Scotland,' and supposed to be composed, not without

---

[39] That Percy's collection was still a dominant point of reference in 1827 – that it had become its own kind of authenticated and authenticating, if disputed, source – is clear in William Motherwell's *Minstrelsy: Ancient and Modern, with an Historical Introduction and Notes* (Glasgow: John Wylie, 1827), Motherwell observes that his first ballad, "Earl Marshall," appeared in Percy's *Reliques*, but he further notes: "The present version has been recovered from recitation" (1).

[40] On this see Harker, *Fakesong*, who notes that there is no evidence of Herd's collecting songs directly, but that his MS does contain such items (29), and further, that "only one piece is known to have been taken by Scott 'from recitation'" (58). The imagined division of balladeering labor here is striking and anticipates splits within anthropology and ethnography, not to mention research in the humanities and natural sciences, quite often dependent on the un- or underacknowledged (not to mention badly paid) labor of graduate students and research assistants. Note, however, that Sutherland and Hewitt believe *pace* Harker that Scott *did* collect.

improvements, out of the two former antient English ones."[41] Percy seems to have handled this ballad, presumably communicated by Lord Hailes, just as he handled "Edom O'Gordon" – accepting the communication from Scotland but "composing" and emending it with "antient English" manuscripts. Jamieson's quotation of Percy's earlier note – "from a MS. copy transmitted from Scotland" – is symptomatic of the compulsive, often adversarial scrutiny of source-authentication which ballad editing fostered. It also confirms that balladeering produced its own chain of quotation and polemical citation, its own transformed transmission route, the links of its chain artifactualized in printed books but also forged through reading, correspondence, and ongoing ballad-hunting. In printing his own "Sweet Willie, and Fair Annie," Jamieson takes the opportunity to criticize aspects of Percy's editorial practice as well as his editorial sensibility:

The text of Lord Thomas and Fair Annet [in Percy] seems to have been adjusted, prior to its leaving Scotland, by some one who was more of a scholar than the reciters of ballads generally are; and, in attempting to give it an antique cast, it has been deprived of somewhat of that easy facility which is the distinguished characteristic of the traditionary ballad narrative. With the text of the following ditty, no such experiment has been made. It is here given pure and entire, as it was taken down by the editor, from the recitation of a lady in Aberbrothick, (Mrs W. Arrot,) to whose politeness and friendship this collection is under considerable obligations. She had no previous intimation of the compiler's visit, or of his undertaking; and the few hours he spent at her friendly fire-side were very busily employed in writing. As she had, when a child, learnt the ballad from an elderly maid-servant, and probably had not repeated it for a dozen years before I had the good fortune to be introduced to her; it may be depended upon, that every line was recited to me as nearly as possible in the exact form in which she learnt it. (23)

This long note quite clearly enacts – or aspires to achieve – the supersession of Percy, of Perceian editorial practice, and of Perceian self-representation. Percy appears as the "experimenter," the last of a series of "adjusters"; Jamieson presents himself as the austere, perfect transmitter, the participant-observer/transcriber sitting by the native-informant's fireside, the last in an authentic chain. Jamieson contrasts Percy's handling of sources with his own collecting procedures and access to native informants. He claims several kinds of authority that he intimates Percy lacked, including stylistic expertise in "traditionary ballad narrative," which enables Jamieson to spot the scholarly "adjustments" of the ballad by the Scottish communicator

---

[41] Jamieson, headnote to "Sweet Willie, and Faire Annie," in *Popular Ballads and Songs from Tradition, Manuscripts, and Scarce Editions* ... (Edinburgh: Constable; London: John Murray, 1806), 2 vols., Vol. I, 22. Hereafter citations will be noted in text by page.

before the ballad left Scotland; Jamieson also proclaims, in his elaborate depiction of his acquisition of the ballad, his ethnographic authority.[42] We note that he authenticates the reciter through the double convention of cited locale ("a lady in Aberbrothick") and cited transmission (Mrs. Arrot's childhood absorption of balladry from an elderly maid-servant)[43]; we note too that he takes care to inform us that Mrs. Arrot had "no previous intimation" of his project, thus warding off the spectre of prepped inform-ants raised by such overly miraculous finds as "Auld Maitland," offered to Scott by Mrs. Hogg for his 1803 edition of the *Minstrelsy* (and later excluded by a wary Francis James Child from his own ballad compendium).

Jamieson's elaborate scene-making and specification is not extrinsic to this ballad; it displays, we might say, his vernacular cultural capital, that which allows him to distinguish both his ballad from Percy's edited text and his balladeering practice, his fieldwork, from Percy's passive reception of imperfectly understood Scottish materials.[44] Describing his practice, authenticating his reciter, and representing their conjunction by the fire-side, Jamieson both re-oralizes the ballad – paradoxically in print – and re-nationalizes it, bringing it home to Scotland after some forty years.

If it was particularly gratifying for a struggling Scottish compiler to correct and supersede Percy by means of cited traffic in the oral, it was almost as gratifying for Scottish balladeers to correct each other and, occa-sionally, themselves. Jamieson footnotes his edition of the ballad "Lamkin" thus: "*This piece was transmitted to the editor by Mrs Brown; and is much more perfect and uniform than the copy printed in the Edinburgh

---

[42] In this nod to "ethnographic authority," which will be developed in later sections of this chapter, I invoke James Clifford's analysis of the discursive construction thereof: see "On Ethnographic Authority," in *The Predicament of Culture* (Cambridge, MA: Harvard University Press, 1988), 21–54. Clifford focuses on twentieth-century ethnographic discourse; as I hope will become clear, I read eighteenth-century balladeering – a species of ethnopoetics – as offering a prehistory, or at the very least a striking foreshadowing, of the methodological and discursive predicament of twentieth-century ethnography.

[43] On the stress placed on childhood, presumably preliterate absorption of ballads, see Ann Rowland, "Fause Nourice,'" 10–12.

[44] I here invoke John Guillory, *Cultural Capital: The Problem of Literary Canon Formation* (University of Chicago Press, 1993): Guillory's striking analysis of the emergence of cultural capital in the vernacular, demonstrated especially in his chapter "Mute Inglorious Miltons: Gray, Wordsworth, and the Vernacular Canon," might be supplemented with an account of the mid-eighteenth-century ascendancy of ballads, that traditional poetry in the vernacular. Gray's "The Bard" is an obvious link, as is his interest in Percy's and Macpherson's projects. Also relevant to the vernacular canon-making projects of this period: Robert Crawford's work on the Scottish invention of English literature (cf. his focus on Hugh Blair's lectures, anthologies like *The British Poets*), and most recently William St. Clair's remarkable analysis of the production of an "Old Canon" within the copyright window, 1774–1808, as well as his meditations on anthology-making, in *The Reading Nation in the Romantic Period* (Cambridge University Press, 2004).

Collection, edited by Mr Herd" (176). Notice how Mrs. Brown becomes the medium not only of Jamieson's ballad but also of the relations among ballad collections and balladeers. In this sense, balladeering could be seen as a particular traffic in women – e.g. Mrs. Brown of Falkland, Mrs. Arrot of Aberbrothick – conducted in the course of homosocial exchange; it could also be seen as a differentiated field of meditations between gender and class, lowly scholar–compilers like Jamieson having to bow and scrape before polite female reciters (as well as before better-positioned editors like Scott). Yet however valuable the redoubtable Mrs. Brown proved to be as an informant, she could herself be corrected by still other recitations, as Scott demonstrated when he noted of his "King Henrie" that it was "edited from the MS of Mrs Brown, *corrected by a recited fragment*" (*MSB*, 168).

As an instance of a double differentiation of what Scott called his "ballad editions," consider Scott's note to his version of "The Battle of Otterbourne," which he declared was "essentially different" from Percy's,[45] and further observed:

This song was first published from Mr. Herd's *Collection of Scottish Songs and Ballads*, Edin. 1774, 2 vols. octavo; but fortunately two copies have since been obtained from the recitation of old persons residing at the head of Ettrick Forest, by which the story is brought out, and completed in a manner much more corresponding to the true history. (*MSB*, 54)

Significant for my argument here is Scott's invocation of recitations as the added ingredient, the differentiating element, in his "Battle of Otterbourne," which is not only not Percy's "English production" but also not the Scotsman Herd's.

Scott's ongoing traffic in balladry – collecting and receiving recitations, corresponding with fellow balladeers, supporting and suborning others' collecting practices – made possible satisfying corrections and completions with each new edition of the *Minstrelsy*. Newly acquired or discovered recitations enabled ballad revision, and since the whole paradoxical point of romantic balladry was to present something simultaneously old and new and as perfect as possible (this including perfect fragments), one would not refrain from amending oneself, as Scott did when he revised several ballads

---

[45] Scott, "Battle of Otterbourne": "The following ballad of the Battle of Otterbourne, being essentially different from that which is published in the *Reliques of Ancient Poetry*, vol. i, and being obviously of Scottish composition, claims a place in this collection" (53). Scott later remarks, "The ballad published in the *Reliques*, is avowedly an English production; and the author, with a natural partiality, leans to the side of his countrymen" (53).

in successive editions of his *Minstrelsy*. Consider, for example, Scott's "Archie of Ca'field," about which he wrote:

> It may perhaps be thought, from the near resemblance which the ballad bears to Kinmont Willie, and Jock o' the Side, the Editor might have dispensed with inserting it in this collection ... The Editor has been enabled to add several stanzas to this ballad, since publication of the first edition. They were obtained from recitation; and as they contrast the brutal indifference of the elder brother with the zeal and spirit of his associates, they add considerably to the dramatic effect of the whole. (*MSB*, 86)

Scott anticipates charges of redundancy here – a redundancy not of re-publication (which more obviously threatens the value of his "Battle of Otterbourne," and his "Johnny Armstrong," and any number of previously published ballads) but of over-similarity and superfluity, his border-raid ballads in sequence beginning to sound quite alike. Recitation here provides Scott with another defended revision: he gets extra stanzas – more ballad goods – and also, in the process, claims to improve his ballad aesthetically (adding to the "dramatic effect of the whole").

As this tour through ballad citation suggests, notices of recitation were coordinated to pre-existing axes of authentication: aesthetic criteria, cultural provenance, linguistic interest, illustration of history or custom or the manners of men. To claim your ballad was obtained through or improved by recitations was, in other words, not a simple claim: a recitation could function like a manuscript (providing new stanzas, correcting old or botched ones), and it could be used to shore up an editor's aesthetics as much as his ethnographics or linguistics or politics. The admission of oral tradition into ballad collections did not solve the problematic of authenticity; it rather added another complicating layer.

CITATION TECHNOLOGY: REPRESENTING MEDIATION IN BALLADEERING

> ... historiographical discourse is constructed as a *knowledge of the other*. It is constructed according to a problematic of procedure and trial, or of *citation*, that can at the same time "subpoena" a referential language that acts therein as reality, and judge it in the name of knowledge. (Michel de Certeau, "The Historiographical Operation"[46])

---

[46] Michel de Certeau, "The Historiographical Operation," in *The Writing of History*, 94.

As the array of excerpted notes above indicates, balladeers addressed the methodological problem of printing recitations, of authenticating oral mediums, by developing a complex system of citation, a system which was for balladeers – as it is today in academic monographs and legal briefs – a kind of technology for authentication as well as remembrance.[47] If in their publications social scientists now use an author–date system, and humanists the MLA or *Chicago Manual of Style* citation system, we might say that in addition to the conventions, however loose, for citing manuscripts, garlands, previously published books, and antiquarian "communications," the Scottish balladeers developed out of antiquarian citation protocols a reciter–transcriber–site system, conjoined to a dating code which marked sometimes the date of recitation, but more usually the age and often the death of the reciter. Thus the recurring "notices" of deceased reciters, and the astonishing proliferation of specifically aged – *dated* – old men and women, in the *Minstrelsy*.

In my reading of eighteenth-century ballad collections, I have seen the reciter's age mentioned exclusively, but quite regularly, when it is a venerable age: reciters are worth dating when they are, like ballads themselves, nearly obsolete relics. Great age indexes authenticity both for ballads and for ballad-mediums: old women and old men possess that which is no longer commonly available – the living tradition now at its end, crossing over into books, transmitted to readers and not hearers, mediated by printed books and not living bodies. They are the living embodiment of ballad historicity, its "situation" in the present, its imminent demise conjoined to its great antiquity. Thus the rather astonishing proliferation and precision of testimonial specification along a chronotopical grid. Consider Ritson's note following the title of "Rookhope Ryde," "A Bishoprick border-song, composed in 1569; taken down from the chanting of George Collingwood the elder, late of Boltsburn, in the neighborhood of Ryhope, who was interred at Stanhope the 16th December 1785; never before printed."[48] (This note was taken over, as was the ballad, by Scott in his *Minstrelsy*, and again by

---

[47] Cf. Grafton, *The Footnote*, for an account of the "citation codes" (253) of historians and their complex debt to Renaissance humanist historiographic disputes and seventeenth-century religious polemic. Also relevant for transhistorical comparison and contrast: Lisa Gitelman's striking analyses of the function of record labels: "The label is a vital cultural nexus, a point where producers meet consumers, where owners meet spectators, where novelty and originality enter the market and commodities perform" (*Scripts, Grooves, and Writing Machines* [Stanford University Press, 1999], 151). How antiquarian headnotes become liner notes and CD inserts is a topic for another essay – yet the lines of force are, I hope, apparent.

[48] Ritson, *The Bishopric Garland*, in *Northern Garlands*, ed. by the late Joseph Ritson (London: R. Triphook, 1810), 54.

Child in his massive collection: such citations were as migratory and as valuable as the ballad texts themselves.) We might remark as well Scott's Rose Smith, "a woman aged upwards of ninety-one," cited as the singer of "Lord Ewrie"; Anne Douglas, the "old woman" who recited "Barthram's Dirge"; the unnamed "woman eighty years of age" who supposedly recited "The Death of Featherstonhaugh"; the numerous notices of "late" minstrels and chanters throughout Scott's introductions and notes in the *Minstrelsy* (e.g. Charles Leslie of Aberdeen, deceased at 104 years old). These aged mediums – these *dated* mediums, in all senses of "dated" – function collectively as a race of last minstrels haunting the ballad collections, which become in most editors' hands an actual or proleptic post-mortem not only for the reciters but for traditionary culture itself. The reciters, then, partake of the chronotopical experiment and consolidation that eighteenth-century balladry undertakes: their lives extending into an almost immemorial past, they provide living access to the "days that are now past."

This developing citation system was both precise and flexible. As Ritson's note to "Rookhope Ryde" shows, citation allowed for the specification of dates of composition or publication, if applicable, but it also allowed for the documentation of ongoing oral transmission right up to the moment of transcription. Consider, again, another exemplary note in Scott's *Minstrelsy*:

This song was written down by my obliging friend, Richard Surtees, Esq., of Mainsforth, from the recitation of Rose Smith, of Bishop Middleham, a woman aged upwards of ninety-one, whose husband's father and two brothers were killed in the affair of 1715. – conclusion of the headnote to "Lord Ewrie" (*MSB*, 66)

Such a note captures in miniature everything we have seen thus far: it traces a path of communication from oral informant Rose Smith to the antiquarian correspondent Robert (here mistakenly called "Richard") Surtees – both specifically located, respectively, in Mainsforth and Bishop Middleham – on to the editor and final mediator, Scott. In Scott's note, the transcriber, site, and reciter are indicated, although the scene of recitation is not conjured; the informant is rather baldly dated, aged upwards of ninety-one; and she is, in a move consonant with Scott's genealogical preoccupations,[49] inserted in a Scottish historical genealogy, with male kin identified as casualties of "the fifteen" (that is, 1715), a shorthand for one of the two major Jacobite uprisings in eighteenth-century Scotland (the other occurring in 1745).

---

[49] On Scott's obsession with genealogy, and his own in particular, see Sutherland, "Scott among the Scotts," esp. 2–7.

We could diagram the represented discourse network thus:

	"Name" Medium	Site	Dating code Age// 'hot' historical date
RECITER	Rose Smith	Bishop Middleham	91+//affair of 1715
TRANSCRIBER	R. Surtees	Mainsforth	

How does it affect our understanding of ballad citation, transmission, and *poiesis* when we learn that almost every aspect of this ballad – the source, her location, her supposed recitation, and her genealogy, not to mention the text of the ballad proper – was invented by Robert Surtees?

One must conclude, as later ballad scholars reluctantly acknowledged, that every step on this path, every node in this discourse network – the reciter, the recitation, and the ballad-text itself – could be created out of discursive air, that is to say, forged. This was particularly disturbing because source-obsessed ballad editors represented themselves as partaking of, on the one hand, what Foucault called "the history of the production of truth," and on the other hand, the aesthetic project of developing cabinets of beauties to be savored by men of taste. One must conclude that the discursive protocols of ballad authentication, not to mention the stylistic features of balladry, had become so formalized, so artifactualized, that they were eminently fake-able.[50]

The notes Scott prefixes to Surtees' ballad communications follow the chronotopical code of romantic balladry: immemorial transmission culminating in living recitation by an aged informant from a specified locale to a respected transcriber–transmitter, Surtees himself. That the content of the note (except for its last juncture, Surtees' writing to Scott) was illusory does not invalidate the power of its form – it rather suggests the triumph of the chronotopical logic of ballad citation, its status as the discursive paradigm of authentication.

---

[50] The case of Surtees' contributions was outlined (with some regret) in George Taylor, *A Memoir of Robert Surtees, Esq. Author of the History of the County Palatine of Durham*. A new edition with additions by Rev. James Raine (Durham: Surtees Society; London: Whittaker; Edinburgh: Blackwood, 1852), as well as in Henry Wheatley's introduction to his edition of Percy's *Reliques*, I [50]. The sharp-eyed Scott never admitted to detecting Surtees' tomfoolery; it was left to later antiquarians to censure Surtees, who persisted nevertheless as a major figure in the history of Northumberland antiquarianism: the still-functioning "Surtees Society," sustained by the Department of History at the University of Durham, is named after him.

Indeed, ballad discourse – a machine for *producing*, as well as *finding*, sources – was sufficiently formalized that Surtees was able to simulate the by-then stock figure of a native informant with a faulty memory whose recitation he had thus to complete:

> The following beautiful fragment was taken down by Mr. Surtees, from the recitation of Anne Douglas, an old woman who weeded in his garden. It is imperfect, and the words within brackets were inserted by my correspondent, to supply such stanzas as the chantress's memory left defective. (Scott's headnote to "Barthram's Dirge"; *MSB*, 85)

One could fabricate not only the desirable path of communication represented by ballad citation but even its pathologies, which the sedulous, imaginative antiquary could both invent and cure, his remedial editorial medicine typographically registered in brackets.[51]

The mediation circuit so fluently traced in ballad citation could be, then, an almost wholly fabricated circuit: herein lies one deep-structural pathology of ballad discourse, a pathology illuminated by the work of Susan Stewart and others. But rather than throw up our hands at the apparently inescapable problematic of authenticity, we might see this possibility of forging not only documents, not only informants, but indeed a whole chain of transmission, as an invitation to pursue further lines of inquiry about evidence and the mediation of evidence.

Surtees' communications to Scott suggest the perils of relying exclusively on one accrediting source. Indeed, it is striking that in the *Minstrelsy*, it was those ballads based on one "copy," with either one named source or no named source, that were later subjected to the most scrutiny and doubt.[52] Scott's usual editorial practice was to collate copies, and while this may have led to the ballad pastiche characteristic of his collection and lamented by rigorous scholars ever since, it paradoxically provided some controls on the evidence base. To collate copies was to treat the notional ideal ballad as a kind of "judgment" or artifact generated by the deliberative gathering and sifting of evidence, the weighing of testimony. Scott's editing was a

---

[51] For another example of the editorially acknowledged memory lapse of an informant, see Ritson on George Collingwood in his footnote to "Rookhope-Ryde": "The reciter, from his advanced age, could not recollect the original line thus imperfectly supplied." Like Surtees, Ritson marked the "supplied line" with brackets: see *The Bishopric Garland* in *Northern Garlands*, 60.

[52] See Hustvedt on the suspiciously acquired "Auld Maitland," rejected by Child; see George Lyman Kittredge on "Kinmont Willie," Child Ballad #186, which he notes is "under vehement suspicion of being the work of Sir Walter Scott," in his introduction to *English and Scottish Popular Ballads*, ed. Kittredge and Helen Child Sargent (Houghton Mifflin, Cambridge Edition, 1904, 1932), xxx; and see of course the three ballads contributed by Surtees.

profoundly juridical as well as a scribal process; he was usually able to call more than one witness to his ballads and thus to insulate himself from the effects (to continue the metaphor) of a single talented perjurer.

Surtees' bogus contributions to Scott's *Minstrelsy* also reveal, albeit negatively, the difference an informant made. To make it into the *Minstrelsy* as an antiquarian communicator, your ballad now benefitted from having a credible oral informant with a specified provenance. The ballad revival offered, then, not only an invitation to forge but also an invitation to fieldwork. After the oral turn in balladry, so long as native informants could still be found, research would be conducted, notionally if not always actually, in the field as well as the library. The balladeer would scour manuscripts, broadsides, correspondents' *materia*, his rivals' collections, and even newspapers; he (or his commissioned emissaries) would also interview, transcribe, record and re-record natives – or represent themselves as doing so.

OUR INFORMANTS, OURSELVES: NATIVES IN THE FIELD OF THE HUMAN SCIENCES

That forgers felt compelled to invent informants and scenes of recitation and transmission suggests how thoroughgoing was the oral-ethnographic turn in balladry. We might sum up this development as the romantic and ethnographic turning of the antiquarian-balladeering operation. I use this phrase by analogy with Michel de Certeau's essay on "The Historiographical Operation." De Certeau writes:

> On a limited scale, envisioning history [balladeering] as an operation would be equivalent to understanding it as the relation between a *place* (a recruitment, milieu, a profession or business, etc.), analytic *procedures* (a discipline), and the construction of a *text* (a literature) … the historical [balladeering] operation refers to the combination of a social *place*, "scientific" *practices*, and *writing*.[53]

Substituting "balladeering" for "history" and "historical" allows us to refine our sense of the discursive logic of which balladeering partook and also furthered. Antiquarianism, inflected by the mid-eighteenth-century fashion for things Gothic, Celtic, and vernacular, provided balladeering with its first milieu; collection, categorization, collation, and comparison constituted its practical and analytic procedures; and the constructed text that emerged, authenticated by formalized citation and documentation, was the "ballad edition," subsumed by the genre of the ballad collection. As we have seen,

---

[53] Michel de Certeau, "The Historiographical Operation," 57.

ballad citation presumes and conjoins practices and discourse, fieldwork and print. Romantic ballad citation remarked the transformation of people (their memories and their speech) as well as manuscripts and books into archives. Processed into sources, these diverse media entered into the sphere of the useful; they became simultaneously "raw material" and authenticating sites: "The convocation of raw data obeys the jurisdiction which is pronounced upon it in the historiographical [balladeering] staging."[54]

If the oral-ethnographic turn opened the balladeering operation to new practices, more specifically to the *representation* of them – collection, transcription, and so on – it also brought to the fore the methodological conjunction of historiographic and ethnographic codes and procedures.[55] Formed and informed by oral-ethnographic transactions, late-eighteenth-century balladeering hovered on the discursive and temporal cusp between history and ethnography, between a discourse of an absent referent (as Barthes famously described history) and one predicated on recently experienced living exchange, however asymmetrical the exchange, however distantiating its final representation (consider, for example, the casually unnamed yet scrupulously cited oral informants in Scott). With Scottish balladeers we see a special preoccupation with the temporal ambiguities generated by the relation of balladry both to history and to living experience. Jamieson was particularly attuned to balladeering's double temporal referent, hoping (he wrote) "to throw as much light as possible upon the state of traditionary Ballad Poetry in this country, *both in former times and at present.*"[56]

Jamieson's inquiry into the present is of course conducted under the pressure of imminent obsolescence; that is to say, his balladeering is always about to become an elegy and he recognizes that it is destined to provide materials for cultural history. Noting that ballads "may be of interest to the curious antiquary, and the philosophical inquirer, into the history of men and manners," Jamieson pointed his readers beyond antiquarian eclecticism to the historiographic discourse most prominent in Scottish intellectual circles, that of philosophical history, known as well as conjectural or stadial history. Scottish Enlightenment historiography famously elaborated a "stadial

[54] Ibid., 94.
[55] James Chandler has persuasively argued that the historian's code – his dating system – requires a mediation between the historiographic and the ethnographic: historicism, he writes, "can be profitably understood in terms of its production of just this kind of coding – the deployment of a dating system for making intelligible the relationship between the representations of culture in those same, then-emerging discourses, historiography and ethnography." See *England in 1819,* 95.
[56] Jamieson, note to "Child Maurice," 3.

theory" of history, variously modeled as a three or four-stage progression of societies through developmental epochs (e.g. barbarism>pastoralism>civilization; hunting>pasturage>farming>commerce). This model of historical periodization and plotting influenced the organization of ballad materials and profoundly informed the historical and critical dissertations and notes of many collections – from Pinkerton's musings in 1781 on poetry as "the original language of men in the infant state of society in all countries," to Ritson's discussion of the shepherd state of society and his analogy to "the savage tribes of America" when discussing the origin and progress of "national song," to Scott's and Jamieson's description of ballads as possessing "considerable interest for the moral philosopher and general historian."[57]

It could be argued that the emerging ballad chronotope put pressure on stadial theory, since what the ethnographic turn in balladeering suggested was the possibility of a heterochronous history, several "times" of cultural development co-existing, albeit under the teleological sign of progress, the British Union and Empire. The irruption of the ethnographic present in Jamieson and to a lesser extent in Scott shows us that balladeering historicism was a complex and ongoing project, its chronotope not wholly laid down in advance. Jamieson's notes often foreground not the obsolescence of a ballad but its continued currency, as in his headnote to "The Trumpeter of Fyvie": "The ballad was taken down by Dr Leyden from the recitation of a young lady (Miss Robson) of Edinburgh, who learned it in Teviotdale. *It was current in the Border counties within these few years, as it still is in the northeast of Scotland, where the scene is laid*" (127–8; emphasis added). Note how Jamieson carefully marks where the ballad "is" and "was current": such a note lays out a geography of living and dying song, as well as the familiar routes and citation protocols of transmission (from Teviotdale to Edinburgh, from Miss Robson to Dr Leyden to Jamieson). Such a note is a chronotopical snapshot (to indulge in anachronistic metaphor) of traditionary culture and transmission.

One must allow that there was no balladeering futurism, as it were: balladeering required historicism, allowed an ethnographic present, but insisted on an economic, political, and cultural dominant – that of early industrial capitalism, its blossoming print organs, and the self-evidence of the British Empire. And indeed, we find such complex layering of social

---

[57] Pinkerton, "On the Oral Tradition of Poetry," in *Scotish Tragic Ballads*, ix–x; Ritson, "A Historical Essay on the Origin and Progress of National Song," *A Select Collection of English Songs* (London: J. Johnson, 1783), iv, ii–iii; Scott, "Introductory Remarks on Popular Poetry," first prefixing the *Minstrelsy* in 1830, 6.

development and temporalities under a teleological sign in that most famous of fictional historiographic genres: the historical novel, founded by Scott once he conceded to Byron the role of world-historical poet.

As we have seen, the balladeering operation was not only historiographic; it was also, by virtue of its increasing openness to fieldwork and the representation of it, ethnographic. This ethnographic turn contributed to a literary version of what we might now call identity politics. In 1794 Joseph Ritson felt he had to apologize for the defect of being English when he ventured his *Scotish Songs* upon the public.

It may be naturally supposed that a publication of this nature would have been rendered *more perfect by a native of North Britain*. Without discussing this question, the editor has only to observe that diligent enquiry, extensive reading, and unwearied assiduity, added to the strictest integrity, and most disinterested views, have possibly tended to lessen *the disadvantages of an English birth*; and that he is persuaded the present collection, such as it is, will not suffer by comparison with any thing of the kind hitherto published in either country.[58]

Here we see Ritson's attempt to overcome what is perceived to be a distinct disadvantage, his status as a non-native collector, with other strengths – his diligence, scholarship, care, and disinterest.

If Ritson could not claim native status, he nevertheless rose to what was by the 1790s an unavoidable ethnographic challenge, noting that for his *Scotish Song in two volumes* he had "even made repeated visits to different parts of Scotland for the purpose of obtaining materials or information upon the subject. How far these pains have been successful must be left to the candour of the intelligent reader, and to the malice of the *Critical Review*."[59] The ascendancy of ethnographic authority as a basis for the ballad editor's authority suggests that earlier charges of "national prejudice" had been transformed: what had been a liability – Scottish birth and upbringing – was now boldly announced as a credential, such that the English antiquarian had to find ways to compete.

Scott and Jamieson devoted prefaces, introductions, and scores of notes to accrediting their ethnographic authority as both natives and sophisticated

---

[58] Ritson, *Scotish Song*, vii–iii. On "North Britain" becoming the preferred term for Scotland in some antiquarian texts after the Union in 1707, see Piggott, *Ruins in a Landscape*, 45. One should consult as well Penny Fielding's work on constructions of "the North" in eighteenth- and nineteenth-century Britain: *Scotland and the Fictions of Geography: North Britain 1760–1840* (Cambridge University Press, 2008); and T. C. Smout, "Scotland as North Britain: The Historical Background, 1707–1918," in *The Edinburgh History of Scottish Literature*, Vol. II, ed. Susan Manning et al. (Edinburgh University Press, 2007), 1–11. "North Britain" was, Fielding observes, a highly charged phrase, one effacing "Scotland" in favor of a notionally unified "Britain." One seems never to encounter a "South Britain."

[59] Ritson, *Scotish Song*, i–ii. On Ritson's fieldtrip in 1786, see Sutherland, *Life of Walter Scott*, 81.

fieldworkers with special expertise (Scott most notably in history and genealogy, Jamieson in comparative linguistics). Historians of anthropology have reminded us that participant observation became the methodological norm for twentieth-century ethnographic fieldwork.[60] We might also observe that the representation of participant observation was for eighteenth-century balladeering if not a norm a highly significant and culturally authorizing card to play. Most authoritative was the native-turned-participant observer, compiler, and editor. Against Percy's long-dead "ancient" (that is, medieval) English minstrels, against Ritson's laborious researches, Scott and his cohort could propose still-living Scottish border minstrels, including themselves. Thus, having discussed the border minstrels of yore, Scott observed:

there was a period in his own life, when a memory that ought to have been charged with more valuable matter, enabled him to recollect as many of these old songs as would have occupied several days in the recitation.
The press, however, at length superseded the necessity of such exertions of recollection ... [61]

Scott's own memory, he intimates, could have furnished the contents of the *Minstrelsy* as well as any manuscript evidence or even the recitations of Mrs. Brown or John Graeme of Sowport, informants he elsewhere acknowledged. The young Scott could "recollect" ballads from himself, a latter minstrel, a living archive. Whether he can now perform such feats, Scott fails to say, but the verbal construction of the sentence ("there *was* a period") suggests that those memorable days, like the days of minstrelsy triumphant, are now past.

As Scott moves from notional minstrels to himself in the persona of Editor, he brings us from a primarily oral culture of prodigious memory to a culture of "the press" which renders such arts of memory obsolete. This passage is one of many in which he constructs the very peculiar ethnographically informed historicizing chronotope of balladry. Unlike English contemporaries, Scottish editors were able to align themselves with their reciter-informants: like their informants – whether peasants or gentlemen, dairymaids or ladies – they had absorbed ballads in childhood. Ballads were their inheritance, they insisted, before they were their objects of study. (That study produces inheritance, that research and ingenuity invent tradition, we must also,

---

[60] One might consult James Clifford, "On Ethnographic Authority" in *The Predicament of Culture*, or Mary Louise Pratt, "Fieldwork in Common Places," in *Writing Culture: The Poetics and Politics of Ethnography*, ed. James Clifford and George E. Marcus, A School of American Research Advanced Seminar (University of California Press, 1986), 32.

[61] Scott, "On Popular Poetry," *MSB*, 9.

along with Hugh Trevor-Roper and other scholars, acknowledge.[62])
Unlike the modernist ethnographers so interesting to late-twentieth-
century critics, Scott and Jamieson and more famously Burns didn't
have to go native; they were native.

But what did it mean to "be native" in balladry? One might consider
whether the balladeer chose to inhabit the editor-function or the poet-
function or both, and when he did which. Again, analyzing the discourse of
citation proves fruitful: self-citation follows the protocols for citing oral
informants. Consider Jamieson's note to "John Barleycorn": "Given by the
Editor, from his own recollection, as he learned it in Morayshire, when he
was a boy, and before the Poems of Burns were published. The two
concluding Stanzas are by the Editor" (240). Such a note conjures a self-
collecting, carefully located native informant (viz. Morayshire), an editor
whose own memory is a cultural archive. We see too, in the defensive nod to
Burns, the ongoing requirement that balladeers distinguish their ballads
from others, particularly those of a paradigmatic native son. And finally, by
acknowledging his completion of the ballad, Jamieson displays what other
editors (Percy, Scott) obscured – exactly where they touched up ballads.
One suspects that Jamieson, unlike an English editor, could so openly
acknowledge "concluding" the poem precisely because Jamieson appears
as a native transmitter, a Scottish maker in the long line of Scottish ballad
poets; one suspects too that he acknowledged such emendations and
completions in order to differentiate himself from Scott (who was often
silent or evasive about editorial emendations), not to mention more flagrant
fabricators like Pinkerton. Jamieson's "John Barleycorn," announced as a
pastiche of recollected and invented stanzas, is a realization, an artifactualization in metrical form, of hybrid temporalities as well as stanzas.

As Scott's and Jamieson's self-representations suggest, the native ballad
editor is always and productively split and doubly informed; he might
historicize, he might ethnographize, but he always *recalls* and *remembers*.
Whether a native's ballad collection is a remembrance of things past or a
representation of things present is the methodological and discursive crux
of late-eighteenth-century Scottish balladry. The question for Scottish

---

[62] See the important volume *The Invention of Tradition*, in particular Eric Hobsbawm, "Introduction:
Inventing Traditions," 1–14, and Hugh Trevor-Roper, "The Invention of Tradition: The Highland
Tradition of Scotland," 15–41. Trevor-Roper's blithe ignoring of the actual eighteenth-century
cultural situation in the Highlands – not least the devastations wreaked on that region post-1745 –
has come in for severe censure, especially by Scottish cultural historians far more alert to the
complexities of Scottish political nationalism and its mutation post-Culloden into a more broadly
dispersed "cultural" form. For a trenchant corrective, see for example Murray Pittock, *Inventing and
Resisting Britain*.

balladeers was not, can the subaltern speak?, but rather, can the native, *as an editor*, historicize? The cultural logic of balladry held out, if it did not fulfill, the promise of integrating historical discourse and ethnographic practice – of historicizing ethnography, ethnographizing history. In its resistance to the unilinear march of stadial history, in its attempts to integrate typological and chronological ordering systems, in its simultaneously ethnographic and historiographic commitments, balladeering offered, albeit often unwittingly, a critique of the human sciences contemporary to it and in some respects of our own. For balladeering discourse struggled to bridge what elsewhere appeared as a chasm, the split between observing, theorizing, writing subjects and the objects of their cultural and historical inquiry (whether ballads or ballad informants).

Balladeering in its Scottish moment became in part a discourse of natives about themselves and to some extent for themselves. Some Scottish intellectuals had been lamenting ever since the Union of the Kingdoms in 1707 the imminent demise of Scottish culture: balladeering and related ethnopoetic ventures like Macpherson's Ossian poems were conducted under this historically alert temporal pressure, their projects envisioned as being (to invoke George Marcus on ethnographic research) either a "salvage" or a "redemptive" operation.[63] As Blair and Hume and Smith had before them, Scott and Jamieson reflected quite lucidly on the predicament of culture and their historical situation. The balladeers were well aware, indeed excruciatingly self-conscious, of the possibility that they were witnessing and perhaps hastening the death of the traditions and ballads they published; they penned epitaphs and eulogies more fulsome if less eloquent than *Tristes Tropiques*. And it is important to recognize that what sharpened their reflections on culture and history was their keen sense of the mediality – not only the temporality and historicity – of the cultural goods they were interested in.

As subtle, agonistic conceptualizers of the problem of the source, of source-mediation, cultural transmission, orders of evidence, and mediality itself, the balladeers developed sophisticated tools for reflecting on method and handling highly differentiated material: perhaps even more important, they created a space for arguing about these methodological issues. Long before the linguistic and anthropological turns in history, long before the critique of textualism and the writing/print monopoly underpinning the human sciences, balladeers were forced to become cultural historians and media theorists. They criticized the wholly textual, written archival basis of

---

[63] In "Contemporary Problems of Ethnography in the Modern World System," George Marcus identifies the "salvage mode" and the "redemptive mode" in a footnote. See *Writing Culture*, 165.

conventional narrative history; they fleshed out and concretized the abstractions of conjectural history; they assessed oral history and recitation alongside more recognizably physical "documents," and they struggled to develop recording technologies adequate to the nature of their desired evidence. Even if balladeers were often more concerned to document *that* a recitation happened than to publish its contents, they nevertheless fed the desire for sound recording technologies that only the wax-cylinder and gramophone recording technologies would begin to fulfill.

BALLADEERING, HISTORICITY, MEDIALITY: FEEDBACK LOOPS AND OSSIAN REDUX

The ballad revival reveals not so much the waning (or the invention) of tradition as the waning of, and the simultaneous preoccupation with, traditional mediation. It is a truism that the ballad revival was part of a cultural revival, especially in Scotland, the zealous efforts of ballad-hunters making clear to singers that their old ballads were of interest and value. Some of these singers were concerned with what printing did to, as well as with, ballads: Mrs. Hogg famously rebuked Scott for having "spoilt" her ballads by printing them: "they were made for singin' and no' for readin'."[64] Regarding such medial transformations, several scholars have recently suggested that printing, and more profoundly writing, kills orality. The antiquarian, scholar, and forger John Pinkerton argued the same two centuries ago: "In proportion as Literature advanced in the world Oral Tradition disappeared."[65] While other critics have found this announcement of the death of orality to be premature,[66] it is true that writing and print technologies transform, in their remediations, oral *materia*; it is also true that print mediates oral materials differentially – consider that for decades, ballads made it into print (for centuries, if we think of the broadside medium), but that it was only in the late eighteenth century that testimonial

---

[64] In a famous, possibly invented passage in her son James Hogg's *Memoirs*, much quoted in the literature since: see Frankie Armstong, "On Singing Child Ballads," in *Ballads into Books*, 249; Sutherland, *The Life of Walter Scott*, 82.

[65] Pinkerton, "On the Oral Tradition of Poetry," *Scotish Tragic Ballads*, xv.

[66] Ruth Finnegan notes: "one sometimes finds the view that writing is incompatible with, or even destructive of, oral literature" (*Oral Poetry*, 160). Finnegan's own view is less extreme: "writing has been in existence for a longer period and over a wider area of the world than is often realized." Regarding British and American ballads, Finnegan asserts, "It is clear that there was and is constant interaction between written and oral forms." She casts further doubt on the distinction between so-called "traditional" ballads and "street" or "broadside" ballads, noting that the latter often passed into oral tradition (161). Groom's microbibliographical analysis of Percy's *Reliques* offers suggestive evidence for Finnegan's broader point about oral-literate feedback loops.

documentation about reciters and traditionary lore began to appear along-side them. It may be that printed ballad collections supported the sustaining as well as the transformation of traditional singing and reciting practice, a phenomenon with which we are so familiar that the "invention of tradition" may be one definition of modernity itself.

Historians of cooking and music and sex and midwifery and any number of human activities have long argued that print lags behind practice; historians of balladeering might argue the same. Print can, however, serve as a spur to further practice – in this case, ballad collecting. We have seen how balladeers returned to the field when confronted with competing publications or when hoping to improve their own: the practice of revising, re-editing, and in some cases completely overhauling ballad collections suggests that we might best describe balladeering as a complex, multiply-mediated feedback loop.

That balladeering might best be modeled as such a complex loop – with all the possibilities of self-correction and amplification such a metaphor implies – is supported by a number of developments, not least Scott's successive editions of the *Minstrelsy*, with its exfoliating apparatus, added "imitations," revisions, reshufflings, and reworkings. We might note that some balladeers and their publishers solicited readers – in advertisements placed in prefaces to their collections and in magazines – to send in new versions of ballads as well as any new or never-before-published finds. Anticipating David Herd's second, revised edition of his *Ancient and Modern Scots Songs, Heroic Ballads, etc.* (first published in 1769, second edition 1776), his publishers solicited readers for "more perfect copies" of ballads and song, for any "Scots songs of merit."[67] *The Scots Magazine* for January 1802 published a "list of desiderata in Scotish Song" that Joseph Ritson had drawn up some years before; the editors exhorted countrymen to furnish "that eminent and accurate antiqua-rian" with any ballad *materia* they had and "invite[d] the communications of every person who can repeat Scotish songs, or who may have an opportunity of transcribing the fleeting words of tradition."[68] Such appeals to native informants persisted through the nineteenth and twentieth centuries, Francis James Child not only corresponding with antiquarians and local historians in Britain but also, through the advertisements prefacing successive volumes of his *English and Scottish Popular Ballads*, inviting less eminent folk to send him material. Child also recommended ballad-collecting closer

---

[67] Harker, *Fakesong*, 29.
[68] Footnote in *Letters from Joseph Ritson, Esq. to Mr. George Paton. To Which is Added, A Critique by John Pinkerton, Esq. upon Ritson's Scotish Songs* (Edinburgh, 1827), 27.

to home, inviting American college students "to unite in an effort to collect popular ballads from oral tradition."[69] Alan Lomax's trip to Scotland in 1950, the collector lugging a new Magnecord tape machine, is only one example of the more recent historical fortunes of the medial technologizing of the endlessly revived ballad word; the digitization of the Child ballads is well underway.[70]

The late-eighteenth-century balladeering feedback loop established one wing of the ongoing project of vernacular cultural *poiesis* – the reciprocal making of poetry through culture and culture through poetry: viz. Percy's "ancient English relics" generated by notionally ancient English minstrels; Scott's border minstrelsy imagined as the work of border minstrels; regional, local, and national poetries and cultures produced and/or sustained by native informants; and of course the Ossian poems, engaged with a traditional vernacular canon. Forty years of balladeering practice, theory, and publication had so transformed cultural poetics that the Ossian poems found themselves on new and more receptive terrain in 1800. It is striking indeed to observe the state of things Ossianic forty years after Macpherson's first fragments appeared: for when, after Macpherson's death in 1796, the Highland Society of Scotland wished to revisit and ascertain the status of the Ossianic corpus and Macpherson's redaction of it, they decided to interview native informants.

Chaired by Henry Mackenzie, a Committee of the Highland Society developed a set of queries to guide its correspondents, who were to ask natives – including themselves-as-natives – whether they knew any of the Ossianic poems; if they could now recite them; if so, how they came to know them; whether they remembered others reciting them; if they could now dictate or transcribe them; if they had ever thus "set them down"; natives were also to be questioned regarding their "traditionary belief" and "traditionary expression." Anyone who could recall Macpherson's collecting expeditions was asked to comment on his behavior and practice, and bi- or tri-lingual Gaelic-speakers were invited to comment on the accuracy of his translations.[71]

---

[69] See Child, "Invitation to unite ... addressed particularly to students in colleges," Cambridge, MA, 1881 (Houghton Library, Harvard University). That college students were asked to collect ballads from Irish-Americans suggests the continuing class stratifications in balladeering as well as its ethnic turn in the US.

[70] For Lomax's apparatus, see the CD: *World Library of Folk and Primitive Music: Scotland*, vol. III of *The Historic Series: the Alan Lomax Collection*, compiled and ed. Alan Lomax; reissued Rounder Records 1998, liner notes and intro. Hamish Henderson with Margaret Bennett.

[71] People fluent, that is, in Scottish Gaelic and English as well as Lallans (Lowland Scots) were best positioned to evaluate Macpherson's translations, since those poems were presented as a rendering into lugubrious English of Gaelic "originals." My discussion here relies on *Report of the Committee of*

The Queries made explicit what we might call, following Foucault, "rules of enunciation," rules which bespeak a discourse that had passed a threshold of formalization.[72] In their incremental specification of questions and directives, the Queries made manifest a subtle set of tools for gathering and sifting among orders of evidence. They also show a Committee mindful of the problems inherent in oral-literate, cross-linguistic transactions, and more specifically inherent in the linguistic and textual mediations constitutive of ethnographic textualization. What is important here is that we recognize in the Queries the formalization of methodological protocols – how to interview, what to ask, what to transcribe, how to cross-check; we can also discern in the Queries the discursive conjunction of ethnographic *praxis* and historical "enquiry" which also distinguished late-eighteenth-century balladeering, as I have argued. For this Enquiry, only certain kinds of speech counted as evidence, as testimony, and native speakers were to be addressed with these enunciative rules in mind. The Queries confirm what historically and culturally informed balladeers had elaborated: in this realm of cultural production (as opposed to "science") what was first at stake was not what was "in the true" but what was "in the evidentiary."

These Queries locate us in the evidentiary problematic which the Ossian poems had in part created. In the 1760s and 70s, doubters demanded that Macpherson produce his "originals" – meaning his manuscripts; in 1805, inquiring Scotsmen set about producing native informants, oral testimonies, or more precisely "oral editions" (to use Dr. Hugh Blair's term), which would most likely be plural and various.[73] The contention over manuscript sources versus oral tradition, textual versus oral transmission, had been definitively altered and nuanced. The *Report on Ossian* demonstrates the legitimation of the practice and concept of collation, the collating of "oral editions" with manuscript and print variants, en route to editorial and cultural judgment. The oral-ethnographic turn which Macpherson had partly (if in spite of himself) initiated had come full circle: if anything was

---

the Highland Society of Scotland, Appointed to Inquire into the Nature and Authenticity of the Poems of Ossian. Drawn up, According to the Directions of the Committee, by Henry Mackenzie, Esq. Its Convener or Chairman. With a Copious Appendix, Containing some of the Principal Documents on which the Report is Founded (Edinburgh: Univ. Press for Constable and London: Longman, 1805). For the full text of the Queries, see the Appendix following this chapter.

[72] Foucault, "The Formation of Strategies," *Archaeology of Knowledge*, 65; "The Enunciative Function," 88ff; "The Formation of Enunciative Modalities," 50 ff.

[73] Blair, Appendix to the Critical Dissertation, 1765, in *The Poems of Ossian and related Works*, ed. Gaskill: "yet by comparing together the different oral editions of them [the Ossianic poems] (if we may use that phrase) in different corners of the country, and by comparing these also with the manuscripts which he obtained, Mr. Macpherson had it in his power to ascertain, in a great measure, the genuine original, to restore the parts to their proper order, and to give the whole to the publick in that degree of correctness, in which it now appears" (404).

going to authenticate the Ossian poems, the Queries make clear, it would be the oral testimony of native informants collated with other documents, including Macpherson's poems, some forty years after publication.

In 1805 the Highland Committee published its *Report on Ossian*, including those Queries that had guided its fieldwork. With its impressive coordination of documents, affidavits, poems in Gaelic, translations into English, and numerous testimonial letters, it was a collection strikingly reminiscent of the apparatus-laden ballad collections with which it was contemporary; and certainly the practices and premises it encoded speak directly to the discursive and cultural logic we have been tracing in the first instance in balladeering. As it turned out, native testimony didn't do much for Macpherson's prestige; the Ossianic material was certainly traditional, but the specific documents Macpherson had produced seemed to be, in the end, his own doing, a reverie on traditionary themes – more eighteenth-century than, say, third-century.[74] Yet if Macpherson had not been whole-heartedly authenticated, native testimony *qua* native testimony had been, however, thoroughly credentialized, its use as evidence formalized.

The 1805 *Report on Ossian* is, I would argue, more significant for its mustering and display of evidence than its conclusions. If the Highland Committee remained somewhat tentative in its rendering of judgment on Macpherson, it was quite definite in its rendering of another kind of historical judgment: Macpherson's Ossian poems, predicated as they were on travel, transcription, collection, and collation – on a poetics of what Mary Louise Pratt has taught us to call "the contact zone" – would have been impossible to create in 1800.[75] Oral culture was dying off, Gaelic-

---

[74] "But the Committee has not been able to obtain any one poem the same in title and tenor with the poems published by him. It is inclined to believe that he was in use to supply chasms, and to give connection, by inserting passages which he did not find, and to add what he conceived to be dignity and delicacy to the original composition, by striking out passages, by softening incidents ... To what degree, however, he exercised these liberties, it is impossible for the Committee to determine." *1805 Report*, 152.

[75] For example in Mary Louise Pratt, "Arts of the Contact Zone," in *Ways of Reading*, 5th edn., ed. David Bartholomae and Anthony Petroksky (New York: Bedford/St. Martin's, 1999); or in her seminal *Imperial Eyes: Travel Writing and Transculturation* (London and New York: Routledge, 1992). I allude to her work tentatively, mindful that Pratt's "contact zones" are, in the words of the "Introduction" to *Imperial Eyes*, "social spaces where disparate cultures meet, clash, and grapple with each other, often as highly asymmetrical relations of domination and subordination – like colonialism, slavery, or their aftermaths as they are lived out across the globe today." The question remains, both for historians of the eighteenth century and for our own moment, just to what extent and in what ways Scottish, English, and/or "British" cultures should be imagined as "disparate." (Murray Pittock, for one, provocatively insists on a British/Irish commonality when many other historians emphasize colonial difference.) British balladeering in its polite modality – the modality I am primarily concerned with here – flourishes after the violent volatility of internal imperial/national conflict is suppressed,

speakers as well, and so too the traditional basis for an Ossianic corpus. The historical window of opportunity – the conditions of Macpherson's ethnographic researches and poetic creation – had closed. The Highland Committee thus arrived at second-order conclusions, a kind of meta-judgment, about the historicity of ethnographically-supported fabrication.

The *Report on Ossian* attested to the historical contingency of poetic making; so too did Scott and Jamieson in their ballad collections, and *The Scots Magazine* in its plea to countrymen. Balladeering in this historical phase anchored itself in a perpetually historicized present: a time of making which knows that its basis (its sources in living memory) will not survive into the future. Balladeering in its broadest sense was a sustained collaborative – if also expropriative – exploration of that contingency, a "making" on the border between documents and informants, texts and speech, books and interviews, historical artifacts and ethnographic transcription, research and invention, custom and rhyme, the historical past and the ethnographic present, "old, far-off forgotten lays" and "familiar matter of today," to invoke Wordsworth's lines from *The Solitary Reaper*.

From this vantage we might venture that the most scandalous aspect of the ballad revival, not to mention the Ossian phenomenon, was its inability, its refusal, to autonomize the aesthetic. Aesthetic values were cited, of course, as criteria for publishing and differentiating among ballads, songs, poems, and fragments. Balladeers like Pinkerton invoked a standard of taste against charges of antiquarian mustiness: "Above all it is to be hoped, from the vast number of pieces rejected, that the editor has in no instance sacrificed the character of a man of taste to that of an antiquary; as of all characters he should the least chuse that of an hoarder of ancient dirt."[76] Most balladeers acknowledged, however, multiple grounds for the interest in and valuing of ballads: aesthetic, historical, cultural, patriotic, philosophical, musical, and antiquarian reasons were all advanced, inflected of course by national and class prejudice. What is important here is that the aesthetic, consistently invoked, never excluded these other bases for valuing ballads. The literary was a broader thing then than now, standards of taste flown when balladeers wished to consolidate cultural identities or historical narratives as much as when they sought to demonstrate the individual distinction of a ballad, a collection, or their own sensibilities.

---

assuaged, or sublimated (i.e. post-Culloden): balladeering typically looks back as it were "sixty years hence," as Scott subtitles *Waverley*, meditating on the turbulences of the contact, resistance, revolution, insurgency.

[76] Pinkerton, *Ancient Scotish Poems* (1786), xv.

Considered as a species of cultural *poiesis*, late eighteenth-century ballad collections offer us a useful way to think through whatever rapprochement there is to be found between "cultural studies" and "the aesthetic," or, to change the axis, between more historicist and more formalist inclinations in the humanities. Many balladeers, after all, understood themselves to be students and defenders of historical and contemporary popular culture: Ritson and Herd were particularly faithful to popular ballad and song, relatively unhampered by temptations to "improve" poems or dress them in more tasteful garb (although they refused like most to publish, if not privately to revel in, bawdy or ribald or scatological verse, arguably the heart of the ballad matter). And if some balladeers weighed down with antiquarian apparatus and polemic their lowly vernacular objects of study, we have only to look at current disquisitions on Madonna or *American Idol* (or indeed, some might say, at this book) to see a similar bureaucratization and hypostatization of the popular by academic discourse. It is not only that the balladeers took popular media seriously: it is how and why they did so that might concern and instruct us. Their example may strike some of us as a cautionary tale about the use and abuse of historicism: Scott historicized some of his contemporaries right out of existence. It is also striking that some of the most dedicated balladeers, most famously Scott, themselves became poets, of an admittedly reactionary stripe: they explored and exploited fully the resources of the media available to them, becoming makers and translators as well as collectors, expropriators, and conservators. Perhaps in this too we might find a useful challenge, or complicated inspiration.

APPENDIX TO CHAPTER 2: QUERIES CIRCULATED BY THE COMMITTEE CONVENED TO "INQUIRE INTO THE NATURE AND AUTHENTICITY OF THE POEMS OF OSSIAN," APPOINTED BY THE HIGHLAND SOCIETY OF SCOTLAND[77]

1 Have you ever heard repeated, or sung, any of the poems ascribed to Ossian, translated and published by Mr. Macpherson? By whom have you heard them so repeated, and at what time or times? Did you ever commit any of them to writing? or can you remember them so well as now to set them down? In either of these cases, be so good to send the Gaelic original to the Committee.

---

[77] Published in *A Report of the Committee of the Highland Society of Scotland, Appointed to Inquire into the Nature and Authenticity of the Poems of Ossian*, 2–3.

2 The same answer is requested concerning any other ancient poems of the same kind, and relating to the same traditionary persons or stories with those in Mr. Macpherson's collection.

3 Are any of the persons from whom you heard any such poems now alive? or are there, in your part of the country, any persons who remember and can repeat or recite such poems? If there are, be so good as to examine them as to the manner of their getting or learning such compositions; and set down, as accurately as possible, such as they can now repeat or recite; and transmit such their account, and such compositions as they repeat, to the Committee.

4 If there are, in your neighborhood, any persons from whom Mr. Macpherson received any poems, enquire particularly what the poems were which he so received, the manner in which he received them, and how he wrote them down; shew those persons, if you have an opportunity, his translation of such poems, and desire them to say if the translation is exact and literal; or, if it differs, in what it differs from the poems, as they repeated them to Mr. Macpherson, and can now recollect them.

5 Be so good as to procure every information you conveniently can, with regard to the traditionary belief, in the country in which you live, concerning the history of Fingal and his followers, and that of Ossian and his poems; particularly those stories and poems published by Mr. Macpherson, and the heroes mentioned in them. Transmit any such account, and any proverbial or traditionary expression in the original Gaelic, relating to the subject, to the Committee.

6 In all the above enquiries, or any that may occur to [blank in text] in elucidation of this subject, he is requested by the Committee to make the enquiry, and to take down the answers, with as much impartiality and precision as possible, in the same manner as if it were a legal question, and that proof to be investigated with a legal strictness.

CHAPTER 3

Tuning the multi-media nation: or, Minstrelsy of the Afro-Scottish border

Regarding the complexities of ballads: let us continue with an experiment in embodied, notionally "national" rhythm. First, count out four beats, several times, and add a snap on "one" and "four" –

1	2	3	4
SNAP	X	X	SNAP

Repeat this several times, such that this rhythmic pattern (let us call it rhythmic pattern 1) becomes easy to sustain.

Next, introduce a variation: maintain the above snapping pattern for several cycles, but then introduce a variant, snapping on beats one and two (rhythmic pattern 2). Alternate between the two patterns:

RHYTHMIC PATTERN 1:				RHYTHMIC PATTERN 2:			
1	2	3	4	1	2	3	4
SN	X	X	SN	SN	SN	X	X

If you have managed to follow these somewhat cumbersome instructions, you will have successfully enacted, in rhythmic pattern 2, a version of the "Scottish snap," a rhythm declared to be a characteristic of Scottish music by authorities from the eighteenth century onward, up to contemporary musicians like the harp teacher Jo Morrison, whose website in 2002 offered tips on "How to Sound Scottish," Scottish snap included.[1] Scottish music was and is known for its uneven rhythms, the forward lilting motion of many songs produced by a rhythm we could represent as a dotted quarter followed by an eighth note (or, equivalently, a dotted eighth followed by a sixteenth note): as in rhythm pattern 1, or the opening bars of "Auld Lang Syne," Fig. 4. The Scottish snap

---

[1] In Morrison's account, "The snap consists of an eighth note followed by a dotted-quarter. You can particularly hear these on Scottish Strathspeys. The reverse snap, a dotted-quarter followed by an eighth, gives an effective contrast to the snap." For other web commentary on the Scottish snap, see www.irish-banjo.com/technique/accompaniment/basic-rhythm-7.html, accessed February 16, 2004.

4 Robert Burns, "Auld Lang Syne," No. 413, James Johnson, *The Scots Musical Museum*

reverses the rhythmic figure, such that an eighth note (for example) is followed by a dotted quarter (or a sixteenth by a dotted eighth): as in the opening snap of "Comin' Thro' the Rye," Fig. 5 (snap asterisked).[2]

I am wondering if, having snapped your way through these instructions, you now feel particularly Scottish. Perhaps if you had grown up in Scotland, or in a US or Canadian or Australian emigrant community with a vital singing, dancing, or fiddling tradition, this snap might have launched you, kinetically and acoustically, into that affective zone which is one dimension of "belonging" to a "nation."

This factitious exercise is meant to snap us once again toward a meditation on that factitious thing, the nation, and toward the question of its historical realization in eighteenth-century Scottish and English song and balladry – or

---

[2] Setts for "Auld Lang Syne' (No. 413) and "Comin' Thro' the Rye" (No. 417 – "written for this Work by Robert Burns") come from Johnson, *Scots Musical Museum*, 426, 430.

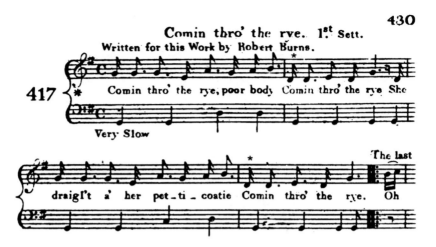

5 Robert Burns, "Comin Thro' the Rye," No. 417, James Johnson,
The Scots Musical Museum

more precisely, to the question of its *represented* realization in various ballad books, antiquarian essays, and historical disquisitions. Those readers who are US citizens are quite familiar with the special cultural charge of rhythm: I got rhythm, wrote Ira Gershwin, his brother George keeping the syncopation lively, but our cultural imaginary everywhere proclaims that it's black and brown Americans who have rhythm, not whites, and certainly not Americans of Scottish, Irish, Welsh, or English descent. If rhythm is now raced, and polyrhythms internationalized and made audible to us via the extension of the world-music commodity, rhythm in the eighteenth century was more often nationalized, as were, of course, such concepts and terms as melody, mode, scale, and instrument: as we see in such eighteenth-century phenomena as the instrument known as "the German flute"; the bagpipes, infamously outlawed as "instruments of war" following the Jacobite uprising of 1745; or the so-called "Strange Irish Key" and "the flat Irish key" derided by the Welsh harper John Parry in *Antient British Music*, his 1742 collection of the "remains" of "Druid" tunes.[3] From this vantage what stands out is not just

---

[3] See John Parry, *Antient British Music; or, A Collection of Tunes Never Before Published, which are Retained by the Cambro-Britons, more Particularly in North Wales, and Supposed, by the Learned, to be the Remains of the Music of the Antient Druids, so much Famed in Roman History* (London: J. Parry and Evan Williams, 1742), 4.

this nationalizing of instruments and keys but their obsolescence – what now appears as their historicity.

If one spends much time reflecting on late-eighteenth-century balladeering (in its full extension: song-collecting, compiling, editing, essay-writing, publishing, inventing, forging), a number of questions soon arise: is cultural nationalism primarily *literary*? Is it, more broadly, to be read as a function of print capitalism, the dissemination of news and ideas, the explosion of mass literacy, the rise of a bookbuying (and songbookbuying) public? How does song, and the idea of song, inflect the idea of the nation? Can one speak of musical nationalisms? Media nationalisms?

These are of course in many respects old questions, familiar in particular to ethno-musicologists, folklorists, and historians of music. These are questions, moreover, inadequate to the balladeering archives themselves, which as we have seen were compiled under the sign of many allegiances, sometimes overlapping – cultural nationalism, regionalism, localism; aesthetic judgment; historical research; moral and philosophical inquiry. This chapter will explore further the interplay of cultural nationalism and historical-medial horizons, as they inform poetry, balladry, and song collections; and here too I will spend more time on the musical, or notionally musical, aspects of these works. For balladeering was never just a matter of books and words, whether recited, chanted, spoken, written, or read; it was also a matter of tunes, of sounds, of "far-off" melodies, as well as modes, keys, and scales. Throughout the eighteenth century, song collections had been appearing alongside and intermixed with ballad collections, the distinction between "ballad" and "song" not then – and still not – formalized.[4] Balladeering involved the collecting, artifactualizing, and remediating of tunes as much as words – this long before Bertrand Bronson undertook the task of collecting and publishing all the tunes and variants of the Child ballads.[5] The developing balladeering archive of tunes, the eighteenth-century theorization of "national keys" and "national song," and the history of the representation of airs, melodies, and accompaniments are

---

[4] Allan Ramsay, for example, published *The Tea-Table Miscellany*, 1724, 2 vols., the influential collection of Scottish and English song from which later balladeers (Percy, Scott) freely poached. He also published in that year *The Ever Green, being a Collection of Scots Poems, Wrote by the Ingenious before 1600*. That the disputed ballad "Hardyknute" appeared in both collections – one a self-described miscellany of song, many newly composed, the other drawn from supposedly ancient manuscripts in the Bannatyne Ms collection – only begins to suggest the historical and categorical flux and interpenetrability of these works. In this chapter, as indeed throughout the book, I move between "ballad" and "song," even as the balladeers themselves did.

[5] See *Traditional Tunes of the Child Ballads*, 4 folio vols., ed. Bertrand H. Bronson (Princeton University Press, 1959–72).

worth a whole other discussion, indeed another book[6]; suffice it to say for the moment that the transcription and representation of ballad tunes was as vexed as the transcription and printed representation of ballad words, if not more so.

"What music is remains open to question at all time and in all places." Thus ethno-musicologist Philip V. Bohlman opens the question of music, cautioning further: "Music may be what we think it is; it may not be."[7] Regarding ballad musics in particular, Dave Harker in *Fakesong* pointedly observes, "Music was never *simply* music: songs were never *simply* songs."[8] So too in the late eighteenth century, ballads were never simply ballads nor airs simply airs.[9] As we have seen, these materials emerged and indeed were produced as objects of national inquiry, literary debate, historical dissertation, and commercial entrepreneurship; they were occasions for cultural fantasy and historical essay, as the voluminous appendices and extensive apparatuses of many eighteenth-century ballad collections make plain. I have argued earlier that from Macpherson and Percy onward, balladeers and other ethno-poetic culture-workers became media theorists *avant la lettre*. They often conducted such media theorization through the discourse of cultural nationalism, as is evident in the way attacks on the Ossian poems mutated rather sharply, especially in Samuel Johnson's hands, into attacks on oral tradition as well as the Scots. (For a later swipe about the Scots' supposed penchant for forgery, one might consult the radical English antiquarian Joseph Ritson, who after reviewing several ballad scandals – including John Pinkerton's many malfeasances – in his "Historical Essay on Scotish Song," observed: "Why the Scotish literati should be more particularly addicted to literary imposition than those of any other country, might be a curious subject of investigation for their new Royal Society" [*Scotish Song*, lxiii].) I have suggested that many eighteenth-century disputes with a decidedly culturally-nationalistic turn – the Ossian controversy, various "scandals of the ballad," and so on – must be understood as *media* controversies: arguments about media, mediation, and mediums.

---

[6] For an inquiry into the Irish case in this period see Leith Davis, *Music, Postcolonialism, and Gender: The Construction of Irish National Identity, 1724–1874* (Notre Dame, IN: University of Notre Dame Press, 2006).

[7] Philip V. Bohlman, "Ontologies of Music," in *Rethinking Music*, ed. Nicholas Cook and Mark Everist (Oxford University Press, 2001), 17.

[8] Harker, *Fakesong*, vii.

[9] My discussion of the mediality of the national air is informed throughout by conversation with Celeste Langan, whose dynamic thinking on these matters is most recently captured in "Scotch Drink & Irish Harps: Mediations of the National Air," in *The Figure of Music in Nineteenth-Century British Poetry*, ed. Phyllis Weliver (Aldershot and Burlington, VT: Ashgate, 2005), 25–49.

"A medium is a medium is a medium." Thus the formidable media theorist Friedrich Kittler rings his variation on Gertrude Stein.[10] But all media are not equal, as Kittler notes, and some media mediate differentially. The dream of a frictionless medium, a perfect transparent conduit, is a dream perhaps left to the condensed matter physicists, with their super-conductors and carbon nanotubes. Only in a digital age of fiber optics, when visual and sound data can be processed, stored, and transmitted via the same stream, can we truly begin to imagine materially how a medium is a medium is a medium. And even now, computer glitches, incompatible software systems, and the mounting piles of technological detritus in my apartment suggest that we are far away from the dream of a world beauti-fully simplified (or horrifically determined) by an integrated universal medium. In the late eighteenth century we are not yet in a fiber optic world. But if Shelley was right in his "Defence of Poetry," that "poets are the hierophants of an unapprehended inspiration, the mirrors of the gigantic shadows which futurity casts upon the present," then perhaps the balladeers might serve as test cases for the gigantic media shadows which our present, their futurity, now casts upon their labors.[11]

Shadows, phantasms: the nation, an imagined community, as Benedict Anderson has influentially argued, bound by print culture and the mass ceremony of daily newspaper-reading – a community of individuals inter-pellated in homogenous empty time, located in a mapped, gridded space. Many have written since the 1980s to complicate the print basis of Anderson's conception of the nation, yet eighteenth-century print culture, in its many exfoliating, energetic manifestations, still stands in most histor-ies and theories as a, if not the, generative matrix of imagined national community.[12] The proliferating British publication of ballad and song allows us to further complicate, or at least refine, our understanding of

---

[10] Kittler, *Discourse Networks, 1800/1900*, 265.

[11] Shelley, "Defence," *Shelley's Poetry and Prose*, 508.

[12] Historians as well as cultural theorists have paid particular attention to the proliferation of newspapers and the emergence of influential magazines and journals in the late eighteenth and early nineteenth centuries, and the impact of these on the formation of audiences and communities: see, for example, Jon Klancher, *The Making of English Reading Audiences, 1790–1832* (Madison, WI: University of Wisconsin Press, 1987); Olivia Smith, *The Politics of Language, 1791–1819* (Oxford, NY: Clarendon Press, 1984); Linda Colley, *Britons: Forging the Nation, 1707–1837* (New Haven: Yale University Press, 1992); Gerald Newman, *The Rise of English Nationalism: A Cultural History, 1740–1830* (Rev. edn. New York: St. Martin's, 1997); and on the German case, Kittler, *Discourse Networks*. Jürgen Habermas' influential work is also crucial, not least as a counter: the literary public sphere as envisioned by Habermas often functions as a cosmopolitan alternative to nationalist and cultural nationalist counterpublics. Colley observes in *Britons* that the materials flying off the eighteenth-century presses were overwhelmingly religious materials: psalmbooks, bibles, tracts. It is also true, however, that secular and politically radical writers were increasingly influential via print culture: see

late-eighteenth-century communities and cultural researches, both "at home" and "abroad."

CULTURAL COMPARISON, TECHNOLOGICAL CONSTRAINT

Cultural nationalism in both literary and musical modes is inherently comparative. Its energy arises as much from the impulse to differentiate as to consolidate. It is striking that, amidst all their cultural comparisons and regional or national specificities, we rarely find in English, Scottish, or "British" ballad collections a clear conceptualization of "European" balladry until later in the nineteenth century.[13] It was for later, more philologically sophisticated and less culturally nationalistic scholars to develop a broader, comparative, "European," purview: such that in 1932 Gordon Hall Gerould – following Francis James Child and numerous other scholars – could write: "Our English and Scottish ballads are not, then, to be considered something peculiar to a single island, but are to be viewed as manifestations of a culture common to European folk as a whole."[14] For the earliest ballad editors, however (e.g. Percy, Ritson, Pinkerton, Jamieson, Scott), balladry was less a zone of a supra- or pre- or proto-national "folk" than of national and indeed regional and local differentiation, investigation, and debate.

A sustained look at the actual texts of ballad collections necessarily complicates our sense of what Katie Trumpener calls "bardic nationalism." One might begin by noting that ambitious Scottish ballad editors envisioned a double, differentiated yet simultaneous audience of Scottish and English readers: this hybrid imagined community (to invoke Anderson again) has much to say about one moment in the historical dialectic between nationalism and imperialism. (These collections also traveled

---

Olivia Smith's re-animation of radical writing and radical thought as an integral part of English identity and political style. See her too on the status of grammars in eighteenth-century Britain, and Kittler on proliferating grammars in Germany circa 1800.

[13] The several invocations of "Europe" in Ritson's and Pinkerton's late eighteenth-century publications most often contrast "Europe" with the "savage tribes" either of North America or of Africa; a fully developed concept of European balladry had to await the full flowering of philology and comparative literary and historical scholarship in the nineteenth century (notwithstanding Thomas Percy's and Robert Jamieson's earlier comparatist forays into Norse and Danish balladry). Francis James Child's compendium, while assembling "English and Scottish ballads," presupposes and maps out in its included variants in many languages a European range of balladry; and less scholarly ballad collections fully reflected this Europeanization of balladry, as we see, for example, in an 1888 volume, *Border Ballads* (ed. Graham R. Tomson [Rosamund Marriott Watson], London: Walter Scott): 'In most countries, certainly in all European countries where narrative ballads are sung, the stories differ in many ways in plot and incident, but in essentials are much alike" (xi); "Of the ballad of *Lord Randal* (of which Professor Child gives no less than fifteen variants) we find versions in German, Dutch, Danish, Swedish, and Italian" (xxi).

[14] Gordon Hall Gerould, *The Ballad of Tradition* (Oxford: Clarendon Press, 1932), 24.

extensively in Ireland and in the North American colonies, even if these audiences weren't so obviously announced within.) One might consider, for example, Allan Ramsay's sub-title to his *Tea-Table Miscellany: A Collection of Choice Songs, Scots and English* (1724), which was dedicated "To ilka lovely BRITISH lass, Frae Ladies Charlotte, Anne, and Jean, Down to ilk bonny singing Bess, Who dances barefoot on the green."[15] To take a later case: the *pièce de résistance* of the 1803 *Minstrelsy* was, tellingly, "The War-Song of the Edinburgh Light Dragoons," a call to British arms against France, which Scott wrote for the regiment he more or less invented as well as quarter-mastered. It is important to observe that the *Minstrelsy of the Scottish Border* was conceived, at its highest geo-political level, as an anti-Jacobinical *British* document. If Scott's "Historical Introduction" focused on Scotland's strug-gle with England up to 1601, the contemporary chronotopical frame of the 1803 *Minstrelsy*, allegorized in "The War-Song," oriented its readers to Britain's struggle with France:

> To horse! To horse! the standard flies,
>   The bugles sound the call;
> The Gallic navy stems the seas,
> The voice of battle's on the breeze,
>   Arouse ye, one and all! (*MSB*, 419)

We can see, then, that the *Border Minstrelsy* simultaneously sustains a power-ful regionalism (the Border, the prominence of Selkirkshire and Ettrick Forest in the notes), nationalism (the *Scottish* Border), and imperialism (the final, definitive British frame). Scottish cultural nationalism appears here not in opposition to Britishness or to British policy but rather as a supporter and mainstay of it.[16]

The late-eighteenth-century axes of balladeering comparisons and differ-entiations were themselves relative and mutable. In English and Scottish balladeering discourse, the Irish, Welsh, Scottish, Native Americans, ancient Greeks, and other so-called savages line up against the refined and artificial triumphs of civilization: and strikingly, the "civilized" nations

[15] Ramsay, *Tea-Table Miscellany* (1724), 14th edn. repr. Glasgow: Robert Forrester, 1876, dedication page.

[16] This observation is indebted to but diverges from Katie Trumpener's discussion of cultural nation-alism in *Bardic Nationalism*, though Trumpener herself offers a corrective to Benedict Anderson, showing how cultural nationalism must be dialectical, its dance between a resistant traditionalism and a progressive modernity constitutive. It is true, moreover, that Scott is a late case, and that his complex coordination of allegiances is both more fluent and more in tune with ideological dominants than the earlier cultural nationalists on whom Trumpener focuses; it is also true that if Britain is embraced in the *Minstrelsy*, England is decidedly not – in this respect Scott's collection confirms Trumpener's analysis.

often lose in the cultural sweepstakes: as we see in the Scottish antiquarian John Pinkerton's ruminations on national musics in *Scotish Tragic Ballads* (1781): "Nay, the music of the most barbarous countries has had effects that not all the sublime pathos of Corelli, or animated strains of Handel, could produce. Have not the Welsh, the Irish, and Scottish tunes, greater influence over the most informed minds at this day than the best Italian concerto?" He continued, "Is not the war-music of the rudest inhabitants of the wilds of America or Scotland more terrible to the ear than that of the best band in the British army?"[17] Savage war-tribes and the British army: both have their musics, and Pinkerton knows which is more fearsome.

Balladeering discourse relies on this habit of cultural comparison, itself variously informed by Enlightenment anthropology, Rousseauvian primitivism, antiquarian eclecticism, and the Scottish mode of conjectural history – in which a "rude age" was imagined to be succeeded by pastoral and ultimately commercial eras. One notes in Pinkerton's remarks the significant absence of English song. Scottish, Irish, and Welsh tunes stand forth as deeply, primally influential; and indeed, if Pinkerton does mention the British army bands, he never anywhere even considers English music *qua* English. This very non-specificity of English music – perhaps analogous to what Trumpener and others have flagged as the systematic underdevelopment of Englishness in the eighteenth- and nineteenth-century British imaginary[18]– fueled the kind of anxiety rebutted vigorously by the English antiquarian Joseph Ritson. In his 1783 *Select Collection of English Songs*, Ritson defended the special "beauties" and "elegance" of English song, heretofore obscured by bawdy and despicable collections. He repeatedly invoked a logic of comparative differentiation, as when he observed in a footnote in his Preface:

* The distinction between *Scotish* and *English* songs, it is conceived, arises – not from the language in which they are written, for *that* may be common to both,

---

[17] Pinkerton, *Scotish Tragic Ballads*, xix.

[18] The status of "Englishness" in the eighteenth-century cultural imaginary is a locus of some controversy among historians and literary scholars: but certainly the period witnesses the efflorescence of John Bulls and roast-beef-eating true-born Englishmen as cultural types, not least in Defoe's poems and novels and Hogarth's works; and of course more persistent local, affective, and ideological allegiances made themselves felt in Wilkeite radicalism and methodism, as Colley argues. Newman also makes plain how robust "Englishness" was in this period, however pressured by its "Celtic peripheries," the cosmopolitan pull of France, and the loss of America, and the production of "Britain" and empire. For a politically alert, persuasive account of Englishness and the politics of "Gothicism" – proposing a vitally contested Englishness in this period, constructed in part through the politics of ancient poetry – see Philip Connell, "British Identities," *The Historical Journal* 49:1 (2006): 161–92. Connell's essay points to a mild, British Gothicism open to plural ethnic identities and a progressivist historical narrative, as opposed to the Scotophobic English radicalism of Wilkes et al.

but – from the country to which they respectively belong, or of which their authors are natives. This discrimination does not so necessarily or properly apply to Ireland; great part of which was colonised from this kingdom, and the descendants of the settlers, the only civilised and cultivated inhabitants, have, consequently, been, ever since, looked upon as *English*: the native *Irish* being, to this day, a very different people. Every one has heard of the ENGLISH PALE.[19]

Note that it is not *language* that distinguishes Scottish from English song, but something like *nativity*, a birthed belonging to a land. Note the effort to keep English-speaking and singing Scots somehow other, their national and musical essence one "belonging" elsewhere. And we note too how the Irish are quite literally, geographically and culturally, beyond the pale. Ritson thus lays out a clear spectrum of belonging, strangeness, and proximity.

Yet this spectrum shifts when Ritson moves from linguistic to musical comparisons. Even as he polices the linguistic border between England and Scotland, between Irish colonials and the native Irish, he is much more musically anxious about the Italians and French. His collection offers, he declares, "the genuine effusions of the English muse, unadulterated with the sentimental refinements of Italy or France" (ix).

Running beneath Ritson's ideational, linguistic, and territorial definitions of community, there is, significantly, another techno-material requirement structuring his *English Songs*: the strictures of print, the constraints imposed by the movable types Ritson could find. In the scrupulous, irritable manner characteristic of him, Ritson informs his readers of these constraints:

The types here made use of presented the only mode of printing the music which could be adopted. The reader may be surprised to learn that, in this great kingdom, where all the arts and sciences are supposed to flourish in their highest perfection, there is not, perhaps, above one printer possessed of a sufficient quantity of these useful characters, and that of no other size.

Ritson goes on to contrast the typographic arts of Britain and France, and praises more broadly those of the Continent, blasting the British monopoly on type: "They who are acquainted with the degree of elegance to which this and every other branch of the typographical arts are arrived upon the continent, or have even looked into that most beautiful specimen of it, the ANTHOLOGIE FRANÇOISE, will have sufficient reason to condemn that pur-blind and selfish policy, which can restrain

[19] Ritson, Preface, *A Select Collection of English Songs with their Original Airs* (London: Longman, Hurst; Cadell and Davies, 1813; 1783 1st edn.), Vol. I of III, 1813, xi.

and prevent all emulation in science in favour of a private monopoly" (xvi–xvii).[20]

Ritson's exasperated note turns us from the agonistic discourse of cultural nationalism, musical and linguistic, to the technical realities of print mediation (themselves inflected by national legal and economic policies). Historians of printed music tell us that most eighteenth-century music published in Britain was engraved, not typeset.[21] While Ritson struggled to find adequate type, most other balladeers – if they deigned to print music – turned to engraving, at least until the spread of lithography. Most ballad collections thus required a multi-media processing of typeset texts and engraved musical staves, notes, key signatures, and ligatures: the music of William Motherwell's 1827 *Minstrelsy: Ancient and Modern* was, for example, engraved, the tunes sequestered in the book's final section.

Motherwell's engraved and Ritson's typeset music (Fig. 6 and Fig. 7, respectively) remind us of the print bases of literary and musical cultural nationalisms – and more broadly, the print basis of histories predicated on such phenomena as ballads. The ballad collection was a strikingly hybrid genre, including anything and everything from manuscripts to broadsides to legal documents to extracts from chronicles to tunes to copperplate illustrations to woodblock prints.[22] As we have seen, the emergent genre of the ballad collection could encompass words and tunes, texts and musics. Yet, as Ritson's complaint highlights, ballad collections did not process

---

[20] In the second edition of *English Songs* in 1813, editor and annotator Thomas Park supplied an additional note to this passage in Ritson's Preface, observing his continuing troubles with type: "The types for the music in this edition were twice cast by Mr. Caslon, before they could be employed: and even the second fount is much more defective in blending the ligatures of notes than might be wished" (Vol. I of III, xvii).

[21] See Charles Humphries and William C. Smith, *Music Publishing in the British Isles from the Earliest Times to the Middle of the Nineteenth Century* (London: Cassell and Co., 1954): "Before the end of the seventeenth century, music printing from engraved metal plates had become the generally accepted method, and this lasted well on into the nineteenth century" (14). "During the eighteenth century little attempt was made to use music type in preference to engraved plates" (28). Humphries notes the emergence of several printing options: Engraved and punched metal plates, movable type, and lithography (post Senefelder's discovery circa 1796). Roger Chartier, in his afterword to *Music and the Cultures of Print*, ed. Kate van Orden (New York and London: Garland, 2000), notes the complex co-existence of two technologies for printing music (movable type and engraving) in seventeenth- and eighteenth-century Europe, and observes that the legal and commercial as well as technical issues involved varied from nation to nation (328).

[22] Here and elsewhere I hope the reader will forgive the author for the relative paucity of discussion of illustrations – a fascinating topic obviously related to the medial-technological questions I here pursue, but alas beyond the scope of this book, or rather of the author. The constant, often amusingly haphazard re-use of woodcuts in broadside ballads is only one exemplary case of a conservative remediation of materials; the increasingly refined illustrations of some late-eighteenth-century ballad books are a striking index of their polite status and cultural desirability.

6 Engraved tunes from William Motherwell, *Minstrelsy, Ancient and Modern* (1827), engraved by Andrew Blaikie

these differential media with equal panache. Most ballad editors eschewed the printing of tunes – notably Walter Scott, who managed to publish several editions of his *Minstrelsy of the Scottish Border* with no music, until the posthumous 1833 edition. So we confront, in Scott, phenomena like the historical ballad, "Sang of the Outlaw Murray," which lacks any song. (There seems in fact to be no surviving music for this song: in his opus, *Traditional Tunes of the Child Ballads*, Bertrand H. Bronson prints no tune for "The Sang of the Outlaw Murray" [Child No. 305].) Scott simply did not define his ballads musically; to him, they were objects of historical, literary, and cultural inquiry, not of musical research. Yet other collectors, Robert Burns famously among them, gathered and transcribed hundreds of tunes for publication in *The Scots Musical Museum* (1787–1803). While the

7 Typeset tune of "The Hunting of Chevy Chase" ("God prosper long our
   noble king"), from Ritson, *A Select Collection of English Songs*

archive of the *Scots Musical Museum* was rather different from that of Scott's
Minstrelsy or Jamieson's *Popular Songs*, nevertheless there was some overlap,
including such traditional Scottish ballads as "Johnny Armstrong."[23]
However different their aims and audiences, such ballad-and-song projects
raised questions in both musical and linguistic domains: How to represent
dialects? Should one represent tunes? If so, how – via imperfect type, or
expensive engraving? Should one include "proper basses for the pianoforte"
(as Johnson did in the *Scots Musical Museum*)? Or should one as a purist
eschew imported harmonies and instrumental settings (as Ritson and
Motherwell did), or should one adopt them (as Scott, 1833, did)? Ritson
in *Scotish Song in Two Volumes* (1794) agreed with Scottish editors and
musicologists that "the words and melody of a Scotish song should be ever
inseparable"[24]– making a point as well about Scottish vs. English song, the
special musicality of the former. Yet whatever the cultural theory animating
his statement, Ritson stood almost alone among antiquarians in recognizing
the value of tunes.[25] His remarks about type above remind us that the

[23] James Johnson even managed to drum up some rather anemic music for Lady Wardlaw's
     "Hardyknute," which one suspects was not sung before or after his publication. See Song 280,
     Vol. I, 289, in *The Scots Musical Museum*, reprint of the 4-volume Blackwood edition of 1853
     (Hatboro, PA: Folklore Associates, 1962).
[24] Ritson, *Scotish Song*, i.
[25] For Ritson's remark, see *Scotish Song*, i; for Ritson's near-singularity, see Gerould, *Ballad of Tradition*:
     "Ritson, indeed, appears to have been the only one of the early editors who was aware of the
     importance of melody to the study of ballads" (67).

separability of tunes and texts was not only a matter of most eighteenth-century editors' preference: it was often an insurmountable technological fact.

There are several historical strands here to be teased out, then: a discursive analysis of balladeering in light of cultural nationalism, and a media analysis of balladeering as a project dependent on the interplay of technology, theory, acoustics, and notation, both alphabetic and pitched. A sustained inquiry into balladeering reminds us of the uneven, differentiated development of interest in and technologies for collecting and reproducing texts and tunes. It also reminds us of the uneven development of that thing we call "print." We tend to forget that "print" is no monolith: there is an uneven development of print independent of the uneven developments of localities, nations, empires, and their peripheries.

Confronted with the range of medial, historiographic, and ideological questions that these balladeering materials present, how might we think through their implications? To offer some speculative proposals, I would like to turn briefly to several examples of ballad and song mediation circa 1800.

FROM THE SCOTTISH BORDER TO THE AFRICAN INTERIOR: CASE STUDIES

Let us first touch down on the border via "The Battle of Otterburn": the border between Scotland and England, the border between oral tradition and literary culture, between Thomas Percy and Walter Scott, between tunes and texts, objects of inquiry and technologies of mediation. A ballad called "The Battle of Otterburn" was published in Percy's *Reliques* in 1765; another, quite different "Battle of Otterbourne" appeared in Scott's *Minstrelsy of the Scottish Border*, there subtitled "The Scottish Edition" (*MSB*, 53). Just as Percy Englished his "ancient minstrels" and Scott Scottished them, so too ballads oscillated on the border, debatable stuff from debatable land.

In the various "Otterburns," as in the more famous "Chevy Chase," the fourteenth-century antagonists are the Earl Douglas on the Scottish side vs. Lord Henry Percy of Northumberland. The literary-historical fortunes of this ballad align with those of cultural nationalism; the ballad is a counter in what Marilyn Butler has called "competing medievalisms" but is also a bone of national contention among editors. Feuding border chieftains modulate with amusing predictability into genteelly feuding editors on either side of the border. Yet we recall that the border itself is not a national region: it is the very space that problematizes "the nation."[26] It is, historically, a contact zone, a war zone, a policed zone. The border does not simply mark the division of nations: it connotes more specifically a Scottish region. Scott's Otterburn, "The Scottish edition," appears in a regional minstrelsy, one which admittedly aspired to promote the region to the status of quasi-nation. And indeed the earlier appearance of this ballad in Ritson's *Northumberland Garland* (1793) further alerts us to the highly regional inflections of much antiquarian balladeering: there were many more intensely imagined communities than nation and empire. Historical study of "The Battle of Otterburn" suggests one way British cultural historians might address Dipesh Chakrabarty's call to "provincialize Europe" (to relativize our archives, to re- and de-center our imaginative and historical geography): it could be argued that the British balladeers were busily provincializing Britain despite themselves, through their successive de- and re-territorializings of such ballad-objects as "The Ballad of Otterburn."

If a ballad like "Otterburn" traveled from one textual realization to another, from one collection to another, it did not travel passively. Editors *produced* the ballad, as Dave Harker reminds us. Scott's "Otterbourne" was one of his infamous "collated editions," a well-stitched patchwork of stanzas poached from previous collections, manuscripts, and opportune recitations, as his headnote to the ballad attests:

This song was first published from Mr. Herd's *Collection of Scottish Songs and Ballads*, Edin. 1774, 2 vols. octavo; but fortunately two copies have since been obtained from the recitation of old persons residing at the head of Ettrick Forest, by which the story is brought out, and completed in a manner much more corresponding to the true history. (*MSB*, 54)

Yet for all these textual mediations, through which Scott orchestrated print and oral media, there is no music to "Otterbourne" until Scott, 1833 (see Fig. 8).

This ballad has appeared in numerous balladeering volumes since, including Child's textual compendium, Bronson's publication of tunes, and *The Pictorial Book of Ancient Ballad Poetry* (1853), which offers, in equal opportunity fashion, Percy's quite antique version followed by Scott's.[27] So "The Battle of Otterburn" exists now primarily as recyclable

---

[26] On the Border as a subset of the problematics of "North Britain," and on Scott's fluent exploiting of the geo-political romance of this imagined geography in his *Minstrelsy* as well as his novels, see Ch. 3, "Great North Roads: the Geometries of the Nation," in Penny Fielding, *Scotland and the Fictions of Geography*.

[27] For these incarnations, see Child, *ESPB*, Vol. VI, 289–302; Bronson, *Traditional Tunes*, Vol. III, 109–12; *The Pictorial Book of Ancient Ballad Poetry*, ed. J. S. Moore (London: Henry Washbourne, 1853), Vol. I of II, 220–7 (Percy's version); 228–31 (Scott's version).

8 Music for "The Battle of Otterburn," Walter Scott, *Minstrelsy of the Scottish Border*

historical evidence: but evidence for what? As an object of inquiry, "Otterburn" has passed through several literary-historical, national, regional, and medial phases: Scott's eventual inclusion of music suggests the possibility of, if not the clear invitation to, "replay." Unlike, say, the ubiquitous "Barbara Allen," or even its fellow historical ballad "Sir Patrick Spens," it has not won a place in the twentieth-century repertoire, in part because at seventy-plus stanzas (according to Bronson, although Scott's edition is shorter) it exceeds the bounds of LP and CD formats for a "ballad single."

Again, what is important in terms of eighteenth-century ballad mediation is this: if Percy and Scott contended over "The Battle of Otterburn," they did not contend over its medial definition *as a text*: neither had any great interest in publishing, much less Englishing or Scottishing, the music. "The Scottish edition" was the edition of the text.

This brings us to our next ballad specimen, another collated edition and like "Otterburn" published as one of Scott's historical ballads: the afore-mentioned "Sang of the Outlaw Murray." As noted in the previous chapter, sources for this ballad included two antiquarian manuscripts, a copy found in the papers of Mrs. Cockburn, and most intriguingly, "the recitation of Mr. Mungo Park, whose toils during his patient and intrepid travels in Africa, have not eradicated from his recollection the legendary lore of his native country" (*MSB*, 57–8). The conjunction here of Mungo Park, the Border native, with Mungo Park, the African explorer, is a historically telling one: for indeed, the figure of Park, like Scott a living archive of Border lore, ushers us from the Scottish Border to the African interior, from one kind of imperial periphery to another.

The casual collaboration of balladeer and explorer points as well to a methodological conjunction which underlies balladeering and other cultural ventures circa 1800 – the interplay of "historiographic" and "ethnographic operations," to invoke again the lexicon of Michel de Certeau. Another way to put this: the ethnographic protocols for cultural collecting that in a very controlled manner inform Scott's *Minstrelsy* informed as well the African explorations of the Scottish physician. We might invoke here Alan Bewell's notion of "domestic anthropology," a concept he developed in light of Wordsworth's moral-philosophical researches.[28] With his open-ness to select oral source-mediums, Scott took up, however gingerly, and with other political allegiances, his own domestic anthropology on the border.

---

[28] See Alan Bewell, *Wordsworth and the Enlightenment: Nature, Man, and Society in the Experimental Poetry* (New Haven, CT: Yale University Press, 1989), 29–42.

A balladeering open to oral tradition, as Scott's very guardedly was, becomes an ethnographic as well as a historiographic project. And a ballad-loving explorer, as Park was, may have been particularly attuned to song-culture and song-mediation abroad as well as at home. In Scott's *Minstrelsy*, Park makes a brief appearance as a native informant; in his *Travels in the Interior Districts of Africa*, Park presents himself as a participant observer, brave, alert, and wily, but often hapless, hungry, robbed, scared, and wet. Among the discourse-objects Park's travels allowed him to produce were glossaries, maps, and, most relevant for this discussion, a document that the ballad scholar Newman White named in 1928 as "the first Negro song printed in English."[29] So beyond the fortuitous linking of Scott's project and African exploration in the figure of Mungo Park, we can see a deeper discursive logic underpinning European, or at least Scottish, cultural researches circa 1800: a song, or the idea of a song, becomes one index of time spent in another place – whether that other place is the Borders' past or truly another African country.

Park's "Negro song" is no simple object. Park was in fact the pathetical subject of the song, sung by village women to cheer up and perhaps tease the miserable traveler. In Chapter 15, Park narrates the occasion of song-making this way: he has reached Sego, the capital of Bambarra, but is told by the King's minion that he must not cross the river. Stymied, he looks for a place to put up for the night, but no one in the city is willing to open their doors to the suspicious white man. Finally, a woman in a nearby village takes pity on him, feeds him, and returns to work with her family members:

They lightened their labor by songs, one of which was composed extempore; for I was myself the subject of it. It was sung by one of the young women, the rest joining in a sort of chorus. The air was sweet and plaintive, and the words, literally translated, were these. – "The winds roared, and the rains fell." " – The poor white man, faint and weary, came and sat under our tree. – He has no mother to bring him milk; no wife to grind his corn. *Chorus.* Let us pity the white man; no mother has he, &c., &c." Trifling as this recital may appear to the reader, to a person in my situation, the circumstance was affecting in the highest degree.[30]

Herein ends Park's relation of the song-event, an appealing ethnographic anecdote. For historians and theorists of orality, this story might have particular interest as a trace of song-composition in action. Yet this is not

[29] See Newman I. White, *American Negro Folk Songs* (Cambridge, MA: Harvard University Press, 1928), 45.
[30] Mungo Park, *Travels in the Interior Districts of Africa* (London: G. and W. Nicol or W. Bulmer, 1799), 198.

the end of the song-matter: the song was reworked back in the metropole, before the publication of Park's *Travels*. As Park tells us in his Postscript, which is actually part of the front-matter of the volume, the "sweet and plaintive" work-song was versified by Georgiana, Duchess of Devonshire, titled "A Negro Song," and prettily set to parlor-room music by G. G. Ferrari (Fig. 9). The Duchess' poem and Ferrari's musical setting stand as metropolitan ornaments, blessings bestowed after the journey but placed before Park's travel narrative.

There are then three "versions" in print of this song: the prose rendering of the oral performance included in Park's narrative; the versification undertaken by the Duchess of Devonshire; and the musical setting by Ferrari – an example of creative remediation if ever there was one. A West African women's work-song found itself transmogrified into a sub-Handelian British anthem. If the ethnographic detail of the song-"recital," as Park called it, reminds us of later anthropologists' memoirs, the musical setting of "A Negro Song" reminds us rather of the fashionable music circulating in London circa 1800.

A further and by now perhaps unsurprising complication arises when we discover that "A Negro Song," variously displayed within Park's own *Travels*, was later published in the second, posthumous edition of Joseph Ritson's *Select Collection of English Songs* (first edition 1783, second edition 1813).[31] Ritson's editor and annotator, Thomas Park, featured "A Negro Song, by Georgiana, Duchess of Devonshire," among the category "Miscellaneous Songs" (a category in this instance embracing everything from old ballads to naval songs to Shakespeare's "Fairy Song" in *The Two Gentleman of Verona* to a sentimental lyric by Anna Letitia Barbauld). Ferrari's music does not figure in Ritson's appendix of typeset tunes. The Duchess's text traveled; the Italian's musical setting didn't. That "negro song" could become its own genteel subgenre, one practiced by benevolent English duchesses as well as enterprising nineteenth-century songsters on both sides of the Atlantic, is something I will pursue in the next chapter. Suffice it to say here that a "Negro Song" in a *Select Collection of English Songs* demonstrates once again the diagnostic heterogeneity of song and ballad collections, even when offered under a supposedly exclusive "national" mandate.

---

[31] See Song LXVII, in Ritson, *Select Collection of English Songs*, vol. II of III, 1813, 200–1.

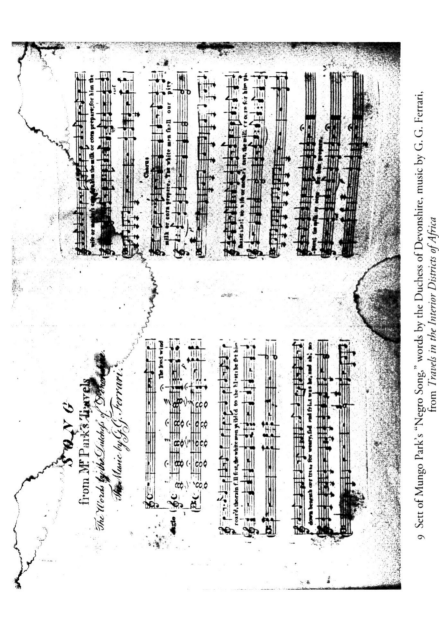

9 Sett of Mungo Park's "Negro Song," words by the Duchess of Devonshire, music by G. G. Ferrari, from *Travels in the Interior Districts of Africa*

FROM ANTIQUARIAN FOOTNOTE TO PARLOR SONG
AND POEM: "THE CHEROKEE DEATH SONG"

For a final example of the cultural, national, and medial complexities of song in this period, let us consider "The Cherokee Death Song," a work that seems to have first appeared in a sheet music version in the confederated states of America in 1780. It appeared as well as a footnote in the introductory essay to Joseph Ritson's *Select Collection of English Songs* (1783). This song – or at least its verbal text – was later revealed to have been composed by Anne Home Hunter, wife of the renowned anatomist and surgeon, John Hunter, a Scottish transplant to London. "The Cherokee Death Song" had a long, complex, transnational career in print, as several scholars (literary as well as musicological) have traced.[32] The song's later migrations included appearances in the first professionally performed American play, Royall Tyler's *The Contrast*, performed in 1787 and published in 1790; Ritson's *Scotish Song in Two Volumes*, 1794; and in Mrs. John Hunter's own *Poems* (London, 1802). These successive textualizations – varying in generic contextualization, musical realization, and authorial/editorial status – offer us a striking opportunity to think about the transatlantic mediation of song, its mutable "nationalizations," and the cultural phantasies song occasioned, whether about Scottish poets or Native American "primitives." As the second act of *The Contrast* begins, for example, we see the heroine Maria "sitting disconsolate at a Table, with Books, &c.": she then reads or sings "The Death Song" (there are no musical cues in the text but we know the sheet music had circulated widely in the republic). She continues with a sentimental disquisition on "the manly virtues of courage" the song portrays, their irresistibility

---

[32] On this remarkable song, which has attracted the attention of musicologists as well as literary historians, see A. Peter Brown's excellent discussion of Hunter's career and several song ventures, including an important collaboration with Haydn, in "Musical Settings of Anne Hunter's Poetry: From National Song to Canzonetta," *Journal of the American Musicological Society* 46:1 (Spring 1994): 39–89; Richard Crawford's brief account in *America's Musical Life: A History* (New York and London: Norton, 2001), 14, 861; the bibliographic information in *Writing American Indian Music: Historical Transcriptions, Notations, and Arrangements*, ed. Victoria Lindsay Levine (published for the American Musicological Society; Middleton, WI: A-R Editions, 2002), 215–16; and Tim Fulford's discussion of this song in particular in *Romantic Indians: Native Americans, British Literature, and Transatlantic Culture, 1756–1830* (Oxford University Press, 2006), 141–3. Fulford focuses on Ritson's mediation of this song, not Hunter's. Levine has the song appearing as London sheet music in 1780 and in a manuscript copybook in 1789, in Absalom Aimwell, pseudonym of Andrew Adgate, *The Philadelphia Songster, Part I: Being a Collection of Choice Songs; Such as Are Calculated to Please the Ear, While They Impress the Mind, and Make the Heart Better* (Philadelphia: John McCulloch, 1789), 8. (Levine, *Writing American Indian Music* 215). I am indebted to Tim Fulford and Ruth Perry for help tracking this extremely mobile song and its scholarship.

to "a female heart," and so on.[33] The terms of the comparative-culturalist readings of such Indian death-songs were so strongly typed that they could thus appear in early federal drama; the gendered discourse occasioned and solicited by such a song is also notable – the stoic hyper-masculine Native Warriors idealized by genteel Anglo femininity.

Certainly "The Cherokee Death Song" partakes of a transcultural fantasy intensified no doubt by Anne Hunter's own marriage – her husband a veteran of New World imperial/military ventures, John Hunter having served as surgeon during the Seven Years War.[34] More broadly, as Tim Fulford argues, this song takes up the protocols of a popular genre, the Indian Death Song, an efflorescence of the transcultural contact and forms of hybridity suggested in the title of his book, *Romantic Indians*.[35] Trafficking in Indians was then a highly conventional thing for a poet and lyrist to do – as we might recall from Wordsworth's "Complaint of a Forsaken Indian Woman," or any of Southey's Indian songs. Hunter's particular Indian and his particular death were especially labile and mobile, as suggested by the long and various course of this song in print, in Ireland and the new USA, as well as in Scotland and England. When Ritson first included the song in his important 1783 "Historical Essay on the Origin and Progress of National Song," prefacing his *Select Collection of English Songs*, he included the text, but not the music, in a footnote. Ritson tucked a mini-antiquarian disquisition into the footnote (a headnote within a footnote, we might say), glossing the songtext thus:

It is a custom with the American savages to put to death the prisoners they take in war by the most lingering and exquisite torments. These it is the height of heroism for the victim to bear with apparent insensibility. During a series of excruciating tortures, of which a European can scarcely form the idea, he sings aloud a song, wherein he strives to aggravate the wrath of his enemies, by recounting the injuries and disgraces they have suffered from him and his nation; derides their tortures, as only adapted to the frame and resolution of children; and expresses his joy in passing with so much honour to the land of spirits. Of one of these songs the following stanzas, which are handed about in manuscript, and have not, it is

---

[33] See Act II, Scene 1 of Royall Tyler, *The Contrast: A Comedy in Five Acts* (Boston and New York: Houghton Mifflin, 1920; first published Philadelphia: Pritchard and Hall, 1790), 32–5.

[34] On Anne Hunter, see A. Peter Brown and also G. T. Bettany, "Hunter, Anne (1742–1821)," rev. M. Clare Loughlin-Chow, in *Oxford Dictionary of National Biography*, ed. H. C. G. Matthew and Brian Harrison (Oxford University Press, 2004), www.oxforddnb.com/view/article/14215 (accessed October 17, 2006). For the life of John Hunter, see Jacob W. Gruber, "Hunter, John (1728–1793)," in *Oxford Dictionary of National Biography*, ed. H. C. G. Matthew and Brian Harrison (Oxford University Press, 2004); online edn., ed. Lawrence Goldman, January 2006, www.oxforddnb.com/view/article/14220 (accessed October 17, 2006).

[35] See Fulford, Ch. 8, "The Indian Song," in *Romantic Indians*, 141–55.

believed, already appeared in print, are said to be a translation. This may, perhaps, turn out not to be the case; but whatever becomes of the authenticity of the composition, it cannot well be denied that the writer has treated the real subject in a manner equally spirited and beautiful.[36]

Here Ritson writes as a comparative anthropologist before the fact, including the song as a specimen of "national song" at a specific stage of society – a striking exemplum of savage cultural production, bristling with martial and stoic and awful virtue, as opposed to the more softened and regulated songs of pastoral and the elaborations of the songs of civil society. In 1783, then, Ritson publishes the Death Song as one kind of primitive cultural specimen for Europeans to ponder; yet he brilliantly suspends the question of its authenticity and authorship (cf. "whatever becomes of the authenticity of the composition"). We observe as well in this note the competitive, careful differentiation so typical of antiquarian protocols, Ritson announcing the song as having "not, it is believed, already appeared in print." Again, the routes of mediation become the explicit content and subject of reflection, even within this minor note: the piece's manuscript circulation is noted, its status as translation nodded to.

By 1794, however, Ritson framed the song as a case of *Scottish* song, as a production of one of the more famous literary ladies who owed a debt to the north country: not the song but the composer became the focus, the song now an example of another kind of semi-residual cultural production – in this case Scottish, not Native American. In this later antiquarian collection, *Scotish Songs*, Ritson significantly publishes the text *with music*: the cultural theory being elaborated here is, as we have seen before, the special inseparability of Scottish words and melody. (For Ritson's version of the song in *Scotish Songs*, see Fig. 10).

When Hunter came herself to publish this poem under her own name – its words, sans music – in her *Poems* of 1802, she included the following note:

The idea of this ballad was suggested several years ago by hearing a gentleman, who had resided several years in America amongst the tribe or nation called the Cherokees, sing a wild air, which he assured me it was customary for those people to chaunt with a barbarous jargon, implying contempt for their enemies in the moments of torture or death. I have endeavored to give something of the characteristic spirit and sentiment of those brave savages. We look upon the fierce and stubborn courage of the dying indian [sic] with a mixture of respect, pity, and

---

[36] Joseph Ritson, "A Historical Essay on the Origin and Progress of National Song," 1783, in *A Select Collection of English Songs*, Vol. I of III, ii.

SONG XI.

THE DEATH SONG OF THE CHEROKEE INDIANS.*

BY MRS HUNTER.

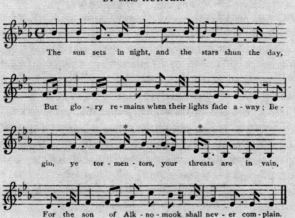

The sun sets in night, and the stars shun the day,

But glo - ry re - mains when their lights fade a - way ; Be -

gin, ye tor - men - tors, your threats are in vain,

For the son of Alk - no - mook shall nev - er com - plain.

Remember the arrows he shot from his bow,
Remember your chiefs by his hatchet laid low :
Why so slow ? Do you wait till I shrink from the pain ?
No, the son of Alknomook will never complain.

Remember the wood where in ambush we lay,
And the scalps which we bore from your nation away ;
Now the flame rises fast, you exult in my pain,
But the son of Alknomook can never complain.

I go to the land where my father is gone,
His ghost shall rejoice in the fame of his son :
Death comes like a friend, he relieves me from pain ;
And thy son, O Alknomook, has scorn'd to complain.

10 "The Death Song of the Cherokee Indians," from Joseph Ritson's *Scotish Song in Two Volumes*

horror; and it is to those sensations excited in the mind of the reader, that the Death Song must owe its effect.

It has already been published with the notes to which it was adapted.[37]

Hunter's compositional anecdote – her note about notes – locates the Death Song in a long tradition of Scottish remediation: old airs finding new words, most famously in the case of Burns' – "My Luv is Like a Red Red Rose"; "Comin Thro' the Rye"; etc. Hunter's reference to "the notes to which it was adapted" points to an interesting ambiguity: the Death Song was adapted as it were to the protocols of antiquarian cultural notes, ethnographic labnotes; it was also notionally adapted to the "notes" of a migratory air. This note shares the ethnographic protocols of English and particularly Scottish ballad-collecting in the period, especially in those collections concerned to claim authority by tracing routes of transmission and remediation. In Hunter's account, the Death Song is an air looking for words; it has crossed the Atlantic to find its lyrist.

Such a specimen as the Cherokee Death Song could move among very different cultural frames over several decades, serving as evidence for several, disparate kinds of cultural argument – all grounded, however, in the conjectural history and stadial models of the Scottish sociological school of history. Such mobility (as well as a peculiar tenacity) suggests how Scottish song distresses any stable concept of cultural or national authenticity and distresses as well the category of literature itself. For in Ritson's 1794 collection the song appears *as song*, musically notated: and here we see how the Indian Death Song might keep company with Burns' sett of "Comin' Thro' the Rye." For Hunter's Indian sings his death song in a rhythm much more associated with Scottish than Cherokee airs: the air turns out to share with Burns' the characteristic rhythmic figure we have already seen, that dotted rhythm typically nationalized in the period as "the Scottish snap" – as we can see and hear when comparing the asterisked measures in Ritson's sett of the song with the opening snap of Burns' "Comin' Thro' the Rye" (Compare Ritson, Fig. 10, with Burns, Fig. 5). It is notable that only when one plays or sings this song (even in one's mind) does its "Scottish" rhythmic aspect appear; here music offers another cultural channel for an audience to tune into. Those attuned to Scottish music, or to the nationalization of rhythms, will get something other than, and additional to, those ignorant of such rhythms, or those who only read the text.

---

[37] Anne Home Hunter, "The Death Song, written for, and adapted to, an original Indian air," *Poems* (London: T. Payne for T. Bensley, 1802), 80.

64

The Flowers of the Foreſt.

63

Adieu, ye Streams that ſmoothly glide, through mazy windings o'er the

Slow

plain! I'll in ſome lonely cave reſide, and ever mourn my faithful ſwain.

Flower of the foreſt was my Love, Soft as the ſighing Summer's gale,

Gentle and conſtant as the dove, Blooming as roſes in the vale.

Alas! by Tweed my Love did ſtray, for me he ſearch'd the banks around, but,

ah! the ſad and fatal day, my Love the pride of ſwains was drown'd.

How droops the willow o'er the ſtream, pale ſtalks his Ghoſt in yonder grove,

dire Fancy paints him in my dream, Awake I mourn my hopeleſs Love.

11 Anne Home Hunter, "The Flowers of the Forest" ("Adieu ye streams"), No. 63,
James Johnson, *The Scots Musical Museum*

Long before the Indian air made its transatlantic crossing, Hunter had undertaken another kind of song remediation so successful that the song passed into oral tradition, as if unauthored: viz. her verbal sett of "Flowers of the Forest," an old air to which Hunter in 1765 provided extremely popular words, such that her version became a Scottish national song, sometimes known by its first phrase, "Adieu ye Streams that Swiftly Glide." It is worth thinking, then, about verbal settings as much as musical settings, and the complex interplay between them. Not words for music perhaps, à la Yeats, but music for words, perhaps – a far older and richer tradition of *poiesis*: a making across media characteristic of balladeering.[38] It is worth contemplating as well the several print genres that could transmit or realize such messages as Hunter's Cherokee Death Song and her "Flowers of the Forest," as well as Burns' songs: for both "Flowers of the Forest" and "Comin' Thro' the Rye" appeared in James Johnson's *Scots Musical Museum* – Hunter's song in the first volume (1787) (see Fig. 11), Burns' in the fourth. And we should recall that, for all their supposed exoticism and ethnographic *frisson*, these songs (like the Duchess of Devonshire's "Negro Song") were circulating or aiming to circulate in this period as parlor songs, with standard genteel accompaniment for piano.

In her "Flowers of the Forest," Anne Home Hunter bids adieu to streams that smoothly glide through mazy windings – and perhaps we should bid adieu to a reification of our literary-theoretical streams. Tunes and texts travel semi-independently, converging and diverging: the air known as "Flowers of the Forest" (also known as "Flodden Field") long preceded Anne Home Hunter and even within her life received several other setts, including two featured in Scott's *Minstrelsy of the Scottish Border* (see Fig. 12 for one sett: note that both were composed by genteel "ladies"). Yet the most successful verbal setts to old airs could enter a feedback loop into oral tradition, their author, even if once known, soon forgotten: many of Burns' songs – both "original" and those set to old airs – circulate even

---

[38] Broadside ballads, for example, were typically printed with the ballad title and a subtitle specifying the carrying tune by name: "to the tune of Rogero," "to the tune of Flying Fame." Tunes thus carried many a different text, and words could sometimes go "with" different tunes. Note that on broadsides musical notation rarely appeared, whereas woodcut illustrations were de rigueur for the broadside, a popular form requiring only one literate reader to broadcast it to a crowd. Tunes were popularly known independent of transcription. Once again we recall that competence in reading or writing musical notation does not coincide with alphabetic literacy, the latter generalized if not universal by 1800, the former still as now a restricted achievement. In the printed, polite books I have mainly focused on here, the interplay between presumed competencies in musical and alphabetic literacy point to the genteel distinction of the work (e.g. Scott's, Johnson's, Mungo Park's).

THE FLOWERS OF THE FOREST 405

IV

At e'en, in the gloaming, nae younkers are
    roaming
'Bout stacks, with the lasses at bogle to play;
But ilk maid sits dreary, lamenting her deary—
    The flowers of the forest are weded awae.

V

Dool and wae for the order, sent our lads to the
    Border!
The English, for ance, by guile wan the day;
The flowers of the forest, that fought aye the
    foremost,
The prime of our land, are cauld in the clay.

VI

We'll hear nae mair lilting, at the ewe milking;
Women and bairns are heartless and wae:
Sighing and moaning, on ilka green loaning—
    The flowers of the forest are a' wede awae.

THE FLOWERS OF THE FOREST

PART FIRST

I

I've heard them lilting, at the ewe milking,
Lasses a' lilting, before dawn of day;
But now they are moaning, on ilka green
    loaning;
The flowers of the forest are a' wede awae.

II

At bughts, in the morning, nae blithe lads are
    scorning;
Lasses are lonely, and dowie, and wae;
Nae daffing, nae gabbing, but sighing and
    sabbing;
Ilk ane lifts her leglin, and hies her awae.

III

In har'st, at the shearing, nae youths now are
    jeering;
Bandsters are runkled, and lyart or gray;
At fair, or at preaching, nae wooing, nae
    fleeching;
The flowers of the forest are a' wede awae.

The following explanation of provincial terms may be found useful:—

Lilting, singing cheerfully. *Loaning*, a broad lane. *Wede awae*, weeded out. *Scorning*, rallying. *Dowie*, dreary. *Daffing and gabbing*, joking and chatting. *Leglin*, milk-pail. *Har'st*, harvest. *Shearing*, reaping. *Bandsters*, sheaf-binders. *Runkled*, wrinkled. *Lyart*, inclining to grey. *Fleeching*, coaxing. *Gloaming*, twilight.

12 Jane Elliott's verbal sett of "Flowers of the Forest," in Walter Scott, *Minstrelsy of the Scottish Border*

now in oral tradition[39]; and Hunter had so far relinquished her authorial property in "Adieu Ye Streams" that she didn't include it in her *Poems* (1802) – though, strikingly, she did include the Cherokee Death Song.

The itinerary of the Cherokee Death Song, moreover, invites us to revisit once again the status of the "invention of tradition." As argued in the last chapter, what we find in such instances as this song is not so much the "invention of tradition" (Cherokee or Scottish or otherwise) as the invention of the concept of traditional mediation – Ritson's mysterious "gentleman

---

[39] On Burns' re-entry into oral tradition, see Mary Ellen Brown, *Burns and Tradition* (London: Macmillan, 1984), in particular Ch. 4, "Tradition's Use of Burns": "Lines, phrases, songs, and poems by Burns have achieved oral currency; nearly anonymous, agreeable to change, these tangible memories of his creativity underline Burns's ability to speak for and to his fellow Scots" (71); on the dangers of prematurely splitting "oral" from "literary" (or popular from elite) streams of balladry and song, see Dianne Dugaw's essay, "The Popular Marketing of 'Old Ballads,'" *Eighteenth-Century Studies* 21 (1987): 71–90.

named Turner" supposedly bringing over an air traditionally (that is, orally) transmitted by Native American informants. We could say too that the invention of tradition emerges precisely as an anthropological, comparative discourse: not only Native Americans, but Scots border-raiders, Morayshire dairy-maids, Highlanders, and African "Negroes" all appear by 1800 as objects of an elaborate English and Scottish discourse on tradition and mediation – a transnational vernacular cultural imaginary.

SONG MEDIATIONS AND METHODOLOGICAL IMPLICATIONS

This rapid run through several song mediations circa 1800 is meant to open further channels for scholars and poets ranging across literary, oral-traditional, musical, and historiographic domains. To move from antiquarians like Ritson and Pinkerton to romantic collector-poets like Scott is to see once again how indebted romantic balladry and indeed romantic historiography was to its antiquarian antecedents; to pivot from Scott to Park is to see how romantic ethnography surfaced in highly disparate texts; to track the Death Song is to see the complex interplay of antiquarian mediation, parlor-song fashions, and transcultural fantasy. If song and the notion of song provided many poets with occasions for reverie – e.g. in Wordsworth's "Solitary Reaper" – song also provided late-eighteenth- and early-nineteenth-century collectors and editors the opportunity for increasingly subtle, complex thinking about history, transmission, national pasts, and national futures. Balladeering thus offers numerous cases for both cross-cultural and trans-medial investigation, and an invitation for further critical and creative work, *poiesis* in its broadest sense: *making*.

Other strains of ballad inquiry point toward such developments as the late-nineteenth-century canonization of the Child ballads and their reverse migration back to Britain (to Scottish and English singers) in the mid-twentieth-century folk revival. One might wish further to explore (as ethno-musicologists certainly have) the recent funneling of "folk" musics (Anglo-Scottish, Appalachian, Cajun, North-Eastern Brazilian, Papua New Guinean, and so on) into the recent media category and commodity-form, "world music."[40] An analysis of "world music" might be usefully informed by Marx and Engels' striking remarks in *The Communist*

---

[40] For an incisive survey of the problematics of "world music," its ongoing dependence on and solicitation of tradition as well as "the nation," see Philip V. Bohlman, *World Music: A Very Short Introduction* (Oxford University Press, 2002), esp. Ch. 4, "Music of the Folk," 64–87, and Ch. 5, "Music of the Nations," 88–110.

Manifesto on the nineteenth-century production of "world literature": "As in material, so in intellectual production. The intellectual creations of individual nations become common property. National one-sidedness and narrow-mindedness become more impossible, and from the numerous national and local literatures [musics] there arises a world literature [music]" (additions/alternatives mine).[41] At this point we can see that a generalized critical history could trace and critique the expropriation, differentiation, proliferation, and imminent integration of these ballad phenomena (no longer partitioned into "literature" and "music") under the rubric, "world media."

Conceived as a historically situated, multi-media project, balladeering asks us – as it asked the balladeers, in slightly different terms – to reconcile discourse analysis with media analysis and communications theory. This chapter has hoped to make a preliminary move in that direction. Friedrich Kittler has remarked on the limits of Foucauldian discourse analysis, which reaches its limit when other media "penetrate the library," when the monopoly of writing ends: "discourse analysis cannot handle film rolls and records."[42] Challenging historians to explore the media (and not simply the artifacts) through which peoples store, record, and process time as well as information, Kittler would have us all become historicizing media analysts as well as media analysts of historical discourse. Invoking Walter Ong's and Milman Parry's work, Kittler notes that oral poetry, oral history, and oral mnemotechnics became areas of investigation only at the time of, and precisely because of, the twentieth-century dissolution of the storage monopoly of writing as a universal medium. Only when one media epoch ends can critics and historians begin to perceive its structuring effects: the dependence, for example, of hermeneutics on a regime of writing as the storage of "spirit" or "soul." Or, to keep to our balladeering zone, the dependence of ballad collections on the medium of the printed book.

Kittler advises us to consider poetic *materia* and mediations not through such concepts as "primary" or "secondary orality" (themselves effects of the historical break they assume) but rather through the category of "media acoustics."[43] Further study of eighteenth-century balladeering is particularly positioned to take up Kittler's challenge, for alongside ballad texts and the many dissertations on ancient minstrels and oral poetry in ballad collections

---

[41] Karl Marx and Friedrich Engels, *Manifesto of the Communist Party*, in *Economic and Philosophic Manuscripts of 1844 and the Communist Manifesto*, trans. Martin Milligan (New York: Prometheus, 1988), 213.
[42] Kittler, *Gramophone, Film, Typewriter*, 37.   [43] In ibid., 37.

were many varieties and formats of printed musics, vocal and instrumental, some of which were meant to be played back, on actual instruments or hallucinatorily in the mind, others of which seemed designed for curatorial display. As I've hoped to suggest, the representation and circulation of ballad musics has its own history which runs alongside but does not wholly coincide with the histories of ballad texts. Joseph Ritson's exasperated comments about the constraints of English typography – echoed by his annotator and editor some thirty years later[44]– only begin to mark out how richly differentiated were the mediations required to get ballad tunes as well as words into books. That a print genre, the ballad collection, found itself complexly coordinating engraving, type, not to mention woodcuts suggests that we need a flexible, subtle way to think of ballad collections as processing, differentially, multiply mediated source data into print, the storage of which might be released in various ways: reading silently or aloud, singing, and/or playing the fiddle or piano. The development of the ballad collection suggests that Romanticism was not only a technology of the letter[45]: it was also – in aspiration if not always in achievement – a technology of the note.

McLuhan's law, that one medium becomes the content of another medium, is perhaps too unidirectional an axiom. We have seen that ballad collections were processing several media contents simultaneously, if not with equal success. We began by considering the ballad collection as an emergent print genre; if we consider poetry, prose, and musical notation to be separate media, we see that the ballad collection strives to subsume them under the supermedia category of the printed book. Some theorists have assumed that print was a more or less silent medium in 1800, that it offered to its alphabetized, literate consumers a transparent vehicle for serving up sensuous inner experience (viz. German Romantic poetry according to Friedrich Kittler) or communal public affiliation (viz. the newspaper according to Benedict Anderson).[46] Ballad collections put pressure on this assumption. We know from Freud's analyses of neurotic fixation as well from radio static, TV fuzz and frozen computer screens that it is precisely when a medium is interrupted that we become aware of it as a medium (whether that medium be the psyche or airwaves or more palpable machinery or this sentence).

---

[44] cf. n. 20.

[45] Viz. David Wellbery, Foreword to Kittler, *Discourse Networks*: "Romanticism, then, is a certain technology of the letter" (xviii); on the "technology of the letter" linking literacy, literature, and epistolary form, e.g. in *Frankenstein*, see McLane, *Romanticism and the Human Sciences*, 15–16.

[46] I here invoke Anderson's influential *Imagined Communities: Reflections on the Origin and Spread of Nationalism*, rev. edn. (London and New York: Verso, 1991) – a book that even when disputed lies behind much of the revitalized scholarship on nationalism since the 1980s.

Breakdowns reveal the hitherto invisible structure of mediation: this premise informs the acerbic brilliance of Kittler's oeuvre as well as many a probing memoir (e.g. Susannah Kaysen's *Girl, Interrupted*), not to mention Deleuze and Guattari's schizanalysis. Balladeering confronted breakdowns and impasses along several media axes: in lapses of informants' memories, missing manuscript pieces, imperfect musical notation, impediments to printing musics. Perhaps even more important than their reckoning with media impasse was the balladeers' *representation* of their reckoning (in prefaces, notes, dissertations): with this, they became media theorists.

The imperfect ligatures of typeset music; the brackets used to mark the place where an informant's memory blanked; the brackets used to enclose the words the balladeer "supplyed"; the asterisks which alerted the reader to speculative emendations: all these marks registered, even as they attempted to remedy in print, a breakdown in those mediations constitutive of the ballad collection. It is striking that these marks are meant not to be pronounced but rather to be seen and processed: they appeal to the intellectual and not to the sensual ear. It was precisely in those marks which would be seen but not heard that print made itself strongly felt both as a medium and as the determinative medium processing all other mediations. In these typographic notations the balladeers made print speak *as print*.

Balladeering thus opens up the space for numerous historical and theoretical questions, among them: was writing indeed the universal medium in 1800, as Friedrich Kittler argues? Was it even possible to have a concept of medium in 1800? The differential processing of words and also sounds, texts and musics, into ballad collections suggests that print is the best choice if we're looking for a "universal medium" circa 1800. And as Celeste Langan has brilliantly argued and as Ritson's complaint about typesetting confirms, print reveals itself by 1800 to be quite "recognizable *as* a medium."[47]

And finally, in terms of balladeering as a particular, historical and historicizing traffic in poetry-as-media: Tom Cheesman and Sigrid Rieuwerts recently observed that "The ballad has always been in and out of whatever media are in existence."[48] True: but it is not the case that ballads

---

[47] See Langan's astonishing essay, "Understanding Media in 1805: Audiovisual Hallucination in *The Lay of the Last Minstrel*," *Studies in Romanticism* 40:1 (Spring 2001): 49–70. Ranging from Scott's *Lay* through prosody-as-medium to reflections on the historicity of the mediated sensorium, this essay has enormous implications beyond its immediate occasion in Scott. Langan observes that "once literacy has become *general* . . . the storage system of 'oral literature' would seem to be obsolete. But precisely for that reason, it becomes available as the ostensible content of the broadcast medium of print." In the *Lay*, she concludes, "the medium of print becomes recognizable *as* a medium (contra Kittler) by its attempt to 'deliver' audiovisual information" (70).

[48] Cheesman and Rieuwerts, *Ballads into Books*, 16, n. 5.

simply fall into whatever media are at hand. Their simultaneous and much-discussed existence in the eighteenth century as oral tradition and printed book, as sung song, antiquarian document, broadside, lyrical ballad, and romantic fragment suggests that we need to consider how media *represent* as well as *present*, how media constitute – as well as impede and conduct – the flow of cultural contents. If the medium is arguably the message, the printed ballad collection sent many messages – about cultural nationalism, of course, but also a message about the historical situation of media.

CHAPTER 4

How to do things with minstrels: Poetry and historicity

"What are the true objects of history?"
"Popular Superstitions and Ballad Literature of England in the Middle Ages,"
– *Putnam's Monthly Magazine*, October 1854

THE CONTENT OF HISTORY WILL BE POETRY.
– Ed Sanders, "Investigative Poetry," 1975

In January 1855, one J. J. Trux contributed an anonymous essay to *Putnam's Monthly Magazine*: "Negro Minstrelsy – Ancient and Modern." Discussing the craze for the song "Jim Crow" and other "negro melodies" like "Zip Coon" and "Long-tailed Blue," the author saluted these compositions as the "golden age of negro literature" – an age forever passed. Now, Trux lamented, "Poetasters who never saw an alligator, or smelt the magnolia blossom in their lives, sit coolly down to write an African ditty, as a pleasant after-dinner pastime, or a daily task."[1]

"Negro Minstrelsy" referred, of course, to the complex phenomenon of "plantation song" and its development into blackface entertainment in the US and abroad.[2] But whence "Ancient and Modern"? This second component of

---

[1] J. J. Trux, "Negro Minstrelsy – Ancient and Modern," *Putnam's Monthly* (January 1855), 72, 75. Internal evidence suggests that Trux had traveled in the south, collected songs in Georgia, fancied himself learned in "negro dialect," and that he was perhaps himself a southern slaveowner; but it may be that he was a Northern aficionado of "negro minstrelsy," his disdain for "northern self-styled minstrels" a jab at fellow would-be connoisseurs as well as imposters. Further references to this article will be cited by page in the text.

[2] It was exactly this popular "modern" efflorescence of blackface entertainment, and the proliferation of neo-plantation songs, that Trux the elite connoisseur decried. In Trux's account, "negro minstrelsy" in its "ancient" moment is uncontaminated by music hall, urban venues, or whites in blackface – it is, so to speak, the spontaneous overflow of powerful feeling in tuneful black slaves. Recent work in American cultural studies has brilliantly illuminated what Trux partly deplored: US blackface minstrelsy as popular entertainment, its origins, its complexities, and its aftermaths. In his influential *Love and Theft: Blackface Minstrelsy and the American Working Class* (Oxford University Press, 1993), Eric Lott undertakes a complex salvaging of minstrelsy from charges of racist expropriation, preferring to see in blackface minstrelsy an enactment of white longing for and homage to black culture as well as

Trux's title, less self-evident than the first, signals an engagement with another cultural discourse: that of late-eighteenth- and early-nineteenth-century antiquarian balladeering in Britain. Decades before there was "negro minstrelsy, ancient and modern," that is, there was Scottish "minstrelsy, ancient and modern."

Trux's "negro minstrelsy, ancient and modern" was an explicitly antiquarianizing gesture – an attempt to pour the songs of African slaves and their descendants into the literary-historical molds that British antiquarians had made for English, Scottish, Welsh, and less often Irish poets and traditions. In British discourse, "minstrelsy" had long denoted the popular, vernacular poetry of a nation. Trux's several references to English and Scottish ballad collections make plain how steeped he was in the literature and discourse of British balladeering, particularly in its "minstrelling" guises. His title itself alludes specifically to *Minstrelsy: Ancient and Modern* (1827), edited by the Scotsman William Motherwell, and to David Herd's important earlier collection *Ancient and Modern Scottish Songs, Heroic Ballads, etc.* (1776, rev. 1791). Like his antiquarian and romantic predecessors, who developed elaborate procedures of scholarly authentication in the course of the eighteenth-century ballad revival, Trux offers stanzaic "specimens" for critical comparison, proposes typologies for classifying ballads ("Historic Plantation Ballad," "descriptive songs," "comic ballad"), and appeals to those who are, like him, "patient and laborious student[s] of negro minstrelsy" (73). Trux's essay is, among other things, a call to collect the remains of "genuine plantation songs" (79), which comprise, he argues, the true national poetry of America: "It will be a proud day for America when these thirty thousand songs [one from each plantation, by Trux's estimate] are collected into several volumes, handsomely bound in Turkey morocco, and superbly embellished"(79).[3] Such calls for cultural conservation via song collection echo the British antiquarians' similar calls (including Joseph Ritson's and Walter Scott's) and intriguingly anticipate Francis James Child's advertised

---

a more obviously derisive and condescending appropriation. In *Blackface, White Noise: Jewish Immigrants in the Hollywood Melting Pot* (Berkeley: University of California Press, 1996), Michael Rogin explores blackface as a kind of technology for Americanization, the assimilation of ethnics (notably Jewish immigrants) facilitated by their appropriation of blackface for their own whitening ends. Rogin is thus less sanguine than Lott about the multiple meanings and uses of minstrelsy as a model of cross-racial desire: "the color line was permeable in only one direction," he notes (37). In *Raising Cain: Blackface Performance from Jim Crow to Hip Hop* (Cambridge, MA: Harvard University Press, 1998), W. T. Lhamon, Jr. tracks performance genealogies, especially the historically elusive transmission of dance.

[3] That Trux advocated the making of gorgeous books out of the expropriated songs of slaves rather baldly confirms Walter Benjamin's observation that every document of civilization is also simultaneously a document of barbarism. See Benjamin, "Theses on the Philosophy of History," *Illuminations*, trans. Harry Zohn, ed. Hannah Arendt (New York: Schocken Books, 1969), 256.

solicitations for ballads in the second half of the nineteenth century. Notwithstanding his discussion of "melodies" and "ditties," Trux approaches "negro minstrelsy" as a species of "literature" which might be periodized into "ages" golden and otherwise. His critical protocols, taxonomizing impulses, and self-fashioning as a culturally informed song arbiter come straight out of antiquarian and romantic British balladeering discourse, as it was formalized from Percy through Scott and beyond.

My second chapter analyzed this formalization of balladeering discourse; Chapter 3 pursued balladeering representation into its medial as well as cultural complexities. This chapter hopes to illuminate the related history of minstrelling discourse that Mr. Trux was drawing on – one that long preceded but was peculiarly adaptable to, and indeed shaped, Mr. Trux's somewhat different preoccupations. Minstrels and minstrelsy marked, we might say, a historical problem (viz. "ancient and modern") and a national problem before they became so conspicuously a racialized phenomenon.[4] Minstrels marked, moreover, a special problem of and for poetry. Minstrels were literary figures, ghosts re-animated in print, before they were entertaining dancers, singers, and comics. And minstrels were in the first instance – that is, from the moment of their first revival in the eighteenth century – objects of historical discourse: poets to think with. With eighteenth-century Britain in mind, we can see that minstrelsy began – or was revived – as a way of talking about the historical and cultural situations of poetry.

Susan Stewart has reminded us that eighteenth-century Britain witnessed the proliferation of notably "distressed genres" – the epic, proverb, fable, and ballad appearing as literary modes vexed and in some cases created by the emergent problematic of authenticity, originality, and modernity in this era of industrial print capital.[5] The later eighteenth century also witnessed the development and refinement of several modern historical discourses and conceptual schemes. We might designate "minstrelsy" as that space where poetry is distressed and vexed by history. By "history," we might be mindful of historical discourse in its several eighteenth-century varieties – antiquarian empiricism, conjectural–philosophical universal history, political narrative, sentimental

---

[4] And here I approach, from another angle but I believe complementarily, one dimension of Rogin's argument. In what he describes as a kind of strategic defamiliarization, Rogin puts American and Americanizing blackface alongside nineteenth-century European nationalisms (*Blackface, White Noise*, 44). He invokes "one European precedent for ethnic nationalism in the service of a conquering empire, and that exception – Scots nationalism – was the major European source for American national culture in both its frontier and blackface forms" (46).

[5] Susan Stewart, "Notes on Distressed Genres," *Crimes of Writing*, 66–101. I would further argue that such modes were distressed by their historiographic self-consciousness, to which they owed their complex status as "revived."

educations.[6] We might also invoke a formula of Ezra Pound – an unlikely tutelary spirit, perhaps, since he favored troubadours over minstrels and largely ignored the Anglo-Scottish tradition in his own canon-building – but it is useful to recall his definition of epic as "a poem including history."[7] How poems included history, how histories included poetry, and more complexly, how poetry confronted and ultimately performed its own historicity: these are the questions "minstrelsy" allows us to pose, particularly in its British keys.

***

The minstrel emerged in eighteenth-century British discourse as a peculiarly resonant figure. He was first revived by the antiquarians, most notably Thomas Percy and Joseph Ritson, who in conducting their debates over balladry also debated minstrel origins theory: were minstrels professional court poets, dignified inventors of their songs, as Percy argued in his 1765 essay "On the Ancient Minstrels in England," or were minstrels lowly itinerants, retailing others' degraded wares, as Percy's antagonist Ritson rejoined?[8] The eighteenth-century minstrel was thus always already a

---

[6] On the range of historical writing and method in the eighteenth-century, and on the methodological debates between *érudits* and *philosophes* (loosely approximating the split between antiquarians and philosophical historians in Scotland), see A. D. Momigliano, "Ancient History and the Antiquarian," *Studies in Historiography* (London: Weidenfeld and Nicolson 1966), 1–39, in particular the sections titled, "The Controversy of the Seventeenth and Eighteenth Centuries on the Value of Historical Evidence" (10–20), and "The Conflicts between Antiquarians and Historians in the Eighteenth and Nineteenth Centuries" (20–7). As an important re-directing of our understanding of eighteenth-century historiography and its relation to sister prose genres (travel writing, biography, the sentimental novel, and so on), Mark Salber Phillips' recent work is essential. See, for example, his "Reconsiderations on History and Antiquarianism: Arnaldo Momigliano and the Historiography of Eighteenth-Century Britain," *Journal of the History of Ideas* 57.2 (1996): 297–316, and his book, *Society and Sentiment* (Princeton University Press, 2000). Susan Manning is also re-animating the Scottish and broader Enlightenment stakes of antiquarian versus conjectural historical method and narration: for example, in her essay, "Notes from the Margin," in *Scotland and the Borders of Romanticism*, ed. Leith Davis, Ian Duncan, and Janet Sorensen (Cambridge University Press, 2004). For an analysis of conjectural history from the perspective of historical epistemology, see Mary Poovey, "Scottish Conjectural History," in *A History of the Modern Fact*, 214–35.

[7] In, for example, Ezra Pound, "Dateline," *The Literary Essays of Ezra Pound* (New York: New Directions, 1968), 86.

[8] For the primary texts of the "minstrel origins" controversy, see Thomas Percy, "An Essay on the Ancient Minstrels in England" (1765), Appendix 1 in *Reliques of Ancient English Poetry*; Joseph Ritson's critical response in his "Historical Essay on the Origin and Progress of National Song," in his *Select Collection of English Songs*, followed by his "Observations on the Ancient English Minstrels," prefacing *Ancient Songs and Ballads from the Time of King Henry the Third to the Revolution* (London, 1790). In "Scandals of the Ballad" (*Crimes of Writing*, 102–31), Stewart locates these debates within the emerging problematic of authenticity: "The character of the minstrel thus becomes as marvelous and opportune an invention as that of the ballads themselves" (115). Nick Groom addresses minstrel polemics primarily from Percy's side, noting that Percy's minstrel theory usefully generated a "cultural provenance" for his *Reliques*, over and against Macpherson's/Ossian's earlier, and influential, Highland provenance. See Groom, *Percy's "Reliques,"* 97.

polemical, debatable, historical figure, and he spawned many a historical dissertation as well as numerous poetic inventions. Considered as a discursive movement, eighteenth-century minstrelsy traverses several discourses and genres: antiquarian polemic, conjectural historical rumination, literary-historical essay on metrical romance, visual art and iconography, and of course poetry and poetics. Revived minstrels appeared in many national and regional domains: and thus we find English minstrels in Percy, French minstrels in Ritson's critique of Percy, Scotticized minstrels in James Beattie's Albion, Scottish border minstrels in Walter Scott's corpus, Irish minstrel boys courtesy of Thomas Moore, and a notably idiot English minstrel in Wordsworth's 1807 poem, "Song at the Feast of Brougham Castle." We also find, by 1860, a conception of British minstrelsy capacious enough to include "negro melodies" under the rubric, *The Minstrelsy of Britain*[9]: evidence that "negro minstrelsy" (*pace* Trux) had its British as well as its American moment.

It is telling, in this regard, that Katie Trumpener called her 1997 book *Bardic*, and not *Minstrel, Nationalism*: for the cultural nationalism she tracks is one of heroic resistance from the periphery, its bardic mouthpieces prophetic, albeit doomed, protestors of the seemingly inevitable march of progress.[10] Compared to bards, minstrels were less obviously heroic or tragic; they lacked the grandeur of Macpherson's Ossian, Gray's Welsh Suicide, or Blake's Ancient Bard.[11] From Percy onward, minstrels are by definition ambiguous figures, caught between their noble predecessors the bards and their entrepreneurial successors in print culture, Elizabethan ballad-mongers and ultimately modern poets. In eighteenth-century representations of minstrels, we might say that bards tended to be prehistoric, minstrels liminal, and ballad-mongers thoroughly and identifiably modern historical phenomena. The project of nationalizing minstrels (viz. Percy's English, Scott's Scottish minstrels) went hand-in-ambiguous-hand with the project of periodizing them, and a survey of minstrel discourse reveals that

---

[9] *The Minstrelsy of Britain: or a Glance at our Lyrical Poetry and Poets from the Reign of Queen Elizabeth to the Present Time, Including a Dissertation on the Genius and Lyrics of Burns*, by Henry Heavisides (Stockton, 1860). Chapter 6 features a discussion of "the negro melodies" alongside "Cockney songs."

[10] I am referring to Trumpener's *Bardic Nationalism*, which, among its many contributions, has opened up numerous archives for scholars of the period and has greatly sharpened critical discussions of genre, historicity, nation, and empire.

[11] Gray's "The Bard" features a Welsh Bard who, rather than submit to Edward I's decree that all Welsh bards be hanged, commits suicide – after delivering himself of a ringing curse on Edward and his line as well as a prophecy hailing the triumph of freedom, poetry, and "Britannia": "with joy I see/The different doom our fates assign./Be thine despair and sceptered care;/To triumph, and to die, are mine." See "The Bard, A Pindaric Ode," in *The Complete English Poems of Thomas Gray*, ed. James Reeves (London: Heinemann, 1973), ll. 139–42, 82.

both projects yielded highly arguable results.[12] Minstrels could be ancient, medieval or modern, depending on the writer and his commitments. The minstrel-figure thus helps us to diagnose an emergent problematic of periodization: Percy and Ritson's minstrels were counters in "competing medievalisms" (in Marilyn Butler's phrase)[13]; Beattie's minstrel witnesses the unfurling of the whole history of man; Scott's minstrels were at various points "ancient oral poets," seventeenth-century professionals, and still-living relics; while Wordsworth tactically represented his hapless minstrel as singing at the end of the Wars of the Roses, rendered implicitly obsolete by the modern poet of humanization, a man speaking to men.

   Yet however he was placed, in whatever ways he was dated, the minstrel raised methodological problems of dating and placing; and dating and placing are those operations crucial to the Scottish Enlightenment formation of the very concept of "the historical situation," as James Chandler has argued in *England in 1819*.[14] So how do we get from the minstrel, a historical figure, to the minstrel as an allegory of the historical situation? To begin to answer this, let us turn to crucial passages in three minstrelling works: James Beattie's poem *The Minstrel* (1771, 1774), Walter Scott's *Minstrelsy of the Scottish Border* (1802–3), and his *Lay of the Last Minstrel* (1805).

"BORN IN A RUDE AGE": HISTORY, TRADITION, AND THE MINSTREL TALENT

Although first revived by English antiquarians, the minstrel was easily adaptable to a Scottish philosophical–historical framework. Beattie's *Minstrel* was inspired, he said, by Percy's 1765 "Essay on the Ancient Order of English Minstrels." Subtitled "The Progress of Genius," the poem loudly professed its allegiance to the progressive conventions of universal history. As Beattie wrote, "The design was, to trace the progress of a Poetical Genius, *born in a rude age*, from the first dawning of fancy and reason, till that period at which he may be supposed capable of appearing in the world as a *MINSTREL, that is, as an itinerant poet and musician*; – a character which, according to the notions of *our forefathers*, was not only respectable,

---

[12] On the polemics of representing "ancient" and "popular" ballads, polemics largely conducted via ostensibly neutral historical narratives, see Paula McDowell, "The Manufacture," *ECTI*, 47:2/3 (Summer 2006). McDowell's analysis reminds us that such periodizing ventures had strong class valences as well as historiographic commitments.

[13] See Marilyn Butler, "Antiquarianism (Popular)," Essay 35, 333.

[14] On the Scottish formulation of the idea of "the historical situation," see James Chandler, *England in 1819*, 203–64.

but sacred."[15] If Percy sang the praises of medieval English minstrels, Beattie gives us (as noted in Chapter 1) a Scottish minstrel "born in a rude age": the "rude age" signifying not a recognizable, date-able historical period – say, the twelfth-through-fourteenth centuries – but rather the first primitive stage of conjectural history. Beattie's introductory remark about "our fore-fathers" reminds us, moreover, that one implied audience here was self-consciously Scottish: minstrelsy here is a call for an explicitly genealogical remembrance, a history of Scotticized Britons modeled as kin – and in this he both Scottishizes minstrelsy and anticipates Scott.

Beattie's historical model is an awkward hybrid of the classical four-ages typology and eighteenth-century stadial progression, the latter model sum-marized by Adam Smith thus: "The four stages of society are hunting, pasturage, farming, and commerce."[16] Beattie puts the conventions of the Progress Poem (e.g. the birth and then flight of the arts and sciences from Greece to Rome to Albion), through some new-modeled conjectural paces. His Minstrel, named Edwin, progresses in fine stadial fashion from the "rude age" (domain of the Beldame, as we have noted) to the threshold of Enlightenment, announced by a severe hermit who salutes the "historic muse."

In these tellingly gendered transactions, the poem both presumes and enacts the internalization of universal history. History appears here, through the hermit's lessons, as the discourse of difficult but necessary enlightenment. To submit to the muse of history is to enter maturity. Thus Beattie coordinates psychological and cultural "progress." Beyond this shift in the gender of authority (from beldame to hermit), indeed determining this shift, is a medial transformation: historical discourse is textualizable, according to poem's metaphorics, whereas "tradition" is oral, transmitted moreover specifically via ballad and "heroic ditty."[17] Despite the hermit–historian's appearance in a rude age, then, the historic muse has, it would seem, learned to write.

[15] James Beattie, "Preface to The Minstrel, or, The Progress of Genius," in *The Minstrel*, 25. Further quotations from the poem will be cited in text by book and stanza. When he first published Book I in 1771, Beattie located his minstrel "in a rude *and illiterate* age" – a phrase which reminds us of the conjunction of primitivity and orality so characteristic of Enlightenment anthropology and historiography.

[16] Quoted in Andrew Skinner, introduction to Adam Smith, *The Wealth of Nations*, 2 vols. (Harmondsworth, 1997), Vol. I, 31. Skinner notes that "it was argued not only that such stages exist and had existed, but also that each society would tend to pass through them in *sequence*" (Vol. I, 31).

[17] On historical discourse as textualized, in figuration if not in the hermit's mediation of it, note the historic muse's "page" (33) and "her transcripts" (35 or 34). For the transmission of oral "tradition hoar," see the previous discussion of the remarkable passage (Bk I, st. 45–7) in which the Beldame educates the minstrel's heart by relating several ballads.

Strikingly, the poem shows our minstrel to be resistant to the lessons of "the Muse of history" as she "unrolls her page" before him (st. 33): Edwin protests the hermit's account of war, destruction, mayhem – the public events, the official contents, of history proper.

> "Ah! what avails," he said, "to trace the springs,
> That whirl of empire the stupendous wheel!
> Ah! What have I to do with conquering kings,
> Hands drenched in blood, and breasts begirt with steel!" (II. st. 34)

Instead of "empire" and conquest – the apparently obvious material of history – Edwin puts forward the claims of poetry and fancy, exalting Nature's lessons over History's:

> To those whom Nature taught to think and feel,
> Heroes, alas! are things of small concern.
> Could History man's secret heart reveal,
> And what imports a heaven-born mind to learn,
> Her transcripts to explore what bosom would not yearn! (II. st 34)

History is ill-equipped to "reveal" "man's secret heart." History fails where interiority and feeling begin: or so it first seems.

If it is somewhat predictable that the sensitive hero resists the martial orientation of the hermit–historian, it is more striking that the young minstrel also critiques history as a hegemonic discourse of the past whose reach exceeds its grasp. Large zones of what Shelley later called "the history of our species"[18] are inaccessible to the historian, the minstrel protests, and here the imagination, or rather the fancy, must do its work:

> O who of man the story will unfold,
> Ere victory and empire wrought annoy,
> In that Elysian age (misnamed of gold)
> The age of love, and innocence, and joy, – (II. st. 36)
>
>   [...]
> But, ah! The historic Muse has never dared
> To pierce those hallowed bowers – 'tis Fancy's beam
> Poured on the vision of the enraptured bard,
> That paints the charms of that delicious theme.
> Then hail, sweet Fancy's ray! ... (II. st. 38)

The minstrel has introduced the question of the "story of Man": the "historic Muse" cannot tell this whole story. Fancy offers us a past inaccessible to history; therein lies its claim, and therein lies poetry's claim on history.

---

[18] The phrase appears in Shelley, "A Defence of Poetry," *Shelley's Poetry and Prose*, 488.

Beattie's minstrel articulates the crucial, diagnostic eighteenth-century predicament of moral philosophical discourse, of the great Enlightenment project Hume called "the science of Man": the story of man, broadly understood, outstrips history proper, understood as the unilinear narration of public events. In this way the minstrel allies himself with conjectural historians; the poem has internalized the broader eighteenth-century critique of the limits of history as a discourse of public events experienced by public men.

Our hermit–historian is ready with his replies, however, and he insists that "the historic Muse" presides over all advances in human development – in politics, law, industry, the arts, and sciences:

> Hail, sacred Polity, by Freedom reared!
> Hail, sacred Freedom, when by law restrained!
> Without you what were man? (II. st. 43)

The hermit decisively harnesses history – the history of man – to what Beattie glosses in a note as "the philosophic spirit" (63). The hermit's account of man's glorious development is so persuasive that –

> Enraptured by the hermit's strain, the youth
> Proceeds the path of science to explore.
> And now, expanding to the beams of truth,
> New energies, and charms unknown before,
> His mind discloses; fancy now no more
> Wantons on fickle pinion through the skies;
> But, fixed in aim, and conscious of her power,
> Aloft from cause to cause exults to rise,
> Creation's blended stores arranging as she flies. (II. st. 55)

A fine conversion to Enlightenment this, with its dialectical residue: the minstrel still cherishes the beldame "who set on fire his infant heart" (II. st. 57 l.1).

That our hero Edwin is a poet-in-training, an emergent minstrel, suggests that the historic muse should teach him lessons applicable to poetry, and Beattie obliges:

> Simplicity apace
> Tempers his rage: he owns her charm divine,
> And clears the ambiguous phrase, and lops the unwieldy line. (II. st. 58)

The end of the historic muse's lesson, we now see, is severer taste and better editing. Enlightenment requires the poet to rid his verse of ornament and ambiguity. When wondering what poetry has to do with history, this poem answers: history chastens poetry, masculinizes the poet, and disciplines his style.

Yet poetry in its turn complicates any straightforward account or theorization of the historical. Beattie's poem raises the problem of a conjectural past, the past before polity: how to access this past? The poem never fully absorbs this aspect of Edwin's resistance and critique. This resistance is as striking as the poem's internalization of universal history. That the historic muse might need the collaboration of fancy, that enlightenment might require first the education of the heart: these are some of the implicit lessons of Beattie's minstrel and of the poem, *The Minstrel.*

It is important to note, however, that Beattie's historic muse is not that historical: it presides over transitions and developments which proceed as if inevitably, according to philosophic plan, in unilinear fashion. Although the minstrel first resists the historic muse, he never disputes the hermit's implicit definition of history and the historical, which is restricted to the progress of official knowledges and arts, transhistorically trackable. What this historic muse lacks, we might say, is a sense of historicity.

FROM "THE HISTORIC MUSE" TO THE HISTORICAL SITUATION: "THEIR DATE WAS FLED"

For a minstrelsy fully alive to historicity, we must consult Walter Scott. Like Beattie, Scott took "the muse of history" as his poetic muse, yet what constituted "the historical" was precisely the recurring question in his work. So how was Scott historical before historical novels? If we accept, provisionally, Arnaldo Momigliano's influential conceptual distinction between historians and antiquarians in the eighteenth century, Scott would seem clearly to fall into the antiquarian camp: and Stuart Piggott has further classified Scott as a romantic, as opposed to an empirically oriented, antiquarian.[19] John Sutherland reminds us that Scott loved what he called "'technical history,' objects that one could handle and which conjured up the past through the fingers that held them," and his Abbotsford estate became the retro-neo mausoleum of Scott's antiquarian fantasia.[20] Yet for all his antiquarian enthusiasms, Scott was also well-versed in the Scottish philosophical school of history, as his biographers attest and

[19] See Momigliano, "Ancient History and the Antiquarian," who for the sake of argument puts forward distinctions he will then refine and complicate – but nevertheless keep – in the course of his essay: "1. Historians write in a chronological order; antiquarians write in a systematic order; 2. Historians produce those facts which serve to illustrate or explain a certain situation; antiquarians collect all the items that are connected with a certain subject, whether they help to solve a problem or not" (3). For Piggott's distinction, *Ruins in a Landscape*: "Scott had chosen between the two streams of antiquarianism and naturally opted for the romantic [over the revived empiric stream]" (128).

[20] Sutherland, *Life of Walter Scott*, 46.

as the prose prefacing the *Minstrelsy* makes clear. What we see in his work is a complicated negotiation of several historical and para-historical discourses, schemes, and methods. And it was "minstrelsy" which offered Scott the space for this negotiation.

The Minstrelsy of the Scottish Border (1802–3) aimed to be the ballad collection to end all eighteenth-century ballad collections. These collections typically took the history of poetry to be co-extensive with the history of "the race" or "the nation": it is less often observed that the cultural nationalism animating ballad collections rested on a prior, if sometimes silent, theorization of the historical.[21] I would further suggest that, through its emphasis on historiographic fluencies, the ballad collection prepares the way for the historical novel (in terms of *materia* but also conceptualization): this is suggested by the allegorically illuminating career of Scott, who moves from collecting and editing ballads to writing poetic romances to authoring his hugely successful and influential historical novels. Scott's first introduction to the *Minstrelsy*, written in 1802 and kept with each successive edition, was, as he pointedly noted decades later, "rather of an historical than a literary nature"[22]: this invocation of the "historical" was intended to legitimize traffic in what critics often regarded as lesser or frivolous materials and genres – ballads and novels.[23] Scott's historical narrative of 1802, a sketch of Scottish border history, was a narrative of hot dates, from Roman times until 1601 – the year of the "Union of the Crowns" in the person known to the Scottish as James VI, to the English as James I. It was this narrative – brief, pointed, fluent, and oriented to public events and public men – that underwrote the display of documents, poems, notes, customary lore, and appendices to follow. In the *Minstrelsy*, then, Scott creates a space for

---

[21] The discussion here might be complemented by Susan Oliver's trenchant reading of Scott's *Minstrelsy* as setting forth an explicitly Unionist political program, over and against the radical republican agitation: see *Scott, Byron, and the Poetics of Cultural Encounter*, particularly Chapter 1, "Collecting Ballads and Resisting Radical Energies: Scott's *Minstrelsy of the Scottish Border*," 19–68. My discussion here emphasizes the historiographic logic of the *Minstrelsy*; Oliver focuses on the politics of cultural encounter carefully framed in the *Minstrelsy*, its representation of "borderlands" artfully designed to culminate in a pacifying British integration.

[22] Scott, "Introductory Remarks on Popular Poetry" (1830), in *The Poetical Works*, 1. Further quotations from the *Minstrelsy* will be cited by page in text.

[23] Ina Ferris compellingly argues this point and illuminates its broader generic, gendered, and cultural implications throughout her book, *The Achievement of Literary Authority: Gender, History, and the Waverley Novels* (Ithaca, NY: Cornell University Press, 1991), particularly in Part I, "Scott and the Status of the Novel." She notes that Scott's *Waverley* "worked in complex ways not only to legitimize novel-writing as a literary activity but to validate novel-reading as a male practice" (10). Scott's constant turn-to-history in his earlier balladeering moment reveals a similar legitimizing, and indeed masculinizing, impulse – ballads presented and framed as documents, as objects of knowledge, not simply as the frivolous albeit moving tales of beldames.

historical narration and antiquarian display to co-exist, the former framing the latter.

Scott taxonomized his ballads thus:

> The Minstrelsy of the Scottish Border consists of three classes of Poems:
>   I.   Historical Ballads
>   II. Romantic
>   III. Imitations of these compositions by modern authors. (36)

Such a taxonomy reveals his, and the genre's, characteristic hybridization of historical chronology and antiquarian typology. If Gibbon emerges in Momigliano's essays on historiography as the great reconciler of antiquarian erudition and philosophical history, we might say that minstrelsy encouraged Scott to develop different but equally striking strategies to mediate among competing historical methods, modes of display, and narrative commitments. With his nod to ballads of "modern date," Scott also signals the retro-neo chronotope of ballad collections which included contemporary imitations. It is striking that historical ballads were those Scott was able to present as "datable" and as documents participating in what Foucault called "the history of the production of truth"[24]: "The Historical Ballad relates events, which we either know actually to have taken place, or which, at least, making due allowance for the exaggerations of poetical tradition, we may readily conceive to have had some foundation in history" (36). Yet if historical ballads existed in para-discursive relation to events tracked in chronicles and legal documenta, romantic ballads existed in a hazier temporal and factual zone. "[T]he second class, here termed ROMANTIC BALLADS, [is] intended to comprehend such legends as are current upon the Border, relating to fictitious and marvellous adventures" (37). In Scott's classificatory scheme, "Historical Ballads" were strongly anchored to event and took "some foundation in history" as their referent, while "romantic ballads" were explicitly fictive, ethnographically "current," and strongly anchored in place, as indicated by the numerous topographical notices heading these ballads.[25] Minstrelsy, then, encouraged Scott to develop a

---

[24] Scott's association of "historical ballad" with verifiable event suggests that these ballads, as objects of knowledge, have reached what Foucault specified as the "threshold of epistemologization." See in particular Foucault's elucidation of several thresholds of emergence for a "discursive formation": positivity, epistemologization, scientificity, and formalization, in Ch. 6, "Science and Knowledge," *The Archaeology of Knowledge*, 186–7. In "The Discourse on Language," Foucault observes that genealogical discourse analysis (unlike, say, the "history of ideas") orients us to "the power of constituting domains of objects, in relation to which one can affirm or deny true or false propositions." (234).

[25] Oliver glosses this taxonomy with "each category representing the oral poetry of a particular period" (*Scott, Byron, and the Poetics of Cultural Encounter*, 72): historical ballads "representative of the early

complex chronotopical code, both historical and topographical, his ballads either dated or placed, and sometimes both.

I believe that minstrelsy increasingly asked its revivers, whether scholars or poets, to confront the chronotope of their work *as a problem*, a configuration *to be constructed*. (This is borne out even in such later occasional pieces as Trux's essay, the aim of which is to construct a plausible periodization and taxonomy for black American song – understood as the "popular minstrelsy" of the American nation.) I would suggest that what mediated in Scott's corpus between the components of his increasingly complex code, between typologies and narration, between antiquarian eclecticism and philosophical–historical integration, was the Editor-function. Scott's Editor-function mediates between the antiquarian fixation on documents, the philosophical historian's love of sociological and developmental schemes, and the narrative requirements of official historical discourse. To borrow terms and conceptual distinctions from Susan Manning, we might say that in its ostentatious juxtaposition of documents, the *Minstrelsy* adheres to a syntactic method more typical of antiquarian historical method, whereas the tendency toward narrative processing fully developed in Scott's novels points to a semantic integration: history as an intelligible, integrated, if complex story.[26] Scott's *Minstrelsy* thus allows us to ask not only the Foucauldian question, "What is an Author," but also, "What is an Editor." Scott invites us to think of the historian not only as a pursuer of clues à la Carlo Ginzburg,[27] or a generalizer up from heterogenous data, or a systematizer of antiquarian erudition, or a narrative artist of the true, but also and in the first instance as an editor: he who undertakes and ideally subsumes all these tasks. So one answer to my earlier question – how was Scott historical before historical novels? – is this: he was a minstrelling Editor.

Scott's move from Editor to Author was accomplished by his first "original" work, *The Lay of the Last Minstrel*, itself generated out of material

feudal period," romantic ballads conjuring "the period of feudal corruption and decline," imitation ballads "reinstat[ing] virtue for a modern age" (72). While suggestive, this may at times simplify the complexities of the chronotopes within each section as well as across the volume; moreover certain ballads found themselves relocated from one class to another, for example when Scott had to concede in later editions that some supposedly feudal ballads were in fact modern imitations.

[26] Susan Manning outlines this distinction in "Antiquarianism, Balladry and the Rehabilitation of Romance."

[27] I here refer to Ginzburg's influential essay, "Morelli, Freud and Sherlock Holmes: Clues and Scientific Method," first published in English in *History Workshop: A Journal of Socialist Historians* 9 (Spring 1980): 5–36. Ginzburg's proposal of a "conjectural paradigm" as the working method of historians – its genealogy pointing back to the medical case and forward to art-historical connoisseurship and detective work – is strikingly consonant with Chandler's very different excavation of the historical "case."

he'd intended for the *Border Minstrelsy*.[28] *The Lay* might well have been subtitled, in the manner of Scott's novels, "150 years since." (*Waverley*, 1814, was subtitled, "or, 'Tis sixty years since.") Scott's last minstrel is imagined as the repository of tradition, a living archive, but also as the *narrator* of tradition, and thus as a primitive or a "naïve" historian, to invoke Schiller's term.[29] Like Beattie, Scott took over from the antiquarians the re-invented minstrel – the professional transmitter of the oral-poetic tradition; unlike Beattie, Scott made the minstrel a historicizable mouthpiece. As "last of all the bards," the minstrel is the figure through whom Scott can both represent minstrelsy and chronicle its obsolescence.

If the minstrel is the medium of *The Lay of the Last Minstrel*, Scott's representation of the minstrel *as* medium authorizes the lay precisely by historicizing his situation, his "case":[30]

> The last of all the Bards was he,
> Who sung of Border chivalry;
> For, welladay! their date was fled,
> His tuneful brethren all were dead;
> And he, neglected and oppress'd,
> Wish'd to be with them, and at rest.
> (Walter Scott, *The Lay of the Last Minstrel*, Introduction to Canto I)

This trope of the fled "date," the chronotope of a hazily but decidedly departed past in a ruined, haunted place, is exactly what constitutes the historical situation of the minstrel. The minstrel thus marks the fatal conjunction of history and literature; through Scott, the re-animated minstrel becomes a figure of the poet's historiographic *method*. In this conjunction of a fled date and a ruined place, Scott explicitly tropes his way through the conceptual coordinates required to locate a historical situation. The minstrel's predicament as "the last of all the bards" thus emerges, particularly in Scott's hands, as an allegory of "the historical situation" itself.

In presenting and representing minstrels, the Romantic poet allowed himself to explore his proximity and distance from minstrel-making and minstrel-culture. The minstrel is inevitably a figure not only of the past or

---

[28] As Scott wrote of "The Lay" in 1830, "It was finally published in 1805, and may be regarded as the first work in which the writer, who has been since so voluminous, laid his claim to be considered as an original author." "Introduction to the Lay of the Last Minstrel," *Poetical Works*, 315.

[29] Here I refer to Friedrich Schiller's influential opposition of the "naïve" to the "sentimental," in *Über naive und sentimentalische Dichtung* (1795). See *Naive and Sentimental Poetry, and On the Sublime; Two Essays*. Transl., with intro. and notes, by Julius A. Elias (New York: F. Ungar Pub. Co. 1966).

[30] On analyzing literary works as "cases," in the full casuistical, grammatical, and psycho-historical senses of the term "case," see Chandler, *England in 1819*, esp. Ch. 4.

of the proleptically past but of the contemporary poet's *method*, both literary and historiographic. As a deeply historicized figure, Scott's minstrel exists in an ironic key – a necessarily ironic key, if we accept Hayden White's argument that the genre of history always partakes of ironic tropologics.[31] If Beattie's minstrel imbibes the lessons of progressive universal history and becomes its poetic vector, the progress of history leaves Scott's minstrel in the dust.

The Lay is predicated on a trope of simultaneously conjunctive and disjunctive analogy. That is, the minstrel is both like and unlike Scott. Displaying the minstrel's obsolescence as Scott did entails a risk: the risk that you too as a poet were forecasting your own obsolescence. Singing on the edge of an abyss (his "date was fled"), the minstrel offers a parable of the modern poet's imminent obsolescence. And yet Scott's confident authority depends precisely on our *not taking* the minstrel as the proper analogue for the modern poet.

It is impossible to avoid the potential bad faith of such minstrel ventriloquization, and it is not surprising that Hazlitt took devastating aim at what he termed Scott's minstrel masquerade, and at the antiquarian origins of the retro-neo minstrelling project. In his Lectures on the Living Poets, delivered at the Surrey Institute in 1818, Hazlitt observed:

There is a modern air in the midst of the antiquarian research of Mr Scott's poetry. It is history or tradition in masquerade. Not only the crust of old words and images is worn off with time, – the substance is grown comparatively light and worthless. The forms are old and uncouth, but the spirit is effeminate and frivolous. This is a deduction from the praise I have given to his pencil for extreme fidelity, although it has been no obstacle to his drawing room success. He has just hit the town between the romantic and the fashionable; and between the two, secured all classes of readers on his side. *In a word, I conceive that he is to a great poet, what an excellent mimic is to a great actor.*[32] [emphases added]

Here we see how Scott's inter- and intra-generic virtuosities unsettled both Hazlitt and his critical categories. Scott's writing project existed in an uncomfortable relation to the official discourses of history – and thus he was charged with offering "history or tradition in masquerade," not in its

---

[31] See Hayden White, *Metahistory: The Historical Imagination in Nineteenth-Century Europe* (Baltimore and London: Johns Hopkins University Press, 1973, 1987), in particular "The Theory of Tropes" (31–8) and "The Phases of Nineteenth-Century Historical Consciousness" (38–42). White traces the nineteenth-century confrontation with Irony back to Enlightenment historiography; see Part One, "The Received Tradition: The Enlightenment and the Problem of Historical Consciousness" (43–131) and his later remarks on Ranke and his followers (277–8). It is striking that, while Ranke acknowledged Scott as a prime influence for his conception of historical method and writing, White does not discuss Scott – a symptom of the restriction of "history" to those specified as professional historians.

[32] William Hazlitt, "On the Living Poets," in *Lectures on the English Poets*, in *The Complete Works of William Hazlitt*, ed. B. P. Howe (London and Toronto: J. M. Dent, 1930), Vol. V of XX, 155.

real, masculine, substance. Neither a sincere historian nor a true antiquarian, Scott emerges in Hazlitt's account as at best an astonishingly successful, fashionable poet.

Hazlitt's recourse to theatrical metaphors – masquerade, mimicry, and acting – brings us to the central, transhistorical problematic of minstrelsy: if minstrels, historically understood, may be seen as the first performance poets, minstrelling discourse constantly poses the problem of what cultural work a modern poet might continue to perform, especially if poetry itself was perhaps obsolete.

TAKING THE MEASURE OF MINSTRELSY: HISTORICIZING MEDIUMS, MESSAGES, METRICS

I suggested earlier that we explore minstrelsy as the place where history and poetry meet, and I have thus far focused on poetic and para-poetic incorporations of historical schemata, antiquarian documenta, and historiographic method. One could trace these minstrelling incorporations of "the historical" through other genres and mediums than the lay, the ballad collection, or the progress poem: scholars have tended to focus on the kinship between the historical novel and the emergent discipline of history within the human sciences.[33] Yet poetry has a particular relationship with history which is different from that between, say, the novel and history, or biography and history, or travel-writing and history: for poetry is that imaginative genre or medium which extends back into what Beattie, Scott, and after him Shelley all called "a rude age": the time before print, indeed before writing, before history as we know it. Poetry not only precedes the discourse of history: it *was* historical discourse, or rather, it was the hegemonic discourse of the past, as numerous eighteenth-century

---

[33] From Lukács through Fredric Jameson (among many others) on the literary-historical side, and from Momigliano to Mark Salber Phillips (among others) on the historians' side, we see a striking orientation to prose genres – an effect, perhaps, of assimilating prose fiction to "the novel" (or "the tale," as Trumpener salutarily reminds us) and "poetry" to "lyric," bypassing the narrative functions of poetry and its inevitable enmeshment with transformations of historical narrative and method. More recent work salutarily reminds us of the overwhelmingly *narrative* nature of romantic poetry (see St. Clair, *Reading Nation*); of the interface of lyric and history (see Newman, *Ballad Collection*, Ch. 3, 96–135; Stewart, *Poetry and the Fate of the Senses*); of profound interconnections between poetry and the novel (see Ann Rowland, "Romantic Poetry and the Romantic Novel," in *The Cambridge Companion to British Romantic Poetry* [Cambridge University Press, 2008], 117–35; G. Gabrielle Starr, *Lyric Generations: Poetry and the Novel in the Long Eighteenth Century* [Baltimore, MD: Johns Hopkins University Press, 2004]; and of the interpenetration of lyric with other genres, narrative modes, discourses, and media (see Goodman, *Georgic Modernity* and McLane, *Romanticism and the Human Sciences*).

conjectural historians observed, as Thomas Love Peacock tartly reminded his readers in his essay "The Four Ages of Poetry," and as twentieth-century ethnographers have confirmed.[34]

As a medium of culture, the minstrel sends us, as he did his eighteenth-century revivers, a complex historical and poetic message. The Scottish Enlightenment, I would argue, invited poets to think new questions: How did poetry intersect with universal history? In what ways was poetry historical and historicizable? Was it true, as Thomas Gray claimed, that "the language of the age is never the language of poetry"?[35] If so, of what age was the language of poetry?

We are on the cusp, it is clear, of questions most actively posed by Wordsworth in his Preface to *Lyrical Ballads*, a text that, against Wordsworth's own poetic practice, virtually predicted the demise of poetry-as-verse. It is worth noting that the minstrel controversy between Percy and Ritson was also a debate over the historicity of verse and poetic style as they intersected with standards of taste: while Percy preferred the rough ragged stanzas of the "ancient" version of the ballad "Chevy Chase," for example, Ritson much preferred the regular stanzas of the Elizabethan version and considered Percy's championing of the former to be an anti-quarian perversion. In antiquarian argument and historical essay, meter mattered; diction too; and poetic style was one contended point of entry into the historicity of poetry and national standards of taste.

Any further exploration of minstrel historicisms and poetics must be prepared to discuss the medium of minstrel messages: to wit, metrical language.[36] That Beattie was not equipped to explore the historicity of

---

[34] Adapting the commonplaces of stadial theory for his own polemical ends (among them, to announce the death of poetry), Peacock wrote: "Poetry is thus in its origin panegyrical. The first rude songs of all nations appear to be a sort of brief historical notices, in a strain of tumid hyperbole, of the exploits and possessions of a few pre-eminent individuals ... This is the first stage of poetry before the invention of written letters." Thomas Love Peacock, "The Four Ages of Poetry," in *Essays, Memoirs, Letters and Unfinished Novels*. The Halliford Edition of the Collected Works of Thomas Love Peacock, ed. H. F. B. Brett-Smith and C. E. Jones, Vol. VIII (New York: AMS Press, 1967), 4–5.

[35] Quoted from Gray's correspondence in Reeves' introduction, *Complete English Poems of Gray*, 25.

[36] And here I am speaking, as I hope by now is clear, of *revived* minstrels, the eighteenth-century discursive phenomenon as it flowed into literary poetics rather than into performance. I defer here the question of British, not to mention US, minstrelsy's multiple *métiers*, not least song, recitation, chanting, and droning – all of which require their own critical inquiries and integrations. The musics and kinesthetics of minstrelsy, as objects of study and sites of representation, have a parallel, sometimes simultaneous but often strikingly different, history from those of minstrel texts and commentaries. Burns vs. Scott is one interesting case here – Burns the avid song-collector, song-writer, hummer of airs and fiddler of tunes, Scott notoriously unmusical, neglecting to print tunes in his *Minstrelsy* until his magnum opus edition, and then scantly (as discussed in the last chapter).

poetry is clear: one measure of this was his chosen measure, the Spenserian stanza – not a stanza any actual minstrel ever deployed. Beattie's metrical medium was explicitly at odds with his historical message: if the muse of history was supposed to chasten the poet and cure him of excessive ornament, the Spenserian stanza would not seem to be his destined *métier*. And thus we see in Beattie's *Minstrel* a constitutive, but unacknowledged, disjunction between its stylistic advice, which is the message of Enlightenment History for poetry, and the Spenserian code of that message.

In *The Lay of the Last Minstrel*, conversely, Scott brilliantly staged the difference between himself and his seventeenth-century minstrel as a metrical difference. In his framing passages, Scott used a minstrel couplet ("the way was long, the wind was cold/the minstrel was infirm and old"); but the minstrel speaks, intriguingly, not in the couplet historically associated with him but in a more fluid stanza poached from Coleridge's "Christabel." Wordsworth similarly, although for different and critical ends, got a grip on minstrelsy through metrical means. When Wordsworth wanted to kill off revived minstrels in the poem "Brougham Castle," he did so by differentiating his elegiac stanza from the octosyllabic couplets through which his bumptious minstrel speaks: "'Quell the Scot!' exclaims the Lance/'Bear me to the heart of France!'"[37] (One wonders whether Wordsworth was not trying to quell one particular Scot – Walter.) However different their takes on minstrelsy, Scott and Wordsworth recognized that the relation of the modern poet to a represented minstrel was always a *metrically* encoded (as well as historically conceptualized) relation.

Scott and after him Wordsworth and Byron realized that the fate of poetry was inextricably bound to the historical problematic we can trace in "minstrelsy." In *Childe Harold*, Byron incorporated aspects of Scott's minstrelsy, modeling Harold's "Goodnight Song" on "Lord Maxwell's Goodnight" from Scott's *Minstrelsy*. Yet Byron boldly collapsed the historical and poetic distances Scott had kept comfortably open between his narrating persona and his ventriloquized minstrel: elaborating in his work a poetic persona virtually indistinct from his tended celebrity, Byron became a truly self-fashioning minstrel, his poetry increasingly imagining itself as co-extensive with recent world-historical developments, most specifically the Napoleonic wars and the Napoleonic career. If poetry ideally is news that stays news (to invoke Pound again), we might say that Byron developed a poetry capable of processing the news, "news" understood as

---

[37] From "Song, at the Feast of Brougham Castle, Upon the Restoration of Lord Clifford, the Shepherd, to the Estates and Honours of his Ancestors," lines 148–9, in *Poems, in Two Volumes*, 263–4.

history-in-the-making. The breadth of the Byronic project encompassed, as Scott recognized his did not, the mapping of interior and erotic life along-side and through contemporary public events, wars, treaties, and tourism. Just as official history had been transformed by its engagement with other historical and ethnographic genres – biography, travel writing, accounts of manners and custom – so too British poetry, for seven years dominated by Scott, found itself in a constant dialogue with powerful prose discourses of sentiment, sensibility, and the private. Byron was in the end better able than Scott to exploit the resources of historiographic and journalistic discourse for poetry. Yet if Scott renounced his minstrel mask in verse, he kept it in another guise, most notably that of editor and author of prose. If in 1812 Byron awoke and found himself famous, it is not surprising that by 1814 Scott awoke and found himself "The Author of Waverley."

MINSTRELSY INTERMINABLE

Despite Scott's move to the novel, poetic minstrelsy continued in various guises. *The Minstrelsy of the Scottish Border* spawned many a lesser collection, including *English Minstrelsy* (anonymously edited by Scott in 1810), William Motherwell's aforementioned *Minstrelsy: Ancient and Modern* (Glasgow, 1827), Frederick Sheldon's *Minstrelsy of the English Border* (1847), and numerous other minstrelling volumes and essays, Scottish, English, and American. So if minstrelsy began again in the mid-eighteenth century, it is not exactly clear when, or if, it ended. I would like to conclude by turning briefly to two examples of the persistence and transmutation of minstrelsy.

For students of US culture, "minstrelsy" inevitably conjures the complex history and ongoing presence of American blackface entertainment. That there might be a connection between Scott's minstrelsy-as-masquerade and minstrelsy as racialized, racist US entertainment is suggested, if only meta-phorically, by the very title of such a recent book as *Inside the Minstrel Mask: Readings in Nineteenth-Century Blackface Minstrelsy.*[38] These connections between the eighteenth-century Anglo-Scottish minstrelsy complex and its nineteenth-century fortunes in Britain and the US are murky and remain fully to be charted, but Trux's article (with which I began) offers one signpost. Another might be found in Henry Heavisides' slim volume of 1860, *The Minstrelsy of Britain*. In Chapter 6, Heavisides proposes to survey: "The vitiated taste of the present age for Cockney songs – their

---

[38] Eds. Annemarie Bean, James V. Hatch, and Brooks McNamara, foreword Mel Watkins (Wesleyan University Press, 1996).

vulgarity – the negro melodies – the lyrics of Tennyson, Gerald Massey etc.": a rather astonishing list of topics ranging across national, class, racial, and performance boundaries in a survey of poetries "of the present age." Heavisides tartly noted that the "class of composition misnamed Negro Melodies" largely "emanated from the Metropolis, and are written by Cockneys who never beheld the Ohio … ." (a charge that chimes nicely with Trux's dismissal of poetasters who "never saw an alligator, or smelt the magnolia blossom in their lives"). Heavisides thus accused English metropolitan poets of putting on melodic, lexical, Americanizing, countrifying blackface. And if Heavisides censures Cockney songs for their "wretched" and "contemptible" vulgarity, he notably castigates the composers of negro melodies for inauthenticity: "Togged out in seedy black suits, with white cravats, curly wigs, and blackened faces, they have attempted by unnatural grimaces, and winks, and nods, and stale conundrums, to impose on the gullibility of poor simple John Bull. These wandering minstrels, however, with their doleful banjos, have had their day – the negro ditties, with their broken English, are fast sinking in public estimation." Heavisides turns then with relief to the lyrics of Tennyson.

The wandering minstrel trope here re-appears, transformed and decisively racialized. Blackened impersonators impose on John Bull: minstrelsy proliferates through such a repertoire of stock characters, national tropes, and equally stock responses. Instead of the long flowing hair and accompanying harp of Scott's last minstrel, these bewigged blackface minstrels strum their doleful banjos – and in the shift from harp to banjo we have another registration, albeit inadvertent, of the historicity of the instruments minstrelsy used. Minstrelsy is an endlessly adaptable system of signification, a flexible instrument, so to speak, which lent itself equally to narratives of historical formation and cultural nationalism – e.g. in Scott's *Lay* – and to cheerfully mongrelizing entertainment. Restricted to its poetic mediations, we see that from Scott onward, late-eighteenth and early nineteenth-century British and American minstrelsy repeatedly splits over crude but powerful questions: is the poet best imagined as an entertainer or a pedagogue? a performer or a figure of enlightenment? A masquerader or a purveyor of truth? And from the first antiquarian revival, with its accompanying tropes of last minstrels, later minstrels, and lately living minstrels, minstrelling discourse posed another question which still persists: minstrelsy – dead or alive? And if alive, in what medium?

Heavisides foresaw the demise of banjo-twanging minstrels, but he was wrong in several senses, as we see in our second example of minstrelsy's later fortunes. Minstrelling discourse survived not only through its popular incarnations – songbooks, shows, jokes, dances, poems – but also through its curators. As Scott's work showed and Hazlitt brilliantly intuited, minstrelsy oscillated between the poles of impersonation and curation, ventriloquization and conservation. These two minstrelling strains coalesced in the caricature catalogued as "Harvard President and Professors as Minstrels" (Fig. 13). We confront here a photomontage made by Harvard's Hasty Pudding Club in 1881, featuring various Harvard luminaries – Charles Eliot, the President of Harvard, and several professors, including William James and Francis James Child, the famous ballad compiler and Harvard's first professor of English Literature. These sober Bostonians are represented as cavorting in the garb, with the instruments, and in the poses made popularly famous by blackface minstrelsy and its stars, including Master Juba and "Daddy" Rice. When minstrelling discourse migrates to America and takes up blackface, we see that a balladeering scholar could find himself straddling that discursive space between minstrelsy as problematic performance and minstrelsy as cultural conservation. Instead of a minstrelling literature conjuring sounds and images, we have here an image of sounds and movements – minstrelsy as parodic, kinesthetic audio-visual hallucination.[39] Such an artifact calls not only for critical race analysis but also for a critical media analysis.[40] About this caricature one hardly knows where to begin, or more precisely where to end, so I will leave it for us to contemplate.

As the place where poetry and history cross, "Minstrelsy" partakes of a specific late-eighteenth-century cultural and intellectual situation; yet the questions minstrelsy raises are, as we have seen, transhistorical and transmedial. Minstrels migrate, mongrelize, and mutate. Endlessly revived, transformed, yet always problematic, always distressed: this is minstrelsy, this is poetry fatally encountering its historical situation. From Scott's last minstrel, barely able to get his harp tuned and his measures flowing, to Henry Heavisides' hopeful assertion that the craze for "negro melodies" had

---

[39] For a suggestive, ingenious reading of audiovisual hallucination engendered by Walter Scott, see Langan, "Understanding Media in 1805," 49–70.

[40] For the kind of media discourse analysis we might undertake regarding minstrelling phenomena in general, one might wish (again) to pursue the implications of Kittler's work, particularly as it illuminates and radically rewrites the romantic "discourse network" circa 1800: see *Discourse Networks, 1800/1900*. During the monopoly of print, Kittler argues, "literature" programs its readers to hallucinate sounds and images; print activates the sensorium and conjures interiority as if there were no mediation. For further meditations on mediality, particularly the impact of sound and visual technologies on the cultural imaginary previously constituted by the discourse network called "literature," see *Gramophone, Film, Typewriter*. For an illuminating discussion of Kittler, "German media science," its antihumanist force, its technophilia and its commitment to an analytic "media a priori," see Geoffrey Winthrop-Young, "Drill and Distraction in the Yellow Submarine: On the Dominance of War in Friedrich Kittler's Media Theory," *Critical Inquiry* 28:4 (Summer 2002): 825–54.

13 "Harvard President and Professors as Minstrels," photocollage, ca. 1881

"had its day," minstrelsy is always imminently obsolete: thus it requires endless revival and equally relentless burial.

Minstrelsy is a Janus-faced muse, a figure of obsolescence but also of a peculiar resilience. It still has much to teach us about poetry, historicity, and ultimately, the condition of mediality. Through minstrelsy, poets began to discover the modern problematic of making which Pound later formulated in two famous dicta – to write "poems including history" while also "making it new." In the mid-twentieth century, John Berryman found in minstrelsy a strategy for voicing, lampooning, sentimentalizing, and racializing the splits in lyric subjectivity: featuring "Henry" (a white American "occasionally in blackface") and the Negro-dialect-speaking "Mr. Bones" (the laconic straightman), Berryman's *Dream Songs* offer perhaps the most famous recent example of the poet-as-minstrelling-maker. Yet minstrelsy even in its American transmutations need not always be in blackface. When Wallace Stevens observes, in his "Notes toward a Supreme Fiction," that "there was such idiot minstrelsy in rain,"[41] we might begin to hear in this minstrelling rain the ingenious persistence of minstrelsy's reign.

---

[41] Wallace Stevens, section 6 in "It must change," "Notes toward a Supreme Fiction," *The Collected Poems* section 3 in "It must change", ll. 7, 394.

CHAPTER 5

Minstrelsy, or, Romantic poetry

> I am the last
> Of all the field that fell
> My name is nearly all that's left
> Of what was Swordy Well.
> – John Clare, "The Lament of Swordy Well"[1]

> O poesy is on the wane
> I hardly know her face again.
> – John Clare, "Decay," *The Rural Muse*[2]

Who was the last minstrel? Perhaps we should award the palm to John Graeme, of Sowport, in Cumberland, "commonly called *The Long Quaker*," whom Walter Scott saluted in 1802: "a person of this latter description, was very lately alive; and several of the songs, now published, have been taken down from his recitation."[3] Or perhaps we should nominate another man Scott commemorated still later in 1830, one Charles Leslie, "more generally known by the nickname of Mussel-mou'd Charlie, from a singular projection of his lip," who was

an old Aberdeenshire minstrel, the very last, probably, of the race, who, according to [Thomas] Percy's definition of the profession, sung his own compositions, and those of others, through the capital of the county, and other towns in that country of gentlemen.[4]

But we mustn't fail to consider the claim of another, later, minstrel, "viz. Francis King, who was well known in the western dales of Yorkshire as 'the Skipton Minstrel,'" of whom the antiquarian J. H. Dixon regretfully announced in 1846: "This poor minstrel, from whose recitation two of

---

[1] John Clare, "The Lament of Swordy Well," *"I Am": The Selected Poetry of John Clare*, ed. Jonathan Bate (New York: Farrar, Straus and Giroux, 2003), 216.
[2] John Clare, "Decay," *The Rural Muse* (1835), *"I Am,"* 181.
[3] Scott, Introduction (historical) to *MSB*, 36.
[4] Scott, "Introductory Remarks on Popular Poetry," *MSB*, 1830, 15.

140

our ballads were obtained, met his death by drowning in December, 1844."[5]

Whether "very lately alive" or quite recently dead, the last minstrel appears as a standard topic, a constitutive *topos*, of antiquarian documentation and essay. Standing as the "last of the race," as Scott had it (and as Fiona Stafford called her illuminating study of this phenomenon), the "last minstrel" configured both the end of a certain strain of poetry and of a cultural epoch, these two obsolescences conjoined in his song and his person. And as suggested in the previous chapter, the last minstrel haunted the poetry of this era as effectively as he did antiquarianism. It becomes increasingly obvious, when canvassing eighteenth- and nineteenth-century British literature, that last minstrels are quite disturbingly everywhere to be found.[6]

In my previous chapter I explored minstrelsy as the place where poetry and historical discourse meet; in this chapter I wish to pursue minstrelsy further as an *intra-poetic* phenomenon, a discourse of and through poetry. I want to explore minstrelsy as another name for *poiesis* in this period. If it was Scott who most fully and obsessively exploited minstrelsy, bringing it repeatedly to a spectacular end, such preoccupations were hardly unique to his oeuvre: Chatterton, Beattie, Crabbe, Goldsmith, Moore, Scott, Hogg, Wordsworth, Coleridge, Byron, Clare, Hemans, L. E. L. (Letitia Landon) – all trafficked in minstrels. For specimens of minstrelsy, one might recall that spell-binding Ancient Mariner, the last of his crew, determined to tell his tale, wedding guest be damned; or we might reflect on any number of passages from Wordsworth:

> O that some Minstrel's harp were near,
> To utter notes of gladness,
> And chase this silence from the air,
> That fills my heart with sadness!
> > "Yarrow Visited," September 1814[7]

---

[5] Henry Wheatley, quoting Dixon, introduction to Thomas Percy, *Reliques*, xxii.

[6] For a discussion of the image of "the last bard" and the trope of "the last of the race," see Stafford, *The Last of the Race*, in particular Ch. 4, "The Last Bards" (83–108) and Ch. 7, "The Sixth Lord Byron," with its discussion of Scott's *The Lay of the Last Minstrel*, 162–6. And indeed, such figures flourished well into the twentieth century: viz. Frost's "The Later Minstrel," addressed to Longfellow, a poem which perfectly exemplifies the mobility and revivability of the last or later minstrel trope, and its especial relevance for poets meditating on the obsolescence of certain national as well as poetic traditions.

[7] "Yarrow Visited, September 1814," in *Shorter Poems, 1807–1820, by William Wordsworth*, ed. Carl H. Ketcham (Ithaca, NY: Cornell University Press, 1989), 137–40, ll. 5–8. Further citations from this poem will be cited in text by line. "Yarrow Visited" itself revisits Wordsworth's "Yarrow Unvisited," composed in 1803 or early 1804, which commemorates William and Dorothy's decision *not* to visit Yarrow during their 1803 tour of Scotland, thereby preserving (so the poem argues) their "vision" (l. 51) of Yarrow from the encroachments of actual encounter. See "Yarrow Unvisited," in *Poems, in Two Volumes*, 198–200, notes, 417.

Or these lines from "Yarrow Revisited" (1831), in which Wordsworth revisits both Yarrow and "Yarrow Visited":

> Once more, by Newark's Castle-gate
> Long left without a warder,
> I stood, looked, listened, and with Thee,
> Great Minstrel of the Border![8]

The "Great Minstrel of the Border" hailed here is Walter Scott, with whom Wordsworth and his sister had walked and talked years before, during their tour of Scotland in 1803.

Thus to the question, "who was the last minstrel?," Romantic poetry could be said to answer, along with Wordsworth: Walter Scott. And indeed, twentieth-century critics have tended to echo Scott's contemporaries in hailing him, albeit in barbed fashion, as the greatest and perhaps the last minstrel: as Harry Levin wrote, "His was a dual role: the last minstrel and the first best-seller."[9] Yet on another level, that of minstrel metaphorics and dispersion, Romantic poets had met the minstrels and found they were themselves.[10]

As the foregoing excerpts suggest, once you begin looking for minstrels, you will find them appearing in poem after Romantic poem, such that minstrelsy may be understood as a central figure of poetic dispersion, historicity, haunting and revivification in this era. One could argue that it was precisely through "metre ballad-mongering" (as Hazlitt later dismissively termed it[11]) and more broadly through a reconstructed minstrelsy that major poets of the period found themselves as poets. There is of course

---

[8] William Wordsworth, "Yarrow Revisited," *Sonnet Series and Itinerary Poems, 1820–1845, by William Wordsworth,* ed. Geoffrey Jackson (Ithaca, NY: Cornell University Press, 2004), 490–93, ll. 1–8. Further citations from this poem will be cited in text by line.

[9] Harry Levin, *The Gates of Horn: A Study of Five French Realists* (Oxford University Press), 45.

[10] See, for example, how early nineteenth-century Scottish poets were easily subsumed under the minstrelling category: in *The Modern Scottish Minstrel; or, the Songs of Scotland of the past half century,* ed. Charles Rogers (Edinburgh: Adam and Charles Black, 1855), 6 vols. From Walter Scott to Robert Jamieson to Mrs. John Hunter (née Ann Home) to Joanna Baillie to James Hogg, Rogers' modern minstrels comprise a remarkable roster of poetic production in late eighteenth- and early nineteenth-century Scotland; and notably, his minstrels are often women. It is also notable that Rogers seeks to claim for Scotland a "Modern Gaelic Minstrelsy," offering "Sketches and Specimens in English Verse of the most celebrated modern Gaelic Bards."

[11] See Hazlitt on Wordsworth and the Lake Poets: "They took the same method in their new-fangled 'metre ballad-mongering' scheme, which Rousseau did in his prose paradoxes, of exciting attention by reversing the established standards of opinion and estimation in the world" ("On the Living Poets," *Lectures on The English Poets,* 163). Hazlitt's sarcastic invocation of their "metre ballad-mongering scheme" recalls and transforms his earlier praise of Robert Burns, who, he writes, "was not a sickly sentimentalist, a namby-pamby poet, a mincing metre ballad-monger, any more than Shakespeare" ("Living Poets," 128).

a long and more recently galvanized critical tradition that acknowledges the impact of revived balladry and romance on what we still conventionally call "Romantic poetry"[12]: this tradition was well established by the time of Scott's 1830 essay "On Imitations of the Ancient Ballad," in which he hailed his fellow innovators in England, Scotland, and Ireland and proposed a balladeering and minstrelling genealogy extending from Percy and Macpherson through Thomas Moore, Southey, Wordsworth, Coleridge, James Hogg, John Leyden, Anne Bannerman, and himself.[13] In this literary history of the period, Scott makes plain the centrality of minstrelsy for a wide array of poets. Having reviewed the controversies attending various ballad scandals (including Thomas Chatterton's Rowley poems and Lady Wardlaw's ballad, "Hardyknute," by which he himself had been duped), Scott explicitly conjoins antiquarian and poetic geneaologies in one stream of minstrel-making. He moves from praise of Percy to Burns, after which he continues:

These, with others of modern date, at the head of whom we must place Thomas Moore, have aimed at striking the ancient harp with the same bold and rough note to which it was awakened by the ancient minstrels. Southey, Wordsworth, and other distinguished names of the present century, have, in repeated instances, dignified this branch of literature; but no one more than Coleridge, in the wild and imaginative tale of the "Ancient Mariner," which displays so much beauty with such eccentricity. We should act most unjustly in this department of Scottish ballad poetry, not to mention the name of Leyden, Hogg, and Allan Cunningham.[14]

Striking again the "ancient harp with the same bold and rough note": Percy's imitations, Burns' songs, Moore's melodies, Southey's metrical romances, Wordsworth's and Coleridge's ballads, and Scott's own "lays" were thus retrospectively aligned with and assimilated to the broader project

---

[12] See, for example, Marilyn Butler, *Romantics, Rebels, and Reactionaries: English Literature and its Background 1760–1830* (Oxford University Press, 1981); Ian Duncan, *Modern Romance and Transformations of the Novel: The Gothic, Scott, Dickens* (Cambridge University Press, 1992); Stewart, "Scandals of the Ballad," in *Crimes of Writing*; Groom, *Percy's "Reliques"*; Trumpener, *Bardic Nationalism*; Newman, *Ballad Collection, Lyric, and the Canon*. These and others scholars have redrawn the map of literary production, such that we can now recognize how central were the ballad revival, and more broadly the "revival of romance" (in Ian Duncan's phrase), to the literary-cultural formation of those poets who came of age in the 1790s. Earlier twentieth-century work by ballad scholars, not least Gordon Gerould in *The Ballad of Tradition* (Oxford University Press [1957, ©1932]) and Albert B. Friedman in *The Ballad Revival: Studies in the Influence of Popular on Sophisticated Poetry* (University of Chicago Press, 1961), had illuminated the links between popular, revived, and literary balladeering in the late eighteenth and early nineteenth centuries.

[13] See Scott, "Imitations of the Ancient Ballad," in *Poetical Works*, 182.

[14] Ibid., 182. The subclausal, belated salute of Leyden, Hogg, and Cunningham enacts and enforces in its syntax the dependent status of these poets, all of whom were patronized (in both senses) by Scott.

of a revivified minstrelsy. Such a passage stands as well as a polemic creation of a poetic genealogy and fraternity, inflected by cultural nationalism but also a "British" canon-making impulse.

By 1800, then, what we might call a "minstrelsy complex" had moved beyond its origins in antiquarian polemic to take up residence within the heart of poetry and poetics. Through minstrelsy, poets explored problems of poetic and cultural authority as well as a history of poetic forms.[15] Working through minstrelsy, moreover, allowed and indeed compelled a poet to consider problems of matter and measure; minstrelsy also forced a poet to grapple with problems of authenticity and historicity. In terms of minstrel-ling *poiesis*, minstrel-making afforded a double focus, a way to think about the internal workings of poetry as well a way to meditate on its legitimating and contextualizing apparatus. "Minstrelsy" became a double and doubling discourse, a set of tropes and operations, simultaneously concerned with processes of *internalization* (that is, in the ways minstrel forms and figures are displayed and transformed in poetry) and processes of *externalization* (that is, in the various authenticating, commentating, and documentary procedures undertaken within and around poems).

"Minstrelsy" also specifies the problematics of a poet's relation to audience and to the broader social and economic negotiations thereof. That Romantic minstrelsy – which is to say, *poiesis* itself – presented a highly stratified, hierarchized "literary field" (in Pierre Bourdieu's terms[16]), only semi-autonomous from the socio-economic field, might perhaps go without saying: what is striking is that poets across Great Britain, across the class spectrum, of both sexes, found in minstrel-making a project. Minstrelsy provided a means for poets to confront their new situation as culture-workers in a commercialized literary era: poets like James Hogg and Felicia Hemans seized minstrel tropologics to explore poetry as a commodity form, the "favor" minstrels sought (often ambivalently) from aristocrats become a figure of the modern poets' desire to find favor from either patrons or commercial audiences or both. Those poets eager for and dependent on success in the market could not afford to create the taste by which they might be enjoyed: they had to find immediate approbation by print publics, just as their minstrel-predecessors sought the favor of aristocratic patrons

---

[15] On the commercial exploration of minstrelsy by women (e.g. Hemans and L.E.L.), and by those men excluded from elite circles of cultural production (e.g., Hogg), see Erik Simpson's seminal essay, "Minstrelsy Goes to Market: Prize Poems, Minstrel Contests, and Romantic Poetry," *ELH* 71:3 (2004): 691–718.

[16] In, for example, Pierre Bourdieu, *The Rules of Art: Genesis and Structure of the Literary Field*, trans. Susan Emanuel (Stanford University Press, 1996).

and immediate audiences.[17] Scott was able to finesse this situation, seeking both patronage and commercial triumph while trying to avoid the taint of mere mercenary service; others less well-placed could neither afford nor maintain such ironic distantiation from the market. (Nor, in the end, could Scott – as the 1826 collapse of his publisher Constable and his own intertwined finances catastrophically proved.)

Through minstrelsy, then, poets addressed and pondered their own socio-economic and political situations; through minstrelsy they also confronted the transhistorical fortunes of poetry. Thus John Clare, so often the plangent ringer in the minstrelling works, saluted his brother plebeian poet, Robert Bloomfield: "Sweet unassuming minstrel, not to thee/The dazzling fashions of the day belong."[18] Clare here points to the ambiguous range of minstrel *poiesis* – minstrelsy as a transhistorical tradition of humble making (by Clare's Bloomfield, for example) vs. minstrelsy as mere poetic fashion (viz. Hazlitt's Scott). Unassuming minstrels tended to lose in the poetico-cultural sweepstakes, yet minstrels still they were – not "Great Minstrels of the Border" but poets of their own socio-cultural location, powerfully articulated. Thus Clare identifies himself in "The Lament of Swordy Well" with the very fields so brutally enclosed in the early nineteenth century: speaking in the voice of the field Swordy Well, Clare extends "the last of the race" trope such that it figures a complete environment, an imperiled cultural and poetic ecology:

> Of all the fields I am the last
> That my own face can tell.
> Yet, what with stone pits' delving holes
> And strife to buy and sell,
> My name will quickly be the whole
> That's left of Swordy Well. (219)

To my opening question, then – who was the last minstrel? – Clare might be said to answer: the very field that used to occasion and support this minstrel's voice. With precise lyrico-critical force, Clare re-directs us from the question of any given last minstrel to the very *ground* of minstrelsy. That the "whole" project of minstrelsy might implode into a black "hole" of merely floating names, that the ground of Clare's poetry – or of any poetry – might be sold out or otherwise excavated beneath the poet: this

---

[17] See Simpson, "Minstrelsy Goes to Market," 712–13.
[18] John Clare, "To the Memory of Bloomfield," *"I Am"*, 196. On Bloomfield's status as best-selling poet, now largely forgotten, see William St. Clair, *The Reading Nation in the Romantic Period*, 217–19, 582.

imminent obsolescence is the recurring matter out of which minstrelsy makes its song.

This chapter pursues the work and ends of minstrelsy, particularly as minstrelsy makes itself felt through Romantic poetry. For if it was the eighteenth-century antiquarians who first revived the figure of the last minstrel, it was the Romantic poets – well-schooled heirs of and sometime participants in the antiquarian project – who found, sometimes to their dismay, that the minstrel and his minstrelsy configured the problem of their own poetry. But before teasing out further minstrelling strains, let us return to its first re-soundings in the voices of the antiquarians. For it is there, in the heart of the ballad scandals, that the minstrelsy problematic acquired its form.

MINSTREL AGONISTES: THE ANTIQUARIAN DEBATE

From the various notices of minstrels with which I began, it would seem that minstrelsy had never decisively died, that it had been decaying from time immemorial, its living remnants always already almost dead. Yet when the antiquarians first revived minstrelsy, they did so, paradoxically, with historical notices of its degradation and death. As Thomas Percy wrote, in his "Essay on the Ancient Minstrels in England,"

Towards the end of the sixteenth century this class of men had lost all credit, and were sunk so low in public opinion, that in the 39th year of Elizabeth, a statute was passed by which "minstrels, wandering abroad," were included among "rogues, vagabonds, and sturdy beggars," and were adjudged to be punished as such. This act seems to have put an end to the profession.[19]

Yet if in this essay Percy remarked an "end to the profession" of minstrelsy, his own editorial practices (which included silently emending ballad texts) and his own poetic ventures (imitations of ancient ballads) suggested that he had continued minstrelsy by other means. Joseph Ritson, Percy's major antagonist, recognized and censured this paradoxical re-vivification. Like Percy, he traced the definitive decline of the profession up to, "[l]astly," an "ordinance of the Commonwealth of 1656, c. 21," which proclaimed that "*fiddlers* or *minstrels*" who attempted to fiddle, sing, or juggle, "are hereby adjudged and declared to be rogues, vagabonds, and sturdy beggars." Having written, like Percy, a version of the legal epitaph of minstrelsy, Ritson gave it a sardonic twist:

---

[19] Percy, "An Essay on the Ancient Minstrels in England," 377.

After this, the word *Minstrel* was scarcely ever mentioned (unless in dictionaries or vagrant acts) till it appeared with such *éclat* in the Essay prefixed to the *Reliques of Ancient English Poetry*.[20]

As Ritson suggests, Percy, editor of the *Reliques*, re-animated minstrelsy in a new, simultaneously historiographic and poetic key. And of course we could argue that the broader antiquarian project aimed precisely to sustain the life of minstrelsy and its "relics" even as it narrated and historicized its obsolescence.

The antiquarian debate over minstrelsy emerged as a function of the ballad revival and its scandals as well as a pervasive medievalism: to revive the ballad was to revive the imagined medium of "ancient" balladry and romance – the minstrel. In reviving the ballad, antiquarians also revived the notion of minstrels, such that, as Susan Stewart observes, "The character of the minstrel thus becomes as marvelous and opportune an invention as that of the ballads themselves."[21] To speak of ballads or minstrels was also, inevitably, to speak of forgery, authenticity, taste, standards of evidence, protocols of editing, and, by 1800, a decades-long history of ballad commentary and apparatus. In 1886, Henry Wheatley published an introduction to his edition of Percy's *Reliques*, the general topics of which handily summed up the array of antiquarian concerns:

> The Minstrels.
> Minstrels and Ballad Writers.
> Imitators and Forgers.
> Authenticity of Certain Ballads.
> Preservers of the Ballads.
> Life of Percy.
> Folio MS. and the *Reliques*.
> Ballad Literature since Percy.[22]

Minstrels lived again, as it were, in this context: the emerging problematic over authenticity, invention, and tradition.

Yet minstrels were not simply invented or revived; they were, like ballads, loudly debated. The most prominent minstrel-combatants were (as noted in the previous chapter) Percy, compiler of the hugely influential *Reliques of Ancient English Poetry* (1765, four editions by 1794), and Ritson, editor and author of several antiquarian volumes, including *Ancient Songs and Ballads from the Reign of King Henry the Second to the Revolution* (1790), which was

---

[20] Ritson, "Observations on the Ancient English Minstrels," *Ancient Songs*, xxi.
[21] Susan Stewart, *Crimes of Writing*, 115.
[22] Wheatley, "General Introduction," *Reliques*, v.

offered to the public as an explicit challenge and corrective to Percy's volume. Percy's encomiastic "Essay on the Ancient Minstrels in England" (prefixed to the third edition of the *Reliques*, 1775) aroused Ritson's ire, as did Percy's habit of silently "improving" ballad texts. Bearing the stern rod of correction, Ritson offered – alongside his scrupulously edited transcriptions of ballad manuscript texts – his own "Observations on the Ancient English Minstrels."

Percy's and Ritson's writings on minstrelsy interrogated poetic and cultural authority but also raised questions of poetic form and style. Surveys of minstrels inevitably modulated into comparisons of "ancient minstrelsy" (the medieval practice and corpus) and the more recent phenomenon, "ballad-mongering" (ascendant with the Elizabethan explosion of broadsides and street songs). What separated the minstrel from the ballad-monger was the technology of print, which transformed the mediation, circulation, and ultimately, if manuscript evidence is any guide, the formal, stylistic features of balladry. In the words of Henry Wheatley, Percy's editor, "The contrast between the construction of minstrel ballads and those of the ballad-mongers who arose as a class in the reign of Elizabeth is very marked."[23] In the incredulous tones of true antiquarian partisanship, Wheatley remarked that Ritson, "with little of Percy's taste ... actually preferred the ballad-writer's songs to those of the minstrel."[24]

Percy praised the minstrel-ballads for their rough immediacy and vigor, whereas Ritson praised the smoother sonorities of the ballad-monger's material. Minstrel theorists often imagined an extended and uneasy period of poetic competition, culminating in the Elizabethan era, during which minstrels and their "rude strains" (in Scott's phrase) lost ground against the smoother productions of the ballad-mongers. Sung to popular airs, the broadside ballads proved more memorable and more circulable amongst the populace; the minstrel, droning to his harp, lost out in this imagined competition of the fittest in the poetic arena. As Joseph Ritson sardonically remarked, "The art of printing was fatal to the Minstrels who sung; people began to read, and, unfortunately for the Minstrels, their compositions would not bear reading."[25] If Ritson focused on the minstrel's changing mediation – his singing versus his being read – Walter Scott focused on

---

[23] Ibid., xxiv.   [24] Ibid., xv.

[25] Ritson, "Ancient English Minstrels," xxii. I discovered some months after finishing this book that Paula McDowell had invoked this very passage in Ritson: see her "'The Art of Printing Was Fatal': Print Culture and the Idea of Oral Tradition Eighteenth-Century Ballad Discourse," in Patricia Fumerton and Anita Guerrini, eds., *Straws in the Wind: Ballads and Broadsides 1500–1800* (forthcoming Ashgate Press, 2008).

the minstrel's *situation*: "The invention of printing necessarily occasioned the downfall of the Order of Minstrels, already reduced to contempt by their bad habits, by the disrepute attached to their profession, and by the laws calculated to repress their license."[26]

At the heart of the minstrel controversy lay this question: was the minstrel a *poet*? It is striking, if perhaps inevitable, that this question was determined by modern – that is, by literate, capitalized, commodified, individualistic – conceptions of that category, "poet." For oral or even primarily chirographic cultures, the rift between "singer" and "poet" may well be inconceivable: they are identical roles. Yet for eighteenth-century antiquarians hot on the trail of genuine "relics" as well as theories of poetic production, transmission, and circulation, the question of whether the minstrel was a celebrated "poet" – that is, a composer, originator, inventor – of *his own* verses, vs. a degraded retailer of others' – was important not only for historical reasons but for aesthetic, social, and nationalistic ones as well.

Walter Scott was still rehearsing this debate in 1830, when he appended his "Introductory Remarks on Popular Poetry" to the "Magnum Opus" edition of his *Minstrelsy*. In response to Percy's contention that the minstrels were "an order of men in the middle ages, who subsisted by the arts of poetry and music, and sung to the harp the verses which they themselves composed," Ritson offered (in Scott's words) a "determined opposition": "He contended, and probably with justice, that the minstrels were not necessarily poets, or in the regular habit of composing the verses which they sung to the harp; and indeed, that the word *minstrel*, in its ordinary acceptation, meant no more than musician."[27]

Taking the characteristically middle road, Scott summed up the anti-quarian debate:

The debate, therefore, resembles the apologue of the gold and silver shield. Dr. Percy looked on the minstrel in the palmy and exalted state to which, no doubt, *many were elevated by their talents, like those who possess excellence in the fine arts in the present day*; and Ritson considered the reverse of the medal, when the poor and wandering glee-man was glad to purchase his bread by singing his ballads at the ale-house, wearing a fantastic habit, and latterly sinking into a mere crowder upon an untuned fiddle, accompanying his rude strains with a ruder ditty.[28] (emphasis added)

---

[26] Scott, "Essay on Imitations of the Ancient Ballad," *MSB*, 179.
[27] Scott, "On Popular Poetry," *MSB*, 11.   [28] Ibid., 12.

Scott's ideal minstrel emerges, in such a passage, as a supremely talented professional who moves to the front ranks of his profession, which is largely populated with mediocrities: this is one description Scott might have offered, if he hadn't been so ostentatiously averse to controversy, of his own career. Scott's turn to "the present day" in this passage is notable: as a writer who first gained literary fame as a collector and imitator of ancient ballads, he was deeply immersed and invested in the stakes of what we might call the antiquarian analogy, that between minstrel and poet. The debate about English minstrels had obvious relevance for a poet intent on finding both a usable past and a bankable literary future in Scottish border minstrelsy, both ancient and modern. And it is no coincidence that after his first success with his collection, *Minstrelsy of the Scottish Border* (1802–3), Scott made a second major literary splash with *The Lay of the Last Minstrel* (1805), the first major work in which Scott appeared as "author" and not, as he had in the *Minstrelsy*, as "Editor."

The most striking theoretical contribution of the minstrel controversy lies in its vexing of the poet. As Susan Stewart notes, "The minstrel origins theory legitimates thereby the professional status of the bard/author." Yet such legitimation worked only if (a) one imagined the minstrel to be an elevated inventor (viz. Percy) or at the very least a highly prized reciter and repository of tradition (viz. Scott), and (b) the contemporary poet styled his work as somehow continuous with the work of minstrelsy. If most writers on minstrel origins focused on the minstrel's legitimizing appeal, nevertheless it was true that to address the question of minstrel origins was to risk emphasizing the differences and discontinuities between the minstrel and the modern professional author. The theory of minstrel origins encoded as well a theory of minstrel ends; and as we have seen, the last minstrels were often represented as decrepit figures, authentic relics valued but also highly differentiated from latter-day minstrelling-authors such as Scott. As a liminal figure, the minstrel hovered on the edge of orality; as a historical figure he mediated the imagined feudal past and the implicitly commercial present.

"Minstrel origins theory" could serve to consolidate cultural nationalism (Percy's markedly English and Scott's specifically Scottish minstrels) but could also provide a usable past for a British present and future (local, regional, and national minstrels subsumed in a grand imperial narrative).[29]

---

[29] On the mutable and often surprising valences of national/imperial relations in minstrelsy, see Simpson, "Minstrelsy Goes to Market." As Simpson notes, minstrelsy could work just as effectively to thwart as to endorse cultural nationalism, "Englishness" and "Scottishness" (and, less often, "Irishness" and "Welshness") put forth precisely to be subsumed within a triumphal British cultural imaginary.

When considering minstrel ends – the solicitation and "noticing" of raconteurs, balladeers, urban "crowders" and rural balladeers – we can see that minstrelsy offered writers other means for cultural and poetic authorization. Mindful of the ethnographic turn in balladeering, we might consider the figure of the "very lately living" minstrel as a native informant as much as a naïve historian. As Scott's work best shows, to invoke minstrel-informants was to make a bid for ethnographic authority. The claim to authenticity, in the case of minstrelsy, derives from the minstrel's imagined organic relation to his tradition, his unmediated access to his material, his embeddedness in place; the modern writer's authority rests on his having such authentic informants, with their authentic materials transmitted in culturally authoritative ways. Minstrelsy thus provides the occasion for a confluence of two projects, antiquarian revival and ethnographic fieldwork.

TOWARD A MINSTRELSY COMPLEX: SPECIFYING THE ELEMENTS

For antiquarians the minstrel debate involved several different points of contention: the social status and function of the minstrel, the nature of his "making" (inventing or merely reciting), the causes of his degradation, the historicity of his medium, and the relative merits of his productions versus those of his successor, the ballad-monger. The antiquarians thus contended over the following issues:
– The definition of minstrels, including the definition of their functions.
– The place of the minstrel in social and cultural life.
– The strengths and weaknesses of minstrel-measures, forms, and styles.
– The status of the minstrel as a medium.
These issues constituted what I have called a minstrelsy complex. At this point I offer several additional working propositions about minstrelsy; we will arrive more formally at these propositions, and their variants, as we move through the next sections of this chapter. But for now, a preliminary offering, the implications of which must exceed the scope of this chapter but which inform the discussions throughout this book:
1 Minstrelsy is a kind of *poiesis.*
2 The minstrel may or may not be a poet.
3 In their persons, performances, and songs, Minstrels testify.
4 Minstrels are always already framed.
5 Represented as both singing songs and the objects of song-theory, minstrels are characterized by a theoretical transitivity.

6 Minstrels mediate and are mediated. If poets take on the job of cultural mediation, they involve themselves in metaphorical minstrelsy.

7 To invoke minstrelsy is, for a Romantic poet as well as for a twenty-first-century critic, to confront the historicity of poetry.

8 In Romantic poems, minstrelsy may be displayed but also may be silently metabolized, or suppressed, or otherwise deflected.

9 Minstrels may be historicized; minstrels may be allegorized; minstrels may be analogized.

10 The relation between minstrelsy and Romanticism may be imagined as that between tenor and vehicle, although which serves as which is open to question.

11 Minstrelsy offers both a history of artifactualization and the promise of perpetual oralization. To represent minstrelsy is to oscillate between two poles: reification and dispersal. These poles are also, intriguingly, the poles of Romantic poetry and theory.

12 To write about minstrelsy is to participate in minstrelsy.

13 Minstrelsy traverses several discourses and genres: in the first instance, it appears as the cultural work proper to oral poets. Minstrels accomplish this work, according to minstrel theory, by reciting traditional poems in traditional performance contexts to traditional audiences. Reconstructed minstrelsy interrogates – even as it represents – every aspect of this cultural work: the form, style, and medium of the poems (i.e. their composition), the context of performance, the authority of performers, the nature of the audience. By the eighteenth century, this first-order minstrelsy is accessible only in its decadent phase, through the speech and remembrance of men and women represented as living relics. Yet each successive mediation of minstrelsy – whether through transcribing ballads, ransacking manuscripts, printing relics, commenting upon them, imitating them, or theorizing them – may also be seen as an extension of minstrelsy.

14 If minstrelsy eludes reification, the representation of minstrelsy requires it.

15 Romantic poetry may be seen as minstrelsy by other means.

In my use of "minstrelsy" here I include the entire range of representations – antiquarian "notices" of minstrels bygone or "very lately living"; Romantic representations of minstrelsy; contemporary scholars' investigations into ballad scandals and the broader vexations of literary culture in eighteenth- and nineteenth-century Britain; my own musings on minstrelsy and the broader critical discussion of it. The extension of this range indicates another aspect of minstrelsy, its tendency to disperse, migrate, wander, and transform itself.

HOW TO REVIVE A MINSTREL: SCOTT'S MINSTRELSY
AND THE CASE OF POETRY

How to use minstrelsy? How to be used by it? Scott's contemporaries asked and answered this question differently. Scott's minstrelsy presumed that the antiquarian project could be redeemed for modern, "original," poetry. In this commitment he was, as he surely recognized, the secret heir of James Macpherson. In his 1830 essay on "Imitations of the Ancient Ballad," Scott rather blithely finessed the question of Macpherson's Ossian poems: "Macpherson was rather an excellent poet than a faithful editor or translator."[30] Macpherson had represented himself, however, precisely as a collector, translator, and transmitter of actual Gaelic fragments and epics; therein lay the scandal of his invention, or at the very least, his heavy remediation, of the poems. As Scott well knew, the appeal and prestige of the Ossian poems lay, in the first instance, in their claim to authenticity *as* retrieved relics of a bardic past. The Ossian controversy made it plain that, under some circumstances, a writer would prefer to appear in the literary public sphere as a translator or editor rather than as a poet. By transforming Macpherson's project into an anticipation of his own, Scott both displayed and sidestepped the very questions of authenticity and authority Macpherson's poems raised. Scott took the bad conscience of the Ossian poems and made it legitimate.

Minstrels, actual and fictive, appear everywhere in Scott's work. *The Lay of the Last Minstrel* (1805) was – as noted in the previous chapter – Scott's first extended attempt to harness minstrelsy to his own efforts at literary self-authorization and legitimation. *The Lay* presents a depressed and decrepit seventeenth-century minstrel, "last of his race," who comes to Newark Tower, finds its lady and her attendants still there, and hesitantly agrees to sing a lay of the noble family's previously high fortunes – a song of the sixteenth century. The minstrel's story has several narrative strands, including a forbidden love between the Scottish Margaret of Branksome Hall and the English Baron Henry of Cranstoun, who belong to rivalrous Border clans; the supernatural mischief of the Baron's Dwarf, a shape-shifting "goblin-page"; and the appearance on the Border of invading Englishmen, who manage to unite the Scottish clans in defense of the young heir to Branksome Hall. All turns out well: the English agree to single combat, which Henry (in disguise) wins. The lovers marry, the heir remains in his Hall, and the goblin-page is unmasked and defeated upon the late revival of the undead and formidable

---

[30] Walter Scott, "Essay on Imitations of the Ancient Ballad," *MSB*, 187–8.

wizard, Michael Scott. If this sounds unwieldy, it is, but *The Lay* is also a briskly paced story, vigorously and dramatically told in six cantos, with judicious splashes of violence, sentiment, and titillation.[31]

For the purposes of this discussion, the plot-content of the minstrel's lay matters less than the elaborate protocols of representation Scott devised, the poem's formal and metrical display, and its narratological ingenuity – an ingenuity informed by Scott's historiographic fluencies, as explored in the previous chapter. A complex yet fluent work, *The Lay* gleefully exploits the figure of the minstrel, the theme of minstrelsy, and the poetic forms appropriate to minstrelsy. Through the minstrel-device, Scott explicitly explores composition-in-performance, audience response, the nature of mediation, and the status of the oral poet as benighted professional – matters which had preoccupied literary antiquarians since the 1760s. Scott was able as well to demonstrate a formal virtuosity and range of ballad styles, as when in the sixth canto, at the marriage feast of Margaret of Branksome and Henry of Cranstoun, Scott's minstrel presents three songs sung by the minstrels at that long-ago feast, each song meant to exemplify a different ballad stanza and balladeering *mentalité*. *The Lay of the Last Minstrel* offers an extensive and layered résumé, then, of the romantic "minstrelsy complex."

Within *The Lay* itself, Scott provides an extended representation and critique of an oral poet in action: a poet attentive to and anxious about audience, composing while performing, re-composing and indeed becoming the song as he sings it once again. Scott's minstrel has several ostentatiously self-reflexive moments when he pauses to reflect on his song, other versions of it, how he came to be fluent in it. The minstrel understands his lay, his corpus, to be an inherited one, and he foregrounds its transmission, his narrative flagged as a tradition learned from another: a "jovial Harper" "taught" him while "yet a youth." This past moment of learning is converted into the "now" of the minstrel's saying: "In guise which now I say" (Canto 4, st. 34). The minstrel, then, understands his lay as a recreation of previous lays, a saying of the same again.[32] For the minstrel, there is no difference between historical and song traditions. The minstrel participates

---

[31] This poem has found a striking number of incisive readers in recent years: see Margaret Russett in *Fictions and Fakes: Forging Romantic Authenticity, 1760–1845* (Cambridge University Press, 2005), Ch. 3, "Unconscious Plagiarism: From "Christabel" to *The Lay of the Last Minstrel*," 70–90; Celeste Langan on the poem's media wizardry in "Understanding Media in 1805," and Susan Oliver's *Scott, Byron, and the Poetics of Cultural Encounter*, 71–82. All current readings are indebted to Nancy Goslee's illuminating discussion of the poem in *Scott the Rhymer*, which for years stood as the rare book-length reckoning with Scott's poetry.

[32] Gregory Nagy argues that the "mimesis" of oral performance should be understood as "dramatic re-enactment." See Nagy, *Poetry as Performance*, 4.

in the competitive ethos of the warrior culture he celebrates: he trumpets his account as one different from, and superior to, "the lay" of other minstrels. An unapologetic rivalry emerges clearly as the engine of minstrelsy, the minstrel's competitive spirit as traditional as his lay. As he proudly reports in Canto IV, his own teacher refused to tolerate "scoffing tongue[s]," and quite readily annihilated bardic adversaries: "The Bard of Reull he slew" (st. 34). "Tuneful hands were stain'd with blood," his former student declares, apparently cheerfully.

The minstrel acknowledges, however, that the romance of continuous transmission, of rivalrous making, is over: he has outlasted his teacher and the bardic community which had heretofore guaranteed the meaningful singing of his song:

> XXXV.
> Who died at Jedwood Air?
> He died! – his scholars, one by one,
> To the cold silent grave are gone;
> And I, alas! survive alone
> To muse o'er rivalries of yore,
> And grieve that I shall hear no more
> The strains, with envy heard before;
> For, with my minstrel brethren fled,
> My jealousy of song is dead.

The lament for the "master" is also a lament for minstrel- and warrior-culture, the end of productive rivalry: "my jealousy of song is dead." It is striking to see that signal romantic lament – "And I, alas! survive alone" – emerge in this context. The minstrel exists as an "I" only inasmuch as he emerges as one of a minstrel band, a band of warrior-scholars. Scott's historicized minstrels, that is, lack individuality, personhood, interiority, subjectivity: they are the vectors of culture, mediums *par excellence*. Having his minstrel reflect on his cultural predicament, Scott develops a theoretically informed and powerful image: that of a native-informant minstrel-maker who can report and meditate as it were "authentically" on oral poetry, song-culture, and its rivalrous ethos – an image the particulars of which contemporary oral theory seems to confirm.

The minstrel's consciousness of his own obsolescence seems to affect his very performance: the cultural supports of his minstrelsy having failed, his own song threatens to collapse as well. An abject minstrelsy emerges, as we see the hapless minstrel at the end of his first "fitt": "gazing timid on the crowd,/He seemed to seek, in every eye,/ If they approved his minstrelsy" (Canto I). For this last minstrel, performance is an arduous task, hesitantly begun and then ecstatically, albeit erratically, continued:

> Amid the strings his fingers stray'd,
> And an uncertain warbling made,
> And oft he shook his hoary head.
> But when he caught the measure wild,
> The old man raised his face, and smiled;
> And lighten'd up his faded eye,
> With all a poet's ecstasy!
> In varying cadence, soft or strong,
> He swept the sounding chords along;
> The present scene, the future lot,
> His toils, his wants, were all forgot:
> Cold diffidence, and age's frost,
> In the full tide of his song were lost;
> And blank in faithless memory void,
> The poet's glowing thought supplied;
> And, while his harp responsive rung,
> 'Twas thus the Latest Minstrel sung.

Such a passage relies, characteristically, on a kind of poetic filter. Scott represents the minstrel's strumming "in varying cadence," at various dynamics ("soft or strong"), finally catching "the measure wild"; such a picture emerges, however, through the medium of Scott's own highly regulated measures, cast in writing and ultimately print, in a more or less standard English, unaccompanied by harp or even, if we are silently reading the lay, audible voice. We have no direct access to such variation in force or volume: we register instead Scott's careful distribution of varying metrics – which he derived in part (and infamously) from the model of "Christabel," and which he discussed in detail (and partly in defense) in his later preface to the poem. Scott's intense focus on the minstrel's activity – his tuning up, his physical movements, his playing, his "uncertain warbling," his anxious consciousness of the audience, his "ecstasy," his intermittent depressions throughout the lay – casts a strange and ambiguous halo over the poem. If the poem often condescends to this minstrel – "infirm and old," barely able to get his harp tuned and his measures flowing – nevertheless the poem ultimately articulates its primary narrative content through this decrepit figure, whom Scott tells us he introduced as a "prolocutor" or "pitch-pipe" "by whom the lay might be sung, or spoken" – a mouthpiece meant to help modern readers more easily swallow the legendary stuff of the poem.[33] (That the lay "might be sung, or spoken": Scott nods here to the antiquarian

---

[33] For Scott's decision to use the minstrel as a framing device, see his "Introduction to 'The Lay of the Last Minstrel,'" *Poetical Works*, 315.

disputes over minstrel recitation. Among some options: droning to a harp, pitched singing, or a kind of *sprechstimme*).

In such passages, Scott takes great pains to represent the oral poet's embodied relation to the audience (conspicuously marked as both noble and female), a relation in which face-to-face contact and immediate somatic feedback are the conditions of recitation and performance. Scott thus marks the historical distance between the situation of the minstrel's recitation and his own poem, bound as it eventually was in printed books, destined for a literate audience of thousands – an audience of men as well as women, of Englishmen as well as Scotsmen, of learned as well as unlearned readers, of lawyers, merchants, academics, and farmers as well as aristocrats. At the level of minstrel metaphorics, then, Scott creates a space for constituting, doubling, differentiating, and historicizing the relation of poet-to-audience. Remembering days when he used to pour out "to lord and lady gay,/The unpremeditated lay," this rather doleful specimen sings a lay that is doubly "of the Last Minstrel" – a lay sung *by* him but also, by virtue of Scott's astonishing poetic and historiographic fluencies, a lay *about* him. Inasmuch as the lay is *his* lay, part of his minstrel-stock, and perhaps *the only lay* the last minstrel now possesses, the lay of the last minstrel is "of" him in yet a third sense. The punning condensation in the preposition "of" offers an allegory in miniature of Scott's interest in the pre-position of the poet, in the poet's *case*.

Scott repeatedly explored minstrelsy as a function of performance situation, contexts themselves historicized and localized as he saw fit. Throughout his romances, as in the *Minstrelsy*, Scott shows listeners responding to, and often *judging*, the poems they hear; almost never do his minstrels or singers sing alone, to or for themselves. Rather, Scott orients us to the communal reception of poetry in specific, elaborate contexts: the focus on highly elaborated dramatic situations gives us a kind of phantasmatic micro-history of minstrelsy-in-action. Thus in the final canto of *The Lay of the Last Minstrel*, the three songs of the marriage feast dramatize the competitive song-making ethos imagined to prevail among minstrels in noble houses; as Francis Jeffrey observed in his review of the poem, each song was meant to illustrate a *poiesis* proper to a period of society (and here again, we see the profound impact of Scottish sociological history on Scott): "It is the author's object, in these songs, to exemplify the different styles of ballad narrative which prevailed in this island at different periods, or in different conditions of society."[34] The first minstrel effort, Albert Graeme's border ballad, offers – in a simple meter, with refrain and additive style – a

[34] Francis Jeffrey, quoted in Lockhart's notes to *The Lay of the Last Minstrel, Poetical Works*, 350.

song that would seem particularly relevant to the immediate occasion of his song: his ballad, just as Scott's romance, tells the story of a union across the border:

> It was an English ladye bright
> (The sun shines on Carlisle wall)
> And she would marry a Scottish knight,
> For love will still be lord of all.

Yet if Margaret and Henry are successfully joined in Scott's *Lay*, Albert Graeme's couple are foiled by the lady's brother, who "swore her death, ere he would see/A Scottish knight the lord of all!" (*Lay* 6.XI, 350). Brother poisons sister, sister dies, suitor slays brother, goes on Crusade, and dies himself: all within three stanzas. The internally sung ballad thus offers a striking tragic variation on the tale-type Scott's *Lay* itself navigates to a more benign resolution.

Beyond Scott's brilliant mobilization of traditionary scenes, plot-elements, and formulas – the jealous or vengeful brother a staple of several love-gone-wrong ballads in Francis James Child's compendium – he has accomplished at least two things: through Albert Graeme, he recasts the outlines of his own border romance into a simple ballad meter, yet he also demonstrates the gulf between his historical romance and this mode of traditionary balladry ("romantic ballads," as he classified them in his *Minstrelsy*) – between his own poem, committed to a code of elaborate historical reference and metrical innovation, and Graeme's song, metrically conservative and largely devoid of much specificity but for the locale, Carlisle.

The song that follows Graeme's marks an advance both in minstrel technique (appreciated within the poem) and historical period: its singer is Fitzraver, bard of Henry, Earl of Surrey, himself famous as the first exponent of the sonnet in English: "As ended Albert's simple lay/Arose a bard of loftier port;/For sonnet, rhyme, and roundelay,/Renowned in haughty Henry's court" (6.XIII). Fitzraver's song features a far more elaborate meter – the Spenserian stanza, in fact – and reads like nothing so much as an anticipation of Keats' "Isabella, or, the Pot of Basil": "'Twas All-soul's eve, and Surrey's heart beat high/He heard the midnight bell with anxious start." (That Fitzraver sings in Spenserian stanzas is an intriguing case of anachronism.) We have moved here into courtly romance, from oral tradition into the elaborate cultivations of Tudor poetry – itself typically circulated in manuscript. Even as the "Scots, and Southern chiefs" applaud Fitzraver's song, which veers from Surrey's love for Geraldine into a diatribe against Henry VIII ("Thou jealous, ruthless tyrant!"), yet another singer rises: Harold, one familiar with "many a Saga's rhyme uncouth," with the poetry of Scalds – and thus Scott has an opportunity to present a more martial, vigorous poem, which ends – as all these set-pieces do – on a piteous note, with a lover dead.

Through his minstrel contest Scott both displays the metrical varieties of and within romance and offers a mini-history of society as a progress-of-poetry; he extends the range of *poiesis* from the Borders to Northern Europe and shows himself a virtuoso of modes, meters, styles, and imagines the contexts in which a particular singer might have acquired or displayed them. Embedded in larger narratives, these set-pieces constantly show us *what poetry is for*, within the narrative, and suggest *how it came to be*, in terms of specified cultural contexts – oral traditionary communities, the Tudor court, Nordic seafarers. Within the narrative, such performed poetry aims both to entertain and to make a bid for aristocratic recognition of poetic supremacy; as narrative episodes themselves, these poems stimulate a series of listener responses and mood changes, such that we are as stunned as the wedding guests in *The Lay of the Last Minstrel* when "sudden, through the darken'd air" lightning strikes and reveals the goblin page (part of the earlier supernatural machinery) struck dead. On this sober note the poem soon closes.

Throughout his romances, particularly in *The Lady of the Lake* (1810) and *Rokeby* (1813), Scott incorporates song, ballad, and story, his set-pieces always alive to the cultural and historical conditions of *poiesis* even as they often ingeniously further his plots. As a Highland romance, *The Lady of The Lake* allows Scott to try out various Gaelic genres, including the coronach, or lament, which Scott had earlier tried his hand at in the *Minstrelsy*. *The Lady of the Lake* features a Highland bard, a minstrel, "white haired Allen-bane" (2.I.445), who seems a dry run for the Highland bard in *Waverley* (1814). Unlike the pathetical, self-consciously residual minstrel of *The Lay of the Last Minstrel*, Allen-bane is wholly contemporary to the action, not a relic but a participant, an index of the vital relationship between a people and its poets. That such a connection was imaginable only in a now inaccessible Highland past bears, of course, its own pointed irony, of which Scott was wholly aware. And here again we see that Scott's ballad turn serves several purposes, both intrinsic and extrinsic, as it were, to the poem: Allen-bane sings the heroine, Ellen, a song, an extended set-piece, the ballad "Alice Brand": "The minstrel tried his simple art/But distant far was Ellen's heart" (4.XV.464). Here Scott's antiquarian hand floridly shows itself, for "this little fairy tale," as he calls it in his note, "is founded upon a very curious Danish ballad" – "The Elfin Gray," the translation of which, from Robert Jamieson's translation from the *Kaempe Viser*, Scott publishes in full in his notes to *The Lady of the Lake*, followed by "The Ghaist's Warning," also taken from Jamieson. If in the notes, the antiquarian editorial procedures of the *Minstrelsy* have continued full force, in the romance proper, Allen-bane and Ellen attend to "Alice Brand," only to be surprised out of their reverie by the sudden reappearance of a hero, James Fitz-James. Significant here is Scott's ability to maintain and display several registers of poetic meaning, interest, and function: the ballad functions as a potentially soothing, distracting narrative for Ellen within the poem, while also appearing in the notes as a curious specimen of Danish poetry, of supernatural poetry, and as the product of translation (by Jamieson) and then adaptation (by Scott).

Scott's wizardly poetics thus encompasses the complex formal, historical, medial, and cultural charges of *poiesis*: his lays are both romances and readings of romance, his minstrelsy both enmeshed in tradition (literary and oral) and a meditation on tradition. At several points in his romances, Scott makes plain where his minstrels lapse (e.g. the last minstrel in *The Lay* thereof, sometimes unable to get his harp going), or where a certain "strain" has been superseded (e.g. Albert Graeme's song bested by Fitzraver's): yet these seem not so much judgments of taste as recognitions of historicity. Most important, we can see that in Scott's hands, the case of minstrelsy becomes a super-subtle instrument for sounding out *the case of poetry itself* – a recognition that has resonance far beyond his own corpus.

HOW TO KILL A MINSTREL: WORDSWORTH'S "SONG, AT THE FEAST OF BROUGHAM CASTLE" AND "HART-LEAP WELL"

Let us consider the rare poem in which Wordsworth explicitly presented and spoke through a minstrel figure: "Song, at the Feast of Brougham Castle, upon the Restoration of Lord Clifford, the Shepherd, to the Estates and Honours of his Ancestors."[35] Set during the Wars of the Roses, the poem presents a minstrel who sings during a reconciliation dinner. Wordsworth briskly sets the scene and lets his minstrel launch his song:

---

[35] See "Song, at the Feast of Brougham Castle, upon the Restoration of Lord Clifford, the Shepherd, to the Estates and Honours of his Ancestors," 1807, in *Poems, in Two Volumes*, 259–64. Quotations from this poem will be cited in text by line.

> High in the breathless Hall the Minstrel sate,
> And Emont's murmur mingled with the Song.–
> The words of ancient time I thus translate,
> A festal Strain that has been silent long.
>
> From Town to Town, from Tower to Tower,
> The Red Rose is a gladsome flower.
> Her thirty years of winter past,
> The Red Rose is revived at last ... (ll. 1–8)

In his opening lines, Wordsworth deftly distinguishes the minstrel's situation from his own. What the minstrel sang, he will "thus translate." The translation involves both linguistic and historical mediations: the "festal Strain ... has been silent long." What we hear is a re-animation, a re-vocalization, the represented mediation of which is the work of the poem, just as it is in Scott's *Lay*. Note how efficiently Wordsworth accomplishes a number of effects in these opening lines and introduces his major formal device: the shift from long measure quatrains to heavily accented four-beat rhyming couplets, the minstrel's own measure (the very measure, we might recall, that Scott rejected for his own minstrel). This shift marks in meter and in form the distance he expressly names between the framing poet-narrator and the minstrel as framed narrator. Wordsworth both thematizes and formalizes the break between the translating "I" and the minstrel: the "I" articulates itself through the stately measures of the elegiac quatrain, a noble ballad measure which barely establishes its governing pace before the Minstrel song begins, in jangling minstrel-couplets, replete with hoary minstrel clichés ("from tower to tower," "gladsome flower").

Securely launched in the minstrel's narration, we hear the story of Lord Clifford, our fifteenth-century hero, dispossessed, endangered, his father slain, a victim of the violence of the Wars of the Roses. Yet the Cliffords must by the end of the minstrel's narration be restored: he sings, after all, at the celebratory restoration feast honoring the young Clifford. As always in reconstructed minstrelsy, the presentation of context is an essential part of the text: the minstrel situates Clifford's life within the strife and ultimate reconciliation of the houses of Lancaster and York, a reconciliation which is the precondition for the restoration both on the level of story (what happened) but also on the level of representation (the minstrel mimicry). The minstrel commemorates the restoration and salutes the Lady and the restored Lord:

> The two that were at strife are blended,
> And all old troubles now are ended.–

> Joy! joy to both! but most to her
> Who is the flower of Lancaster!

Wordsworth energetically pursues the minstrel narration through all its stereotypical functions and commitments: its celebration of aristocracy, chivalry, genealogy, romance, and martial vigor. The minstrel imagines the ancestral weapons clamoring for their noble lord, no longer a child, to put them to good use:

> "Quell the Scot," exclaims the Lance –
> Bear me to the heart of France,
> Is the longing of the Shield –
> Tell thy name, thou trembling Field;
> Field of death, where'er thou be,
> Groan thou with our victory! (ll. 148–53)

This rather comic series of exclamations has roused the minstrel, and the poem, to a kind of fury. And it is here, at the height of the jingoistic clanging of the weapons' voices, resounding through the minstrel's voice, that Wordsworth abruptly changes course.

The minstrel ventriloquizes the weapons' salute to the lord only to be superseded by the return of the Wordsworthian narrator, with his own "Alas!," his own meter, and his own measure, that is to say, his own judgment:

> Alas! The fervent Harper did not know
> That for a tranquil Soul the Lay was framed,
> Who, long compell'd in humble walks to go,
> Was softened into feeling, sooth'd, and tamed.
>
> Love had he found in huts where poor Men lie;
> His daily Teachers had been Woods and Rills,
> The silence that is in the starry sky,
> The sleep that is among the lonely hills.
>
> In him the savage virtues of the Race,
> Revenge, and all ferocious thoughts were dead:
> Nor did he change; but kept in lofty place
> The wisdom which adversity had bred.
>
> Glad were the Vales, and every cottage hearth;
> The Shepherd Lord was honoured more and more;
> And, ages after he was laid in earth,
> "The Good Lord Clifford" was the name he bore. (ll. 161–76)

Returning to his opening measures, Wordsworth re-establishes the initial and now starkly authoritative voice of the poet–translator. He reveals the

song to have been framed with a difference: what had initially seemed a
presentation, albeit translated, of the minstrel at the hall is now revealed to
be a representation of a past event – to wit, the minstrel's singing of his
misdirected restoration song. Wordsworth purposely renders the minstrel
song *as a fragment*: the poem breaks off its presentation, first figured as a
faithful translation, to veer into critique. We might contrast the minstrel's
ostentatiously formulaic "Alas!" lament – "Alas! When evil men are strong/
No life is good, no pleasure long" – with the Wordsworthian narrator's. The
minstrel's lament is twice repeated (viz. lines 89–90 and 106–7), as if to
emphasize its formulaic quality – its status as easily available metrical
"filler." Wordsworth's "Alas" marks the return of the historically and poetically reflective narrating consciousness. Wordsworth's "Alas!," the signal
exclamation of lament and regret, is here aimed not at bad men, nor the
passing of the heroic age, nor even at the obsolescence of the minstrel, but
rather at *the minstrel's misdirection of his song*: "Alas! The fervent Harper did
not know/That for a tranquil Soul the Lay was framed." The minstrel got it
wrong. He was singing the wrong story to the wrong person in, we now see
and hear, the wrong measure. His dependence on an antique stock of motifs
and phrases led him into the wrong kind of poetic frenzy, a comically and
pathetically ventriloquial violence: Quell the Scot! Exclaims the Lance. If in
Scott's *Lay* the minstrel is deeply solicitous of and anxiously attuned to his
audience, Wordsworth's harper deeply misjudges his:

> Alas! The fervent Harper did not know
> That for a tranquil Soul the Lay was framed,
> Who, long compell'd in humble walks to go,
> Was softened into feeling, sooth'd, and tamed.

Wordsworth's Lord Clifford is no war-like victor of a feudal code of
revenge, as the Harper presumes: the Lord stands, rather, as a proleptic
emblem of Wordsworthian humanization, a "softened," "soothed," and
"tamed" soul. In good stadial fashion, the good Lord Clifford has passed
through his own pastoral stage (viz. the shepherd exile) to emerge as a
guarantor of civil society. If Scott commemorated, through a sanitizing
historicizing scrim, the savage and tempestuous appeal of border chieftains
and unruly clans, Wordsworth here decisively turns away from this appeal,
writing the epitaph of its sensibility and ethos:

> In him the savage virtues of the Race,
> Revenge, and all ferocious thoughts were dead.

The hapless minstrel chants himself unwittingly into obsolescence, singing
"dead" virtues as if they were live. Through this figure Wordsworth offers a

negative critique, carving out by negation the space a modern poet might inhabit and sound out through his meters. Intriguingly, Wordsworth makes plain that it is the minstrel here who is retrograde, not the pacified Lord. This careful management suggests a canny acknowledgment: the aristocracy, albeit not aristocratic minstrels, had persisted unto 1807 – and should ever persist, if humanized, according to the broader ideologics of the poem.

"Song at the Feast of Brougham Castle" revives minstrelsy, then, in order to kill it: to display minstrelsy is here to put it under critique. Wordsworth's poem offers a critical insight. The poem focuses on the lag between poetic commitments and social progress; casting this drama into the fifteenth century, he allegorizes the predicament of the modern poet, who must figure out how to stand regarding his poetic past as well as his ethico-political present. Not the glamor of minstrelsy and of medieval history but its bumptious tragi-comedy, its fatal aporias: this Wordsworth presents.

A misdirected, superannuated, historically superseded and metrically displaced minstrel: by presenting and critiquing such a figure Wordsworth critically enacts his own poetics of humanization and suggests other modern ends for poetry than the praise and blame of presiding rulers – the oldest and most enduring function of poets, as Peacock tartly reminded his readers in his 1820 "Four Ages of Poetry," and as ethno-poetic scholarship continues to suggest. From this vantage, it is true, it is hard to see how "Brougham Castle," a flattering genealogical poem aimed at Wordsworth's aristocratic neighbors and possible patrons, is significantly different from Scott's *Lay of the Last Minstrel*, in which both last minstrel (in the seventeenth century) and Scott himself (in the early nineteenth) look to the Buccleuchs for patronage. For all Wordsworth's stunning meditations on poetry and power, and poetry-as-power (as in signal passages in *The Prelude*), and for all his witty thrashing of the abject minstrel-poet (who in singing songs to glorify aristocratic patrons is quite seriously merely trying to do his job, and well), we should not look to "Brougham Castle" for a strong critique of Wordsworth's own relation to local aristocratic powers.

What we get in "Brougham Castle," instead, is a metrical encoding of socio-poetic supercession; in this, "Brougham Castle" shares the broader periodizing concerns of Scott's *Lay*. But strikingly, Wordsworth's minstrel (unlike Scott's last minstrel) *performs badly within the terms of his own social context*. Social structure emerges as the determining horizon for a viable poetics in a given socio-historical epoch, yet within a given occasion or situation – say, a fifteenth-century feudal hall, or an early nineteenth-century print run – a poet may perform well, middlingly, or badly. Within a phase of cultural development, or a "period of society," as the

Scottish sociological school would have it, there are a multitude of occasions in which a poet may thrive or flounder; what minstrelsy brings home is a strong analysis of the poet and of poetry *as both occasioned and determined*. It is not surprising that minstrelling poets less certain of their social and economic position – James Hogg, say, or John Clare – would explore this binding of and through poetry from other, more urgently critical angles.

If we consider minstrelsy to be the name for a *poiesis* highly attuned to its social and cultural situation, then we can see that Wordsworth continues minstrelsy by other means, even as he subjects its medieval and traditionary forms and the revival thereof to critique. Violently suspending his minstrel's narration, Wordsworth insists on a modern poetry critically open to an incomplete past – a poetic past that must be imagined and critically remediated into a contemporary poetry. Minstrelsy is the opposite of art for art's sake; the minstrel is a poet *for the culture's or community's sake*. Wordsworth's poetics of humanization may be read as a minstrelsy transformed and perfected for "softened," "soothed, and tamed" liberalism.[36]

The Wordsworthian critique proposes a minstrelling dialectic – progressive minstrels (poets of general humanization) overcoming retrograde minstrels (poets resistant to generalized humanization), Wordsworth's quatrains subsuming, negating, and surpassing minstrel couplets. This critique resists being assimilated into a curative historicism (which is one way we might assess Scott's metrico-historiographic project). Wordsworth, that is, foregrounds the possibility that the residual (in Raymond Williams' terms) might persist long into a new dominant formation[37]: part of the work of "Brougham Castle" is to display and enforce the residual status of Clifford's minstrel, evaluated by what the poem endorses as ascendant, indeed regnant, sociopoetic values. Wordsworth had invested enormous capital in an emergent poetics, a self-proclaimed "experimental" poetics of sympathy divine, human capacity, and "the still sad music of humanity." The critical and poetic energy Wordsworth devoted to cordoning off other poetics – say, a more transparent poetics of social hierarchy – suggests his anxiety about what kind of poetry and poetic stance would indeed turn out to be residual.

---

[36] And here, as in so many other respects, we can see how the ideologics of Wordsworth's project aligns with Scott's: as in Ian Duncan's trenchant formulations about Scott's novels as generating the fictive space for liberal consent to civil society – see Duncan, "Authenticity Effects." Duncan focuses here on Scott's (vs. Hogg's) fictions, but the broader ideological work he specifies as accomplished through Scott's novels is consonant with the complex subject formation promoted throughout Wordsworth's oeuvre.

[37] For a discussion of the "residual," see Raymond Williams, *Marxism and Literature*, esp. Chapter 8, "Dominant, Residual, and Emergent," 121–7. Williams calls for an "'epochal' analysis," through which we might "seize" cultural process "as a cultural system."

Consigning certain poetries to the historical and ethical dustbin while asserting the power of his own: this is one way to understand as well the logic of "Hart-Leap Well," that *Lyrical Ballad* in which minstrels briefly appear yet again as indices of a superseded past. In part a poem about hunting, "Hart-Leap Well" is also a poem about poetry and its relation to power.[38] (It is not wholly fanciful to suggest that the poem might be called, à la John Lomax's memoir, *Adventures of a Ballad Hunter*.) In "Hart-Leap Well" we see Wordsworth mobilizing ballad form and style against what we might call an antiquarian ballad ethic. "Hart-Leap Well" stands, then, simultaneously as a monument to and a critique of balladeering.[39]

Readers may recall that the pseudo-medieval chase in part one of "Hart-Leap Well" concludes with a hunted hart leaping, terrified, to its death, after which its mesmerized hunter Sir Walter announces his plans to commemorate the spot – to acculturate it, and memorialize it:

> I'll build a Pleasure-house upon this spot,
> And a small Arbour, made for rural joy;
> 'Twill be the traveller's shed, the pilgrim's cot,
> A place of love for damsels that are coy.
>
> A cunning Artist will I have to frame
> A basin for that fountain in the dell
> And they, who do make mention of the same,
> From this day forth, shall call it Hart-Leap Well.

Sir Walter's monumentalizing impulse emerges as a species of remembrance. In his memorializing plans Wordsworth gives us a kind of poetic etiology on the naming of places – exactly the kind of back-formation antiquarians loved to traffic in.

The culminating image of knightly delight features minstrels, dancers, and a paramour, all cavorting at the dread "spot" where the Hart died:

---

[38] See David Perkins, "Wordsworth and the Polemic Against Hunting: 'Hart-Leap Well,'" *Nineteenth-Century Literature*, 52:4 (March 1998): 421–45.

[39] In "The Politics of 'Hart-Leap Well," *Charles Lamb Bulletin* NS 111 (July 2000): 109–19, David Chandler offers a reading of the poem as a meditation on and critique of romance as well as Wordsworth's youthful commitments. Chandler reads "Sir Walter" as a kind of young Wordsworth manqué under sympathetic critique: "In so far as Sir Walter represents the young, 'savage' Wordsworth the question became, as it would in *Home at Grasmere*, one of inheritance, continuity, and the preservation of high – but transformed – ideals. More pointedly: could the young disciple of French 'Liberty' be redeemed?" (113). Chandler's reading, while far more sympathetic to the Wordsworthian trajectory, echoes aspects of Marjorie Levinson's influential reading of Wordsworth's Immortality Ode as an autobiographical reckoning with the "fading light" of French hopes.

> And thither, when the summer days were long,
> Sir Walter journey'd with his paramour;
> And with the dancer's and the minstrel's song
> Made merriment within that pleasant bower.

In part two of the poem, such "merriment" comes in for strong critique, both by the shepherd informant who re-tells the story, imagining the dying hart's thoughts, and the poet-interlocutor, who ultimately instructs the shepherd that they, unlike Sir Walter and his minions, share a common ethic: "sympathy divine." In its critique of the ballad pageantry of part one, fully visible only in retrospect, "Hart-Leap Well" transforms a hunting ballad into a balladized progress-poem – or rather, the progress-poem here finds its ballad *métier*. Among the necessary casualties of this operation are Sir Walter's minstrels, wanton celebrators of power, presumably as unable as Sir Walter to subscribe to the doctrine of "sympathy divine" that underwrites the modern poet's legitimacy.

Sir Walter is hardly a primitive hunter: he is rather imagined as an extremely cultivated savorer of artful displays of power. He is a back-formation of modernity, a figure of modern romance as Ian Duncan has so helpfully defined it – "romance as modern culture's construction of a symbolic form prior to itself."[40] This definition could be applied to the late-eighteenth- and nineteenth-century ballad itself, and more broadly to romantic minstrelsy *tout court*. It is also true that skeptical readers could find in the Wordsworthian narrator's quite typical arrival in part two of this ballad at a shepherd-informant and a shared *moralitas* – the "sympathy divine" that displaces Sir Walter's "joy" in the hart's fate – not so much an advance to a fantasized equalitarian pastoral mode as a repression and displacement of the actual politico-economical factors structuring the exercise of sympathy and violence circa 1800. Somehow "Nature" has arrived once again to teach us lessons.

Whatever the peculiarities and deformations of Wordsworth's pedagogy, we can see that here again minstrelsy appears as that mode of poetry which has been *and should have been* superseded; and in a characteristic dialectic, Wordsworth delivers this knockout punch against a minstrelling epoch and ethic in the very form associated with minstrels – the ballad. The poem implicitly tracks a sequence of human epochs, socio-cultural stages, and *mentalités*, and it does so through the very ballad form that had so often

---

[40] Duncan, *Modern Romance*, 10–11. Duncan argues that it is Scott who formalizes this version of romance; I would suggest Wordsworth and other poets and writers are similarly mobilizing and formalizing this symbolic form, though certainly Scott perfects it.

been used to demonstrate a single notional epic or period (be it "ancient," "medieval," "primitive," "oral," or some other gloss for prior phases). From the mid-eighteenth century, antiquarians and literary scholars had presented ballads as "ancient" relics and "old" songs; had read them as documents in a history of sensibility, national emergence, and cultural formation, or occasionally as still-persisting "songs of the common people" (cf. Addison): Wordsworth internalized these readings of ballads, such that his ballads are everywhere a *reading of ballads*. Minstrelsy testifies against itself; modern balladry trumps medieval balladry (and aspires as well, one can't but feel, to trump the pseudo-medieval balladry so typical of Scott, so powerful in Coleridge). By writing such a modern ballad, moreover, Wordsworth resists consigning balladry to a "closed past"[41]: his ballad moves into an utterly contemporary chronotope, featuring speech "in the now." Reflecting on and thus connected to the past, "Hart-Leap Well" demonstrates a continuing, localized inheritance of ballad *matter* – e.g. in the Shepherd's relating of the story – which is itself generalized into the universal, disciplined, officially humanized ethic of Wordsworthian *poiesis*.

MINSTRELSY FROM BELOW: JOHN CLARE AND THE
CRITIQUE OF THE PROGRESS OF POETRY

As I hope the foregoing discussion makes plain, Romantic minstrelsy – and Romanticism-as-minstrelsy – repeatedly poses a profound question: how should poets formalize – that is, how should they render into poetic *form* – their relation to culture? Through minstrelsy poets explored the pasts and futurities of poetry; through such exploration they could make both their own poetries and their cases for their poetries. As previously noted, minstrelsy is an ongoing inquiry into the poet's situation. If Scott's minstrelsy constituted a poetics of display, of outward show, mummery, and masquerade, Wordsworth's minstrelsy relied on what we now see as a characteristically Wordsworthian movement of internalization.

Scott and Wordsworth ventured into minstrelsy with what we might call strong socio-psychological capital; however different their minstrelling engagements, they had the ambiguous privilege of representing – and not merely *being* – last or residual minstrels. For other poets less well situated,

---

[41] This phrase I adopt from Ina Ferris, who suggests that Scott moved from "the 'closed past' of his poetry and achieved the 'fullness of time necessary for the historical novel'" (133). Yet in the Introductions to the Cantos of *The Lay of the Last Minstrel* and *Marmion*, Scott insists on keeping open the dialogue between modern poetry and oral-traditional past: even in his romances, his past is not so closed, nor is his historiographic technique so remote from that of his later novels.

minstrelsy named an explicitly benighted social horizon of poetic aspiration and failure: and to sketch this "minstrelsy-from-below," we might consider John Clare.

For Clare was – as his second book, *The Village Minstrel and Other Poems* (1821) announced – ostentatiously indebted to minstrelsy and a continuer of the minstrelling strain.[42] The title poem of that book offers a re-doing, in fact, of Beattie's *Minstrel*, covering some of the same developmental ground in the same Spenserian stanzas (albeit of very different texture and stance): absorption of shepherd wisdom, immersion in women's tales, education of the heart, the progress of the young-minstrel-in-training from youth onward. Beattie's minstrel was however explicitly *British*, a Unionist minstrel singing the song of Albion's (as well as Edwin's) arrival at the pinnacle of the arts and sciences. Clare's minstrel accrues no such cultural capital. Clare appears in the public sphere not as a national (or transnational) minstrel but rather as a *village* minstrel; he is also glossed as "The Northamptonshire peasant" on the title page of that volume. Region and class locate this village minstrel in a social and literary field. If Beattie's Edwin bespoke aspects of Beattie's own development, Clare's shepherd Lubin was even closer to the poet: Clare was a laborer throughout his adult working life (when not confined in institutions), and his shepherds, farmers, and other workers are not prettified projections of pastoral nor objects of stadial inquiry but figures in a politically and economically transforming landscape.

The formerly mute inglorious Miltons had become less mute by the early nineteenth century, and through minstrelsy some sought their glory, only to find that they would remain confined within a straightened minstrelsy – a "peasant" poetry welcomed so long as it was confined to regional interest, rural beauties, local or sub-national color, fondly remembered games, pasttimes, customs; a minstrelsy-from-below welcomed so long as it figured "lower orders" as quiescent: that is to say, a minstrelsy purged of political or

---

[42] Indeed, when Clare suggested "Village Minstrelsy" as an alternative to "The Village Minstrel" for the title of his book, his publisher John Taylor objected because similarly titled works (including Scott's anonymously edited "English Minstrelsy") had not sold well, and also because he preferred Clare's old title, "The Peasant Boy," and would consider too "The Village Muse." These alternatives, with their different yet related lines of force, suggest how readily and strongly branded Clare would be as a peasant minstrel, and how readily he was fashioning himself as such – partly along the lines of Robert Bloomfield, author of "The Farmer's Boy," and other peasant poets. That Clare proposed "Village Minstrelsy" suggests how strongly located he understood his work to be – a poetry of a common ground. For this exchange I am indebted to Zachary Leader's "*Lyrical Ballads*: The Title Revisited," in *1800: The New Lyrical Ballads*, ed. Nicola Trott and Seamus Perry (New York: Palgrave, 2001), 23.

social insurgence.[43] Precisely because Clare did not thus purge his minstrelsy, his poetry proved unwieldy for his publishers and some readers; even
now a lingering condescension colors Clare, who is too often read exclusively as a touchingly precise nature poet, always already mad.

In "Helpstone" (1809) the earliest poem of his we can date, Clare salutes
the eponymous village and environs and establishes the low coordinates of
his minstrelsy:

> Hail, humble Helpstone, where thy valleys spread
> And thy mean village lifts its lowly head,
> Unknown to grandeur and unknown to fame,
> No minstrel boasting to advance thy name:
> Unlettered spot, unheard in poets' song,
> Where bustling labour drives the hours along,
> Where dawning genius never met the day,
> Where useless ignorance slumbers life away
> Unknown nor heeded, where low genius tries
> Above the vulgar and the vain to rise.[44]

Here the poet proposes himself as minstrel and his subject, Helpstone, as
appropriate for minstrelsy: and significantly, this requires a supercession of
negation, Helpstone heretofore having "no minstrel boasting to advance thy
name." "Unknown," "unlettered," "unheard" – the spot and the poet both.
This is both a traditional poetic gambit – *my song shall now render unto fame
a previously unstoried spot* – and a powerful articulation of actual and not
only rhetorical difficulty: what we feel throughout these lines is the "labour"
of "low genius" who "tries ... to rise." Minstrelsy as a song of labor, from
labor, minstrelsy as a labored song: here we have the underside of the
spectacular, magical, as if unlabored fluencies of Walter Scott.

Instead of compliant last minstrels (viz. Scott) or pacified Lords (viz.
Wordsworth), Clare gives us a minstrelsy of outraged, impassioned, yet also
tender plebeian witness: his Lubin in "The Village Minstrel" (1821) proceeds
as it were in Beattian fashion to imbibe local knowledge, popular superstitions, and so on, yet instead of progressing to the tutelage of the hermit
and muse of history – figures of the professoriat–literati if ever there were –
young Lubin indicts enclosure and the trampling of English liberties:

---

[43] For a pathbreaking account of "peasant poets," their fashionability, and their complex relation to
patrons (including more genteel poets), see Anne F. Janowitz, *Lyric and Labor in the Romantic
Tradition* (Cambridge University Press, 1998), particularly for her incisive take on the "thresher-poet"
Stephen Duck and the "milkmaid" poet Anne Yearsley.

[44] Clare, "Helpstone," *Poems, Descriptive of Rural Life and Scenery* (1820), *"I Am,"* 15.

There once were lanes in nature's freedom dropt,
There once were paths that every valley wound –
Enclosure came and every path was stopped;
Each tyrant fixed his sign where paths were found,
To hint a trespass now who crossed the ground:
Justice is made to speak as they command;
The high road now must be each stinted bound:
– Enclosure, thou'rt a curse upon the land
And tasteless was the wretch who thy existence planned. (St. 94; 36–7)

O England, boasted land of liberty,
With strangers still thou mayst thy title own,
But thy poor slaves the alteration see,
With many a loss to them the truth is known:
[…]
And every village owns its tyrants now,
And parish-slaves must live as parish-kings allow. (St. 95; 37)

This eruption of the time-of-the-now, the *Jetzeit* in Walter Benjamin's terms, blows minstrelsy open to an ongoing, *contested* history:[45] a poetics of conflict and contest, not supercession or sublimation (as in Beattie and, more complicatedly, in Scott and Wordsworth). This violent collision of ringing critique and tender remembrance-recreation is a hallmark of Clare's work, and indeed we can see it in other poets – Blake and Hogg for example – unable or unwilling to claim the mantle of middle- and upper-class politesse.

A poet advertised as "The Northhamptonshire peasant" would clearly bear powerful marks of his distressed situation vis-à-vis the class politics of polite, genteel "literature"; and Clare's poetry is a lacerating, brilliant mediation on distressed production – minstrelsy made precisely out of impediments to minstrelsy. If Wordsworth ostentatiously purges his poetry of the threat of bogus minstrels and their misdirected minstrelsy, Clare offers us an anti-minstrelsy, a minstrelsy of negation, of precarious arrival and tenuous achievement. As we have seen, "minstrelsy" conjoins problems of matter, measure, and maker. Minstrelsy specifies, to put it in Marxian terms, the means of poetic production, the nature of poetic materials, and

---

[45] Walter Benjamin, "Thesis on the Philosophy of History," *Illuminations*, 263. Criticizing a historicism that relies on a concept of time as "homogenous empty time," a historicism concerned only to establish "causal connection[s] between various moments in history," Benjamin calls for a method through which the historian would "establish … a conception of the present as the 'time of the now,'" which is shot through with chips of Messianic time" (261, 263). Clare's "time of the now" is admittedly more Jeremiahic than Messianic.

the status of the poet-producer. Minstrelsy explicitly links the status of poetry to the problem of the "progress of society" – most obviously in the progress poem, which had its efflorescence in the eighteenth century and continued to attract nineteenth-century poets. As the space of an always already historical and historicizeable poetry, a poetry always already enmeshed in social situation, "minstrelsy" was an instrument especially suited to such meditations on progress. As we have seen, Beattie's minstrel progresses through discourses, media, and bodies of knowledge, more or less in harmony with an allegorized vision of a progression from pastoral to civil society; and in more elaborate, sophisticated ways Scott's *Lay of the Last Minstrel* lays out an analogous development, though his minstrel remains a fixed emblem of an earlier stage of society, re-animated, theorized, and historicized by Scott, the modern minstrel of civil society. And Wordsworth lays out a similar pattern of sociological development, with which a poet might be in or out of tune. Clare shows us a far more radical, and more painful, minstrelsy, a minstrelsy in which the progress of society might leave progressive poets behind: in which a zone of perpetual futurity, once guaranteed by poetry, is violently emptied into a devastated present. Thus his poem "The Progress of Rhyme" (composed in the 1820s, unpublished until the twentieth century) – which together with "The Village Minstrel" (1821) shows his tremendous facility in the protocols of the progress poem – offers an elegy for the very idea of the progress of rhyme, and for Clare's own youthful self-conception.

For Clare, minstrelsy is the name of a realm he is not sure he has a right to join. Invoking the harp and lyre and the traditional tropes of minstrelsy, Clare lays bare the political economy of poetry as it bore upon a powerfully determined (in all senses) poet. A charged language of rights pervades "The Progress of Rhyme," a poem that Jonathan Bate considers Clare's "Prelude," the "growth of this poet's mind":

> No friends had I to guide or aid
> The struggles young ambition made.
> In silent shame the harp was tried
> And rapture's guess the tune applied,
> Yet o'er the songs my parents sung
> My ear in silent musings hung;
> Their kindness wishes did regard,
> They sung and joy was my reward.
> All else was but a proud decree,
> *The right of bards and nought to me,*
> A title that I dare not claim
> And hid it like a private shame. (127, emphasis added)

Poetic stirrings arousing "private shame"; ambition checked by a strong sense of exclusion; poetry a matter of rights and claims not his, "the right of bards and nought to me": What we have here is not bardic nationalism but minstrelling class critique. Clare offers a moving anatomy, recollected not quite in tranquillity, of the "literary destitution"[46] such an aspiring poet confronted. Drawing on the language of the American Declaration of Independence, the poet politicizes the question of his "right to song" and points to the enormous difficulty in sustaining his inner conviction:

> I felt that I'd *a right to song*
> And sung – but in a timid strain
> Of fondness for my native plain. (122, emphasis added)

Thus the aspiring poet fortifies and cheers himself while contemplating flowers –

> And so it cheered me while I lay
> Among their beautiful array
> To think that I in humble dress
> Might have *a right to happiness*
> *And sing as well as greater men,*
> And then I strung the lyre again. (123, emphasis added)

Clare's radical discourse on minstrel rights, English liberty, and human happiness reminds us that minstrelsy did not always have to be allied with a conservative (or, in our terms, "liberal") politics.

Scott's last minstrel is anxious about his reception, and whether he can perform up to standard; he does not manifest anxiety about *whether he is or is not a minstrel*. We might put Clare's concerns alongside Keats', say, or Wordsworth's representations of his own self-interrogations in *The Prelude*: again what impresses this reader is that, while Wordsworth agonizes over theme, he never questions that "vows were made to him," that he was always already a consecrated poet, nature's son. Through minstrelsy Clare moves the question of poetic aspiration right back into the heart of social being, from where it must always launch: and the very nature of his fears and shames illuminates the underside of the more comfortably socialized anxieties of Wordsworth, and even Keats, whose lower-middle-class background and education gave him the edge over such a figure as Clare.

---

[46] I draw this phrase from Pascale Casanova, *The World Republic of Letters*, trans. M. B. DeBevoise (Cambridge, MA: Harvard University Press, 2004), 181. Casanova is herself drawing upon Pierre Bourdieu and ascribes such destitution to disadvantaged national literatures, not classed writers.

The enormous pathos of Clare's project arises from his overwhelming investment in "poesy" per se, signal poems attesting to his recourse to poetry as a comfort, balm, a "cheer," as crucial self-sustenance. Minstrelsy was, Clare shows us in "The Progress of Rhyme," a horizon and a prospect, not a zone of retrospect:

> My master's frowns might force the tear
> But poesy came to check and cheer –
> It glistened in my shamed eye
> But ere it fell the swoof was by –
> *I thought of luck in future days*
> *When even he might find a praise.*
> I looked on poesy like a friend
> To cheer me till my life should end.[47] (emphasis added)

Clare had enormous ambitions for himself *through poetry*. Ambition is a social hope, and his poems often track the course of that ambition, his disappointments, his flares of triumph and sudden crashes into bitterness and despondency.

Clare's work raises the question of a minstrelsy unallied with social power: could it work, would it move, through the literary field as constituted circa 1820? Certainly Clare was well-received in London, his first book selling out three print-runs. But the social anxiety his poems and his person presented are clear, for example in the elaborately mock-apologetic introduction his publisher John Taylor affixed to *The Village Minstrel*. As his much-loved Burns had been before him, Clare was very much enmired in problems of metropolitan patronage and had a notoriously vexed relationship with his publishers. Beyond the difficulties of his publishing career – including the longstanding debates over the editing of Clare – we see that the poems internalize the question of poetic power, ambition unbacked by worldly inheritance.

In "The Progress of Rhyme" Clare explores the possibility that minstrelsy might be a route to dispossession rather than self-possession and "happiness." As an itinerant laborer, he like Hogg faced insinuations that he could not have written the poems attributed to him. Reflecting on his quondam "friends," the editors, publishers, and sponsors who helped him into print, the poet sardonically writes:

> Hope came, storms calmed, and hue and cry
> With her false pictures herded by,

---

[47] "The Progress of Rhyme," *The Midsummer Cushion* (unpublished in Clare's life), *"I Am,"* 120–1.

With tales of help when help was not,
Of friends who urged to write or blot,
Whose taste were such that mine were shame
Had they not helped it into fame.
Poh! Let the idle rumour ill,
Their vanity is never still –
My harp though simple was my own. (124, emphasis added)

And still later, Clare again insists:

No matter how the lyre was strung,
From *my own heart* the music sprung. (126, emphasis added)

Rebutting charges that he was a mere tool in the hands of his better-placed "friends," the instrument here claims possession of his own minstrelling instruments. Clare's harp, hard-won, hard-strung, stands here as his "own," self-made, defiantly local, in solidarity with others in the community – animal, floral, and arboreal as well as human.

There is of course a great risk in sentimentalizing Clare – but why not acknowledge the great power his project still bears? Clare's work, when heard through the minstrelling strains he so explicitly sounded, resonates all the more critically with and against Scott's, Hogg's, Wordsworth's, and Byron's – this last the poet he so famously thought himself to be when mad.

MINSTRELSY AS ONGOING DIAGNOSIS: A MODERNIST CRITIQUE OF THE ROMANTIC IN WALLACE STEVENS

It means the distaste we feel for this withered scene
Is that it has not changed enough. It remains,
It is a repetition.
[...]
It must change. (Wallace Stevens, "Notes toward a Supreme Fiction"[48])

Minstrelsy exhausts itself. This Walter Scott discovered when *Rokeby* (1813), though still very successful, failed to sell as well as his previous efforts.[49] Minstrelsy, we might say, exacted its own perfect revenge. Trafficking in the tropologics and problematics of last minstrels, Scott found himself to be perilously close to his vexed "brethren," quite possibly himself the last

---

[48] Wallace Stevens, "Notes toward a Supreme Fiction," *The Collected Poems*, 390.

[49] For the relative disappointment regarding the distribution of *Rokeby* (1813) and the subsequent *Lord of the Isles* (1815), see David Hewitt, "Scott, Sir Walter (1771–1832)," in *Oxford Dictionary of National Biography*, ed. H. C. G. Matthew and Brian Harrison (Oxford University Press, 2004); online edn., ed. Lawrence Goldman, May 2006, www.oxforddnb.com/view/article/24928 (accessed October 17, 2006).

minstrel. Confronting the abandonment of his audience as well as a changed cultural situation (changed not least by Byron's huge success with the first two cantos of *Childe Harold* [1812]), and perhaps having reached the limits of what even he could do with the syncretic options minstrelsy afforded, Scott did what any self-respecting self-fashioning modern minstrel could do, that is, he became a novelist.

The exhaustion of poetry is a constitutive trope of minstrelsy (e.g. Clare's "Decay": "O poesy is on the wane"); minstrelsy emerges, as we have seen, as a scheme for working through, for sounding out, a multiply determined exhaustion and obsolescence on the one hand and perpetual revivability on the other. Wallace Stevens intuited as much when he introduced minstrel-figuration into his meditation on the end of poetry in "Notes toward a Supreme Fiction":

[VI]

Bethou me, said sparrow, to the cracked blade,
And you, and you, bethou me as you blow,
When in my coppice you behold me be.

Ah, ké! the bloody wren, the felon jay,
Ké-ké, the jug-throated robin pouring out,
Bethou, bethou, bethou me in my glade.

There was such idiot minstrelsy in rain,
So many clappers going without bells,
That these bethous compose a heavenly gong.

One voice repeating, one tireless chorister,
The phrases of a single phrase, ké-ké,
A single text, granite monotony,

One sole face, like a photograph of fate,
Glass-blower's destiny, bloodless episcopus,
Eye without lid, mind without any dream –

These are of minstrels lacking minstrelsy,
Of an earth in which the first leaf is the tale
Of leaves, in which the sparrow is a bird

Of stone, that never changes. Bethou him, you
And you, bethou him and bethou. It is
A sound like any other. It will end.[50]

---

[50] Wallace Stevens, "Notes toward a Supreme Fiction," 393–4.

This passage offers an extraordinary meditation on, and sublation of, Romanticism, minstrelsy, and Romanticism-as-minstrelsy. Stevens here directly invokes the problem of poetic vocation and invocation perhaps most powerfully, even notoriously, formulated in the culminating appeal of Shelley's "Ode to the West Wind":

> Make me thy lyre, even as the forest is:
> What if my leaves are falling like its own!
> The tumult of thy mighty harmonies
>
> Will take from both a deep autumnal tone,
> Sweet though in sadness. Be thou, Spirit fierce,
> My spirit! Be thou me, impetuous one!
>
> (Shelley, "Ode to the West Wind" (1819), ll. 57–62[51])

Be thou me, says the Shelleyan poet to the wind, to the world, to the spirit of Nature/Imagination/the Awful Shaping Power; Make me thy medium; Make thyself me. Shelley's climax can be read with microscopically playful attention to syntax, as Stevens does, rendering his appeal thus: Bethou me: that is, make *me* a *you*, a *thou*, an addressable *subject*; ratify me as an other in an exchange that will prove the adequacy of mind to world, poet to situation. It is as if the urgency of Lacan's mirror stage had found its voice; or, to turn things differently, as if the problem of intersubjectivity had discovered its linguistic base.[52] This plea, in all its registers, Stevens insistently sounds, and resounds throughout the passage, the poet become a bird in his monotonous clamor for mirror-making, every bird, like every poet, crying out for a predetermined responsiveness from the world: "Bethou, bethou, bethou me in my glade." This, Stevens seems to be saying, is what Shelley, and a Shelleyan strain of Romanticism, has come to.[53]

Working through the longstanding trope equating birdsong and poet's song, Stevens offers a characteristically modern critique, itself a higher romantic critique, of romantic *poiesis*. It is as if the brilliant cadences of Shelley's Ode had dissolved, over time, in the air, in the wind, into an "idiot minstrelsy," the "one voice repeating, one tireless chorister/The phrases of a single phrase": "Bethou him, you/And you, bethou him and bethou." It is

---

[51] Percy Bysshe Shelley, "Ode to the West Wind," *Shelley's Poetry and Prose*, 221–3. Further quotations will be cited by line in text.
[52] On the discursive basis of intersubjectivity, see Emile Benveniste, "Subjectivity in Language," *Problems in General Linguistics*, trans. Mary Elizabeth Meek. Miami Linguistics Series No. 8 (Coral Gables, Florida: University of Miami Press, 1971).
[53] That Stevens is profoundly engaged with Shelley is evident in other allusions, however playful, including the subsequent encounter between Nanza Nunzio and Ozymandias, "It Must Change," VIII, 395.

hard to think of a more devastating diagnosis of certain aspects of Romantic ideology, egotistical sublime and all.

Stevens' complex metaphorics of fixity, monotony, repetition – figured through such artistic practices as photography and glass-blowing – points us to a poetry of exhaustion, many voices reduced to "one voice repeating," to a degraded cohort of "minstrels lacking minstrelsy." Yet in this phrase we arrive at the signal moment in the passage. In a stunning transvaluation of minstrelsy, Stevens moves us from the "idiot minstrelsy" of rain, and of ceaseless iteration of the same, to another possibility: that of minstrels *in possession* of minstrelsy – poets alive to a renewed *poiesis*. The whole passage may be read as a brilliant exorcism of one aspect of minstrelsy: its idiocy, its fixity in "single text[s]," its mindless repetitiveness "that never changes." (Note the textualism of this imagery: this is truly the Derridean tyranny of the letter, rendering even speech, or figured speech, "the same"). Of this debased minstrelsy, Stevens writes the epitaph: "It is/A sound like any other. It will end." Yet still unfulfilled is the promise subliminally offered, as if by negation: if the chorus of "bethous" is wittily, thoroughly, elegantly done in (though, we notice, also *sung*, and thus carried on), there remains the possibility of a poetry – a minstrelsy – committed to the modernist mandate: "It must change." It is as if Stevens were indicting a stream of poetry that had forgotten the mandate of medieval minstrels and troubadours – to *move* the song.

"Notes toward a Supreme Fiction" is a manifesto and an enactment of a potentially revived poetry, revived out of the very exhausted materials it would seem to repudiate. The poem stations itself on the brink of a new invention: "Begin, ephebe, by perceiving the idea/Of this invention, this invented world,/The inconceivable idea of the sun.//You must become an ignorant man again/And see the sun again with an ignorant eye." This desire for the world made new, and the claim the poetry will remake the world anew, is of course an ancient one, its utterance itself a repetition: but nevertheless, to utter it anew is potentially to make it new. Yet everywhere Stevens shows the conditions out of which this desire springs: a sense of disgust, revulsion against the merely iterated and recycled:

> It means the distaste we feel for this withered scene
> Is that it has not changed enough. It remains,
> It is a repetition.

"It" is a repetition indeed: a rep-"it"-"it"-ion, since "it" has not changed enough, though Stevens is putting "it" through its changes. Iterated four times in three lines in this passage (with *it* morphemes snuck in as well), and compulsively invoked in signal passages, "it" is the subject of the poem and the space toward which all Stevensian subjects gather: "*It* must change," yet "*It* will end." "*It* is a sound like any other," yet *it* is not a sign like any other. Between sounds and significance, both of which will end, poetry moves. Mindless sounds endlessly repeated: the ké-ké of the felon jay and of an "idiot" – itty-it – "minstrelsy." Stevens literally, iterally hangs his critique of minstrelsy, of an unmoving poiesis, on "it": the threat of "it," a single text, gran-"it" monotony. Truly "it" must change for "it" no longer to evoke the distaste we might feel for a withered poetry, a poetry in which "it" has not changed enough. It (and "it") is typical of Stevens' brilliance – grammatical, morphemic, and lexical: he draws us ever onward, acoustically as well as orthographically, to ponder the "it"-erability of "it." "It" does not only *refer* to the "supreme fiction," then: "it" *is* the supreme fiction. "It" functions ultimately not as a neutral personal pronoun of reference but as a proper global name for the totality of what must change: "IT must change."

Stevens thus models and enacts a subtle, exquisite oscillation within his *poiesis* as "it" moves "to and fro." He strikingly moves us, and "it," through the metaphorics of the oral-literate, high-low problematics recurrent in Romanticism and in literary theory more broadly.

[IX]

The poem goes from the poet's gibberish to
The gibberish of the vulgate and back again.
Does it move to and fro or is it of both

At once? Is it a luminous flittering
Or the concentration of a cloudy day?
Is there a poem that never reaches words

And one that chaffers the time away?[54]

Moving between "the poet's gibberish" and that "of the vulgate" – between the poet's idiolect (his it-iolect) and the vernacular, here brilliantly cast in the poet's Latinate gibberish ("vulgate") – Stevens' work suggests the complex legacy of minstrelsy for modernism and beyond.

Walter Scott announced in his "Introductory Remarks on Popular Poetry" that "*tongue* is chief of minstrelsy"; Stevens suggested that the poet was "the speaker/Of a speech only a little of the tongue."[55] Perhaps

---

[54] Wallace Stevens, "Notes toward a Supreme Fiction," *The Collected Poems*, 396.
[55] Walter Scott, "Popular Poetry," *Poetical Works*, ii; Stevens, "Supreme Fiction," "It Must Change," IX, 397.

here we have a figure for the rift between a genuinely popular literary poet and a modern poet grappling with what was by then a century-old condition of alienation from audience. Yet a reconciliation sounds forth as "it" moves between poet's gibberish and the vulgate's, and between literary and traditionary poetries: "it is of both," and *poiesis* is of both. Both obsolete and the horizon of futurity, poetry as minstrelsy may continue in new media and new situations "to move to and fro," to be that "luminous flittering" in and of human language.

CHAPTER 6

Seven types of poetic authority circa 1800: Romantic poiesis reconsidered

In previous chapters I described how antiquarians, balladeers, and poets made their bids for cultural and editorial authority, variously grounding their authority in ethnographic, linguistic, aesthetic and/or historiographic expertise. Between 1750 and 1800, balladeering created a zone of *poiesis* in which a "minstrelsy complex" moved to the heart of romantic making; in which literary and oral and manuscript traditions and materials could be equally solicited; in which national, nativist, experiential, and scholarly bona fides might be advanced; in which many kinds of authority were displayed and debated. Poetry emerged as both the object and the medium of debate, debates both indebted to and shaping of emergent disciplines in the human sciences. Under these conditions *poiesis* fostered historiographic, ethnographic, and linguistic speculation and research, as well as many modes of making: the making of new poems, but also (as we have seen) essays, dissertations, citations, screeds, letters, incipient genres (the ballad collection), translations. With this horizon of *poiesis* in mind, this chapter will sketch, speculatively and briefly, a discursive map for *poiesis* more generally in this period. What we conventionally call "Romantic poetry" (that is, literary, author-branded poetry that has made it into anthologies and twentieth- and twenty-first-century classrooms) looks somewhat different when viewed with these other, contemporary aspects of *poiesis* in mind. This chapter offers then a heuristic for thinking and perhaps for teaching: a fuller range and different conceptualization of poetries in several Englishes circa 1800 might become more apparent, and differently interesting, to our students as well as ourselves.

This discussion, while informed by a sense of oral-literate interactions, is primarily oriented to those poetries made on the literate side of that boundary, poems and poetic addenda written and typically destined for print; one could imagine a different kind of map that accounted for poetry-as-performance, and for the local and regional pre-eminence of various oral-traditional poets, singers, and transmitters in this era: Mrs. Hogg,

Mussel-Mou'd Charlie, and so on – though here too one must realize that even those poets who worked from tradition, apparently *sans texte*, were usually literate and surrounded by print culture; and they often extended their repertoire via song- and ballad-books. As always, one cannot work with simple oral vs. literate, or oral vs. writing/print, binaries.

With my previous discussions of eighteenth-century balladeering and minstrelsy in mind, I want to point to the more or less simultaneous emergence and convergence of two functions which have often been held apart in the criticism until very recently:
– The radical authority of deep, extended, "authentic" subjectivity
– The elaborated authority of editorial objectivity.
In other words, the project here is to suggest preliminary routes for charting the relationship between the representation and discourse of Editorial Exteriority and that of Lyric Interiority: we might call these functions, *Scott* and *Wordsworth* – though under each poet's proper name we find explorations of both functions, as this essay will argue. (The modes of authoritative enunciation listed below might be considered "thresholds of poetic enunciation," following Foucault's scheme in the *Archaeology of Knowledge* of thresholds of enunciation and formalization in the human sciences.) With such thresholds of *poiesis* in mind, Wordsworth's *Prelude, or the Growth of the Poet's Mind*, begins to speak in striking ways to the many editions of Scott's *Minstrelsy of the Scottish Border* (or, the Growth of the Cultural Anthology). Under the sign of *poiesis* one could make editions of the self as well as editions of ballads: and one might fashion oneself precisely through the persona of Editor conjoined to the practice of literary authorship (viz. Scott's novels),[1] or one might become the custodian of one's own

---

[1] On the complexities of Scott's career, his complex legitimation and re-masculinization of the novel through hybrid generic practices (viz. "historical novel") and the critical support of the *Edinburgh Review*, see Ina Ferris's *The Achievement of Literary Authority*, especially 5–6, 10. For the complexities of his anonymous publication of *Waverley* and the emergence of that phenomenon, the "Waverley novels" and "The Author of Waverley" (itself become a brand and a proper name of a kind), see her final chapter, "Establishing the Author of Waverley: The Canonical Moment of *Ivanhoe*." See as well Penny Fielding's discussion of "The Author of Waverley" (*not*, one observes, the same as "The Author of *Waverley*"), Scott's creation of a brand name, and his use of anonymity in the literary marketplace: Ch. 2, "Grammar and Glamour: Writing and Authority," in *Writing and Orality*, 55–60. More recently Margaret Russett in *Fictions and Fakes* diagnoses Scott's anonymity as a bravura brand-naming, a deft exploitation of literary property in all senses (see 155–91). Ian Duncan offers a persuasive account of Scott's studied anonymity as "a condition of the author's unprecedented cultural visibility, a mask that advertised itself"; he writes of this "anonymity game" as a venture as much superstitious and apotropaic as a bid for gentility (*Modern Romance*, 185). Duncan like Russett points us to Scott's adventures in authorship vs. Hogg's. In his essay on Scott for the new *Oxford Dictionary of National Biography*, David Hewitt observes that there is still no wholly satisfactory account of Scott's motivations for maintaining anonymity for so long.

works, such that one became primarily an editor of oneself (which is the way Lee Erickson describes Wordsworth's late career, including his involvement with the editor William Moxon).[2]

In order to arrive at this double-sided extension of *poiesis* – this double movement of internalization and externalization – we might first consider more fully the several ways *poiesis* authorized itself in the period.[3] What is especially striking is the impact of emergent orally-based, literarily-mediated authority; the complex oral-literate conjunctions of this period led to an expansion of poetic activities (editing as well as making, forging as well as collecting traditions) and contributed as well to an internalization of the complex meanings of "the oral" (which is one way to understand the prominence of children and rustics in Wordsworth's *oeuvre*). For diagnostic purposes I will continue to focus on Scott and Wordsworth as two examples of a *poiesis* indebted to a mediated orality, though I will have occasion to invoke Hogg and Clare as well. I hope that those readers more immersed in these and other Romantic poets (Burns, Southey, Byron) might find here a heuristic useful beyond the examples discussed. I offer first a preliminary sketch of seven types of poetic authority prevailing in this period.[4] What follows is a brief taxonomy of categories, sometimes overlapping, of some

---

[2] On Wordsworth's retreat into a long, avid curation of his corpus, see Erickson's rather severe yet just observations in *The Economy of Literary Form: English Literature and the Industrialization of Publishing, 1800–1850* (Baltimore and London: Johns Hopkins University Press, 1996): "When his poetic powers declined, he served as the editorial custodian of his early aspirations" (49).

[3] This discussion is indebted to many works on the construction of poetic authority, though in its brevity it can by no means address the full range of issues only suggested here. One model of such sustained historical-theoretical inquiry is John Guillory, *Poetic Authority: Spenser, Milton, and Literary History* (New York: Columbia University Press, 1983). For discussions of Walter Scott's construction of literary authority, including his display of oral materials throughout his novels, see Ina Ferris, *The Achievement of Literary Authority*; for nineteenth-century literary production in light of techno-material transformations, see Erickson, *The Economy of Literary Form*. Erickson suggests that poetry *per se* has a brief early nineteenth-century boomlet because of expensive paper costs: but once the Continent is reopened, new papermaking techniques and printing methods are invented, there is no longer a need for highly concentrated verse forms, and the expansive novel triumphs: "Cheaper printing strips poetry of its cultural pre-eminence and mnemonic force" (19). This does seem a rather bald explanation but is suggestive. On the use and abuse of orality in nineteenth-century Scottish discourse, particularly as a way for ambitious literary men to establish themselves, see Fielding, *Writing and Orality* and Newman, *Ballad Collection, Lyric*. And in "Authenticity Effects: The Work of Fiction in Romantic Scotland," *The South Atlantic Quarterly* 102:1 (Winter 2003): 93–116, Ian Duncan offers, via the case of Hogg, a stunning analysis of the literary field in this period, particularly in its Scottish specificities. There is of course a vast scholarship on Romantic poets and their several constructions of authority, authorship, and their *auctors*: this chapter hope not to replicate but rather turn in different directions the discursive horizon of poetic authority in the period.

[4] My chapter title is of course an homage to William Empson's brilliant *Seven Types of Ambiguity* (1930). I expect this title may function as a provocation: other readers might discern more than seven types of British Romantic poetic authority, still others may find fewer: the typological proposal is offered as a heuristic, not as a rigid taxonomy.

available modes of poetic authority circa 1800; the essay opens out en route into a longer discussion of several modes of authorization within and around Romantic poems.

I THE AUTHORITY OF INSPIRATION

Following Weber's tripartite model of authority outlined in his 1947 *Theory of Social and Economic Organization*, we might explore the authority of inspiration in its traditional, charismatic, and rational variants and combinations. Under this rubric we could include Bardic Authority, Vatic Authority, Prophetic Authority – though Bardic Authority *qua* Bardic more typically grounds itself in an appeal to tradition *per se*: tradition as inspiration. What had been a longstanding topos of charismatic and traditional authority – the prophet, the bard, Isaiah, Homer – became a basis for an increasingly rationalized authority: cf. Wordsworth's invocations of "rational sympathy" and "sympathy divine." We might see (for example) Wordsworth's rationalizing and democratizing of the vatic as a way to preserve it in an increasingly rationalistic era. A survey of Romantic apostrophes might be one way to explore this zone: "Imagination! Lifting up itself before the eye and prospect of my song!" (Wordsworth, *Prelude*, XII)[5]; "O wild west wind, thou breath of autumn's being!" (Shelley, "Ode to the West Wind").

The traditional and charismatic varieties of authoritative inspiration persisted (and persist), of course: Blake's epics are nothing if not a stunning continuation, albeit often esoteric, of this line. And this period's preoccupation with tradition and revival manifested itself not least in its revived or channeled bards: Macpherson's Ossian, Blake's Ancient Bard, Irish and Welsh bards reimagined as heroic resisters of English domination, a much-cited Homer (though the ancient Greek bard was himself the new subject of rational analysis and speculation). What is striking in such figures as Ossian is that Macpherson needed a poet-figure to authorize tradition: it was not enough for him to present the fragments and epics of the Highlands as the *poiesis* of a culture or community. He sought a proper name, a bardic "author," for the tradition. The analogy here with classicists' ongoing debate over Homer – historical figure? the name of the tradition itself? – is striking.[6]

---

[5] William Wordsworth, *The Thirteen Book Prelude*, ed. Mark L. Reed (Ithaca, NY and London: Cornell University Press, 1991), Vol. I of II. Further quotations will be cited from this volume in text.

[6] On ancient and modern formulations of the Homeric question, see for example Barbara Graziosi, *Inventing Homer: The Early Reception of Epic* (Cambridge University Press, 2002).

The authority of inspiration presupposes that poems come from else-where, even if that elsewhere is, as Wordsworth would have it, within. Imagination, God, the muses, the tradition, Milton, the west wind, Blake's brother Robert, Shelley's serial beloveds, the spirit of Liberty: each are figured as inspirators. And if such inspiration was fueled by more chemical means – e.g. the opiate haze perfuming "Kubla Khan" – it seems clear that such authority is not to be gainsaid, except perhaps by a man from Porlock.

II THE AUTHORITY OF ANONYMITY

Virginia Woolf strikingly observed in "A Room of One's Own" that "anon-ymous" was both a famous author and also, quite likely, a woman. This glosses quite nicely certain aspects of *poiesis* in this period. "Anonymous" was the author of such much-circulated ballads as Barbara Allen, The Cruel Mother, and The Twa Sisters. (Anonymous continues to be their author, if not their performer or editor.) Anonymous floated on the tongues of the people. Anonymous may have been an author, long since forgotten; anonymous may have been the name for communal memory or communal invention; anonymous worked equally well as a literary or commercial strategy or mask (viz. Walter Scott's novels, published first by "Anonymous," then by "the Author of Waverley"). Anonymous was Scottish, English, Welsh, Irish, male, and female, Jacobite, Jacobin, Anti-Jacobin, Tory, Whig; anonymous was alternately scurrilous, genteel, traditional, innovative. Anonymous was the most protean authority of the romantic period, the most elusive, and the least celebrated – though often the most cited in ballad collections.

In this period, as most likely in all, "Anonymity" itself was a much-distressed category, and thus we might first distinguish between:

II.a. Oral anonymity: traditionary ("Traditional ballads" by anon; ballad collections), and

II.b. Literary Anonymity: as in the first edition of *Lyrical Ballads*, or Lady Caroline Nairne's poems, or Scott's "The Bridal of Triermain" and "Harold the Dauntless," his two "experiments" in anonymous impos-ture, as Lockhart put it: the latter poem was inserted in the Register as "under the guise of *Imitations of Walter Scott*."[7]

---

[7] Note that these poems, minor ventures in romance, were Scott's attempts to test public taste, as well as the critical mettle of Francis Jeffrey and other reviewers: his previous romances had been published under his name, while these anonymous poems were reviewed as either lesser imitations of Scott or of Coleridge, and among the candidates proposed as their author was James Hogg. Their relative failure seems to have confirmed Scott in his turn to prose genres, and to have inaugurated the complex anonymity game associated – but not exclusively – with his novels.

Clearly both modes of anonymity, whether understood as "oral" or "literate," were effects of a well-developed literary print culture: the privation of name encoded in "anonymous" suggests the normative condition of a work-as-authored, irrespective of that author's status as unknown or unwilling-to-be-known (cf. Lady Wardlaw, Lady Caroline Nairne, the numerous unnamed ladies in Scott's *Minstrelsy*, and later Mrs. Brown, who desired to remain anonymous in Scott's and Jamieson's collections and whose express wishes were overruled).[8] The boundaries between IIa (Oral Anonymity) and IIb (Literary Anonymity) were notoriously and newly porous by the late eighteenth century, thereby laying the ground for ballad impostures and editorial "touchings-up." Anonymous was of course a convenient and sometimes necessary haven for women authors who for whatever reason – gentility, fear of opprobrium, and so on – wished not to be known as authors in the public sphere, or to come in for hostile scrutiny from the very active reviews; it served as well to protect those who ventured politically volatile works on the public. And related orthogonally both to anonymity and the authorial name is that phenomenon of pseudonymity which so flourished in eighteenth- and nineteenth-century cultural production.[9]

III   THE AUTHORITY OF IMITATIVE AUTHORSHIP

Here we encounter the other side of ballad scandals and forgeries, their "legitimate" and not counterfeit coin (to use the metaphor Scott used, as if anticipating Derrida): those many instances in which poets *acknowledged* and *avowed* imitation of antiquity. Coleridge's "Ancyent Marinere" (to use his original antiqued spelling) was, as Wordsworth wrote and announced to the new reader, "professedly written in imitation of the *style*, as well as of the spirit of the elder poets."[10] Tour de force though it is, the poem looks less singular when read alongside the many ballad collections with which it was contemporary: Scott's *Minstrelsy*, for example, featured a third section expressly devoted to "Imitations of the Ancient Ballad." Indeed this

---

[8] For one of the anonymous lady balladeers, see Henry Wheatley, Percy's nineteenth-century editor, on Lady Anne Barnard and her authorship of "Auld Robin Gray": "Lady Anne Barnard kept her secret for fifty years, and did not acknowledge herself the author of it until 1823, when she disclosed the fact in a letter to Sir Walter Scott." Wheatley, Introduction to Thomas Percy, *Reliques of Ancient English Poetry*, xlvi.

[9] For an incisive account of the complex interrelations of anonymity and pseudonymity, and their interface with a more standard "author's name," see Margaret Russett, *Fictions and Fakes*, especially her final chapter, "The Gothic Violence of the Letter: Naming the Scotch Novelist," 155–91.

[10] See Wordsworth's 1798 Advertisement to the *Lyrical Ballads*, 8.

department of the *Minstrelsy* was so successful that later editions expanded to include a virtual roll-call of prominent poets and Scott's associates: Anna Seward, M. G. ("Monk") Lewis, John Leyden, and of course Scott himself. And Margaret Russett has argued that the collection of imitations – forged, faked, refurbished, or otherwise – becomes a hallmark of literary production in this period. James Hogg was perhaps the most notable exploiter and subverter of the imitation protocols Scott so dexterously deployed.[11] *The Mountain Bard* (1807), a collection of ballad imitations, marked Hogg's bid for literary fame via the authority of acknowledged imitative authorship (type III); here the poet showed his hand as a master and not merely a passive redactor of a wide-range of ballad forms, traditionary and literary. His first and greatest poetic success, *The Queen's Wake* (1813), was received in part as a kind of imitation of Scott's *Lay of the Last Minstrel*, its elaborate bardic contest (seventeen bards gathering to sing competitively over three nights, to commemorate the return of Mary Queen of Scots from France in 1561) taking imaginative and metrical wing from Scott's far briefer representation of minstrel-contest in Canto 6 of *The Lay of the Last Minstrel*. In addition to its brilliant display of regional and historical ballad styles from all over Scotland, the poem is accompanied by the testimonial, ethno-poetic notes we should by now see as virtually de rigueur across the range of Romantic *poiesis*.[12]

Imitation went far beyond imitation of ballads, ancient or medieval, of course: parodies and satires of contemporary poets proliferated as property in style and motif became brand-recognizable counters in the literary public sphere: as in Hogg's hilarious send-ups of Scott, Campbell, Wordsworth, and indeed himself in *The Poetic Mirror: The Living Bards of Britain* (1816) – a work which laid bare the ongoing threat of Romantic *poiesis*: self-imitation, advertent and inadvertent (see Wordsworth). Linking more famously satiric ventures as *Peter Bell the Third* to the underlying logic of

---

[11] That imitation could be as much satiric-parodic as emulative must of course be remembered: Claude Rawson invites us to understand Chatterton in this Augustan vein (see Rawson, "Unparodying and Forgery: the Augustan Chatterton." *Thomas Chatterton and Romantic Culture*, ed. Nick Groom [London: Macmillan; New York: St. Martin's, 1999], 15–31); and certainly Hogg was a brilliant sender-up of contemporaries' as well as of traditionary and medieval-literary modes. So too several of Peacock's ventures – the parodies of Wordsworth, Scott, etc. in his "Paper Money Lyrics," or the hilarious set-pieces throughout his novels – might be seen as part of this tradition, and this mode of authority.

[12] On Hogg's ingenious turning of the question of bardic nationalism, see Douglas S. Mack's introduction to *The Queen's Wake*, ed. Douglas S. Mack (Edinburgh University Press, 2004), xxxiv–xxxviii. As Mack observes, "the main contest of *The Queen's Wake* will not lie between Scottish and non-Scottish poetry [but] … will lie between rival aristocratic and popular strands within the Scottish poetic tradition" (xxxiv).

ballad and romance imitation might open up further the politics and poetics of style in this period.

It is important to note that IIb ("Literary Anonymity") and III ("Acknowledged, Imitative Authorship") may account for the "same object," as it emerges in different discursive space: Coleridge's "Ancyent Marinere," first published in the anonymous *Lyrical Ballads*, appeared as an anonymous yet acknowledged imitation of the ancient and was later published under the author's name with marginalia. The ballad "Hardyknute" ran through the full discursive circuit from IIa to IIb to III: what first seemed an "ancient" anonymous poem from tradition was by the mid eighteenth century speculatively identified as authored (it was in fact written by Elizabeth Halket, Lady Wardlaw, and anonymously published in a folio pamphlet in 1719; it appeared in Ramsay's *Tea-Table Miscellany* and had a long, vexed career through the eighteenth century, some believing its author John Bruce). John Pinkerton published in 1781 what he claimed was a "full" version of the poem, only later to retract the second part as authored by himself.[13]

IV AUTHORITATIVE TRANSLATION

These linguistic and cultural mediations, especially of European vernaculars past and present, had an enormous impact on post-1750 English-language poetry, not least Macpherson's *Ossian* (which however vexed was presented as a translation, Gaelic "originals" being rustled up later). So too Walter Scott's ventures into translation – of Bürger's "Leonore" and "Die Wilde Jäger" – propelled him further into balladeering and more deeply into a literary career. Percy's translations of Norwegian and Jamieson's of Danish balladry launched one strain of comparative scholarship which would only reach fuller efflorescence with the development of comparative philology and linguistics. Charlotte Brooke's *Reliques of Irish Poetry* (1789) itself conjuring Percy's *Reliques of Ancient English Poetry* (1765), featured Irish originals for the comparison of the learned, even as Macpherson had ultimately furnished Gaelic originals for the Ossian poems.[14] And alongside these vernacular translations persisted of course the longstanding

---

[13] On the strange career of "Hardyknute," see Chapter 2, n. 11.

[14] See Charlotte Brooke, *Reliques of Irish Poetry: Consisting of Heroic Poems, Odes, Elegies, and Songs, Translated into English Verse: with Notes Explanatory and Historical, and The Originals in the Irish Character, to which is Subjoined an Irish Tale* (Dublin: J. Christie, 1816). The epigraph on the title page, in Irish, is immediately translated below: "Melodious, Oisin, are thy strains to me." This is Ossian repatriated.

engagement with Latin and Greek – an investment in the latter particularly enriching the mythographic, liberal, critical, erotic poetry of Moore, Peacock, Shelley, and Keats.[15]

V EDITORIAL AUTHORITY

As suggested before, particularly in my second chapter, the late eighteenth century witnessed a rapid development of scholarly editing and its protocols, fostered by the efforts of antiquarians and poet–editors. Nick Groom reads Percy's *Reliques* as a significant episode in the history of scholarly editing; balladeering more broadly may be understood as a central moment in that history – an agonistic, combative yet collaborative process by which men and a few women worked out standards of authentication, criteria for evidence, protocols for citation.

Editorial authority increasingly required a complex coordination of multiple axes of authority: the authoritative editor would strive to mediate distinct kinds of sources, oral, manuscript, and print; he might find himself working with literate, semi-literate, or (very rarely) pre- or a-literate informants; and an aspirationally magisterial editor could find himself simultaneously taking on the roles of scholar, collector, historian, antiquarian, etymologist, genealogist, paleographer, and geographer. It was a rare editor who did not also harbor his own poetic ambitions: viz. Percy's 1771 "Hermit of Warkworth," and Scott's imitations and translations, included in his *Minstrelsy of the Scottish Border* from the first edition.

Scott's ostentatiously elaborate headnotes show how editing offered him an opportunity to meditate on and discriminate among kinds of sources and kinds of mediation and, in turn, among kinds of authority. Throughout the *Minstrelsy*, Scott reflected on the historical basis of oral-traditionary authority and his complex mediation of the same into print culture. Particularly striking is Scott's scrupulous documenting of each link in the mediating chain. Consider his note to "The Raid of the Reidswire":

This poem is published from a copy in the Bannatyne MS., in the handwriting of the Hon. Mr. Carmichael, advocate. It first appeared in *Allan Ramsay's Evergreen*, but some liberties have been taken by him in transcribing it; and, what is altogether

---

[15] On the liberal and radical valences of mythographic poetry in second-generation Romantic writing (particularly that of Peacock), see Marilyn Butler, "Myth and Mythmaking in the Shelley Circle," in *Shelley Revalued: Essays from the Gregynog Conference*, ed. Kelvin Everest (Barnes and Noble, 1983), 1–19. On the force of Moore's Anacreontic lyrics – and for a compelling, persuasive recovery of an eighteenth-century Anacreontic pre-history of Romantic lyric – see Marshall Brown's essay, "Passion and Love: Anacreontic Song and the Roots of Romantic Lyric," *ELH* 66:2 (1999): 373–404.

unpardonable, the MS., which is itself rather inaccurate, has been interpolated to favor his readings: of which there remain many obvious marks.[16]

Tracing an arc from manuscript through an earlier printed collection to his own strictly edited (we are encouraged to think) publication, Scott marks each phase of mediation, strictly re-marking the faults at each preceding level – the inaccuracies of the manuscript, Ramsay's errors in transcription, his "unpardonable" interpolations. As important as Scott's implied claim that he redresses, in all senses, the "unpardonable" injuries done to this ballad, is Scott's mode of representing that redress: his focus on the circuit of mediation. Scott sends two messages here: the first and most obvious, that he corrects the past mediations; secondly, that this ballad is a product of a history of such mediations.

For indeed Scott's notes are all meditations on method and therefore, meditations on the historicity of mediation. Concerning the aforementioned ballad, "Death of Featherstonhaugh," Scott writes,

It was taken down from the recitation of a woman eighty years of age, mother of one of the miners of Alston-Moor, by the agent of the lead mines there, who communicated it to my friend and correspondent, R. Surtees, Esq. of Mainsforth. She has not, she said, heard it for many years; but, when she was a girl, it used to be sung at merry-makings, "till the roof rung again."[17]

From the eighty-year-old mother to the agent of the lead mines to R. Surtees, friend and correspondent of Scott, to the *Minstrelsy* itself: Scott here records an astonishing metamorphosis from oral communication through writing to print, as well as a series of appropriations up the socio-economic ladder, not to mention a shift in the gendering of mediation as one moves from the female source-medium to her son's overseer. (One wonders, here, how the agent came to know of his miner's mother: what kinds of commerce and communication went on at the mines, such that this ballad ore could be mined, refined, and commodified?) We notice as well the inclusion of the woman's non-balladeering, testimonial speech – "till the roof rung again" – which intensifies the illusion of immediacy and the aura of authenticity. Such speech is a species of testimony, an "I was there, I remember" performance, which further authenticates both Scott's primary source-medium and his matter. The woman's speech also vivifies for us the customary scene of recitation, the "merry-makings" she can still remember. In two sentences, then, Scott manages to represent several successive

---

[16] Scott, prefatory note to "The Raid of the Reidswire," *MSB*, 69.
[17] Scott, prefatory note to "The Death of Featherstonhaugh," *MSB*, 81.

operations of mediation and to trace the textualization which together have produced this particular artifact; moreover, by quoting the woman's speech, he recreates the communal, customary world out of which "this curious, though rude rhyme" emerged. The note thus serves a double function, marking the route of transmission and textualization but also sustaining the illusion of orality which best guarantees the authenticity of the poem as a popular ballad. That "The Death of Featherstonhaugh" was one of Surtees' forgeries ("Lord Ewrie" and "Bartram's Dirge" were the other two palmed off on Scott) does not affect the discursive ground of Scott's authoritative bid.

In Scott's critical apparatus and poems, we can see traces and explicit representations of several strata of "orality," from casual anecdotes to carefully transmitted border lore to ballads obtainable both from living reciters and centuries-old manuscripts. After decades of antiquarian revival and many popular ballad collections, it is not that surprising to find such a complex representation of layers and kinds of "orality." What is striking is Scott's deft handling and theorization of these layers. As such notes as those prefacing "The Raid of the Reidswire" and "The Death of Featherstonhaugh" suggest, Scott's editing involved a specific, elaborate *poiesis*, simultaneously a making of culture through poetry, both oral and literate, and a making of poetry through the representation of culture – "culture" here understood in the old-fashioned anthropological sense as lore, custom, tradition.

Under the rubric of Editorial Authority, the editor would mobilize not only textual but other forms of evidence – oral tradition, custom, topography, and so on. Ear- and eye-witness became, as we have seen, admissible evidence for editorial arbitration: and thus we move from Editorial Authority to two explicitly testimonial modes of authority.

VI ETHNOGRAPHIC AUTHORITY

Here we encounter a species of authority more familiar perhaps through the discourse of twentieth-century social science and critiques thereof, for example James Clifford's discussion in his *Predicament of Culture*, Clifford Geertz's and George Marcus' many discussions of anthropology and its discontents, the debate between Marshall Sahlins and Gannath Obeysekere conducted in the 1990s.[18] One finds in the poems and poetic apparatus of

[18] For key texts on this debate over the meaning of Captain Cook's death, and the supposed *mentalité* of Pacific islanders, see Gannath Obeyesekere, *The Apotheosis of Captain Cook: European Mythmaking in the Pacific; with a New Afterword* (Princeton University Press; Honolulu, Hawai'i: Bishop Museum Press, 1997; originally pub. 1992); and Marshall Sahlins, *How "Natives" Think; about Captain Cook, for Example* (University of Chicago Press, 1995). For a summary of this debate and its larger implications

this period a striking, increasing reliance (or claimed reliance) on informants, eyewitness reports, and transcribed recitation – all prominently
noticed, if not always fully included, in Scott's *Minstrelsy*; all drawn upon
as well in the 1805 *Report on the Poems of Ossian*; all suggested in and around
several of Wordsworth's *Lyrical Ballads*. We see editors like Scott and
Jamieson styling themselves as both native informants and participant
observers, and we see poets doing the same; and we witness the emergence
of the poet-as-informant – from Macpherson to Burns and Scott and Hogg
to Wordsworth to Byron to Clare. Within or alongside ethnographic
authority we might place other modes of explicitly cultural authority:
knowledge about geography, topography, local language/dialect, lore, bot-
any, custom, dress, building practices, etc.

A poet coming from the "lower orders" could invoke ethnographic
authority but did so at his or her own risk: he or she would always be
received as a permanently and merely "natural" poet, "natural" bearing its
old connotations of "idiot" and "illegitimate" as well as "inborn." As several
scholars have sharply reminded us – Ian Duncan and Margaret Russett in
particular – the case of "The Ettrick Shepherd" James Hogg exemplifies the
class strains attendant on this kind of bid for authority. In Hogg's case, as in
a different key his fellow "peasant-poet" John Clare's, ethnographic authority could be used to combat class prejudice (native genius steeped in native
lore earning the respect of literary Edinburgh and London); yet as Burns
had discovered previously, metropolitan elites would never allow a plough-
man-poet (or a shepherd-poet, or a peasant-poet, or a thresher-poet, or a
milkmaid-poet) to forget his or her determination as such.

If Scott worked from the *Minstrelsy* onwards to establish his bona fides as
native informant as well as editor and *Makar*, Hogg risked being confined to
the status of mere native informant – the charismatic, lore- and ballad-
stuffed bumptious shepherd hailed, often condescendingly, in the
Minstrelsy, whose third volume Hogg later claimed was largely his own
work. And indeed, in his complex relation with Scott – whom he admired,
emulated, envied, and continuously rivaled – it was the native card that
Hogg found best to play: according to Hogg it was Hogg, that is, not Scott,
who had properly native access to Scottish border lore; Hogg who had best
naturalized Highland verse forms into Scots English; Hogg who deserved

for anthropology, see Clifford Geertz' review of Sahlins in *The New York Review of Books*, November
30, 1995: 4; as well as Robert Borofsky, "Cook, Lono, Obeyesekere, and Sahlins," *Current
Anthropology* 38:2 (April 1997), 255–82.

the Burnsian mantle of "native son."[19] Thus the tenth bard in *The Queen's Wake* emerges as native son of the border region of Ettrick:

> The bard on Ettrick's mountains green
> In Nature's bosom nursed had been
> (Night the Second, 259–60, 62)

– a sly rebuke to Scott, who ostentatiously grounded most of the *Minstrelsy's* "romantic ballads" in Ettrick Forest, which he had so productively "raided" with the help of native informants like Hogg. The tenth bard's song in *The Queen's Wake*, "Old David," reinscribes the natal claim, as David exclaims: "O Ettrick! Shelter of my youth!/Thou sweetest glen in all the south" (*The Queen's Wake*, Night the Second, lines 684–85, 73). And indeed in the conclusion to *The Queen's Wake*, Hogg makes explicit the rivalry, resentment, and gratitude he all felt due Scott, and pitched this complex homage in a competitively native key. After saluting Scott for his "generous heart" (330), and his sponsorship of Hogg's early minstrelsy, Hogg continues:

> He little weened, a parent's tongue
> Such strains had o'er my cradle sung.
> But when, to native feelings true,
> I struck upon a chord was new;
> When by myself I 'gan to play,
> He tried to wile my harp away. (ll. 332–7, 171)

Hogg announced himself, moreover, as the definitive superseder and surpasser of Macpherson, Percy, and Scott by appearing as an authoritative editor of and commentator upon the full range Scottish tradition, Lowland and Highland, Covenanter and Jacobite, island and mainland, Catholic and Presbyterian.[20] We might see Hogg's ongoing contest with Scott on the field of cultural authority as a replaying in a later poetic and editorial key, and on the competitive fields of commercial, literary Edinburgh and London, the imagined contest between Scott and Percy, or Scott and

---

[19] For Hogg's complex relation to Scott, and his competitive bids for authority, see for example Jill Rubinstein's introduction to James Hogg, *Anecdotes of Scott* (Edinburgh University Press, 1999); she astutely observes that Hogg in his anecdotes "farther marginalizes Scott by highlighting his status as an outsider in Ettrick Forest, the locus of authenticity and valued" (xxiii). Invoking H. Porter Abbott, Rubinstein suggests we read *Anecdotes* as "identity-related performative acts" (xvii). In "Authenticity Effects," Ian Duncan offers a brilliant anatomy of Hogg's critical performativity and his vexed cultural situation; Duncan's Hogg conducts a relentless exposure of the liberal machinery of the ideology of early nineteenth-century fiction, especially with regard to Scott's elaborate protocols thereof.

[20] See for example his elaborate, pointed notes to *The Queen's Wake*, with their intricate citations of tradition as well as linguistic expertise; or his edition of *The Jacobite Relics*, which suggests, as Murray Pittock has argued, how complex were Hogg's relations to persisting Jacobitism, Catholicism, and the supernatural.

Ritson. The class animadversions Scott could insinuate against the petit-bourgeois Englishman Ritson were all the more sharply focused in his relation to Hogg and Hogg's work; and the *Blackwood's* circle in later years worked successfully, with Hogg's ambivalent complicity, to create and sustain the figure of Hogg as *naive* as well as *native* son.

Any appeals to ethno-cultural authority slide quite easily, of course, into the bordering category of experiential authority below: what is special about ethnographic authority is its relation to the emergent concept of culture, to a discourse of the human sciences that takes as its object not the individual but the group, periodized, localized, sociologized, or historicized. One invokes authority here not simply over one's experience but rather over one's experience *as culturally symptomatic or characteristic*.

VII   EXPERIENTIAL AUTHORITY

As is true with many categories listed above, the editor and the poet could both appeal to (or simulate) experiential authority, not least through the conventions of the lyric or editorial "I." Beyond the convention of the first-person persona, we see that the preoccupation with experience and its internalization is the very matter of such works as "Tintern Abbey" and *The Prelude*. And as we have seen, experiential authority was also tactically invoked by antiquarians and editors – Ritson noting the trips he made into Scotland to search out manuscripts, Scott trumpeting his "border-raids" for ballads.

It is also true that a poet circa 1800 could mobilize experiential authority against tradition, or pretended tradition: this is one way to understand 1815 Wordsworth's diatribe against Macpherson:

Having had the good fortune to be born and reared in a mountainous country, from my very childhood I have felt the falsehood that pervades the volumes imposed upon the world under the name of Ossian. From what I saw with my own eyes, I knew that the imagery was spurious. In nature everything is distinct, yet nothing defined into absolute independent singleness. In Macpherson's work, it is exactly the reverse.

To say that the characters never could exist, that the manners are impossible, and that a dream has more substance than the whole state of society, as there depicted, is doing nothing more than pronouncing a censure which Macpherson defied; when, with the steeps of Morven before his eyes, he could talk so familiarly of his Car-borne heroes; – of Morven, which, if one may judge from its appearance at the distance of a few miles, contains scarcely an acre of ground sufficiently accommodating for a sledge to be trailed along its surface.[21]

---

[21]   William Wordsworth, *Essay, Supplementary to the Preface*, in *The Prose Works of William Wordsworth*, ed. W. J. B. Owen and J. W. Smyser, Vol. III of III (Oxford University Press, 1974), 77.

Here Wordsworth mobilizes all the tropes of nativism, nativity, of eye-witness and immediate topographical knowledge, to counter the force of a poetry that had perhaps done more than any other to promote the aura of native-traditional authenticity.

For evidence of the pervasiveness of such authority-bestowing tropes, and their ramifying complexity, we might turn almost at will to Burns, or Hogg, or Clare, who in "The Village Minstrel" hails "[h]is native scenes!" (st. 105, l. 1) and salutes "O dear delightful spots, his native place!" (st. 109, l. 1). Yet as is so frequent in Clare, the very grounds for authority become sites of dispossession: as if re-doing Gray's "Elegy in a Country Churchyard," Clare's minstrel addresses the dead in his native churchyard:

> Looking and list'ning for the brook in vain, -
> Ye'd little think such was your natal scene;
> Ye'd little now distinguish field from plain,
> Or where to look for each departed green;
> All plough'd and buried now, as though there nought had been. (st. 111)

Claiming the authority as a native to measure what has disappeared from the "natal scene": therein lies the critical force and pathos of Clare's project. His work rings several variations on experiential authority, as in "January" in *The Shepherd's Calendar* (1827), which is shot through with testimonial bona fides, local knowledges, observations of animal behavior. The poet appears as native informant, stationed in a line of oral transmission –

> The witching spells of winter nights,
> Where are they fled with their delights,
> When list'ning on the corner seat,
> The winter's evening length to cheat,
> I heard my mother's memory tell
> Tales superstition loves so well,
> Things said or sung a thousand times,
> In simple prose or simpler rhymes?
> Ah, where is page of poesy
> So sweet as theirs was wont to be?[22]

This potentially bathetic contest between homespun stories and inadequate "page[s] of poesy" points to something far more critical in Clare: a keen awareness that in such a case as his, childhood memory and cultural memory overlapped, and that the agricultural ecology sustaining such tale-ridden winter nights was fast fading – and not because of the

---

[22] Clare, "January," "The Shepherd's Calendar," "*I Am*," 71.

work of invisible hands but rather the all too visible enclosures pauperizing the population.

The complex orchestration of editorial, ethnographic, and experiential authorities in particular is a hallmark of romantic *poiesis*, with poets adjusting the ratios of these depending on their situations and aspirations. Poets could and did often appeal to several registers of poetic authority: *Lyrical Ballads* as a collection navigates between a kind of documentary, ethnographic authority and that of represented subjectivity – between, say, "The Complaint of a Forsaken Indian Woman" and "Tintern Abbey." In his Preface, Wordsworth made clear this double-sided project, remarking of the "poems in the collection," "it may be proper to say that they are either absolute inventions of the author, or facts which took place within his personal observation or that of his friends."[23] Either absolute inventions or personally observed facts: here Wordsworth lays out the horizon of his *poiesis*, grounded in either authorial "invention" or in attested "fact."

Any number of poetic projects in this period display such heteronymous authority: Byron's *Childe Harold* displays coordinates experiential authority (the flirting with and through the Harold-persona), ethnographic authority (thus were my travels and transcriptions), authority of translation (cf. the Albanian war-song) and of literary simulation/imitation, in such moments as the "Good Night Song," modeled on "Lord Maxwell's Goodnight." Southey's *Thalaba* suggests the editor's hand in its florid apparatus, the English ballad tradition in its various songs, the frisson of ethnographic authority in various footnotes. And of course, as previously suggested, Scott's *Minstrelsy* offered a striking orchestration of modes of authority, all subsumed under the role of editor-cum-native.

HETERONYMOUS AUTHORITY: COORDINATING INTERIORITY AND EXTERIORITY

A Editorial authority and inward turns: Scott's Minstrelsy *and* Marmion

Scott's developing editorial persona clearly did not preclude the autobiographical I: it was precisely through his emendations, retrospective essays, prefaces, and postmarks that Scott mobilized, testified to and reworked his experience, as well as in his more conspicuously "life-writing" projects as his *Memoirs* and *Journals*. Whether appearing as minstrel-manqué, half-hiding as "the Author of Waverley," pranking as the willfully anonymous author of

---

[23] Wordsworth, "Advertisement" to *Lyrical Ballads*, 8.

"The Bridal of Triermain" and "Harold the Dauntless," or styling himself the Sheriff of Selkirk or the Laird of Abbotsford, Scott's self-representations suggested a complex negotiation and management of class, status, authorship, authority, property, and public persona.

Perhaps too little remarked are Scott's attempts to track an explicit minstrel autobiography *within* his work, most notably in his second metrical romance *Marmion; or, A Tale of Flodden Field* (1808). If in *The Lay of the Last Minstrel*, the minstrel-poet is distanced into a seventeenth-century past, mediated by a framing, modern narrator, *Marmion* strikingly alters the ratio of historical and poetic distances. Scott prefaces each of its six cantos with an "Introduction" *in propria persona*, addressed to friends and comrades, including the Rev. John Marriott, tutor to the son of Scott's patron, the Duke of Buccleuch, and William Erskine, his close friend, fellow lawyer, and literary sounding-board. Each of these introductions is retrospective, full of reflections on his early experience, the "growth of the poet's mind," and shared ventures; each is in a regular octosyllabic couplet, the "minstrel measure."

> We marked each memorable scene,
> And held poetic talk between;
> Nor hill, nor brook, we paced along,
> But had its legend or its song.
> > Introduction to Canto II, To the Rev.
> > John Marriott, A. M., Ashestiel, Ettrick Forest, *Marmion*[24]

It is as if Scott were launching each canto with a sociable epistle, as if he were Pope to Marriott's Arbuthnot, or perhaps (more to the contemporary point) Coleridge addressing Wordsworth or Lamb.[25] Metrical romance here offers a space for multiple modes of historical narration, from the biographical remembrance to the military campaign to the course of love in the seventeenth century; it also allows Scott to take over certain Augustan modes – e.g. the epistle – he would have seemed to abjure.

The introduction addressed to Erskine, Canto III, moves from Scott's present work, his poetry, to a portrait of the artist as a young man:

---

[24] Scott, Introduction to Canto II, *Marmion; or, A Tale of Flodden Field*, *Poetical Works*, 535. Future citations from these and other romances will be by Canto, section, and page.

[25] On these Introductory passages in *Marmion* as Scott's soon-to-be-abandoned version of a Coleridgean conversation poem, see David Hewitt, "Scott, Sir Walter (1771–1832)," in *Oxford Dictionary of National Biography*, ed. H. C. G. Matthew and Brian Harrison (Oxford University Press, 2004); online edn., ed. Lawrence Goldman, May 2006, www.oxforddnb.com/view/article/24928 (accessed October 17, 2006).

> Thus while I ape the measure wild
> Of tales that charmed me yet a child,
> Rude though they be, still with the chime
> Return the thoughts of early time;
> And feelings, roused in life's first day,
> Glow in the line, and prompt the lay.
>
> (Introduction, Canto III, 394–5)

Though Scott ostentatiously and characteristically condescends to his efforts (aping wild measures and so on), he nevertheless "return[s]" through them to "thoughts of early time;/and feelings," to which he never condescends. Such a passage is reminiscent of nothing so much as certain passages in the *Prelude* – "fair seed-time had my soul" (I, 306) – when Wordsworth traces in his infancy the springs of later poetic vocation.

> Was it for this
> That one, the fairest of all Rivers, lov'd
> To blend his murmurs with my Nurse's song,
> And from his alder shades and rocky falls,
> And form his fords and shallows, sent a voice
> That flow'd along my dreams? For this didst Thou,
> O Derwent! travelling over the green Plains
> Near my sweet Birthplace, didst Thou, beauteous Stream,
> Make ceaseless music ... (*Prelude*, I, 272–80)

and later, as Wordsworth recalls the long summer days in his youth when he

> stood alone
> Beneath the sky, as if I had been born
> On Indian Plains, and from my Mother's hut
> Had run abroad in wantonness, to sport,
> A naked Savage, in the thunder shower. (*Prelude*, I, 301–5)

From Wordsworth's River Derwent to Scott's Sandyknowe to other youthful haunts, the child finds in his environs the seeds of his vocation:

> Yet was poetic impulse given,
> By the green hill and clear blue heaven.
> It was a barren scene, and wild,
> Where naked cliffs were rudely piled
> But ever and anon between
> Lay velvet tufts of loveliest green:
> And well the lonely infant knew
> Recesses where the wall flower grew ...
>
> (*Marmion*, Introduction to Canto III, To William Erskine,
> Esq. Ashestiel [394–5])

Common to both poets is the pronounced figuration of *nativity*, *native clime*, and *natality*: the condition of having been born, as Hannah Arendt uses the term,[26] and of having been born *in a specific place*: "It was a barren scene, and wild," Scott writes, thereby linking his infant scenery to his "measure wild."

This unusual elaboration of autobiography in Scott – characteristically elaborated as part of a conversation and/or epistolary network – suggests that in *Marmion* Scott attempted to make good on James Beattie's blocked attempts to use the minstrel as a vehicle for the poet's, and not just the notional culture's, *Bildung*.[27] That is to say: both Scott and Wordsworth made inward turns, were capable of "the internalization of quest romance," as Harold Bloom put it in his famous essay[28]; both understood minstrelling *poiesis* as an opportunity to explore autobiographical as well as ethnographic or historical figuration. Yet, as David Hewitt observes, Scott never tried such a poetic experiment again.[29] The experiment in *Marmion*, an experiment in autobiographical, inter-generic writing pushing on from the metrical and generic innovations of *The Lay of the Last Minstrel*, was never to be repeated: the Editor-function was a more successful place (judged by sales) from which to launch future attempts on the public. Thus, while Scott continued in the romance mode, he abandoned the reflexive lyric "I": self-reflexivity would be channeled, extended, and authorized through his editorial persona, in whatever genre he publicly pursued.

The point here, with which this essay began, is to emphasize the reciprocity of lyric subjectivity and editorial exteriority, however much a particular author might have more vigorously pursued one option. The multiply mediated *poiesis* represented in Scott was not limited to his work, or even to the genre of ballad collections: the preoccupation with ethnographic authority, oral-literate interactions, and mediation so conspicuous in Scott equally informs the work of William Wordsworth. This is all the

---

[26] See Hannah Arendt, "Prologue," *The Human Condition* (University of Chicago Press, 1958, 1989), 1–11, in particular her invocation of "the most general condition of human existence: birth and death, natality and mortality" (8).

[27] See Sutherland's illuminating article, "The Native Poet: The Influence of Percy's Minstrel from Beattie to Wordsworth," *Review of English Studies*, New Series 33 (132) [November 1982]: 414–33.

[28] See Harold Bloom, "The Internalization of Quest-Romance," *Romanticism and Consciousness: Essays in Criticism*, ed. Harold Bloom (New York: Norton, 1970), 3–24.

[29] See David Hewitt, "Scott, Sir Walter (1771–1832)," *ODNB*: "The six epistles in Marmion are wholly different [from Scott's other work]: they are Scott's personal meditations on who he is, and on the status of his art; they explore the Romantic themes of memory, consciousness, and identity. They are Scott's finest poems, yet when they appeared they were universally criticized … Never again did he use his own voice; never again did he attempt to explore his own mind and personality in the genre most closely associated with Coleridge, the conversation poem."

more striking because Wordsworth's ballads were presented as original, novel poems, poems composed by an author (even if he sometimes chose, as in the 1798 Lyrical Ballads, to be anonymous) and certainly not by tradition. Yet if Wordsworth polemically rejected certain aspects of poetic inheritance and tradition (personifications, poetic diction, and so on), he embraced a notion of "human inheritance," which included oral tradition, oral poetries, and local lore.[30]

B *Oral materia and ethnographic authority in Wordsworth*

The discourse of oral authentication appears throughout Wordsworth, especially when – as with Scott – he has chosen to present himself as a kind of poetic native-informant, participant observer, or listener-researcher within the rustic community. Consider, for example, the note he prefaces to one of his most celebrated poems, "Hart-Leap Well":

Hart-Leap Well is a small spring of water, about five miles from Richmond in Yorkshire, and near the side of the road which leads from Richmond to Askrigg. Its name is derived from a remarkable chace, the memory of which is preserved by the monuments spoken of in the second Part of the following Poem, which monuments do exist as I have there described them.[31]

Moving from topographical description to the tradition of the "chace" or hunt that the poem recounts, here we see Wordsworth deploying the testimonial mode so favored by Romantic poets when they wished to use traditional stories and places in their own work. Note as well his purveying of the folk etymology for the well's name, which becomes, of course, the poem's title. "Hart-Leap Well" emerges, then, not only as a much-storied site – a place saturated with oral lore – but also as a site marked by Wordsworth's handling.[32] But Wordsworth makes sure that in his later intervention, the literary transformation, he ostentatiously pays his debt to the oral materials which made the poem possible.

---

[30] On Wordsworth's strong engagement with oral history, particularly local lore and custom, see Barbara T. Gates, "Wordsworth's Use of Oral History," *Folklore* 85:4 (Winter 1974): 254–67.

[31] Wordsworth, prefatory note to "Hart-Leap Well," *Lyrical Ballads*, 127.

[32] For comments on the site, and its ongoing literary-local significance in part due to Wordsworth's poem, see David Chandler, "Hart-Leap Well: A History of the Site of Wordsworth's Poem," *Notes and Queries* (March 2002): 19–25. Chandler suggests that the poem "was probably an attempt to preserve a genuine piece of folklore" (20). He returns to this argument in "The Politics of 'Hart-Leap Well,'" *Charles Lamb Bulletin* NS 111 (July 2000), writing that the ballad "preserves ... the substance of a true story" (117). He also suggests that Wordsworth himself bestowed the name on the spring, which previous to his poem was known as Bowes Well. Here Wordsworth's poem not only drew on tradition: the poem entered tradition and indeed *named the place*.

What we see here is not only the usefulness of oral traditions for poetry but the desire to build acknowledgments of such usefulness into the poem. The turn to orality, that is, could have been suppressed or obscured; but time and again Wordsworth announces his debt to and interest in lore, story, report, rumor, and tradition. Through such announcements he, like Scott, marks his own poetry as a particular kind of poetry, one made out of an explicit dialogue with, and handling of, oral materials. Indeed it was Wordsworth, as Barbara Gates argues, who more strongly engaged oral history, while Scott advised the mining of texts, not locals, for intriguing tales, customs, and mores.[33] Again, it is the representation of orality, and not simply the use of it, that is most striking and most important for considering Romantic *poiesis*.

Throughout *Lyrical Ballads* we find a testimonial rhetoric, an authoritative claim. Consider "The Childless Father," to which Wordsworth appended the following asterisked note:

*In several parts of the North of England, when a funeral takes place, a bason full of Sprigs of Box-wood is placed at the door of the house from which the Coffin is taken up, and each person who attends the funeral ordinarily takes a Sprig of this Box-wood, and throws it into the grave of the deceased.[34]

Such notes, attached to the poems and meant to be read with them, certainly put pressure on the admittedly moth-eaten requirement that poems be, in John Donne's phrase, "well-wrought urns." The constant recourse to the oral breaks open the seamless closure of the poem-as-artifact; indeed, the notes and commentary throughout *Lyrical Ballads* suggest that Romantic poetry, read in its first published incarnations, would often resist later New and post-New Critical formulations about poetry. So often presented as the writer of exquisite, anthologizable lyrics requiring no external information for interpretation, Wordsworth was also the writer of poems stuffed with their own critical commentary, a commentary that often reflected his debt to oral communications, his turn to oral traditions, and his desire to offer himself as a transmitter or curator of these traditions (as in the funerary customs in the note above). Oral tradition could appear, in Wordsworth as in Scott, both in the prose surrounding poems or indeed within the fabric of poems themselves. As Wordsworth, speaking of his

---

[33] See Barbara T. Gates, "Wordsworth's Use of Oral History," for her account of Scott's and Wordsworth's exchange over *The White Doe of Rylstone*, during which Scott offered textual material which he said would correct aspects of that poem; to this Wordsworth tersely replied he would rather rely on oral materials and not antiquarian research.

[34] Wordsworth, asterisked note to "The Childless Father," in *Lyrical Ballads*, 204.

poem, "The Horn of Egremont Castle," reported to the amanuensis of his last years, Isabella Fenwick: "This story is a Cumberland Tradition; I have heard it also related of the Hall of Hutton John, and antient residence of the Huddlestons, in a sequestered Valley upon the river Dacor."[35]

And indeed, if we understand "orality" to be a huge, catch-all term covering everything from age-old oral tradition to yesterday's gossip, we see that Wordsworth's poetic project ran through a vast range of oral possibilities and resources. Many of his poems were worked up from local exchanges of stories and bits of news that he, his sister, and his friends gleaned in their rural retreat. One could say, in fact, that in retiring to the Lake District Wordsworth had chosen to live in a community that was in many ways still an oral community; many of the figures he depicts seem to be at most partially literate, and all are accustomed to regular exchanges of gossip, story, and lore. More important for our purposes is the privileged place of oral communications and traditions in Wordsworth's verses as well as his life. His later remarks to Isabella Fenwick emphasize this aspect of the genesis of several poems. Such remarks, however remote from the actual time-of-composition of these poems, could be considered part of the dis-course of oral authentication around, or extrinsic to, Wordsworth's work – and thus are part of the function of exteriority to which I drew attention above. Indeed, the proliferation of testimonial discourse in his remarks to Fenwick suggests that, for Wordsworth, the truth of much of his poetry inhered in the truth – in the authority – of the traditions and incidents recounted therein. Thus:

On "The Sailor's Mother": "I met this woman near the Wishing-Gate, on the high road that then led from Grasmere to Ambleside. Her appearance was exactly as here described, and such was her account, nearly to the letter." (404)

Regarding "Beggars": "Town-End. 1802. Met and described by me to my Sister near the Quarry at the head of Rydal Lake – a place still a chosen resort of migrants travelling with their families." (407)

On "Alice Fell": "1801. Written to gratify Mr. Graham of Glasgow, brother of the Author of the Sabbath ... The incident had happened to himself, and he urged me to put it into verse, for humanity's sake." (408)

Regarding "Resolution and Independence": "Town-End. 1807. This Old Man I met a few hundred yards from my cottage at Town-End, Grasmere, and the account of him is taken from his own mouth." (408)

---

[35] William Wordsworth, Notes of Isabella Fenwick, *Poems, in Two Volumes*, 405. Further citations from this volume will be in text by page.

On "The Blind Highland Boy": "The incident upon which this Poem is founded was related to me by an eye witness ...." (420)

Wordsworth's remarks rely on the pervasive discourse of experiential authority ("the incident had happened to himself"), of immediate transmission ("such was her account, nearly to the letter," "the account of him is taken from his own mouth"), of "eye witness"– in short, on the discourse of ethnographic and ethnopoetic authority that also marked Scott's, Hogg's, and Clare's *poiesis*. And in fact, Wordsworth and Scott occasionally worked up the same incident in their verse. Of the poem, "Fidelity," about a dog faithfully keeping watch over its dead master, Wordsworth reported, "Walter Scott heard of the [master's] accident, and both he and I, without either of us knowing that the other had taken up the subject, each wrote a poem in admiration of the dog's fidelity" (404). Notable here is that Scott *heard* of the accident, as did Wordsworth: oral reports, once again, became the stuff of their verse.

Whether local reports of "accidents" or authoritative accounts of traditionary lore, such oral *materia* could present problems for the literary poet committed to trafficking in orally based authority. Oral information could, of course, be wrong, as Wordsworth acknowledged in his note to "Rob Roy's Grave": "I have since been told that I was misinformed as to the burial-place of Rob Roy. If so, I may plead in excuse that I wrote on apparently good authority, namely that of a well-educated Lady who lived at the head of the Lake within a mile or less of the point indicated as containing the remains of one so famous in that neighborhood" (415). And here we see how Wordsworth shifts the responsibility for promulgating error from himself and his poem to the "well-educated Lady" who had seemed an "apparently good authority." That Wordsworth even considered making such concessive, corrective remarks is striking: they reveal how strongly invested he was – and how powerfully dependent he considered some of his poems to be – in the authority of local oral traditions.

AUTHORIZATION AND REMEDIATION IN *THE PRELUDE*

That Wordsworth's lyrical ballads both solicited and aimed to surpass the cultural authority of traditional ballads is not surprising: what is striking is the way the double logic of his balladeering *poiesis* – editorial authority displayed around poems, lyric interiority explored within them – migrated into epic. *The Prelude* is famously preoccupied with the problem of authorizing its subject – the growth of the poet's mind, and the growth of

Wordsworth's as a type thereof. As critics have long observed, the poem is the *summa* of Wordsworthian internalization. It is perhaps less often emphasized that Wordsworth's ceaseless poetic self-authorization is complexly grounded in ethnographic and editorial protocols. The ethnographic and testimonial turns so prominent in *Lyrical Ballads* recur throughout *The Prelude* in an extended figuration and implicit defense of ear- and eye-witness. And Wordsworth emerges not only as inquirer into his own history but conspicuous editor and remediator of others' tales.[36]

The work of the *Prelude* is to authorize Wordsworth as both native and informant: here we can see the convergence of Wordsworth's poetics with self-testifying moments in Scott's *Minstrelsy*, or *Marmion*: ethnopoetics meets autobiography – My Informant, Myself.

> How shall I trace the history, where seek
> The origin of what I then have felt? (2. 365–66)[37]

> Relating simply as my wish hath been,
> A Poet's history. (4.70–1)

What would seem to be a merely autobiographical history – however exceptional the subject – reveals itself to be a far more ambitious project. The ceaseless retracing of an individual life, a "poet's history," soon involves the poet in a retracing of a much more general history – what Shelley later called "the history of our species." Cultural history meets personal history, as the progress of this poet's being coordinates itself with "the progress of our being" (2.239) – a generalized human being:

> Bless'd the infant Babe,
> (for with my best conjectures I would trace
> The progress of our being) blest the Babe,
> Nurs'd in his Mother's arms, the Babe who sleeps
> Upon his Mother's breast, who, when his soul
> Claims manifest kindred with an earthly soul,
> Doth gather passion from his Mother's eye! (2. 237–43)

The Prelude everywhere bespeaks its internalization of conjectural history, the "progress of society" model so powerfully developed by the Scottish sociological school and manifested in everything from Beattie's *Minstrel* to

---

[36] Any discussion of Wordsworth's tale-telling is deeply indebted to a brilliant critical heritage, which I will not attempt to survey here: but among the most incisive explorations is surely Don H. Bialostosky, *Making Tales: The Poetics of Wordsworth's Narrative Experiments* (University of Chicago Press, 1984).

[37] William Wordsworth, *The Thirteen Book Prelude*. All quotations will be cited by book and line in text.

Scott's oeuvre to Peacock's *Four Ages of Poetry*. Here we see how *poiesis* took up the project Mary Poovey discerns in Scottish conjectural history: that of reconciling moral-experimental maps of subjectivity with accounts of sociality.[38] As critics have long noted, Wordsworth's childhood becomes a type of the ideal childhood of the race; it does so through the logic of an internalized conjectural history – the growth of his mind become a type of the stadial growth of human mind *tout court*. It is no accident that Book 8, "love of nature leading to love of mankind," tracks a passage through a pastoral mode, that crucial phase in stadial history preceding the emergence of civil society and the commercial epoch. Wordsworth's pastoral is ostentatiously anti-literary; we note too the profoundly *sociological* and *ethno-historical* nature of Wordsworth's shepherd sociability phase.[39]

Wordsworth ushers us from pastoral to civil society and the ego-formations and affects appropriate to each; part of the tension of *The Prelude* is its fixation on the pastoral mode, shepherd heroes and affections, which the poem itself recognizes as a superseded or residual state. For all the fascinated loathing of the London passages, and the repeated homages to rural retirement, this is a profoundly metropolitan work, its "retracing" and retreat itself a mark of privilege and arrival elsewhere. Wordsworth could always leave the woods and fields. Burns and Clare couldn't, and had to work them in more obviously labored ways.

In a mode of ethnographic pastoral, Wordsworth takes pains to identify his shepherds as *real shepherds*, actually encountered:

> A rambling School-boy, thus
> Have I beheld him, without knowing why
> Have felt his presence in his own domain,
> As of a Lord and Master (8.390–3)

---

[38] See in particular Poovey's remarks in "Scottish Conjectural History," in *A History of the Modern Fact*, 218–29. Poovey is more interested in the interface of theories of subjectivity with those of liberal governmentality, but her account of stadial theory and its inquiries into "human nature" complements the analysis of *poiesis* offered here.

[39] Wordsworth's extended engagement with the human sciences (moral philosophy, political economy, and other emergent discourses) has received new attention in the past twenty years, in part a function of humanists' attempt to metabolize Foucault, particularly *Les Mots et Les Choses*, but also because of Romanticists' renewed orientation to the British Enlightenment. For the sociologics and anthropologics of Wordsworth's project, see Regina Hewitt, *The Possibilities of Society: Wordsworth, Coleridge, and the Sociological Viewpoint of English Romanticism* (Albany, NY: State University of New York Press, 1997), which explores the Romantic project as "poetic sociology." Reading backward from the institution of sociology, Hewitt reads selected poems and essays as models both of and for "learning how a coherent society can function" (98). See also Bewell, with his striking analysis of *Lyrical Ballads* as a kind of "domestic anthropology," in *Wordsworth and the Enlightenment*, and McLane, *Romanticism and the Human Sciences*, for an inquiry into the anthropo-logic of British Romanticism.

In a typically dialectical move, Wordsworth takes conjectural shepherds out of the pastoral stage of society and puts them within his own experiential space: here, as in "Hart-Leap Well," there are still shepherds to teach us lessons. And there are tales of shepherds to remediate. Most important, these shepherds and tales are *eye- and ear-witnessed*: therein lies Wordsworth's special claim, this grounding of Fancy and ultimately imagination in this natively informed *I*:

> I myself, mature
> In manhood then, have seen a pastoral Tract
> Like one of these, where Fancy might run wild. (8.324–6)

There is then a complex coordination of sociological and individual axes throughout *The Prelude*, individual memory saluted but always re-grounded in cultural location: and the second half of this operation is too often forgotten in the focus on Wordsworthian mind – even with a generation of incisive historicist criticism behind us. Thus the egotistical sublime of signal passages becomes a social condition, a generalized human condition:

> And here, O Friend! have I retrac'd my life
> Up to an eminence, and told a tale
> Of matters which, not falsly, I may call
> The Glory of my youth. Of Genius, Power
> Creation and Divinity itself
> I have been speaking, for my theme has been
> What pass'd within me. Not of outward things
> Done visibly for other minds, words, signs,
> Symbols or action; but of my own heart
> Have I been speaking, and my youthful mind. (3. 168–77)

What would seem to be a conspicuous emphasis on Wordsworthian singularity is quickly generalized: "Yet each man is a memory to himself" (3.189). The very passage that points to a culmination of an inward turn – "my theme has been/What pass'd within me" (3.173–4); "of my own heart/Have I been speaking" (3.176–7); "to shape out/Some Tale from my own heart" (1. 221–2) – segues immediately into a species logic. The individual is the social being, as Marx reminds us. Tales are after all *that which can be told to others*, those stories that might be circulated and retold: as the poet reminds us in "Simon Lee," "should you think,/Perhaps a tale you'll make it." The "Tale from my own heart" launched in Book 1 expands to encompass, among the many tales of *The Prelude*, "a Soldier's Tale" (4. 445), a "simply fashion'd tale" recalled from childhood (5.177), "the Matron's Tale" (8. 224) of the shepherd and his son in Book 8, the mediation of which Wordsworth so ostentatiously marks:

> Here may be told
> One, as recorded by my Household Dame.
> At the first falling of autumnal snow
> A Shepherd and his son one day went forth
> (Thus did the Matron's Tale begin) to seek
> A Straggler of their flock. (8. 220–5)

Indeed one way to understand the notorious evasions and bizarrerie of the Julia and Vaudracour episode is to see Wordsworth effortfully pivoting from referent to mediator of this tale, a story of transgressive sex, illegitimacy, and paternity gone awry – a tale told (with variants) by any number of ballads.

The Prelude thus installs Wordsworth as a culture-poet as much as a poet of individual consciousness and sets forth a dynamic movement between socialized poetries and inward turns. Wordsworth operates in *The Prelude* as much as an editor and remediator of cultural contents as a figurer of lyric subjectivity: as we have seen, these are profoundly interwoven poetic functions, themselves indebted to the balladeering and minstrelling *poiesis* detailed in previous chapters. *The Prelude* is an epic chock-full of remediated tales and ballads, these materials ostentatiously flagged as such in Wordsworth's serial iteration of his "recording" and "retracing" – to wit, the Miltonic formulation about his task ("Nor sedulous as I have been to trace/How nature by extrinsic passion" was transformed); or any number of formulations foregrounding the (re)tracing, telling, and recording of matters (viz. "I would relate" [1. 186]; "I would record/how in tyrannic times ... " [1. 203–4], "Nor should this, perchance/Pass unrecorded" [2. 395–6], or the address to Coleridge in Book 3: "And here, O Friend, have I retrac'd my life/Up to an eminence" (3. 168–9). Indeed in the closing passage of the 1805 *Prelude*, Wordsworth converts *Lyrical Ballads*, and more touchingly the remembered project of *Lyrical Ballads*, into a spot of time: the conclusion of Book 13 celebrates his and Coleridge's walking –

> That summer when on Quantock's grassy Hills
> Far ranging, and among her sylvan Coombs,
> Thou in delicious words with happy heart,
> Didst speak the Vision of that Ancient Man,
> The bright-eyed Mariner, and rueful woes
> Didst utter of the Lady Christabel
> And I associate with such labour, walk'd
> Murmuring of him who, joyous hap! Was found,

> After the perils of his moonlight ride
> Near the loud Waterfall; or her who sate
> In misery near the miserable Thorn ... (13.393–403)

Offering a mini-résumé of the tales he had so brilliantly swapped and formalized with Coleridge, Wordsworth here as it were dissolves *Lyrical Ballads* back into their prior form as material commonly available for poetic (and more broadly human) conversability.

Wordsworth's authority as poet is at stake here, not simply his authority as generic cultural arbiter: and in the several moments in which he lays out his specifically poetic project we see his diagnostic sifting through several types of authority we by now are well-prepared to recognize. Wordsworth's prehistory of poetic inspiration bears a striking resemblance to antiquarian efforts. Making inquiry of himself, and of possible poetic theme, he observes that he "wanted not a store/of primitive hours" (4.340). An archive unto himself,

> a longing in me rose
> To brace myself to some determin'd aim,
> Reading or thinking, *either to lay up*
> *New stores, or rescue from decay the old*
> *By timely interference.* (1. 124–8, emphasis added)

"Rescu[ing] from decay" old "stores": this evokes nothing so much as Percy's conception of his project, or Scott's in the *Minstrelsy*, or indeed more current ethno-cultural efforts – the "salvage anthropology" described by George Marcus. The work of the poet is to generate further stores, for a perpetually revivable futurity: "I would enshrine the spirit of the past/For future restoration" (2. 342–3).

Wordsworth's laid up or rescued "stores" are both cultural and individual; they are simultaneously inherited and introspected "stores," harvests from within and without. A Wordsworthian spot of time is, significantly, a storied spot, as the extended figuration of such throughout the Prelude suggests. In Book 5, for example, Wordsworth invokes Dorothy and their days spent

> wandering, as we did,
> Through heights and hollows, and bye spots of tales
> Rich with indigenous produce, open ground
> Of Fancy, happy pasture rang'd at will! (5. 234–7)

These "bye spots of tales" are harvested throughout *The Prelude*, linking the poet, local culture, human inheritance, and cultural-transmitters from beldames to Milton, as suggested in the elaborate genealogy of "inspired souls" saluted in Book 5:

> And yet it seems
> That here, in memory of all books which lay
> Their sure foundations in the heart of Man;
> Whether by native prose or numerous verse,
> That in the name of all inspired souls,
> From Homer, the great Thunderer; from the voice
> Which roars along the bed of Jewish Song;
> And that, more varied and elaborate,
> Those trumpet-tones of harmony that shake
> Our Shores in England; from those loftiest notes
> Down to the low and wren-like warblings, made
> For Cottagers and Spinners at the wheel,
> And weary Travellers when they rest themselves
> By the highways and hedges; ballad tunes,
> Food for the hungry ears of little Ones,
> And of old Men who have surviv'd their joy:
> It seemeth, in behalf of these, the works
> And of the Men who fram'd them, whether known
> Or sleeping nameless in their scatter'd graves,
> That I should here assert their rights, attest
> Their Honours; and should, once for all, pronounce
> Their benediction; speak of them as Powers
> For ever to be hallowed ... (5. 198–220)

From Homeric epic to "ballad tunes," from Jewish prophets to cottagers and spinners, Wordsworth here maps a world-historical and, significantly, *transmedial poiesis*: encompassing not only a multitude of genres but a variety of oral and literary poetries. Poetry here moves through "books" and their memory as well as "tunes," and all these "works" are granted "[t]heir Honours." This is obviously a strongly hierarchized accounting – from "loftiest notes" to "low ... warblings" – but it aspires to be a total accounting.

Wordsworth's sifting of themes in *The Prelude* – extensively in Book 1, and then again in Book 8 – points up how polemical is his construction of authority. He is as engaged with low spinners, cottagers, and balladeers as with contemporaries, with notionally oral informants (e.g. that deserted soldier, his old beldame) as with Spenser and Milton. And just as some antiquarians found in oral informants the living archive that would distinguish their work from text-bound colleagues, Wordsworth announces himself as a poet hostile to a merely textual, merely literary *poiesis*. In Book 8 of the *Prelude*, Wordsworth revisits the matter of history, British themes, and authorized poetics, and in a remarkable passage he implicitly distinguishes the ground of his poetics from that of his contemporaries:

> 'Tis true the History of my native Land,
> With those of Greece compared and popular Rome,
> Events not lovely nor magnanimous,
> But harsh and unaffecting in themselves
> And in our high-wrought modern narratives
> Stript of their harmonizing soul, the life
> Of manners and familiar incidents,
> Had never much delighted me. And less
> Than other minds I had been used to owe
> The pleasure which I found in place or thing
> To extrinsic, transitory accidents,
> Of record or traditions; but a sense
> Of what had been here done, and suffer'd here
> Through ages, and was doing, suffering, still
> Weigh'd with me, could support the test of thought,
> Was like the enduring majesty and power
> Of independent nature; and not seldom
> Even individual remembrances,
> By working on the shapes before my eyes
> Became like vital functions of the soul. (8.770–89)

Not "native land" but native "suffering" "here": this is the ground of Wordsworth's poetics. Wordsworth makes a sharp distinction here between "record or tradition" and a more nebulous "sense/of what had been done here, and suffer'd here/Through ages": not development but recurrence; not record or tradition but "a sense" of doings; not events, manners, incidents, or the traditions of lore but ongoing "suffering": not Scott, say (with his conspicuous mining of "record" and "tradition"), but Wordsworth and "a sense" of "suffering." This and this alone "could support the test of thought" and could provide true matter for the "awful burthen" of "philosophic Song."

That Wordsworth authorized a poetics of sensible suffering, that he ostentatiously rejected what seemed to him merely literary definitions of *poiesis*: these are now commonplaces of his reception, and rightly so. What is striking is the specific way Wordsworth arrives at such authorization in *The Prelude*: his poetics requires an extensive working through, sifting, and arbitration of several grounds of poetic authority – rejecting in the passage above, for example, "record or tradition," while elsewhere ceaselessly iterating his own kinds of "recording." When we recall that "record" (manuscripts, previously printed books) and "tradition" (orally transmitted legend, lore, and ballad) were the core and often competing bases of balladeers' authority, we are prepared to feel the force of Wordsworth's polemical "recording" and "relating" over other poets', whether "oral" or "literary." When we recall as well that minstrels, those culture-poets par excellence, were imagined – by antiquarians as well as Romantic poets – to function precisely as cultural archives, we can see how Wordsworth both inherits and transforms the cultural basis of poetic authority.

At once an archive in himself and an editor of others' – his several informants functioning à la Scott's Mrs. Hogg, that "living miscellany" – Wordsworth presents himself as if externalizing his memory of himself while simultaneously internalizing the contents of others'. The representations of these operations constitute "the growth of the poet's mind" – a growth we can see as indebted to historiographic and ethnographic discourses of mind, its development, and its testifiability. And perhaps we are now in a better position to see how that mind coordinated several medial streams under the sign of Wordsworth's own authority: for truly, here the medium was the message. Yet the medium was no rigid, reified thing: the poet is a privileged node in an endlessly amplifying feedback loop, in which the "stores" of subjectivity become "related" to cultural "stores" and vice-versa. Wordsworth expects us to understand the critical, reflexive mobility of the poet-as-medium. "A Traveller I am/And all my tale is of myself," Wordsworth observes in Book 3, ll. 195–7. We should hear a strongly mock-epic note here, a satire on the egotistical sublime as well as an homage: for Wordsworth opened up for us in ways we too often forget a space for poetry to move forward. At the very moment the novel seemed the imaginative genre most capable of totalizing the situation, in Marxist terms, poets saw a threat and an opportunity. If Scott has many heirs in Hollywood as well as in blockbuster historical fictions, Wordsworth has had surprising, unacknowledged poetic heirs and may yet. "I am large, I contain multitudes."

CHAPTER 7

British Romantic mediality and beyond:
Reflections on the fate of "orality"

In *Tristes Tropiques*, Claude Lévi-Strauss suggests that we think of so-called primitive peoples not as "peoples without history" but as "peoples without writing."[1] British poets of the late eighteenth and early nineteenth centuries discovered themselves to be indisputably and perhaps regrettably both historical and literate. Not that Chaucer, Spenser, or Milton lacked either a sense of history or the resources of writing; but none of these luminaries had to consider, as did so many of the English and Scottish Romantics, the fate of poetry as a cultural project set adrift from its imagined origins – origins in speech and gesture, in what Percy Shelley called a more "vitally metaphorical" language.[2] To restore poetry to those origins, or at the very least to remind readers of those origins, was the explicit aim of such poets as William Wordsworth and Walter Scott. Shelley described poetry as "connate with the origin of man"; Wordsworth lauded the almost mystical connection between the first bards and their audiences; and Scott derived his own poetic genealogy from minstrels who, he maintained, served the Scottish "National Muse" even as Homer served that of the Greeks.[3]

This search for origins was a function of this period's heightened consciousness of the history and mediality of poetry. It is not an overstatement

---

[1] See Claude Lévi-Strauss, "A Writing Lesson," in *Tristes Tropiques*, trans. John and Doreen Weightman (Penguin, 1992), 298: "After eliminating all other criteria which have been put forward to distinguish between barbarism and civilization, it is tempting to retain this one at least: there are peoples with, or without, writing; the former are able to store up their past achievements and to move with ever-increasing rapidity towards the goal they have set themselves, whereas the latter, being incapable of remembering the past beyond the narrow margin of individual memory, seem bound to remain imprisoned in a fluctuating history which will always lack both a beginning and any lasting awareness of an aim."

[2] For this phrase, see Shelley, "Defence," *Shelley's Poetry and Prose*, 482.

[3] See Shelley, "Defence," 480. For Wordsworth's ruminations on "the earliest poets of all nations" see his "Appendix on Poetic Diction," appended in 1802 to Wordsworth and Coleridge's *Lyrical Ballads*, 317–18. After a brief discourse on Homer and his imagined editor Pisistratus, Walter Scott informs us that Scottish ballads offer a glimpse of "the National Muse in her cradle" ("Introductory Remarks on Popular Poetry," *MSB*, 7).

to say that, in the last decades of the eighteenth and the first of the nine-teenth centuries, almost every major British literary poet found him- or herself engaging with oral tradition, as well as with the figure of the oral poet, his work, his cultural position, and his method of composition. As we have seen, oral tradition acquired new status not only as a legitimate fund of cultural authority but also a resource for the making and annotating of "original," literary poetry. Balladeering protocols and a minstrelsy complex informed and galvanized Romantic *poiesis*, such that we can trace a trans-formation of poetic possibility in eighteenth-century Britain: the emergence of a new literary orality. Recent scholarship on eighteenth- and nineteenth-century literature has illuminated the cultural and political stakes of what we might call "the oral turn" in the late eighteenth century; oral theory and more recent developments in media theory help us to reflect further on the processes of mediation (for example, transcription, printing, and other forms of textual "fixing") required and displayed by literary uses of orality. With a complex inheritance of work by theorists of the oral and media theory *tout court*, we may propose for this period a poetic spectrum, one which carefully ranges through the cultural meanings and stylistic possibil-ities of literary orality.

In the following pages I propose to discuss further what has been called "the romance of orality"[4] as a particularly lively and vexed opportunity for Romantic poets. "Orality" of course always threatens to devolve into a virtually contentless word, a reified counter to "literacy" or "the literary": and one aim of this chapter is to resist that, to explore the very different meanings and uses of the notional "oralities" we find in Romantic poetry. It is in fact more precise to conduct such an exploration under the sign of "mediality" rather than "orality" *per se*, because (as I have argued regarding antiquarians, James Beattie's "Minstrel," and numerous other ventures in *poiesis* in this epoch) any conjuring of "orality" in writing or print invites us to reckon with what Friedrich Kittler calls "a transposition of media."[5] Oral-literate conjunctions abound in the work of Romantic poets just as they do in the collections of balladeers, and the poets found themselves thinking along equally theoretical lines: what was the difference between hearing a

---

[4] See Maureen N. McLane, "Ballads and Bards: British Romantic Orality," *Modern Philology* 98:3 (February 2001): 423–43; and see Penny Fielding, *Writing and Orality*: Fielding notes that when the "romance of orality" is "constructed by a dominant ideology it begins to look suspiciously like writing" (10) – that is, as fixed, authoritative, monologic, and culturally hegemonic. Some oralities, that is, are better than others, and in a "graphocentric society" (10), it is the elite literati who sift and determine the values and meanings of the oral.

[5] Kittler, *Discourse Networks, 1800/1900*, in particular the section "Untranslatability and the Transposition of Media," in "Rebus," 265–73. See too Ch. 1, n. 25.

poem and reading it? Between oral tradition and literary inheritance? What were their interfaces, their impasses? Inasmuch as Romantic poets wrote poems about poetry, and lyrics about song, they were also writing poems about media. In its preoccupation with mediality, British Romantic poetry offers a strong test case for what scholars have termed the "double logic of remediation"[6]: a simultaneous drive toward immediacy on the one hand, hypermediacy on the other (what some gloss as the tension between medium as window vs. medium as mirror – this opposition itself a vexed metaphor). The apparent or phantasized immediacies of "orality" repeatedly confront – and indeed are often generated as an effect of – the ostentatious efforts of literate mediators: as in antiquarians' headnotes; Scott's and Hogg's narrators, elaborately framing their minstrels; Wordsworth's, Scott's, Hogg's, and Southey's annotations; Blake's multimedia books, his children, bards, and pipers severely incised by the engraver's hand, pictured and watercolored.[7] Romantic poetries offer exemplary cases of "remediation" – "the cycling of different media through one another," as one scholar glosses it.[8] "Cycling" may be, however, too loosely directional and benign a gerund, for as we've seen, it's not as if poems simply appeared in, or cycled through, any medium at hand: beyond literary and artisanal traditions, there were strong economic and cultural incentives and payoffs for appropriating the glamor of the oral in specific ways, and those poets with pre-existing cultural capital tended to make the best of the print commercial deal.

At the risk of scanting the historico-material specificities attending the making, distribution, and circulation of the specific poems and works here discussed, I hope here to show how an alertness to oral-literate conjunctions might re-open some poems and poetic passages many readers may feel they know all too well. I hope as well in this chapter to suggest how instances of "close-reading," fueled by explicit historical and theoretical concerns, might continue to interest both scholars and students – given that close-reading

---

[6] See (again) Jay David Bolter and Richard Grusin, *Remediation*; and *Rethinking Media Change*, ed. David Thorburn and Henry Jenkins, Introduction, 1–16. The invocation of "window" and "mirror" can't but remind us of M. H. Abrams' *Mirror and the Lamp*, a book that in many ways could be transposed into a newer medial key for ongoing illumination.

[7] Clearly a full account of such interfaces should include the visual not to mention the determinations of print *per se*, especially in Blake's case; and as in Chapter 3 the question of actual and not only notional musics is also relevant. This chapter pursues a subsection of conjunctions within *poiesis* but is certainly not meant to be exhaustive.

[8] In *Writing Machines* (Cambridge, MA: MIT Press, 2002), N. Katherine Hayles invokes Jay David Bolter's and Richard Grusin's influential formulation of "remediation" thus: "*Remediation*, the cycling of different media through one another" (5).

has so nearly bitten the critical-theoretical dust, albeit not in classrooms. I focus then not on orality or literacy *per se*, nor on "oral poetry," nor even or exclusively on "orality-effects" as a function of "literariness." Rather, I will try to sketch in a necessarily preliminary fashion the relations of the "oral" to the "literate" and the "literary" as figured within Romantic literary poems, with a foray into late-twentieth-century poetics. My interest here as elsewhere is on the ways Romantic poets transposed actual and notional oral materials and represented themselves as doing so.

FROM PIPING TO PRINT: BLAKE'S ALLEGORY OF POETIC MEDIATION

William Blake's "Introduction," the first poem in his *Songs of Innocence*, offers a swift résumé of some aspects of Romantic mediality. Critics have brilliantly anatomized the dynamic and often disjunctive interplay between visual and verbal elements of Blake's work[9]; we have perhaps less often attended to his equally complex negotiation of "oral" and "literary" streams in his "composite" *poiesis*. Blake's "Introduction" (Fig. 14) and the other *Songs of Innocence* straddle that fertile ground between song, ballad, and nursery rhyme, the generic and formal definitions of which seem to vary depending on the socio-historical and formal commitments of the classifier.[10] The inaugurating song establishes the occasion, scene, and mode of poetic composition: we first see and hear the poet as a piper casually "piping down the valleys wild."[11] As if to confirm John Stuart Mill's dictum that poetry is not heard but rather overheard, Blake introduces a fey child who has apparently overheard the piper. Asked by the child to "Pipe a song about a Lamb," the Pan-like piper obliges. We may assume that, since he pipes and thus occupies his mouth, the poet-figure pipes a tune of pure music, devoid of words (and yet the child through his request has already made the

---

[9] On the often critically disjunctive relation of Blake's words and pictures, see W. J. T. Mitchell, *Blake's Composite Art: A Study of the Illuminated Poetry* (Princeton University Press, 1978).

[10] A brief glance at some standard books on English metrics and poetic forms confirms this elasticity: John Hollander in *Rhyme's Reason: A Guide to English Verse* (New Haven, CT: Yale University Press, 1989) has several witty, exemplary definitions of the generic ballad stanza and its variants, but none for "song." Whereas Hollander first introduces "quatrain," then "ballad" as a special kind of quatrain, Paul Fussell in *Poetic Meter and Poetic Form* (New York: Random House, 1979, rev. edn.) informs us that the "simplest quatrain is the ballad stanza" (133). Fussell also has no entry for song, which seems to be a far more elastic term than ballad; this may derive from the ballad's strong association with poetry as an art of arranged words, whereas "song" powerfully connotes a tune.

[11] William Blake, "Introduction," *Songs of Innocence*, in *Songs of Innocence and of Experience*, intro. Geoffrey Keynes (Oxford University Press, 1967), plate 4, line 1. Further references to this poem will be cited by line in the text.

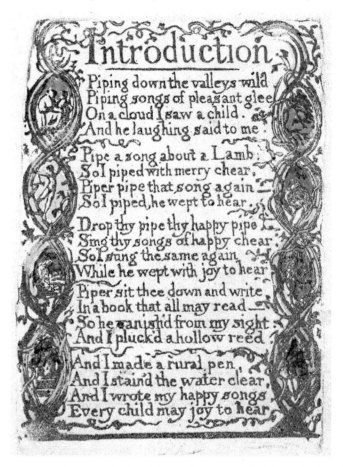

14 William Blake, "Introduction," *Songs of Innocence*, 1789 (Copy C, plate 4);
Lessing J. Rosenwald Collection, Library of Congress, © 2007 the William Blake
Archive. Used with permission.

song "about a Lamb"). This assumption (that the song begins as purely or
primarily instrumental tune) is confirmed by the child's next request for a
song to be sung, not piped: "Drop they pipe thy happy pipe!/Sing thy songs
of happy chear" (ll. 9–10). The poet again obliges, singing, as he asserts, "the
same" (l. 11). (Yet we are induced to wonder: in what way is the song, sung
and no longer piped, "the same"?) The child then exhorts the poet: "Piper
sit thee down and write/In a book that all may read" (ll. 13–14). Again, the

poet obliges, plucking a hollow reed: "And I wrote my happy songs/Every child may joy to hear" (ll. 19–20).

Blake's Introduction is a lovely fable about the origin of the *Songs of Innocence*; the poem is also a whimsical allegory about performance, composition, and mediation. The poem imagines the preconditions of its existence: the book in our hands was desired, requested, by a child "on a cloud" (l. 3). The child here serves as an imagined audience and as a kind of media muse: his requests usher us through a set of poetic mediations. The inner stanzas each mark a new moment and a different medium of performance. What we might call absolute music becomes a kind of program music ("a song about a Lamb" [l. 5]), which in turn becomes sung text and finally the written song. This sequence could be seen as a progressive sophistication of the acoustic and verbal arts, culminating in the written poem; these transformations would then appear in sequence as a kind of unfolding hierarchy of technologies and arts. Unmediated piping, a kind of primitive pastoral, gives way to verbal articulation and ultimately to writing. Yet both the imagined origin and destination of the work remain somewhat ambiguously in the oral despite this progressive displacement toward writing, literacy, and the literary. Note the closing lines: "And I wrote my happy songs/Every child may joy to hear." The potentially pleased children, the imagined future audiences, are just that – imagined as auditors, not readers: they "may joy to hear."

Yet these songs are now decisively written, albeit with a "rural pen." Blake's song invites us to consider what is gained and what is lost in the fixing of form implied by writing. The child urges the piper to write "in a book that all may read" (l. 14). The bookform amplifies the potential audience (to include "all") but also decisively sunders the "song," the poem, from the scene of performance. We see that as soon as the piper begins to write, the child "vanish'd from" the piper's sight: no longer is the child's presence necessary to inspire or guarantee the offering and occasion of song. The very turn to writing banishes the child: in terms of the internal drama of the poem, both muse and audience are gone. Or rather, the audience is implicitly transformed: just as piping yields to writing, so too the single child-interlocutor gives way to the imagined community of child auditors.

Yet for children "to hear" this song, it must be read or recited aloud. Someone must get his or her hands on this book, or must learn this poem by heart, for it to be transmitted as Blake envisions. Blake's poem thus indicates other potential scenes than the dramatized dialogue, the scene of reading and the scene of recitation. Blake prefers to imagine children as auditors, not readers; yet he slyly tips his writing hand in the third stanza, in which he rhymes "read" – the deciphering operation which will presumably bring the book to "all" – with "reed," the instrument which allows him to transcribe his song. The homonym captures in miniature one aspect of the oral-literate conjunction: as the grammar school definition has it, homonyms are words that sound alike but are spelled differently. Such a definition, and such a pun, depend on a fixed orthography: we are clearly far from primitive orality, clearly *après la lettre*. The lexical puns have the fullest force for the reader who sees but also hears the joke. And yet the imagined children still remain relatively in the oral, relying on a literate interlocutor to recite this poem so that they "may joy to hear."

Thus we see that a *Song of Innocence* is also a Song about a complex oral–literate conjunction. The poem takes into account the acoustic and cognitive dimensions of speech, the rhetorical uses of orthography in its puns, and the vital interaction of reading, writing, and hearing. Readers are after all made not born. Blake both acknowledges the mediation of reading and represents a viable pre-literate audience of children. In this way he gestures toward the social, generational aspect of the oral–literate conjunction: we have both children in the oral domain, and also the unrepresented but implicitly mediating literate elders.

A final and brief word on Blake's oral–literate conjunction: a word about pictures. The first plates of *Songs of Innocence* – the plates that immediately precede the poem, "Introduction" – illustrate almost perfectly the transition from the orally-oriented world of piping to the literarily-mediated scene of reading. It is as if Blake gives us a preview, as it were, of the cultural allegory to follow in words. On the Frontispiece, plate 2 (Fig. 15), the boldly sculptural Adamic piper looks up to the child, who has apparently just addressed him (the piper pauses, as it were, mid-stride); on the title page, plate 3 (Fig. 16), we see children leaning on their seated nanny or mother and the book she holds – a volume, quite possibly, of these songs. These images are almost inexhaustibly rich, in their juxtaposition of genders, poses, bodies, clothing, and children, who appear as both flying inspirers and subjects of domestic and pedagogical care. Before we even arrive at the first poem, then, Blake offers us images of the transition he will soon encode in words as well as pictures. To invoke anachronistically another medium, it is as if Blake gives us two silent film stills, which retrospectively become intelligible as a "before" (piping) and an "after" (print). We might say, then, that the frontispiece conjures an oral pre-history (replete with pastoral iconography – Pan, pipers, Arcadia, the conventions of the idyll): such a pre-history is, of course, an invention of literature. The title page conjures,

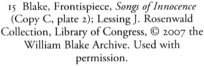

15 Blake, Frontispiece, *Songs of Innocence*
(Copy C, plate 2); Lessing J. Rosenwald
Collection, Library of Congress, © 2007 the
William Blake Archive. Used with
permission.

16 Blake, Title page, *Songs of Innocence*
(Copy C, plate 3); Lessing J. Rosenwald
Collection, Library of Congress, © 2007 the
William Blake Archive. Used with
permission.

by contrast, a "contemporary" and highly mediated oral sphere, the one inhabited by pre- and semi-literate children then and now. It is perhaps unnecessary to observe that what I'm calling a more contemporary scene of reading is as allegorically dense, as fictive, and as visionary, as the preceding plate: we notice that the woman and children sit under an ever-symbolic and ambiguous tree, its branches sinuous and twining, a vine wound around its trunk. It is, interestingly, under the relatively domesticated scene of reading and not under the sculpted, striding, frontal body of the piper that Blake puts his title, his name, and his joint occupation, author and printer. However primitivist his allegiances, Blake had no particular nostalgia for the "piping" phase of poetry, just as he had no longing for the infantine preserve of Innocence, which he in other works derided as the saccharine land of Beulah. It was the *Songs of Experience*, after all, that ultimately gave the *Songs of Innocence* their dialectical spin; so too it was William Blake, as author, printer, and urban poet, who reached back across the divide separating him from primary orality to conjure and critique the primarily oral world of pipers, lambs, and children.

THE ETHNOGRAPHIC ROMANCE: THE ALBANIAN
WAR-SONG IN *CHILDE HAROLD*

We can ascertain a whole other domain of Romantic orality in Byron's *Childe Harold*, the first two cantos of which were published in 1812. A fabulously self-promoting travel poem, *Childe Harold* ushers its eponymous and self-exiled hero through a wide-ranging European terrain. Harold, like Byron, fancies himself a true-born son of Greece, and as he nears the imagined cradle of his much-loved civilization he offers many observations about the peoples now dwelling in the formerly Hellenized mountain region. The world-weary Harold is especially delighted by the primitive hospitality afforded him by the motley crew of soldiers loyal to the Ali Pasha. As he rests in a military camp the Albanian soldiers begin their war-chant. Harold assures us that:

> In sooth, it was no vulgar sight to see
> Their barbarous, yet their not indecent, glee.
> *(Childe Harold*, II. st. LXXII)[12]

Of the Albanians he notes

> the long wild locks that to their girdles stream'd,
> While thus in concert they this lay half sang, half scream'd
> (II. st. LXXII).

The song then begins:

> [1.]
> Tambourgi! Tambourgi! Thy 'larum afar
> Gives hope to the valiant, and promise of war;
> All the sons of the mountains arise at the note,
> Chimariot, Illyrian, and dark Suliote!

In Harold's pleased contemplation of the chanting soldiers, we have an ethnographic scene made literary. The Albanians' performance is notably unrefined: the soldiers "half sang, half-scream'd" the song. The piling on of ethnographic detail – the "wild locks," the "kirtled" style of dress (II. st. LVIII, LXXI) – helps to establish the scene of ballad recitation.

---

[12] Byron, George Gordon, Baron, *Childe Harold's Pilgrimage*, in *The Complete Poetical Works*, ed. Jerome McGann (Oxford University Press, 1980–93), Vol. II of VII, 66. Further quotations from this poem will be cited by canto and stanza in text.

The Albanians, specified throughout as exotic "Mussulmans," conveniently generate a song assimilable to Byron's loose generic categories. Formally, the Tambourgi song (tambourgi being the name of the war-drum) is a ballad specimen isolated within a larger poetic romance composed in Spenserian stanzas. For the war-song itself Byron resorts to a ballad stanza, four lines of four stresses each in running rhythm; his assignation of Arabic numbers to its stanzas (as opposed to the Roman numerals that order the Spenserian narrative) further marks the song as a set-piece. The formal and numerical shifts constitute a new poetic moment in the poem, in which the ballad serves handily as the form appropriate for rendering, indeed translating and transposing, the Albanians' "barbarous, yet [...] not indecent glee."

This ballad moment, both embedded in and set off from what is already a notably archaizing romance, allows us to make several observations about genre, form, and the socio-cultural code of Romantic poetry. When Byron chose the Spenserian stanza for his long romance, he paid homage to the Renaissance master of what was already in Spenser's hands a medievalizing genre, the romance epic; he was also participating in a late-eighteenth- and early nineteenth-century vogue for Spenserian romance (viz. Beattie's *Minstrel*, Shelley's *Laon and Cythna*, Clare's *The Village Minstrel*).[13] Byron wrote in his Preface to the First and Second Cantos, "The stanza of Spenser, according to one of our most successful poets, admits of every variety." To sustain the complex music of this stanza was to establish one's claim to a certain poetic pedigree: learned, aristocratic, masterful. Spenser's intricately rhymed nine-line stanza, with its closing alexandrine, is decidedly literary and classically allusive; the use of the stanza clearly signifies both Byron's comprehensive familiarity with literary history and the nature of his poetic ambition. To choose to write in Spenser's stanza was also to avail oneself of its sweetly archaic, and to Byron poetical, potential. Indeed, his hero's very epithet – Childe – is only one of a series of archaisms that Byron employed. As he observed: "It is almost superfluous to mention that the appellation 'Childe,' as in 'Childe Waters,' 'Childe Childers,' &c. is used as more consonant with the old structure of versification which I have adopted."

Yet even as the versification and such diction as "wight," "in sooth," and "whilome" (all these in only the second stanza of the first Canto) already left in 1812 an archaic taste on the tongue, the poetic project of *Childe Harold* was decidedly modern, journalistically contemporary and immediate. As

[13] The crucial study of this vogue is Greg Kucich's *Keats, Shelley, and Romantic Spenserianism*, which reminds us of Beattie's influence and also suggests the critical power of Spenser's divided poetics for radical and liberal poets in the Romantic era.

Byron declared, "The following poem was written, for the most part, amidst the scenes which it attempts to describe." The devastation of the Peninsular War, the sexiness of Spanish girls, the degradation of modern Greeks, the outrage of Lord Elgin's appropriation of the marbles – these are only a sampling of the topics Byron addressed in his versified travels. We have then, a distinct gap between the modernity of Byron's persona and project and the self-styled "old" poetic resources he chose to execute that project. Or rather, the self-consciously archaic touches in diction and versification must be seen as indices of Byron's decadent modernity.

When we return to the Albanian war-song, the disjunction between archaizing verse technique and modern self-production arises in another form. Byron calls the Albanian war-song a "lay" – a notably archaic term suggestive of medieval minstrels and their songs. The distance between Harold, the entertained and apparently scribbling guest, and the unselfconscious and dancing Albanians, is rendered in part as a difference in poetic forms. Harold, we might say, speaks Spenser; the Albanians scream ballad. The ballad stanza, unlike the Spenserian, lacks a proper name; it is a quintessentially popular stanza; its serviceability for this scene reveals how closely allied was the concept of the ballad with the oral, the exotic, and the primitive. Of course, Byron's fluency in ballad forms came in part through his deep acquaintance with Walter Scott's collection: as he wrote in his Preface, he modeled another ballad in *Childe Harold*, the "Good Night" song, upon "'Lord Maxwell's Good Night,' in the Border Minstrelsy, edited by Mr. Scott."[14] The extensive scholarship on oral poetry, with its emphasis on composition during performance, its debates over the status of memorization, and its demoting or erasing of the category "author," allows us to distinguish between these two ballad instances in *Childe Harold*.[15] Byron represents Harold as the sole singer spontaneously moved by his grief to sing and perhaps compose his "Good Night" ballad, whereas the Albanians sing as an undifferentiated wild group. Of course, Byron authored each ballad, however indebted he was to his sources, literary or ethnographic. Yet he very carefully orchestrated the respective scenes of their occasion in the poem. These two instances suggest how the ballad could simultaneously uphold literary, capitalized conceptions of authorship and romantic theories of collective folk utterance; the ballad as a form could mark out a continuum

---

[14] Byron, Preface, 4.
[15] For one partisan version of the contentious history of this scholarship, see Ruth Finnegan, *Oral Poetry*; Walter Ong's critical assessment of the term, "oral literature," launches a series of useful observations in his *Orality and Literacy: The Technologizing of the Word* (London and New York: Routledge, 1982).

from primitive to civilized in one long poem. So we see that the ballad could be used to signify both the alterity of *another* primitive culture, such as the Albanians', and the primitive *within* one's own culture, as in the case of Scott's border-ballads and Harold's "Good Night." The ballad form in *Childe Harold* acquires its cultural meaning, then, from its contextualization in the larger romance. If it is true that, as Walter Ong says, "Popular ballads . . . develop on the edge of orality," we may say that literary ballads explore the cultural meaning of that edge and indeed render it a quasi-anthropological trope: ballad form as the figure of the primitive, the popular, and the authentically emotive, whether encountered at home or abroad.[16]

The significance of this ballad specimen ramifies when we turn to the notes to *Childe Harold*. Byron published his cantos with notes; the poem was read and reviewed in light of these notes, which feature Byron *in propria persona* relating various details of and observations from his actual travels in 1810 and 1811. Byron's notes might be read as a late, decisive intervention in the discourse and practice of antiquarian documentation and annotation, consolidated most notably through the publication of ballad collections (e.g. Percy's, Ritson's, and contemporary to Byron, Scott's). The elaborate footnoting, prefacing, and appending which marked these eighteenth-century productions in Britain as well as on the Continent (e.g. Herder's *Stimmen der Völker in Liedern*) partook, as we have seen, of the system of textual protocols governing the genre of the ballad collection. That these protocols could and did migrate into poetry presumably free of antiquarian aspirations is suggestive. Witty, learned, opinionated, self-dramatizing, the notes are as much a project of poetic self-presentation as the poem proper: it is in the notes that Byron makes his bids for linguistic and ethnographic authority. In his note to the war-song, Byron provides what he claims are actual transcriptions and transliterations of Albanian popular song. He begins:

As a specimen of the Albanian or Arnaout dialect of the Illyric, I here insert two of their most popular choral songs, which are generally chaunted in dancing by men or women indiscriminately. The first words are merely a kind of chorus without meaning, like some in our own and all other languages.

1. Bo, Bo, Bo, Bo, Bo, Bo,
   Naciarura, popuso.
2. Naciarura na civin
   Ha pen derini nderini ti hin . . .

---

[16] Walter Ong, *Orality and Literacy*, 159.

(Which he translates as:)

1. Lo, Lo, I come, I come; be thou silent.
2. I come, I run; open the door that I may enter.[17]

Byron also includes a song "preserved" by the Arnaout girls, who he informs us "are much handsomer than the Greeks, and their dress is far more picturesque":

1. Ndi sefda tinde ulavossa
   Vettimi upri vi lofsa.
1. I am wounded by thy love, and have loved but to scorch myself.[18]

This series of transcriptions, transliterations and translations provides extremely suggestive material for thinking about the oral, the written, and (to invoke Ong) technologies of the word; moreover, Byron's two-tiered structure of poem and notes juxtaposes the war-song as a kind of ballad signifier against an ethnographic and linguistic signified. Crucial to the interest of the war-song and of the Albanians themselves, in both the poem and notes, is their "picturesque" primitivity. In the poem, the Albanians appear as a "barbarous" people; in the notes, we are informed that they are also an oral people. Byron observes "that the Arnaout is not a *written* language: the words of this song, as well as the one which follows, are spelt according to their pronunciation. They are copied by one who speaks and understands the dialect perfectly, and who is a native of Athens" (197).

In Byron's case, as in Scott's *Minstrelsy*, the ballad with its apparatus of notes provides an opportunity both for literary invention and for establishing ethnographic and linguistic bona fides. In his use of the ballad as a literary, linguistic, and ethnographic resource, Byron resembles many of his contemporaries; special to Byron is the harnessing of those resources to yet another project, the production of a cosmopolitan public poetic persona. Constantly emphasizing the cultural and historical distance between himself and the peoples he encounters, Byron anoints himself as cultural mediator and commentator – poetic tour guide. He will present their barbarity for us; he will ventriloquize their wild songs for us; and he will conspicuously suffer from historically induced melancholia as a result of such encounters. (Indeed, the Albanian war-song segues immediately into Byron's signal lament: "Fair Greece! sad relic of departed worth!"[II. st. LXXIII].

Such differently oriented theorists of ethnographic writing like James Clifford and Michel de Certeau might say, with good reason, that Byron

---

[17] Byron, Notes, 196.   [18] Ibid., 197.

produces and aestheticizes the gap between himself as civilized and the Albanians as savages.[19] Yet, recalling my opening quotation from Lévi-Strauss, we can foreground another rift between poet-observer and Albanian-observed: the rift between the literate writer and the apparently a-literate Albanians. And we note as well the presence of that wonderfully shadowy character in so much ethnographic writing, the native informant, who in this case, Byron informs us, is a "native of Athens" – not an Albanian – who nevertheless "understands the dialect perfectly." With his fluency in Albanian and his skill at transcription, the informant is the embodiment, the personification as it were, of a complex oral-literate conjunction. This conjunction, imagined in Blake as taking place both within language and across generations, here appears as an ethnographic and linguistic encounter across a multiply mediated and aesthetically useful divide. This divide, and the multiple literary and linguistic realizations of it, are characteristic of what I have proposed we call the ethnographic strain of romantic orality.

WORDSWORTHIAN TRANSMISSIONS: "SIMON LEE"

Unlike Byron's use of the ballad for the Albanian war-song, the ballad in Wordsworth's hands becomes the space for encounter, not the sign of the exotic or of primitivity *per se*. Nor is the ballad reserved for especially "romantic" utterance, as in Harold's swooning "Good Night." Instead the ballad in Wordsworth's corpus provides the metric for increasingly serious poems of counter-enlightenment. The oral–literate conjunction appears in

---

[19] I here refer again to two signal works for thinking about the links between ethnographic writing, historiography, and poetry: James Clifford, *The Predicament of Culture* and Michel de Certeau, *The Writing of History*. Clifford observes that by the early twentieth century, participant observation, in the mode of fieldwork, becomes a necessary component of the anthropologist's discursive and disciplinary legitimation. See in particular Clifford's first chapter, "On Ethnographic Authority," 21–54. Byron's footnotes, as I've suggested, make an intriguingly analogous bid for ethnographic and ethno-poetic authority. In discussing Byron's textual strategies, I am mindful as well of de Certeau's account of the "ethnographic operation" (the ideological and textualizing practices he describes in the essay, "Ethno-Graphy: Speech, or the Space of the Other: Jean de Léry" [209–43]). De Certeau outlines a "hermeneutics of the other" inscribed by and through ethnographic writing, with a narrative structure organized around "The Break" and the subsequent "Work of Returning" (218–26). *Childe Harold* raises a number of questions, not least: where is "the break," in de Certeau's sense? between England and the Continent? Greece and Albania? That the poem is itself a "work of returning" seems clear, as are Byron's letters, later folded into his notes. De Certeau also helps us to see how Byron's ethnopoetics rely and ring variations on the binaries constitutive of the scientific field of "ethnology," in which (according to De Certeau) primitive society is characterized by orality, spatiality, alterity, and unconsciousness, whereas civilized, Christian society and its subjects emerge, over and against this "primitive" other, as possessing writing, temporality, identity, and consciousness (209). Such an ethnological scheme, historically specified and particularly elaborated, is clearly embedded in, indeed displayed by, Byron's poem and notes.

the *Lyrical Ballads* not as a border between primitivity and modernity, or between Scotland and England, or between the contemporary and the residual, but rather as a lived and living speech situation. Of course, these are "balladized" speech situations, as Scott would say; moreover, Wordsworth's ballads could be seen as instituting another rift, that between child and adult, or between rustic and sophisticate. Yet in refusing to relegate "orality" to the margins or the footnotes or to the merely residual, Wordsworth's poems offer a way to re-think the relation of orality to literacy and more specifically the relation of the oral to the literate *within* literature. Wordsworth's poems diagnose the oral–literate conjunction as a symptom of literature itself.

"Simon Lee," for example, begins as a kind of popular yarn, with Wordsworth emphasizing the sometimes dubious nature of oral transmission:

> In the sweet shire of Cardigan
> Not far from pleasant Ivor-hall,
> An old man dwells, a little man,
> I've heard he once was tall.
> Of years he has upon his back,
> No doubt, a burthen weighty;
> He says he is three score and ten,
> But others say he's eighty. (ll. 1–8)[20]

Simon Lee – the man and the poem – seems to come from an oral world of rumor, report, and long if arguable communal memory. Yet the poet – clearly not a rustic, probably more sure of his age than Simon – also moves in this world: the poet speaks to Simon Lee as the old man struggles to cut a tangled root, and the poet ultimately lends "poor Simon" a hand. Speech and contact appear as the very formal condition for the generation and indeed the transmission of this ballad.

Wordsworth complicates the orality-effect of this poem when in the ninth of thirteen stanzas he addresses the "gentle reader." Wordsworth introduces the mediation of reading even as he promotes an orality-effect through his jaunty versification, the rustic social space of the poem, and his simulation of talk. He apostrophizes the reader as a possible transmitter of the poem in the future. In his comically circumlocutory address the poet says:

---

[20] Wordsworth, "Simon Lee," *Lyrical Ballads*, 60–3. Further quotations from this poem will be cited by line in text.

> What more I have to say is short
> I hope you'll kindly take it;
> It is no tale; but should you think,
> Perhaps a tale you'll make it.

What follows then is the account of the poet's lending his hand to Simon, and Simon's astonishing gratitude after. This is "no tale," Wordsworth insists, yet it may become one: this claim reads several ways. Wordsworth may be suggesting that the pathetic scene with Simon should not be cheerfully assimilated into the category, "tale"; he may also be suggesting that what is here a printed account may yet be circulated as a "tale" among a community of readers, hearers, overhearers, and raconteurs. The poem imagines its other lives, as a printed object (thus "O Reader!") and less assuredly as a told "tale" ("perhaps a tale you'll make it"). Wordsworth would not have his "tale" passively transmitted, as if the reader were a mindlessly memorizing conduit: only if she should "think" will the reader "make" it a tale. Here the reader becomes, like the poet, a "maker," which is, as Walter Scott and Percy Shelley both noted, the English approximation of the term "poetas."[21] The future of the poem, then, involves a collaboration between the author, the reader, and possible auditors. Expanding upon Wordsworth's apostrophe, we could also describe the life of the poem through an array of linguistic and social practices – composing, writing, printing, bookselling, reading, reciting, revising.

Significant for my argument: the poem "Simon Lee" imagines several avenues of poetic transmission; in doing so the poem also reveals mutually permeable domains of orality, semi-literacy, and sophisticated literacy. These terms, after all, are reifications: the "oral" and the "literate" are not in the end abstractions but rather markers of the complex linguistic, cognitive, and technological capacities and orientations of individuals and communities. Even more than my example from Blake, who keeps his oral-literate conjunction mostly on the plain of visionary imagination, Wordsworth's ballads gesture to a complex social and linguistic reality. The rustics and children of his poems show habits of mind and speech that linguistic and cultural anthropologists would designate as partially "oral," yet it is also crucial to Wordsworth's vision that these characters freely interact with more literate interlocutors. And if these poems run the risk of condescending to or sentimentalizing the a-literate or pre-literate

---

[21] Walter Scott, in his "Introductory Remarks on Popular Poetry," notes that "the bards of Greece [earned] the term 'POETAS,' which, as it singularly happens, is literally translated by the Scottish epithet for the same class of persons, whom they term the *Makers*" (4).

figure, as Coleridge and other critics then and now have claimed, never-theless Wordsworth's poems consistently and compassionately reach across a divide that other poets and theorists of the human sciences would have kept rigidly unbridgeable.

Wordsworth was keenly aware of the contingent modalities through which people might encounter his, or any poetry: from oral through manu-script through writing to print or combinations and simultaneities thereof. In an astonishing series of remarks on the sonnet, "Though narrow be that Old Man's cares, and near" (1807), Wordsworth spoke of his source and inspiration, "Old Mitchell of Coleorton," the Old Man of the sonnet, as well as of a laborer who had taken an interest in Wordsworth's verses:

He [Old Mitchell] was, in all his ways and conversation, a great curiosity, both individually and as a representative of past times ... there was also a laborer of whom I regret I had not personal knowledge; for, more than forty years after, when he had become an old man, I learnt that while I was composing verses, which I usually did aloud, he took much pleasure, unknown to me, in following my steps that he might catch the words I uttered, and, what is not a little remarkable, several lines caught in this way kept their place in his memory. My volumes have lately been given to him by my informant, and surely he must have been gratified to meet in print his old acquaintance.[22]

From Old Mitchell, the antique "curiosity" who is a "representative of past times" and a useful "informant," to the unnamed, unknown laborer who followed the poet as he composed his verses, Wordsworth here traces several layers of oral–literate interaction over time, as well as a wonderfully surpris-ing arc of poetic inspiration, composition, mediation, and reception. As reported here, Wordsworth's poems travel a strange, illuminating route, from his own tentative soundings-out, remembered by the attentive eaves-dropping laborer, to the published volumes in which the laborer, decades later, can now "meet in print his old acquaintance." The poetic network he describes here links oral and literate media, technologies of memory with print technologies, local knowledge and cosmopolitan poetry. Such notes offer crucial sites for ongoing investigations and appreciations of Romantic (and indeed contemporary) *poiesis* in its full medial complexities.

LYRICAL BALLADS AND MEDIA CIRCUITRY

That his own poems might be broadcast by oral means: this was a point of pride for Wordsworth, who observed in the 1800 *Preface* of his poem,

---

[22] Wordsworth, Fenwick notes, 422.

"Goody Blake and Harry Gill": "I have the satisfaction of knowing that it has been communicated to many hundreds of people who would never have heard of it, had it not been narrated as a Ballad, and in a more impressive metre than is usual in Ballads." Here Wordsworth announces the oral transmission of an "impressive" literary ballad: the ballad itself is implicitly saluted as a more effective medium of communication than other literary forms, indeed than other print forms such as newspapers.

The case of "Goody Blake and Harry Gill" is exemplary for such medial transformations. Wordsworth introduced the poem in his *Preface* thus:

> The tale of Goody Blake and Harry Gill is founded on a well-authenticated fact which happened in Warwickshire. Of the other poems in the collection, it may be proper to say that they are either absolute inventions of the author, or facts which took place within his personal observation or that of his friends.[23]

Wordsworth does not here offer the grounds by which this tale is "well-authenticated," but we know that "Goody Blake and Harry Gill" was based on a story Wordsworth encountered in Erasmus Darwin's *Zoonomia, or the Laws of Organic Life* (2 vols., 1794–6). There, Darwin had written that he had "received good information of the truth of the following case, which was published a few years ago in the newspapers." In "Goody Blake and Harry Gill," as in Scott, we encounter multiple mediations of "a true story" (Wordsworth's subtitle to the ballad – the only ballad he marked in this way).

The transmission of this ballad and its ongoing circulation might be represented thus:

[oral stories] > newspapers > Darwin's *Zoonomia* > WW's "Goody Blake and Harry Gill" in *Lyrical Ballads* > readers/reciters of WW's poem > WW's *Preface*

and could also be coded in the following way:

oral communication/curious lore > printed ephemera > "case" in scientific treatise > "balladization" and framing in WW > re-oralization and simultaneous reprinting

All these operations (printing, reciting, editing, framing, balladizing) are as it were external to the ballad's "content," the "tale," as Wordsworth calls it: such operations are the medial "envelope" through which the notional "matter" passes. Regarding the "matter" itself, the poem is compulsively self-reflexive about its interrogation: "What's the matter? What's the matter?/What is't that ails young Harry Gill?/That evermore his teeth they chatter,/Chatter, chatter, chatter, still" (ll. 1–4). We follow the organized, measured "chatter" that is verse to learn that Goody Blake, a poor neighboring woman, has

---

[23] Wordsworth, "Advertisement" to *Lyrical Ballads*, 8.

been stealing firewood from Harry's property (localized, as so often in Wordsworth's work – here in Dorsetshire); when the comparatively well-off Harry discovers this "trespass" (l. 66), he beats her off, and she in turn curses him: thus his incessant teeth-chattering, his perpetual cold.

What in Darwin's hands is a psycho-physiological "case" becomes in Wordsworth an opportunity for community-based moral reflection, a meditation on the limits of property, possessive individualism, the persistence of witchery and curses, the rough justice of the folktale brought into modernity; the ballad stands as well as a kind of natural-supernatural ballad, curses and spells relocated into the moral economy of social, sentimental circulation. For this discussion it is important to observe that the poem also offers, within and without, a media allegory. If Wordsworth's notes point to transmission circuits outside the poem, the poem itself offers a *represented transmission* of the case:

> In March, December, and in July,
> 'Tis all the same with Harry Gill;
> The neighbors tell, and tell you truly,
> His teeth they chatter, chatter still. (ll. 9–12)

The neighbors' chatter, like Harry Gill's, *communicates* something: the meaning of that communication is part of the poem's residue, what the reader must process, as it were. The chatter establishes both that there is a social channel and that it is open; the phatic function is in full flower.

Wordsworth represents a community that will ponder this case: he urges his notional listeners/readers – here figured as "ye farmers all" – to "think . . . of Goody Blake and Harry Gill." Thus the final stanza concludes:

> A-bed or up, by night or day;
> His teeth they chatter, chatter still.
> Now think, ye farmers all, I pray,
> Of Goody Blake and Harry Gill. (ll. 125–8)

This is a characteristically Wordsworthian invitation (made also in "Simon Lee" and other ballads), a request that the reader internalize what the poet has just communicated. Behind the poet's communications lie his own history of received transmissions (whether of lore, Darwin's physiological anecdotes, or news-bits) and his profound internalization. Wordsworth asks the reader within the poem to continue the communication circuit; in his Preface, he made plain his delight that readers had done so not only by *thinking about* but by *re-oralizing* the poem. Here *thinking* would seem almost to require such deliberative re-oralizing, as if thought were always already social, socialized, and further socializable.

REPRESENTING ORALITY AND IMPASSE IN "THE SOLITARY REAPER"

For all the phantasies of immediacy and multi-media broadcast we can find in Wordsworth's oeuvre, he is also famously a poet of impasse and opacity: and this too we might consider as a function of Wordsworth's inquiry into poetic mediality. As an evocation of the historical and material distances that oral poetry could (and could not) travel, consider one of Wordsworth's best-known poems, "The Solitary Reaper." Beholding "yon solitary Highland Lass," and enjoining us to do so as well, Wordsworth in the third stanza bursts forth impatiently:

> Will no one tell me what she sings?
> Perhaps the plaintive numbers flow
> For old, unhappy, far-off things,
> And battles long ago:
> Or is it some more humble lay,
> Familiar matter of today?
> Some natural sorrow, loss, or pain,
> That has been, and may be again!
>
> Whate'er the theme, the Maiden sang
> As if her song could have no ending;
> I saw her singing at her work,
> And o'er the sickle bending; –
> I listened till I had my fill,
> And, as I mounted up the hill,
> The music in my heart I bore,
> Long after it was heard no more.[24]

As Peter Manning reminds us, Wordsworth worked up this poem not from an actual encounter recalled from his and Dorothy's 1803 tour of Scotland but more directly from "a beautiful sentence" in his friend Thomas Wilkinson's manuscript, *Tours to the British Mountains*.[25] That a poem presenting a personally experienced, unmediated (if vexing) overhearing of

---

[24] William Wordsworth, "The Solitary Reaper," *Poems, in Two Volumes*, 185, ll. 17–32.
[25] Peter Manning, "'Will No One Tell Me What She Sings?': *The Solitary Reaper* and the Contexts of Criticism," Ch. 11 of his *Reading Romantics: Texts and Contexts* (Oxford University Press, 1990), 241–72. Manning's elegant, trenchant essay offers a historicist corrective to and complication of Geoffrey Hartman's previously dominant, and permanently powerful, reading of the poem as another Wordsworthian movement of consciousness. Thanks to Ann Rowland for referring me to Manning's essay. Of "The Solitary Reaper," Wordsworth remarked, "This Poem was suggested by a beautiful sentence in a MS. Tour in Scotland written by a Friend, the last line being taken from it *verbatim*." See his note to the poem in *Poems, in Two Volumes*, 415. Curtis identifies the friend as

oral lyric had its origins in – and drew its closing line from – another tourist's written document only begins to suggest the always already fictive and "written" nature of "oral" encounters as they appear in Romantic poetry (not to mention the textually mediated vision of all eighteenth- and nineteenth-century tourists). The poetic economy here, material and meta-phorical, is obviously rich and potentially disquieting.[26] If the poem lends itself to readings as a Romantic expropriation of women's, workers', or Highlanders' oral poetry (or, in a less sinister gloss, as an obfuscated appropriation of a friend's manuscript), it also offers us the chance to read it as a melancholy methodological inquiry. The almost absurd question, "Will no one tell me what she sings?" propels a set of provisional responses and meditations on ballad genres: "what she sings" may be a "historical ballad" (to invoke Scott's taxonomy)[27] – a tale of "old unhappy, far-off things,/And battles long ago"; but on the other hand, the song may be a "more humble lay, familiar matter of today." The mysteriousness of the song lies not only in its linguistic inaccessibility – the Highland lass sang in Erse (Scottish Gaelic), Wordsworth's source reports – but in this temporal ambiguity: the ballad may gesture back to time immemorial or may equally commemorate "today's" news, news which, moreover, may be repeated in the future – she may well be singing of "pain/That has been, and may be again!"

The ballad chronotope – the space-time configuration of oral *poiesis* – here emerges as temporally extensive (from "long ago" to a possible future "again") but spatially restrictive: Wordsworth offers in the Highland singer an image of a traditional culture recreating itself over time, from time immemorial; it is the image, perhaps nostalgic, of a rooted human community in its full temporal extension. That such a community appears in

Thomas Wilkinson, and adds that his "*Tours to the British Mountains* (London, 1824) circulated among friends in MS. for years before it was published; the passage reads: 'Passed a female who was reaping alone: she sung in Erse as she bended over her sickle; the sweetest human voice I ever heard: her strains were tenderly melancholy, and felt delicious, long after they were heard no more' [12]" (415).

26 A fuller account of this poem would have much to say about the exoticism of the Highland girl, Wordsworth's eroticizing of her, his focus on her song as his pleasure, his taking of his "fill" at the expense of "her work," his unrepresented transformation of source materials in generating a lyric of represented spontaneity. Luke Gibbons has recently discussed this poem, for example, in terms of its diagnostic unknowingness regarding the Irish Gaelic tune carrying the opaque words of such a worksong: the overlooking of the Scottish and Irish linkage here is a problem both in Wordsworth and in his critics, including the author of this book (Luke Gibbons, on "Acoustics," plenary lecture, "Scottish Romanticism in World Literatures" Conference, University of California, Berkeley, Sept. 9, 2006).

27 The reader may recall that Scott identifies the "three classes of poems" included in his collection: historical ballads, romantic ballads, and imitations of these compositions by modern authors. See his "Introduction" to *MSB*, in *Poetical Works*, 36,

the highly marked regional figure of a Highland lass should not obscure the general point of Wordsworth's inquiry; it was Wordsworth's frequent strategy to meditate on the universal human through such "exotic" or "marginal" figures. It is of course striking and characteristically Wordsworthian that she be "single in the field," solitary as the tree in the Immortality Ode, the one that gives him terrible pause. Despite her being "single," she is hardly individuated: Wordsworth is less interested in the oral poet than in oral poetry.

Oral poetry here emerges not as the province of trained professional rivals (*pace* Scott's minstrel corps) but rather as that haunting song that drifts through and between individuals. If Scott's minstrel emphasizes the work of learning his lay, Wordsworth's lass seems to know her song as it were unconsciously: her work is reaping, not singing, and her song comes unbidden, sung for none other (she thinks) than herself. In his romances, Scott emphasizes the institutional situation, the explicit cultural-formation, of song culture; Wordsworth finds in this song an occasion for meditating on the ambiguities of song, song-transmission, and song-matter. Note that Scott's minstrel has no expectation that any of his audience will go out and repeat his lay; his is a professional recitation bespeaking years of training and specialization. The Highland lass shows us another aspect of oral poetry, song as a popular, unprofessional, communal inheritance, an inheritance, notably, represented as inaccessible – or, to be more precise, as only partially accessible – to Wordsworth. *That* she sings, he appreciates; *what* she sings, he cannot know. The tune carries, the semantic import doesn't. In terms of ballad *poiesis*, Wordsworth in "The Solitary Reaper" seems to anticipate an insight later theorists, most notably Bertrand Harris Bronson, have also enunciated: that a ballad is a ballad only when it has a tune.[28]

"The Solitary Reaper" may be seen, then, as a performance in print of transformed and ostentatiously imperfect transmission. The reaper's "song" becomes, of course, Wordsworth's poem, "Solitary Reaper": sung song becomes artifact. The poem explicitly offers a splitting between music and meaning, between measures and melody on the one hand – her "plaintive numbers" – and the verbal and thematic content of her words, the "matter." The poem traces an allegory of translation and textualization but also of dispersal: she sings "as if her song could have no ending." Is this not the dream

---

[28] For a version of this dictum, see Bertrand Harris Bronson, *The Traditional Tunes of the Child Ballads* (Princeton University Press, 1972), Vol. I of IV: "*Question*: When is a ballad not a ballad? *Answer*: When it has no tune" (ix).

of poetry, and of those cultures, professions, and individuals who produce it? Wordsworth's "as if" delicately places the pivot of the poem between perpetual presence (the time of singing, the sung "now") and inevitable passing.

The pathos of this encounter is figured, perhaps inadvertently, in Wordsworth's closing couplet. Having asked "what she sings," having proposed possible answers, Wordsworth leaves "the Vale profound":

> And, as I mounted up the hill,
> The music in my heart I bore,
> Long after it was heard no more. (ll. 30–2)

The poem offers us, of course, not her music but his, not her matter but his reflections on the indeterminacy of the song's matter; the impasse between the reaping singer and the walking poet persists, a rebuke to fantasies of transparency and unobstructed mediation. It is striking that Wordsworth focuses most on the poet's preoccupation, as it were, with "the matter"; he notably swerves from ventriloquizing the lass, preferring to emblazon her figure and to re-channel her music into his lines. This representation of listening, and his insistence that we listen – "O listen!" – creates an immediacy and a contemporaneity that Scott's poems, with their scrupulously historicizing spectacle, abjure. Yet it is appropriate that, however different these poems, we recognize in them a haunting by questions raised by oral *poiesis*. The oscillation between Wordsworth's "O listen!" ("The Solitary Reaper") and his "O Reader!" ("Simon Lee") might be seen, moreover, as diagnostic of the media situation of Romantic poetry: listening and reading both figured in, and solicited by, print – print the generalized medium of all streams of *poiesis*.

Perhaps, given the frequency with which oral communications become the stuff of Wordsworthian lyrics – with their enunciators witting or unwitting providers of "matter" – we should both revisit and revise a New Critical dictum. Wordsworth's poems are often not so much poems about poetry as poems about the complex encounters between oral and literary *poiesis*. His most compact and penetrating exploration of oral–literate complexities – particularly those inhering in problems of textual mediation – may be found in the lyric he wrote as if to preface Macpherson's Ossian poems, the most vexed and famous orally based texts of the period.

BINDING MEDIATIONS: WORDSWORTH'S OSSIAN UNBOUND

"The Solitary Reaper" shows Wordsworth thinking about the textualization he represents himself as enacting. We might also bear in mind, as a further complication, what we know and what Wordsworth later acknowledged, that the poem was in a sense always pre-textualized, a manuscript its muse. Whether displayed or occluded, such textualizing operations were, of course, practices central to romantic traffic in the oral. Wordsworth's poem, "Written on a Blank Leaf of Macpherson's Ossian," proposes in its title that Wordsworth's "lines" be taken as a continuation of, as well as a supplement to, Macpherson's work. What has been left "blank" by Macpherson's Ossian will be written in and over. The poem may be read as a commentary on the Ossian problematic, which Wordsworth astutely diagnoses as a problematic of poetry itself.

Wordsworth begins by offering natural similes as figures for poetic reception:

> Oft have I caught from fitful breeze,
> Fragments of far-off melodies,
> With ear not coveting the whole,
> A part so charmed the pensive soul:
> While a dark storm before my sight
> Was yielding, on a mountain height
> Loose vapours have I watched, that won
> Prismatic colours from the sun;
> Nor felt a wish that Heaven would show
> The image of its perfect bow.
> What need, then, of these finished strains?
> Away with counterfeit remains![29]

Wordsworth naturalizes the process by which we receive poetry, particularly poetry that exists, like Ossian's, only in "fragments." Figuring the reception of poetic "fragments" as a kind of overhearing of "far-off melodies," Wordsworth hovers between oral/aural and literate "strains" of poetry. The "fragment" here is positively valued, while "the whole" stands uncoveted. In this astonishingly modulated and understated simile, Wordsworth pits an ethic and a poetic of the authentic fragment against, in a richly suggestive phrase, "counterfeit remains" (akin to the unsought rainbow). Macpherson's "finished strains" appear in rhyme as they did, in Wordsworth's opinion, in literary history – as "counterfeit remains."

It is telling that the counterfeiter here, Macpherson, remains unnamed – as if he shall remain nameless. That there might be a fragment or partial remain of Ossian does, however, continue to intrigue Wordsworth, who

---

[29] "Written on a Blank Leaf of Macpherson's Ossian," in *Sonnet Series and Itinerary Poems, 1820–1845, by William Wordsworth*, ed. Geoffrey Jackson (Ithaca, NY: Cornell University Press, 2004), 610–12, ll. 1–12. Further quotations from this poem will be cited by line in text.

boldly invokes Ossian as poet, having refused to name his translator/
mediator:

> Spirit of Ossian! if imbound
> In language thou may'st yet be found,
> If aught (intrusted to the pen
> Or floating on the tongues of men,
> Albeit shattered and impaired)
> Subsist thy dignity to guard,
> In concert with memorial claim
> Of old gray stone, and high-born name,
> That cleaves to rock or pillared cave,
> Where moans the blast or beats the wave,
> Let Truth, stern arbitress of all,
> Interpret that original,
> And for presumptuous wrongs atone;
> Authentic words be given, or none! (ll. 17–30)

In this central movement of the poem, Wordsworth shows himself thinking
through – in incredibly concentrated lines – the oral–literate problematic
that the Ossian controversy made into a famously debatable topic. In his
apostrophe – "Spirit of Ossian!" – Wordsworth re-opens the question of
Ossian. Wordsworth stringently dissociates the "spirit of Ossian" from the
texts through which he supposedly is heard, that is, Macpherson's "translations." Wordsworth's apostrophe to Ossian's spirit is a kind of dis-interral,
a revivification, with a difference. Conjuring and appealing to his presence
in a significantly conditional clause: "if imbound/In language thou may'st
yet be found ..." Wordsworth tellingly reverses the operation of textualization to which Macpherson had subjected Ossian: we might say that, in
spiritualizing Ossian, rendering him a presence in nature, Wordsworth
imaginatively re-oralizes Ossian.

Wordsworth deftly represents several layers of mediation, presenting
them in reverse order, as if peeling away the "counterfeit" layers to reach
the ineffable, mysterious and yet authentic core. Having dispensed with
Macpherson's "finished strains," Wordsworth further problematizes the
question of any access to Ossian "in language." Wordsworth recognizes
that the problem of Ossian is, even aside from Macpherson, a problem of
mediation. To consider whether Ossian "may'st yet be found" leads one to
wonder whether he might be "intrusted to the pen/Or floating on the
tongues of men,/Albeit shattered and impaired": the uncertainty of reference in this last apposition raises an intriguing question: is it the "tongues of
men" which are "shattered and impaired," or the paltry "aught" (anything)

one might still find, or indeed the "Spirit of Ossian" perhaps found "floating" there which is shattered?

The question of Ossian hinges, then, not only on "authentic words" but also on the state of men's tongues and the reliability of human mediations. One wonders how exactly we might ascertain the authenticity of "authentic words": original Ossianic words, could they be found or reconstructed, would be Gaelic; yet perhaps Wordsworth might have been satisfied by faithfully edited, fragmentary Ossianic translations, in which case "authentic words" would still be heavily mediated ones. Wordsworth traces very efficiently a romantic economy of poetic mediation and realization, ascending up several layers of artifactualization. The "spirit" appears as the raw material, the driving pulse, of poetry; it may be "imbound/in language" – this is the first, linguistic mediation of poetic spirit. It is notable that language itself appears here as a binding, a medium; this linguistic binding may be rendered orally (in the "tongues of men") or may be textualized ("intrusted to the pen"). Wordsworth privileges neither mode of transmission or fixing; he offers both, in a rapid parenthetical, as options. In the first movement of the poem, Wordsworth strenuously criticizes the distortions engendered by our longing for artifactual "wholes" – for "finished strains." But we see that it is not the *writing* of oral poetry that vexes Wordsworth; it is, rather, the obscuring of what may yet actually "subsist" – whether in oral or written form.

It becomes apparent, as one rounds through the poem's arc, that Ossian serves as a case for lost poetry in general:

> No tongue is able to rehearse
> One measure, Orpheus! of thy verse;
> Musaeus, stationed with his lyre
> Supreme among the Elysian quire,
> Is, for the dwellers upon earth,
> Mute as a Lark ere morning's birth. (ll. 37–42)

Ossian is thus the latest in a long line of poets whose "verses" are lost, no longer "rehearsable." Only their names persist. Note that here, Wordsworth explores the oral-poetic problematic as a problem not so much of *authorship* or *source* as of *poetic work*, most specifically the mediating work of cultural transmission. Here he foregrounds a different issue from that, for example, in "Solitary Reaper," where the "author" of the lass's song – like those of most English and Scottish ballads – is presumably anonymous, lost in the mists of time: Wordsworth there confronts a mysterious song, a winsome singer, but no "original source," and more importantly, no problem of origination. In the case of Ossian, Musaeus, and Orpheus, however, we have names and not works, origins but no surviving poetic destinations. Yet Wordsworth's catalogue of lost beauties leads him to a surprising interrogation:

> Why grieve for these, though past away
> The Music, and extinct the Lay?
> When thousands, by severer doom,
> Full early to the silent tomb
> Have sunk, at Nature's call ... (ll. 43–7)

Here, with stunning economy, Wordsworth both diagnoses the melancholy and longing which fueled the antiquarian/historicist project and counter-prescribes for it. If it was the desire to provide a national epic and a heroic, dignified past that fueled Macpherson, as well as Percy and Scott, this longing – however profound – should not, according to this poem, be indulged. In this remarkable passage Wordsworth moves beyond his stern critique of counterfeiting and false finishing to criticize the psycho-cultural impulses propelling that bad project. Again, he poses the crux of his critique as a question, for this is truly an interrogation of the "griefs" that lead men to create bad "memorials": "Why grieve for these, though past away/The Music, and extinct the Lay?" Well, indeed, why grieve? To this Percy and Macpherson and Scott could have given extended, albeit differently inflected, responses. Yet Wordsworth objects to the emotional economy of antiquarian grief precisely because such grief privileges and fetishizes lost rarities – whether poets, poems, or musics – over vaster, unnamed human and poetic losses. "[T]housands, by severer doom,/Full early to the silent tomb/Have sunk."

The poem then becomes an homage to and invocation of "Bards of mightier grasp!" – the "chosen few" who persisted, unsung, in their vocation. In the closing lines of the poem, Wordsworth rounds back to the Ossian problematic that underlies the whole, and provides a reconstructed poetic genealogy for British poetry. Imagining poets in all ages and climes comforting their fellow men, Wordsworth analogizes:

> Such, haply, to the rugged Chief
> By fortune crushed, or tamed by grief,
> Appears, on Morven's lonely shore,
> Dim-gleaming through imperfect lore,
> The Son of Fingal; such was blind
> Maeonides of ampler mind;
> Such Milton, to the fountain head
> Of Glory by Urania led! (ll. 75–82)

In these closing lines, Ossian is reclaimed and inserted into a pantheon of poets whom Wordsworth addresses as his "Brothers in Soul!" In soul, we might add, but not in textual body. Even in these last lines Wordsworth keeps us alert to the problem of mediation: the final turn to Ossian – the "Son of Fingal" – is a conspicuously mediated apparition. He "appears, on Morven's lonely shore,/Dim-gleaming through imperfect lore." Not Ossian's fragments but his spirit, not his historical, verifiable existence but his continued fame preserved and sustained through "imperfect lore": Wordsworth ends his lines here, with the shadowy image of the barely and imperfectly mediated poet. Yet this Ossian, however shattered and impaired, is the poetically powerful Ossian. Converting Ossian into a muse rather than a source, proposing him as spiritual forebear rather than as fragmentary text, Wordsworth reaches an uneasy reconciliation with Ossian, whose influence he would elsewhere furiously and improbably deny.[30]

Again, what is remarkable here is not the turn to Ossian, and to the oral–literate problematic surrounding his purported works, but the terms and lines through which Wordsworth thinks and renders that problematic. Transmission, oral or not, and textualization, are the cruces of this poem, and more broadly, for any poet intent on a rigorous engagement with dubious but compelling "remains." Such a poem allows us to re-think certain critical insights about Romanticism: for example, that it was pre-occupied with notions of "spirit" and transcendence; that it privileged a discourse of inspiration over imitation; that it developed a poetics of the fragment. These general propositions seem true enough, especially for poets like Wordsworth who often employed vatic strains. But perhaps we could refine these propositions by considering them, as it were, in an oral key: in such a poem as Wordsworth's on Ossian, we see that his commitment to the fragment rests on a complex theorization of literate mediations of the oral as well as a nod to ongoing oral mediations (e.g. "tongues of men," "imperfect lore"). We also see that the invocation of Spirit is no transparent operation: the apostrophe – perhaps the stereotypical Romantic trope (O wild west wind, O Derwent, etc.) – immediately propels a conditional clause ("*if* imbound …) and parenthetical options (e.g. possible preservation by

---

[30] See Wordsworth's extraordinary attack (already invoked in Chapter 6) in his *Essay, Supplementary to the Preface*, in *The Prose Works*: "Yet, much as those pretended treasures of antiquity have been admired [Macpherson's Ossian poems], they have been wholly uninfluential upon the literature of the Country. No succeeding writer appears to have caught from them a ray of inspiration; no author, in the least distinguished, has ventured formally to imitate them – except the boy, Chatterton, on their first appearance" (78).

tongues or pen). With their qualifications and clarifications, Wordsworth's lines scrupulously enact the difficulty we have in "getting," not to mention "getting to," Ossian.

Wordsworth's poem allows us to see that there is no Ossian, and indeed no poetry, without mediation, whether oral or literate. One can only discriminate among kinds of mediation and kinds of remains ("counterfeit" or authentic). All poetry depends, however regrettably, on binding mediations. In a stunning paradox, it is through the rhetoric of immediate access, of unimpeded inspiration – "Spirit of Ossian!" – that Wordsworth most cannily argues his point: no poetry without mediation. Here then we see a powerful case of the double logic of remediation: immediacy and hypermediacy both conjured within one poem, the two sides of Romantic mediality sounded out and displayed.

ROMANTIC MEDIALITY: WORDSWORTH VS. SCOTT

Representing orality means theorizing orality. For Romantic literary poets, representing orality required a confrontation with the cultural situation and historicity of poetry. Was oral poetry dead? If "oral poetry" meant "minstrelsy," sung by trained minstrels to Scottish aristocrats, as in Scott's *Lay of the Last Minstrel*, then yes. If "oral poetry" meant "popular poetry," as Scott has it in the "Introduction to Popular Poetry" prefacing the *Minstrelsy*, then no, oral poetry was not at all dead: the contents of the *Minstrelsy*, Scott frequently notes, were often taken "from the mouths" of contemporary singers and reciters, and such testimonia also pervade Burns' notes, Hogg's too, and – as we have seen – Wordsworth's. Was oral poetry a viable inheritance for literate poets? Again, the question has no one answer: for Scott, immersed in as well as cultivating and commodifying Border song-culture, there was a vital continuity from his edition of the *Minstrelsy* to his first "original work," the *Lay of the Last Minstrel*. Yet Scott's relation to Border lore and Border poetry may be read, to borrow terms from Schiller, as a relation of the sentimental to the naïve. Conspicuous in Scott's works are his mediating, ironizing, historicizing hand and voice. On the question of viable encounters with orality, moreover, Wordsworth's work also reveals a profound recognition of a barrier – whether linguistic, cultural, or educational – between the modern, literate, publishing poet and what he represents as his oral contemporaries. The drama of Wordsworth's poems often arises from his represented recognition of just such a barrier. His poems offer a savoring of such impasse, even as he strains to transcend it: as he asks, concerning the Highland lass's enigmatic song: "will no one tell me what she sings?"

It is striking that Scott always published his ballads as hyper-mediated acts of *poiesis*: they appeared as translations (from Bürger), as "imitations of the ancient ballad" (Part 3 of the *Minstrelsy*), or as insets within metrical romances or historical novels. Scott relentlessly investigates and represents the cultural context in which a ballad might be sung, composed, re-worked, or abandoned. His ballads could migrate to new sites within his corpus, or come from another's: "Glenfinlas; or, Lord Ronald's Coronach" and "The Eve of St. John" both first appeared in M. G. Lewis' *Tales of Wonder* and found a subsequent home in Part 3 of the *Minstrelsy*; "The Death of Featherstonhaugh" first appeared in a footnote in *Marmion* (1808) but by the 1810 edition of the *Minstrelsy* had made its way into that collection as a specimen of an historical ballad – there "in its proper place," as Scott saw it, as a foregrounded, framed, authenticated artifact.[31] Such shifts in voicing, local framing, dramatic situation, and generic context shows Scott fluently moving his materials, re-making, as it were, the song.

In *Lyrical Ballads*, Wordsworth proposes the ballad as the medium through which he will simultaneously arouse feeling and conduct meditations on tradition, ethics, politics, and community; in his romances, Scott invokes ballads and other related lyric and song set-pieces as indices of cultural development and socio-cultural situation. Both poets explore poetry as a species of communication and as a possible transmission channel. In the cases discussed above, Wordsworth aims to make the ballad the very *medium* of his message, the *determinate conduit* of reflexive thought and surcharged affect; Scott uses such ballads as a *content* of his medium – whether his medium was antiquarian collection, romance, or, ultimately, novel. Wordsworth's Preface to *Lyrical Ballads* offers an intricate, sustained, vexing account of poetry as a metrical medium, transmitting via regular and irregular pulses carefully calibrated surges of pressure to the psychesoma; he distinguishes poetry from prose not by their respective languages but through the special psycho-physiological *techne* that is meter. Such a fine-grained theorization of poetry *per se* is largely alien to Scott's project: while he often reflected on the comparative impacts and utilities of meters (viz. his remarks in his "Introduction to the *Lay of the Last Minstrel*," on ballad measure vs. octosyllabic couplets vs. the varied measures of "Christabel"), there is a way in which Scott is indifferent to medium, aside from his

---

[31] Scott, prefatory note to "The Death of Featherstonhaugh," *MSB, Poetical Works*. 81. This ballad was one of Surtees' three forgeries, clearly a very successful one, serving a variety of poetic purposes.

supreme orientation to the supermedium of print. The mobility and flexibility and success of Scott's writing career, his supremely opportunistic relation to materials, his truly experimental literary entrepreneurship, his constant attunement to audience, has led one of the most prominent scholars of Scott, David Hewitt, to remark: "There is a sense in which Scott's work is literature only because of the need for a medium, and that it is closer to performance, a permanent negotiation between tale teller and audience, in which the excitement of the moment takes both parties through to the end."[32]

It was this very compact between poet and audience – or "tale teller and audience" – that Wordsworth struggled with and Scott brilliantly negotiated by the mid-1810s. This divergence in Wordsworth's and Scott's careers might be read as a diagnostic case in media history: committed to poetry (that is, to a certain stream of poetry), Wordsworth lost his audience; committed to audience, Scott abandoned poetry.[33] Such a statement grossly simplifies these authors' situations circa 1815, as well as the social and commercial structuring of genres and reading publics. Yet such a comparison, on the field of media history as opposed to, say, the history of genres, may better illuminate just what was at stake for imaginative writers, particularly those staked in poetry *qua* poetry, in the early nineteenth century. In his "Defence of Poetry," Shelley famously transvalued "poetry" such that it came to signify any humanly important and transformative cultural project – Bacon's science, Jesus' ethics, Dante's *Commedia*. And "poetry" has long since oscillated between its status as a particular kind of metrical or lineated linguistic product or performance and a pseudo-metaphysical category (for "greatness," "imagination," what have you). In his faux vernacular wisdom, William Carlos Williams proclaimed, "If it ain't a pleasure, it ain't a poem." By these lights, for many contemporary readers Wordsworth's *Excursion* (for example) was no poem; Scott's *Waverley* was. What does a poet want? To write poems. What does a medium want? To conduct. Wordsworth continued to write poems and to curate himself; Scott ceaselessly conducted the flow of old and new contents. Wordsworth has entered the history of literature and the psyches of those still structured by print; Scott has since gone to the movies.

---

[32] See David Hewitt, "Scott, Sir Walter (1771–1832)," in the *Oxford Dictionary of National Biography* online (accessed October 17, 2006).

[33] Scott of course never wholly abandoned poetry, but his work post-1814 was primarily in prose genres: novels and biographies and editions of major authors, including himself.

ORALITY INTERMINABLE: ORAL TURNS IN
LATE-TWENTIETH-CENTURY POETRY

I would argue that the Romantic encounter with orality – its complex representations of and debts to oral poetry, its exploration of song-culture and traditional forms like the ballad, its privileging of ethnographic authority as a poetic resource, its focus on mediation – inaugurated a long imaginative exchange that we are still witnessing. It is striking that, however different their poems, aims, and commitments, poets as diverse as Scott, Wordsworth, and Coleridge understood their balladry to be both innovations and interventions in what they saw as moribund poetic state. Their work presents the by now familiarly paradoxical face of many modern literary movements: they strove, in Ezra Pound's words, to "make it new," and did so by reviving what they saw as the old, the traditional, the popular, the naïve. Among the traditional things ready for re-working: oral poetry, which from one angle seemed decidedly past, and yet from another was everywhere around them, in the popular ballads they knew from childhood, or the songs their grandfathers knew, or tales carried in the minds of vagrants they might encounter on the public way, or tunes sung by their nurses.

This paradoxical movement, of literary revivification through the romance of orality, persists in contemporary experimental poetry, albeit in newly determined forms. We can debate, as critics have on the front page of *The New York Times*, whether rap is poetry; leaving aside that revealingly vexed and racialized controversy, we find in the heart of high-cultural North American poetry a telling turn toward the oral and toward theories of the oral. Among the more recent, sophisticated investigations of twentieth-century oral–literate interactions are John Foley's *How To Read An Oral Poem* (2002) – with its extended discussion of a Nuyorican slam poet juxtaposed against the Beowulf-poet, a Serbian bard, and Homer – and the collection of essays, *Close Listening: Poetry and the Performed Word* (1998), edited by Charles Bernstein, poet, critic, and longtime impresario of experimental writing in North America. With contributions from scholars, poets, language- and non-language-identified writers, *Close Listening* investigates a specifically trans- and inter-medial *poiesis*: its essays feature meditations on noise, concrete poetry, poetry readings, discrepant sounds, translatability, aural and visual "performances" of "the poetic text" (to invoke Johanna Drucker's essay within).[34] The very title of Section 3, "close hearings," aligns

---

[34] See *Close Listening: Poetry and the Performed Word*, ed. Charles Bernstein (New York: Oxford University Press, 1998), including Drucker's "Visual Performance of the Poetic Text." Particularly

with my remarks in Chapter 2 regarding the challenges ballads gave and
continue to give those of us trained as primarily *textual* scholars and critics: a
historically and critically informed close listening is certainly crucial for a
historical media analysis of *poiesis*.

Alongside, and surely fueled by, the massive transformations in communications technology in the past century, we can trace in late-twentieth-
century poetry a marked persistence and tactical renewal of the ethnographic
romance of orality, with some poets rejecting what they perceive as
the merely literary and the culturally insular. Jerome Rothenberg's
manifesto, "New Models, New Visions: Some Notes Toward a Poetics of
Performance," first presented in 1977, proposes an oral turn as a route out
of the imagined etiolation of Western thought and culture.[35] Just as our
understanding of oral poetry and performance has been illuminated by the
conversation between philologists and anthropologists, so too we see
Rothenberg turning to anthropologists of ritual, notably Victor Turner, in
an attempt to imagine a new, postmodern poetic practice free from literary
constraints:

> The model – or better, the vision – has shifted: away from a "great tradition"
> centered in a single stream of art and literature in the West, to a *greater* tradition
> that includes, sometimes as its central fact, preliterate and oral cultures throughout
> the world, with a sense of their connection to subterranean but literate traditions in
> civilizations both East and West. (640)

Outlining this new paradigm, Rothenberg calls for the dissolution of the
artwork, for an emphasis on process over product, and for the disappearance
of the distinction between artist and audience. On this last point, he notes,
"the tribal/oral is a particularly clear model, often referred to by the creators
of 1960s happenings and the theatrical pieces that invited, even coerced,
audience participation toward an ultimate democratization of the arts"
(643). Again, what is important here is Rothenberg's telling impulse to
find in the "tribal/oral" an alternative to Western high-cultural models of
art-making.

If it was the Romantics who first conceptualized the idea of "poet-as-
informant," the postmoderns continue to find it compelling. Rothenberg,

---

relevant to this discussion are Bob Perelman, "Speech Effects: The Talk as a Genre" (200–16)
and Ron Silliman, "Afterword: Who Speaks: Ventriloquism and the Self in the Poetry Reading"
(360–78).

[35] Jerome Rothenberg, "New Models, New Visions: Some Notes toward a Poetics of Performance," first
presented and published in 1977; now published in *Postmodern American Poetry*, 640–4 ed. Paul
Hoover (New York and London: W. W. Norton, 1994). Further quotations from the essay will be
cited in text by page.

for example, makes a polemical, volatile analogy in the closing paragraphs of his essay, styling his new-modeled poet as a post-literate, native informant:

> The model switch is here apparent. But in addition the poet-as-informant stands in the same relation to those who speak of poetry or art from outside the sphere of its making as do any of the world's aboriginals. The antagonism to literature and to criticism is, for the poet and artist, no different from that to anthropology, say, on the part of the Native American militant. It is a question in short of the right to self-definition. (644)

It is by now a cliché that such avant-garde announcements of the death of art and literature are accompanied by an exaltation of the "primitive," the collective, and, more important for our purposes, the oral. We observe here, as we can in eighteenth-century writing, a characteristic blurring of these terms into one another. Such an extended, if confused, analogy reveals how politically and ethically problematic the turn to the oral can be. In his great drive to liberate artists from the shackles of convention, critical apparatus, elitism, and commodification, Rothenberg turns to a fantasy of pre-capitalist, communitarian societies and ritual practices. In doing so, his rhetoric ultimately lapses in its elision of actual aboriginal and Native American claims, histories, and predicaments. Readers informed by decades of post-colonial critique – not to mention so-called "native" readers who might encounter this essay – can't help but hear neo-colonial tropes in this manifesto. One could discuss such moments in this and other essays under the title, "On the Use and Abuse of the Oral Native for Art."

This is not to mount what at this point can only be a tired prosecution of Rothenberg or other voyagers into ethno-poetics; more interesting than the ideologics embedded in what we should recall was a utopian moment are the terms through which such a project was proposed: transmedial as well as transcultural encounter. "The model switch is here apparent," Rothenberg declares: we might take this as a referendum on a poetic communications model as well as on first-world canon-making. Rothenberg was focusing on poetics at a particular moment in the late 1970s: his manifesto has clearly become a synecdoche for those interested in constructing a postmodern, post-western, post-literate canon, however quixotic such a venture may be. And Rothenberg has long been a prominent and hugely influential compiler, translator, anthologist, and advocate of various world poetries and alternative poetics.[36] Poetics for him merges into the making of culture, and the

---

[36] Among his many contributions, alongside his own volumes of poetry, are the important *Technicians of the Sacred: A Range of Poetries from Africa, America, Asia, Europe & Oceania*, ed. with commentaries by Jerome Rothenberg (2nd edn., revised, Berkeley: University of California Press, 1985); *Revolution of the*

democratization of culture, thereby involving art-making in a political and ethical project. But Rothenberg's analogy raises yet again the disquieting asymmetry confronting students and theorists of so-called oral cultures, poetries, and peoples, whom we almost inevitably approach from the literate, capitalized side of the oral/literate boundary. If natives should be wary of anthropologists, in what ways should the South Slavic guslars have been more wary, say, of Milman Parry, or Leadbelly of John and Alan Lomax?

What is notable, for our purposes, is the continuation of the romance of orality in this manifesto housed within the typeset, mass-produced pages of *Postmodern American Poetry*. Postmodern poets, even more pointedly than their Romantic forebears, invoke orality as a mode of critique: it reveals what most prevailing poetry *is not*, what it lacks, what it needs; it shows the way, for these poets, to a new consideration of performance, language, and relation to audience. The ascendant regime of electronic media has transformed the horizon for thinking such that "orality," "talk," "performance," and so on must now be considered in light of new technologies, formats, and media: TV, broadcast news, cable news, blogs, webcams, talkshows, stand-up comedy (to which Charles Bernstein's own poems owe much). The very concept of "making" had come to look very different by the late 1960s, as Rothenberg suggests. "Happenings," "Mail Art," and other expressive and critical modes put pressure on *poiesis*: Dick Higgins, one of the founders of Mail Art, suggests in his "Intermedia Chart" (Fig. 17) how we might locate various poetic projects within historical reconfigurations of media. Higgins' set-theory approach to intermedia offers a provisional, synchronic picture of *poiesis* in the broadest sense (albeit with a marked emphasis on more experimental ventures and movements – Fluxus, Concrete Poetry, Conceptual Art); by now readers will understand that one aim of this book has been to offer in words if not images a similar picture or map of some aspects of Romantic *poiesis*, and to suggest how the intermediality discernible circa 1800 might speak to that of 2000. For a final example of a medially reflexive poetic project, let us turn to David Antin's "talk poems."

Since the 1970s Antin has set himself the task of becoming a post-literate performance poet, a truly improvisatory poet who comes to events, he claims, with no prepared text, just the readiness to talk, to perform, and to be open to the occasion. Antin's "talk poems" explicitly interrogate

INTERMEDIA CHART

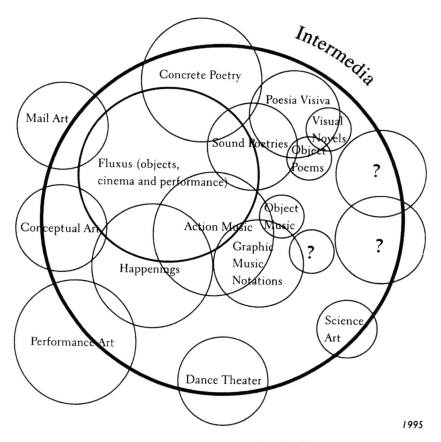

17 Dick Higgins, "Intermedia Chart"

poiesis, highlighting the interplay of oral and literate streams of making. As he polemically declared in "a private occasion in a public place,"

> i came here in order to make a
> poem talking to talk a poem which it will be all
> other things being equal[37]

[37] David Antin, "a private occasion in a public place," in *Postmodern American Poetry*, 231. Further quotations of Antin's preface and poem-talk will be cited in text by page.

For Antin, "to make a poem" is "to talk a poem"; he makes as he goes, he claims, on his feet. Antin's work is obviously a highly sophisticated meditation on *poiesis* as well as an apparently free-form "talk."

Evoking aspects of comic monologue, confessional poem, jazz improvisation, free association, and obsessional diatribe, his pieces are intriguing examples of a reconstructed orality used to jumpstart contemporary poetry.[38] Antin is, moreover, extremely self-reflexive in his pieces, meditating explicitly on his compositional choices and the stakes of his poetic gambits. In his introduction to "a public occasion in a private place," republished in *Postmodern American Poetry*, Antin notes that he'd been called to do a reading:

> *i had to explain that i wasnt doing any reading any*
> *more   or not at that time anyway   that i went to a*
> *place and talked to an occasion and that was the only*
> *kind of poetry i was doing now   but if that was all*
> *right with them id like to read with jackson maclow* (230)

Antin thus announces a reading involving no reading, a reading in which "reading" becomes the name not for the practice of reading out words from books or manuscripts but rather for the occasion itself, an occasion which, he proudly declares in his opening lines, is unmediated by books, text, print, or writing:

> i consider myself a poet but im not reading poetry   as you see
>   i bring no books with me   thought ive written books   i
> have a funny relationship to the idea of reading   if you cant hear
> i would appreciate it if youd come closer (231)

Swerving here from "the idea of reading" to the problem of hearing, Antin gestures explicitly to the audience. This gesture is both an interactive solicitation – a thing said to the audience concerning the audience – and a theoretical proposition. Antin goes so far as to announce the death of all poetry that is not, as he claims his is, "complete improvisation"; this extreme pronouncement he then quickly and characteristically re-works:

> ive
> said you cant possibly make a poem that isnt a complete improvi-
>   sation say   or something like that   and then i figured   as

---

[38] For an illuminating discussion of Antin and the stakes of his work, see Marjorie Perloff, "'No More Margins': John Cage, David Antin, and the Poetry of Performance," in *The Poetics of Indeterminacy: Rimbaud to Cage* (Princeton University Press, 1981), 288–340. Perloff reads Antin's exploratory *poiesis* as specially engaged with "opsis," that is, with spectacle: "Performance . . . is, by definition, an art form that involves *opsis*: it establishes a unique relationship between artist and audience" (289).

soon as i said it   a week later i made exactly the opposite kind of
poem   because as soon as you take a position very forcefully
youre immediately at the boundary of that position (234)

Antin constantly invokes the implicit contract between poet and audience,
revising the contract as he names it:

... youre here at a private experience in a public
place   its what one expects of a poet isnt it? (236)

Antin's semi-serious characterization of poetry as a typically "private
experience" relies on a literate, literary, bourgeois conception of poetry,
in which poems are imagined as intimate, written, page-bound communications read alone, in silence, in private. Using oral performance to
confound the literate conventions associated with poetic experience,
Antin explores the social situation of poetry, its "place," its status as
"private" or "public." Antin has undertaken as kind of meta-performance
poetry, a *poiesis* obviously informed by a deep literary sophistication that
nevertheless privileges – or claims to privilege – the "composition-in-
performance" one associates with oral poetry. Yet however much Antin
has recourse to the oral, Antin's performance poetry is not, to be sure, the
"saying of the same again" of traditional oral poetry: his works are not
re-creations but rather one-time-only improvisations. And we can see that,
by allowing the printing and anthologizing of transcriptions of his poem-
talks, Antin also embraces – notwithstanding his avoidance of conventional capitalization and punctuation – the same means of mediation and
transmission as his more text-oriented, literary-minded peers. The contra-
dictions of Antin's project are obvious, not least to Antin, who revels in
paradox.

More broadly Antin asks us to attune ourselves to the trans- and inter-
medial stakes of *poiesis*, as the title of his 1984 work, *Tuning*, suggests.
Tuning – the title itself a ramifying transhistorical media pun – might be
read as a latter-day take on Beattie's *Minstrel* crossed with Wordsworth's
Prelude, a kind of "growth of the poet's mind" fueled by a transmediation of
tales: for one of the striking aspects of Antin's work is the way he incorporates anecdotes, lore, gossip, and other oral *materia* into his work, which
becomes a kind of talking-through of the egotistical sublime that is also a
generous offering of the self as a reflective medium of and for others. Antin
is both living archive – a "living miscellany," far kin to Mrs. Hogg – and
improvisatory editor/performer. In terms of transmedial poetics, *Tuning* is
especially rich, for example in the status of the remembered radio transmissions and TV shows featured in "whos listening out there," the final

piece in the book.[39] "whos listening out there" is the printed version of a piece Antin performed on the radio; here the "talk poem" meets the delivery system and techno-ideologics of radio, the peculiarities of which become one subject of the work.

As Antin demonstrates, radio offers a new medial horizon for *poiesis*, a new channel for performance and a reconstructed oral *poiesis*. For the postmodern poet-cum-child of the 1940s, radio and not Aeolian harps becomes the strange instrument of and analogue for *poiesis*. "whos listening out there" might be read in fact as a bravura riff on Roman Jakobson's communications model, outlined in his "Closing Statements: Linguistics and Poetics" (1960).[40] Antin activates what Jakobson called the phatic function of poetics: he frequently checks the channel, assessing the contact between speaker and addressee. Several passages invoke the "conative function," orienting us to the addressee:

> the only thing thats disturbing you now   if its disturbing you
> at all   is the possibility that because of the way im speaking
>   about speaking on the radio that maybe i will violate your
> confidence and trust by saying something else (270)

Antin makes explicit how certain media heighten our consciousness of certain communicative functions: the conative function here becomes a site of potential opacity, since the broadcast radio medium (as opposed to older historical forms of radio transmission, point-to-point) specifically disrupts the feedback loop, listeners unable freely to "talk back" over the same channel. This peculiar simultaneity, shared time sustained over a non-transitive, non-reciprocal channel, creates a kind of poetic vertigo: is this radio-lyrico-utterance *heard*, much less overheard? Thus Antin recalls a previous radio piece he'd done:

> it was very hard to believe that i was really on the
> air at all   and that seemed to be my basic feeling about being
> on the radio   a kind of uncertainty about whether i was talking
>   to anybody out there at all   (270)

Flagging this "uncertainty," Antin brings the conative function to the fore. If in "The Solitary Reaper," Wordsworth foregrounds the problem of the message and its receivability – "Will no one tell me what she sings?" – Antin's radio'd work concerns himself with the problem of addressee. Radio

[39] See David Antin, "whos listening out there," *Tuning* (New York: New Directions, 1984), 267–95. Quotations from this work will be cited by page in text.
[40] In Thomas A. Sebeok, ed., *Style In Language*, (Cambridge, MA: MIT Press, 1960), 350–77.

Poetry re-constitutes the relation among (to use Jakobson's terms) message, addresser, addressee, code, channel, and context.

That media impede as well as conduct, that they are determinate channels, introducing noise, static, and specific constraints, that they imagine specifically trained or prepared receivers – all this Antin elegantly glosses all en route:

                                              as each
        medium   each way has something in it   inherently
            some price you pay for being able to go through it or transmit
            through it   or receive   maybe not much more than my
            attempt to find out   who im talking to out there   or whos
        listening   while im trying to find out   (278)

Trying to find out not only one's subject, but one's channel, addressee, and code: this is a flagrantly meta-medial *poiesis*, a transposition into a new multi-medial key of the long tradition of poems about poetry. Through the question of "whos listening," poised against the sound-image of who's talking, Antin re-introduces into his radio'd talk piece the question of the linguistic circuit. There are "voices in the air" indeed, to invoke the spirits of Shelley's *Prometheus Unbound*: that the history of media gives us new technologies for transmitting these voices shouldn't obscure their transhistorical force. Whether there are ears to hear is another albeit related matter.

Whether radio'd, digitized, slammed, blogged, downloaded, printed, or performed, the romance of orality has proven to be surprisingly resilient, persisting through the birth of new media and the concomitant re-organization of old. Many of us – scholars, critics, and poets – long ago internalized a concept of poetry founded on the hegemony of print and the ideal of the fixed, perfected, replicable artifact. It seems unavoidably true that, as Walter J. Ong suggested, we now live in a world governed by "secondary orality" (as he called it) – in which the oral/aural domain, newly mediated and amplified by electronic and digital technologies, has displaced the primacy of text and print.[41] Whether oral or literate or hovering in the twilight zone between the two, poetry has always been, in the first instance, an art of

[41] Ong discusses "secondary orality" (as opposed to the "primary orality" of peoples untouched by writing) in light of Marshall McLuhan's notion of the "global village" – the mass-mediated group-consciousness promoted by electronic, and now digital, media. See Ong, *Orality and Literacy*, 136–7. As I have previously observed (in Chapter 3 in particular), Kittler salutarily criticizes Ong for partitioning "primary" and "secondary" orality, which division is, as Kittler observes, an effect of literature itself. "Secondary orality" suggests, then, too neat a continuation with "primary," as if there were some reified thing "orality" that might be "revived" or superadded to print. Still the "secondariness" of "secondary orality" does carry some useful sense of a revivification of some aspects of a media ecology perhaps suppressed during the Typographic Era, as McLuhan might have put it.

language. The vitality of poetry will surely continue to depend on this ongoing negotiation between a history of linguistically based traditions – whether "oral" or not – and an embrace of new media. The *critical* vitality of poetry and poetics will depend on our consciousness of this negotiation, on our refusals as well as affirmations: our refusing to take "orality" – whatever that may be – as residual; refusing both technophilia and technophobia; refusing to idealize or lament poetry; refusing the reactionary partitioning of "poetry" into "poetry vs. verse," or vs. prose, etc. – oppositions which the Romantics long ago put paid to. For poets will continue, as Adorno put it in *Aesthetic Theory*, "[t]o make things of which we do not know what they are."[42] Whether we are prepared to receive unanticipated messages: this is the challenge of future poetries that are, in Wordsworth's terms, "ever more about to be."

---

[42] Quoted in Robert Kaufman, "A Future for Modernism: Barbara Guest's Recent Poetry," *American Poetry Review* Jul/Aug 2000, n. 8.

Conclusion: Thirteen (or more) ways of looking at a black bird: or, Poiesis unbound

[1.]

I was of three minds
Like a tree
In which there are three blackbirds.
    – Wallace Stevens, "Thirteen Ways of Looking at a Blackbird"

[2.]

There were three ravens sat on a tree.
Down a down, hay down, hay down
There were three ravens sat on a tree.
With a down
There were three ravens sat on a tree,
There were as blacke as they might be.
With a down derry, derry, derry, down down.
    – "The Three Ravens," traditional, from Thomas Ravenscroft's
    Melismata, 1611

[3.]

Hi! says the hawk unto the crow
If you ain't black then I don't know.
    – from *Songs from the Hills of Vermont*, 1919

[4.]

Then I heard it, inside the swarm, the single cry

of the crow. One syllable-one-inside the screeching and the
        skittering,

inside the constant repatterning of a thing…
    – Jorie Graham, "The Dream of the Unified Field"

As these epigraphs suggest, black birds have long perched emblematically on balladized, sung, and poeticized trees. As ravens, corbies, and crows, as English, Scottish, and American creatures, black birds have winged their

26

THE THREE RAVENS

a. Melismata. Musicall Phansies. Fitting the Court, Cittie, and Countrey Humours. London, 1611, No 20.* [T. Ravenscroft.]

b. 'The Three Ravens,' Motherwell's Minstrelsy, Appendix, p. xviii, No XII.

---

a was printed from Melismata, by Ritson, in his Ancient Songs, 1790, p. 155. Mr. Chappell remarked, about 1855, Popular Music of the Olden Time, I, 59, that this ballad was still so popular in some parts of the country that he had "been favored with a variety of copies of it, written down from memory, and all differing in some respects, both as to words and tune, but with sufficient resemblance to prove a similar origin." Motherwell, Minstrelsy, Introduction, p. lxxvii, note 49, says he had met with several copies almost the same as **a**. **b** is the first stanza of one of these (traditional) versions, "very popular in Scotland."

The following verses, first printed in the Minstrelsy of the Scottish Border, and known in several versions in Scotland, are treated by Motherwell and others as a traditionary form of 'The Three Ravens.' They are, however, as Scott says, "rather a counterpart than a copy of the other," and sound something like a cynical variation of the tender little English ballad. Dr Rimbault (Notes and Queries, Ser. v, III, 518) speaks of unprinted copies taken down by Mr Blaikie and by Mr Thomas Lyle of Airth.

THE TWA CORBIES.

a. Minstrelsy of the Scottish Border, III, 239, ed. 1803, communicated by C. K. Sharpe, as written down from tradition by a lady. **b.** Albyn's Anthology, II, 27, 1818, "from the singing of Mr Thomas Shortreed, of Jedburgh, as sung and recited by his mother." **c.** Chambers's Scottish Ballads, p. 283, partly from recitation and partly from the Border Minstrelsy. **d.** Fraser-Tytler MS., p. 70.

* Misprinted 22.

1 As I was walking all alane,
   I heard twa corbies making a mane;
   The tane unto the t'other say,
   'Where sall we gang and dine to-day?'

2 'In behint yon auld fail dyke,
   I wot there lies a new slain knight;
   And naebody kens that he lies there,
   But his hawk, his hound, and lady fair.

3 'His hound is to the hunting gane,
   His hawk to fetch the wild-fowl hame,
   His lady's ta'en another mate,
   So we may mak our dinner sweet.

4 'Ye'll sit on his white hause-bane,
   And I'll pike out his bonny blue een;
   Wi ae lock o his gowden hair
   We'll theek our nest when it grows bare.

5 'Mony a one for him makes mane,
   But nane sall ken where he is gane;
   Oer his white banes, when they are bare,
   The wind sall blaw for evermair.'

'The Three Ravens' is translated by Grundtvig, Engelske og skotske Folkeviser, p. 145, No 23; by Henrietta Schubart, p. 155; Gerhard, p. 95; Rosa Warrens, Schottische V. l. der Vorzeit, p. 198; Wolff, Halle der Völker, I, 12, Hausschatz, p. 205.

'The Twa Corbies' (Scott), by Grundtvig, p. 143, No 22; Arndt, p. 224; Gerhard, p. 94; Schubart, p. 157; Knortz, L. u. R. Alt-Englands, p. 194; Rosa Warrens, p. 89. The three first stanzas, a little freely rendered into four, pass for Pushkin's: Works, 1855, II, 462, xxiv.

26. THE THREE RAVENS

1 THERE were three rauens sat on a tree,
   Downe a downe, hay down, hay downe
There were three rauens sat on a tree,
   With a downe
There were three rauens sat on a tree,
They were as blacke as they might be.
   With a downe derrie, derrie, derrie, downe,
    downe

2 The one of them said to his mate,
  'Where shall we our breakefast take?'

3 'Downe in yonder greene field,
There lies a knight slain vnder his shield.

4 'His hounds they lie downe at his feete,
So well they can their master keepe.

5 'His haukes they flie so eagerly,
There's no fowle dare him come nie.'

6 Downe there comes a fallow doe,
As great with yong as she might goe.

7 She lift vp his bloudy hed,
And kist his wounds that were so red.

8 She got him vp vpon her backe,
And carried him to earthen lake.

9 She buried him before the prime,
She was dead herselfe ere euen-song time.

10 God send euery gentleman,
Such haukes, such hounds, and such a leman.

---

b. THREE ravens sat upon a tree,
  Hey down, hey derry day
Three ravens sat upon a tree,
  Hey down
Three ravens sat upon a tree,
And they were black as black could be.
  And sing lay doo and la doo and day

Variations of The Twa Corbies.

b. 1. As I cam by yon auld house end,
   I saw twa corbies sittin thereon.

2¹. Whare but by yon new fa'en birk.

3. We'll sit upon his bonny breast-bane,
   And we'll pick out his bonny gray
    een;
   We'll set our claws intil his yallow
    hair,
   And big our bowr, it's a' blawn bare.

4. My mother clekit me o an egg,
   And brought me up i the feathers gray,

And bade me flee whereer I wad,
For winter wad be my dying day.

5. Now winter it is come and past,
   And a' the birds are biggin their
    nests,
   But I'll flee high aboon them a',
   And sing a sang for summer's sake.

c. 1. As I gaed doun by yon hous-en,
   Twa corbies there were sittand their
    lane.
2¹. O down beside yon new-faun birk.
3¹. His horse. 3². His hounds to bring the
    wild deer hame.
4. O we'll sit on his bonnie breist-bane,
   And we'll pyke out his bonnie grey
    een.

d. 1¹. walking forth. 1². the ither. 1ᵇ. we twa
    dine.
3². wild bird.
5². naebody kens.
5ᵇ. when we've laid them bare. 5⁴. win
    may blaw.

way through traditional balladry, nursery rhyme, courtly song, literary poetry, blackface minstrelsy, and twentieth-century pop music (viz. the jazz standard, "Bye Bye Blackbird," the Beatles' "Blackbird"). For centuries blackbirds have been metered and baked four-and-twenty in a pie –

> Sing a song of sixpence a pocket full of rye
> Four and twenty blackbirds baked in a pie.
> When the pie was opened the birds began to sing,
> Oh wasn't that a dainty dish to set before the king?[1]

– while in more recent decades a black bird offered the Poet Laureate of Great Britain an *imago* of the mythic trickster animal intelligence he so prized: thus Ted Hughes' *Crow* (1970).[2]

These final pages propose not a survey of the black bird motif in lore and literature but a tactical selection of its several crucial incarnations, particularly in two ballads, "The Three Ravens" and "The Twa Corbies," both known – since Francis James Child's compendium – as Child No. 26 (see Fig. 18): for as the black bird wends its way through balladeering books, raising its head in blackface minstrelsy, lending its inscrutable presence to Wallace Stevens' serial imagist *punctum*, it allows us to revisit and, I hope, distill some of the concerns of this book: the problematics of mediation, the poetics of editing, the interface of oral and literate poetries, the historicity of poetry in print and in the air. The first part of this conclusion aligns with my previous inquiries into the representation of ballads; the latter part hopes to move such inquiry into a final meditation on the ends of *poiesis* itself, and here I hope to suggest how an exclusively *literary* poetics might be transformed through a sustained encounter with oral poetics. Through the black bird we may encounter the full range of *poiesis* once again as both the dispersable, dematerialized "beauty of inflections" (viz. Stevens) as well as the materialized, printed black marks, those notes and letters through which these birds and our poetries have moved, sounded, and had their being in various Englishes.

In speaking of various Englishes, I point to the transhistorical and transnational fortunes of the ballad that became Child No. 26 – its attestations in seventeenth-century English, eighteenth-century Scottish, and twentieth-century American and Canadian idioms; I point as well to the gap in tone and feeling between "The Three Ravens" and "The Twa Corbies," a gap which has long exercised editors. In both ballad versions, birds confer on the matter of where to find a meal; in both, a bird reports that a knight lies dead on a nearby field. In "The Three Ravens," often denominated the "English" ballad, the birds then offer an elegy (or

---

[1] In the spirit of Scott and Jamieson, I will note myself as the oral informant here: collected from myself, July 10, 2008; checked via Google, July 25, 2008, www.allaboutspace.com/Blackbirdrhyme.html.

The rhyme may also be found as "Song of Sixpence" in Joseph Ritson's wonderful collection of nursery rhymes, *Gammer Gurton's Garland: or, the Nursery Parnassus. A Choice Collection of Pretty Songs and Verses, for the Amusement of All Little Good Children who can Neither Read nor Run* (London: R. Triphook, 1810), 10, annotated in full antiquarian fashion. From antiquarian garlands to living memory to the web: a diagnostic trajectory.

[2] See Ted Hughes, *Crow: From the Life and Songs of the Crow* (London: Faber, 1970).

"dirge," as Joseph Ritson called it) for this knight, enumerating his faithful attendants: hawk, hound, leman (the beloved, sometimes a figurative "fallow doe," other times a gravid lady). In "The Twa Corbies," the Scottish counterpart, the birds enumerate these attendants *precisely* because they are absent: they have heartlessly abandoned the knight, leaving him as carrion for the corbies, who plan to "pike [pluck] out his bonny blue een." Over the centuries we find these birds, in both ballads, variously localized: in one Child variant, three ravens lament a dead knight in Lincolnshire; in James Reed's *Border Ballads*, twa corbies croak hungrily over a dead knight in the Middle Marches of Scotland; and in its transatlantic migration, raucous American crows often caw over a dead horse (the horse having replaced the dead knight in some versions).[3] The gregarious birds continue to seek out their food, alternately pitying or exulting over the dead creature which lies "on yonder green field" (in England), "behint yon auld fail dyke" (in Scotland), or "on yonders plain" (in the US).[4]

It is worth noting that these ballads do draw on somewhat different lexical stock: here is one case where the cultural nationalism of editors circa 1800 seems to be supported by the actual language of the poems. That is to say, labeling these ballad counterparts "English" and "Scottish" is not, in this case, simply the strained bid for cultural distinction and differentiation that it is with other such ballad labels, e.g. in Scott's "Sir Patrick Spens," subtitled, "The Scottish Edition." "Corbies" is, as the *OED* notes, a Scottish word, deriving from Old French; its first meaning is "A Raven; also, often, the carrion crow." And "The Twa Corbies" has a markedly Scottish diction. "Raven" conversely has a Teutonic lineage, from Old English through Old High German, with cognates in Old Norse.[5] Yet both versions move with adjustments into the American vernacular, and both were to be found (and may well still be) in Scotland, despite the frequent "nationalization" of the versions.[6]

---

[3] For the Lincolnshire localization, see the version sent by R. Brimley Johnson to Child, included in *English and Scottish Popular Ballads*, ed. Francis James Child, corrected 2nd edn. Mark F. Heiman and Laura Saxton Heiman (Northfield, MN: Loomis House Press, 2001), Vol. I of V, Appendix, 353; for corbies in the Scottish marshes, see James Reed, *Border Ballads* (Manchester: Carcanet Press, 1991); for the cawing of American crows (whether two or three) over dead horses or knights, see Bertrand Harris Bronson, *The Traditional Tunes of the Child Ballads* (Princeton University Press, 1959), Vol. I of IV, Child No. 26, in particular "Three Black Crows" (B. 6), 311.

[4] The phrases come from, respectively, "The Three Ravens," "The Twa Corbies," and "The Three Crows" (cf Bronson, Group B, Three Black Crows, 4, 6), Bronson, *Traditional Tunes*, 310, 311.

[5] See the *Oxford English Dictionary*, entries for "corbie" and "raven," respectively.

[6] William Motherwell, while including "The Twa Corbies" as "A Scottish Ballad" in his 1827 *Minstrelsy*, also observed in his notes that "The Three Ravens" was equally current in Scotland. See Motherwell, *Minstrelsy* (1827), Appendix "Musick," xvii. More recently, Emily Lyle includes both "The Twa Corbies" and "The Thrie Ravens" as her final ballad specimens: she adopts the version of "The Twa Corbies" printed in Child from Scott's 1803 *Minstrelsy*, but she publishes a version of "Thrie Ravens"

TOWARD CHILD NO. 26:CLASSIFYING, NATIONALIZING, LOCALIZING BALLADS' BLACK BIRDS

"The Three Ravens" first appeared in print in 1611, in Thomas Ravenscroft's songbook *Melismata: Musicall Phansies. Fitting the Court, Cittie, and Countrey Humours*. Ravenscroft divided his songbook into five sections: Court Varieties, Cittie Rounds, Cittie Conceits, Country Rounds, Country Pastimes. "The Three Ravens" appears as the twentieth of twenty-three songs, leading off the fourth section, "Country Pastimes" (Fig. 19). Taking the music and text over from Ravenscroft, Joseph Ritson appears to have been the first eighteenth-century balladeer to include the song in his *Ancient Songs* (1790). He observed there that the ballad, though published in the early seventeenth century, surely went back much further in oral tradition – an observation with which Bertrand Bronson later agreed in his *Traditional Tunes of the English and Scottish Popular Ballads*.

Given the logic of eighteenth-century balladeering, it's not surprising that "The Three Ravens," like many another ballad, found itself a coin in culturally nationalist traffic. "The Three Ravens" and the "Twa Corbies" have a long history of difficult coupling. These ballads were filtered through cultural nationalisms, editorial protocols, and the technical limitations conditioning such printings. What for Ritson was a specimen of Ancient English Song became for Scott a foil for a ballad he presented as a Scottish ballad, "The Twa Corbies." Scott introduces "The Twa Corbies" thus:

> This poem was communicated to me by Charles Kirkpatrick Sharpe, Esq. jun. of Hoddom, as written down, from tradition, by a lady. It is a singular circumstance that it should coincide so very nearly with the ancient dirge called *The Three Ravens*, published by Mr. Ritson, in his *Ancient Songs*; and that, at the same time, there should exist such a difference, as to make the one appear rather a counterpart than copy of the other.

Here we see once again the logic of ballad citation – the compulsion to present transmission circuits as an index of authentication and distinction. Scott's publication is in a complex dialogue with Ritson's, both acknowledging but also subsuming Ritson's *Ancient Songs*, for Scott goes on to (re) publish "The Three Ravens" within the space of his headnote – this all before getting to his own text of "The Twa Corbies." Scott publishes "The Three Ravens," moreover, not simply as an English variant, but as evidence for

---

from Andrew Crawfurd's nineteenth-century collecting in Scotland, and notes that it comes "with tune, from Mary Macqueen (Mrs. Storie)." See Emily Lyle, *Scottish Ballads* (Edinburgh: Canongate Press, 1994), 284, n. 82 and 83.

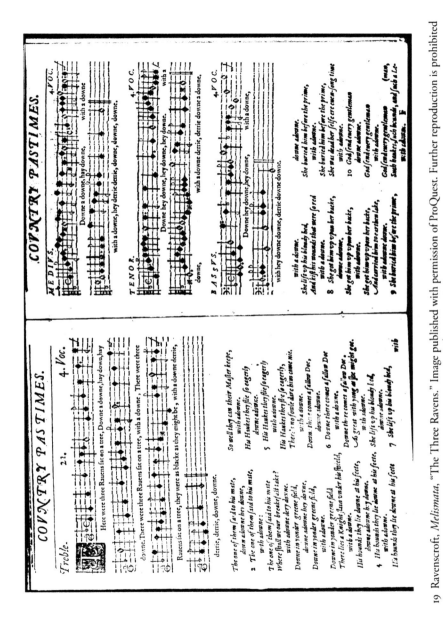

19 Ravenscroft, *Melismata*, "The Three Ravens." Image published with permission of ProQuest. Further reproduction is prohibited without permission.

the reader's arbitration and judgment: "In order to enable the curious reader to contrast these two singular poems, and to form a judgment which may be the original, I take the liberty of copying the English ballad from Mr Ritson's Collection, omitting only the burden and repetition of the first line."[7]

In Scott we have what I believe is the first contrastive publication of "The Three Ravens" and "The Twa Corbies." Here "The Three Ravens" is subordinated, contained and framed within the headnote. This coupling of ballads is offered for close-reading and scrutiny. That Scott invites the reader to compare is not so striking as the aim of comparative judgment: establishing priority as to "which may be the original." Scott's "Twa Corbies"/"Three Ravens" exemplifies both the cultural nationalism (here fairly muted) underlying his collection but also the agonistic and collaborative antiquarian discourse network lying behind the collection: from Sharpe, the antiquarian communicator who sent Scott the ballad transcription, to Ritson, the previous publisher, Scott orchestrates his fellows under the sign of magisterial editing.[8]

The more recent textual fortunes of these ballads suggest that, alongside their de facto canonization as Child No. 26, they persisted as material for other kinds of editorial and historical rumination than the comparative–philological (cf. Child) or comparative–musicological (cf. Bronson). Later twentieth-century editors have not abandoned the more local, regional, or national strains of ballad editing – James Reed, for example, publishing "The Twa Corbies" in his *Border Ballads* (1991). If Child surveyed balladry as ultimately a portion of a broad European (and Indo-European) inheritance, Reed sets his sights closer to home: "Border ballads belong to a period, a place, and its people." He thus emphasizes "the environment in which they flourished."[9] Reed publishes "The Twa Corbies" in his third

---

[7] Scott, "Twa Corbies," *MSB, Poetical Works,* 127.

[8] Child ups the editorial ante and quotes from Sharpe's Letter to Scott, August 8, 1802: "The song of 'The Twa Corbies' was given to me by Miss Erskine of Alva (now Mrs. Kerr), who, I think, said that she had written it down from the recitation of an old woman at Alva" (*ESPB,* 351). Thus Child further re-authenticates the ballad transmission, shows his access to Abbotsford documents, and provides new documentary information, namely, the name and locale of the transcriber; we see here again that the reciter is that paradigmatically unnamed old woman.

[9] *Border Ballads,* selected and intro. James Reed, 9. Reed's text comes from Scott, and he credits the *Minstrelsy* in brackets below the ballad's title (140). He does not however elect to adopt any part of Scott's headnote – the dialogue with Ritson, "The Three Ravens," etc. Eschewing the idea of collating ballad versions, opting for a single-text principle, he elsewhere takes his ballad texts from Child as easily as from Scott, though one observes that, in terms of classifying affinities, "The Ballads of the Middle Marches 1" are drawn largely from Scott's outlaw/border-raid ballads, those Scott published in the *Minstrelsy* under the rubric, "Historical Ballads." And his "Ballads of the Middle Marches 2" draws heavily upon those ballads Scott classified as "romantic," many of them taken from Mrs. Brown's manuscripts.

section, "Ballads of the Middle Marches (2)," thereby stationing his Scottish corbies in a specific, historically and geographically inflected landscape.

A question emerges: when does a variation or a "counterpart" (as Scott put it) become an autonomous poem? From Scott onward this question has loomed, sometimes in the background, sometimes in the fore, and it remains, for this ballad, unresolved. For Child, unlike Scott, the question was not one of Scottish versus English "originals" but rather of plaintive elegy versus cynical dialogue: to him the Scottish verses "sound[ed] something like a cynical variation of the tender little English ballad."[10] Note how Child considers "The Twa Corbies" a "variation": we have moved into the more nuanced field of philologically grounded textual editing, in which editors seek to publish variants (however cynical or degraded), not to arbitrate "originals." Child presents "The Twa Corbies" as a lesser variant (viz. "traditional form") of "The Three Ravens" (see again Fig. 19); but the most recent *Norton Anthology of Poetry* (2005) presents the poems as more or less companionable and distinct (viz. Scott's idea of "counterparts"): only the footnotes alert the reader to the fact that *both* are Child No. 26.[11] Thus the *NAP*, like Scott, presents "The Twa Corbies" as an autonomous poem. Yet the question of variants, their encroachments, degradations, and transmutations, persisted, especially when the ballad migrated to North America and kept alive both the English elegiac strain and the Scottish cynical strain.

THIRTEEN (OR MORE) WAYS OF LOOKING AT
A BLACKBIRD: A RECAPITULATION

These balladized blackbirds have crossed the threshold of poetic enunciation in many ways, casting their metrical shadows in many print modalities, from songbook to broadside to philological compendium to school anthology and beyond. To review these Ways of Looking At (Framing, Labelling, and Mediating) a Black Bird, it is worth noting that this ballad has appeared variously –

---

[10] Child, headnote to "The Three Ravens," in *ESPB*, Vol. I of V, 253.
[11] See *The Norton Anthology of Poetry*, ed. Margaret Ferguson, Mary Jo Salter, and John Stallworthy, 5th edn. (New York: Norton, 2005). Among the twelve "Early Modern Ballads" we find both "The Three Ravens" (101–2) and "The Twa Corbies" (102): that the first is glossed as "Child No. 26" in the notes shows how the Norton remediates Child; yet only in the notes is the reader invited to consider the poems as linked, much less as "versions" or variants of each other – rather than as free-standing autonomous lyrics, each a singular Norton-sanctioned poem. On the problematics of placing and dating ballads within the Norton, see Mary Ellen Brown, "Placed, Replaced, or Misplaced?," *ECTI* 42:2/3, 115–29.

- As a song among English renaissance songs; a "country pastime" in Ravenscroft's *Melismata*, and a period song in twentieth-century CD compendiums such as Alfred Deller and Desmond Dupre's *The Three Ravens: Elizabethan Folk and Minstrel Songs.*[12]
- As "ancient" song: in Ritson: *Ancient Songs* (1790).
- As an "original," or debatable original (as in Scott's *Minstrelsy*).
- As antiquarian communication: in Scott, who salutes his "communicator" Charles K. Sharpe of Hoddom, and in Child, who takes over and elaborates this citation, and who in his appendix to Child No. 26 included this further communication from R. Brimley Johnson:

From E. Peacock, Esq. F.S. A., of Dunstan House, Kirton-in-Lindsay, Lincolnshire, whose father, born in 1793, heard it as a boy at harvest-suppers and sheep-shearings, and took down a copy from the recitation of Harry Richard, a laborer, who could not read, and had learnt it "from his fore-elders." He lived at Horthorpe, where a grass-field joining a little stream, called Ea, Ee, and Hay, is pointed out as the scene of the tragedy.[13]

- As English: "The Three Ravens," in Ritson, and residually in Child and Bronson.
- As Scottish: "The Twa Corbies," nationally and/or regionally marked as such in Scott, and Motherwell, Child, Bronson, Reed, and Lyle, though to different editorial ends.
- As British: in such anthologies as R. Brimley Johnson's *Popular British Ballads* (1894).
- As American: "The Three Black Crows" and "The Two Black Crows" in Child and Bronson, and also those minstrel songs supposedly affiliated with it.[14] (For a minstrel variant mentioned by Bronson, see "The Crow Family" [Fig. 20]).[15]

---

[12] See the first track of Alfred Deller and Desmond Dupre, *The Three Ravens: Elizabethan Folk and Minstrel Songs,* Vanguard Classics, 2003 (a remastering of LPs from 1956 and 1957).

[13] Child, *ESPB,* Appendix, 353.

[14] See "The Bird Song," version of Child No. 26, "The Three Ravens," on Lesley Nelson, "The Contemplator," www.contemplator.com/child/birdsong.html, accessed July 26, 2007. See too "Says the Blackbird to the Crow," version of Child No. 26, "Three Ravens," on "Digital Tradition Mirror," http://sniff.numachi.com/pages/tiTHRERAV6;ttTHRERAV6.html, accessed July 25, 2007. Note that the page features a tune. Regarding "Says the Blackbird," both The Digital Tradition and Bronson refer us to one H. M. Belden, who in his *Ballads and Songs: Collected by the Missouri Folk-lore Society* (Columbia: University of Missouri Press, 1973,1940) considered this song yet another variant of Child No. 26. See Bronson, *Traditional Tunes,* Vol. I, 308.

[15] See for example "The Crow Family," Bodleian Library *allegro* Catalogue of Ballads, Harding B 18 (606). The song is perhaps less a racist ditty – though surely it is that too – than a typical specimen of cultural nationalism turned along American ethno-racial lines.

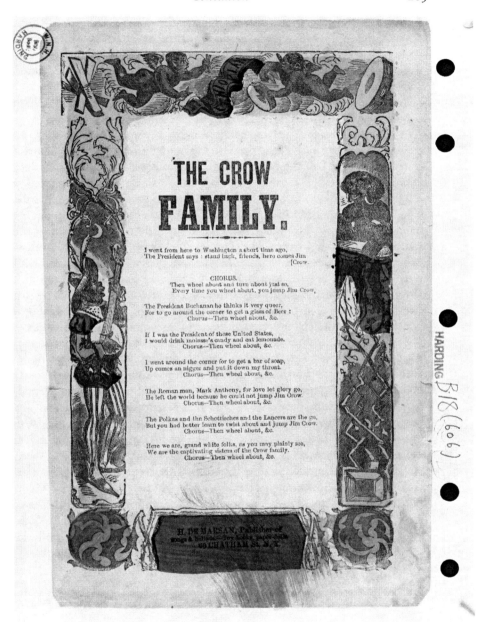

20 "The Crow Family," American broadside ca. 1860

- As musically notated: from Ravenscroft's 1611 songbook through Ritson to Motherwell to varieties of modern musical notation, in Bronson and other songbooks.
- As specimens of "popular ballads": Child (viz. *English and Scottish Popular Ballads*), and the *Norton Anthology of Poetry*, 3rd edn., 1983.
- As specimens of "early modern ballads" under the rubric of "English Poetry": *Norton Anthology of Poetry* 4th edn. 1996, 5th edn., 2005.

"The Three Ravens" has appeared, then, as a country pastime song, an ancient song, an English text proffered for comparison with the Scottish "Twa Corbies," a ballad among ballads, a popular ballad, an early modern ballad, a link to English carols (see Bronson), a Dorian tune (Bronson), a CD track; "The Twa Corbies" has appeared as a Scottish ballad, a romantic ballad, an antiquarian communication, a border ballad of the middle marches (see Reed), a popular ballad, and an early modern ballad in the tradition of English poetry. "The Twa Corbies" and "The Three Ravens," separate and conjoined, have thus served a variety of editorial ends and have lived in multiple medial incarnations. The ballad has been realized as a performance (recited, sung, spoken); as documented and textualized by (for example) Sharpe, and in Scott, Child, Cecil Sharp, Bronson, Crawfurd, Lyle; and as recorded by newer sound-recording technologies "in the field," on stage, and in recording studios. It flourished, as we have seen, as a broadside with several offshoots; the broadsides are now themselves remediated on the web.[16] The ballads appear in several web incarnations, closely linked as they have been since Scott and then Child ratified and systematized the connection, the "Twa Corbies" typically subordinated to "The Three Ravens" (*pace* Scott). "The Three Ravens" and "The Twa Corbies" now appear as well as audio tracks on numerous compilations, themselves often digital remasterings of older recording technologies – e.g. Alfred Deller's LPs, now on CD; Peter, Paul and Mary recorded in concert, now a CD downloadable through iTunes. And at Lesley Nelson-Burns' Child Ballad website (www.contemplator.com) you can download MIDI files of "The Three Ravens" (www.contemplator.com/child/3ravens.html), "The Twa Corbies" (www.contemplator.com/child/twacorbies.html), and the American "Bird Song" (www.contemplator.com/child/birdsong.html).

---

[16] See Bodleian Library *allegro* Catalogue of Ballads online: www.bodley.ox.ac.uk/ballads/ballads.htm, which yields, after a search for "blackbird," many ballads and songs about unrequited love, sailors, crime and other typical ballad matters but also a final entry for the ballad, "The Crow Family," Harding B 18 (606), New York: H. De Marsan, c. 1860; subject, Blackface Minstrelsy. This is most likely the minstrelsy song that Bronson alludes to in his volume, which he and some web editors are willing to consider in "the family" of Child No. 26.

These several medial realizations do not represent a history of super-cession but rather an arrival at a historically determinate medial simulta-neity: printed and digitized versions of the poem continue to appear even as singers remake the song in concerts or at home; texts are printed and digitized independently of, as well as concurrently with, the tunes. It is striking that when twentieth-century singers and ensembles have returned to the song, they most often sing Ravenscroft's version: print has here served as a resource for re-oralization and new performance and has fostered, some 400 years after Ravenscroft's publication, new forms of remediation. It is also true that the newest media return us to the oldest modes of trans-mission (thus "secondary orality" allows us at times to bypass print): those children who learn "The Three Ravens" from recordings might become the nodes of a newly mediated oral transmission: not face-to-face, but mouth-to-ear nonetheless.

REMAKING AND UNMAKING *POIESIS*: BETWEEN MEDIAL INDIFFERENCE AND MEANINGFUL MESSAGES

From the point of view of song, so to speak, it matters not who moves it, what medium carries or determines it: it is simply enough that the song – that *poiesis* – go on. In this peculiar sense poetry is supremely indifferent to its mediums, whether humans, books, or CDs. "The Three Ravens"/"The Twa Corbies" raises the spectre of such indifference *in its content*: most obviously in the corbies' ostentatious lack of sympathy with the knight, as if to show by contrast that the ravens' sympathy is a another instance of human susceptibility to the pathetic fallacy. As "The Twa Corbies" cheer-fully makes plain, birds just don't care. To think otherwise is wish-fulfillment.

Between disenchantment and wish-fulfillment the human meanings of poetry emerge. Consider the last stanza of "The Twa Corbies," which takes us from the immediate situation of dead knight and hungry birds to the *longue durée* of death on the indifferent earth:

> Mony a one for him makes mane,
> But nane sall ken where he is gane;
> Oer his white banes, when they are bare,
> The wind sall blaw for evermair.

Humans may elegize, may "make mane" and acculturate their dead, but this does not transform the total situation: that over his bones and ours "the wind sall blaw for evermair." This line – a prophecy and a judgment, an epitaph for the knight, his kind, and poetry itself – may be read simultaneously as a consolation and a curse. Though men may die, the wind blows on. In this wind we have the figure of a nonsentient, indifferent medium, a medium without messages except the sole message that the medium exists – "for evermair." It is this possibility of a non-responsive, disinterested wind that Shelley's "Ode to the West Wind" works so strenuously to master, lending to the wind what he would borrow from it:

> Make me thy lyre, even as the forest is:
> What if my leaves are falling like its own!
> The tumult of thy mighty harmonies
>
> Will take from both a deep autumnal tone,
> Sweet though in sadness. Be thou, Spirit fierce,
> My spirit! Be thou me, impetuous one!

In contrast to the prevailing figurative logic of Romantic poetry, traditional balladry here offers a wind purged of humanized spirit; its winds blow not through forests or Aeolian harps, making music as if by nature, but rather over dead bodies, waste lands, unredeemable flesh. The ballad sings a hard, alien yet still human knowledge. Perhaps it was this haunting, inscrutable "evermair" that Edgar Allen Poe heard and channeled through the voice of yet another ominously vocal (yet lexically limited) black bird, his "Raven." In his relentless "Nevermore," the raven's negation contains within it the perpetual work of *poiesis*, "evermore."

If Wordsworth figured in his "gentle breeze," that "correspondent breeze" blowing through his *Prelude*, a correspondence between Mind and Nature, traditional balladry insists on the difference between the moving air and human breath. Inspiration is mortal; breathing is mortal; the wind is not. The air, that medium in which we live and move and have our being, outlasts our being; in this, the air is an intriguing metaphor – but only a metaphor – for a poetry which outlasts any individual singer or maker.

In its final four lines (" … the wind sall blaw for evermair"), "The Twa Corbies" achieves an astonishing figurative complex, linking and assessing the relations between human song, birdsong, and windblow. The birds mediate between the insentient wind and the once-sentient knight; between inanimate nature and the cognitive sentience of *poiesis*. Birds like humans send out their vocal, animal communications; unlike humans, birds (apparently) cannot conduct a reflection on the nature of these communications. In the ballad and song texts I have been considering, we confront not lone birds but rather a notionally communal *poiesis*, a kind of choral back-and-forth, an interested avian community chorus (elegiac or acerbic) speaking of the nearby dead, and by extension, of values like loyalty and fidelity. Birds here offer an image of sociable commentary in which humans might recognize themselves. The internal dialogue launching both "The Three Ravens" and "The Twa Corbies," as well as the returning chorus of "The Crow Song": these all suggest a communal, intersubjective responsiveness we know as the condition of being-in-language.

Certainly traditional balladry anthropomorphizes its birds. Yet their song possesses within it the ghost of a wholly alien species communication. In the US versions of Child No. 26 we find a much stronger emphasis on the question of avian *vocalization*: if the refrain in "The Three Ravens" stands as a kind of generic time filler, its *down-a-down* syllables moving us through the dance and the tune, the refrains in "The Three Crows" (sometimes "Two Crows"), increasingly exploit the onomatopoeic potential of poetry-as-bird-song. The American birds caw, craw, and Billy McGee McGaw[17]: in American versions, the refrain is explicitly *in the birds' voice*, and the birds are thus imagined as hovering between raucous, nonsensical vocalization and articulate speech – between what Stevens called "idiot minstrelsy" ("Notes toward a Supreme Fiction") and "lucid, inescapable rhythms" ("Thirteen Ways of Looking at a Blackbird").

Traditional balladry thus shares with literary poetry an interest in the relation of birdsong to human song and works out its own meditation on temporality, mortality, and indeed, mediality. Poets have often explored birdsong as a lesser yet kindred *poiesis* – an *ahistorical* song, a *non-artifactual* song, an unindividuated *species* song – as opposed to the historical, mortal, artifactual, individual work of human making. That the nightingale's song in Keats' Ode – the "self-same song" – was heard centuries ago by emperor and clown, that it shall persist even when the poet has "become a sod"[18]: this is Keats' simultaneous homage to and critique of birdsong, its endless iterability, its persistence through the deaths of generations of birds unto new generations. A perfect wrought thing, of "hammered gold and gold enamelling," is what Yeats seeks in "Sailing to Byzantium," over and against the vital yet fleeting music of a perishable bird and by extension a perishable song.[19] Such poems traffic in a metaphorics of aesthetic permanence over "fled music," of singularly wrought works over generically iterated songs, of a phantasized triumph-of-life in art over death and mutability.

---

[17] See Bronson, *Traditional Tunes*, Vol. I, 310–11.
[18] John Keats, "Ode to a Nightingale," *NAP*, 936, l. 65, l. 60.
[19] William Butler Yeats, "Sailing to Byzantium," *NAP*, 1200, l. 28.

Traditional balladry will of course have none of that and indeed inverts the metaphorics of such *poiesis*, returning poetry to the domain of communal re-creation. Elegies may be sung, yet "The wind sall blaw for evermair." And that is the way it is. Yet so too, says balladry, shall the poem persist "for evermair," as long as it finds its singers, readers, or recreators in any medium.

That birds might not continue to sing, that poetry might be done in by its own refusal to move: this is one way to understand the force of Keats' "La Belle Dame sans Merci" (1819). In this poem, literary balladry famously meets traditionary balladry. Reworking plot and motifs from faery ballads, notably "Thomas the Rhymer," "La Belle Dame" features a knight who explains his lone and "palely-loitering" condition as a kind of death-in-life subsequent to his erotic encounter with a faery maid.[20] If the knight is "in thrall," the poem plays with its own thralldom to and mastery over tradition. "La Belle Dame" turns aspects of "The Three Ravens/The Twa Corbies" inside out: in the traditional ballad, we have a dead knight discussed by birds; in "La Belle Dame," we have an undead knight for whom the lack of birdsong is an index of his larger situation:

> And this is why I sojourn here
> Alone and palely loitering,
> Though the sedge is wither'd from the lake,
> And no birds sing.

We are, significantly, in a domain *without* birdsong. The link between human song and birdsong – a link explored throughout world poetry, traditional and literary – is here broken. From the fulsome ravens and garrulous corbies of traditional balladry we have moved into a peculiar silence, a diagnostic silence. The absent birdsong is marked throughout the ballad in its absent sounds, the strikingly missing feet in the last line of each stanza. We expect a full abcb ballad stanza, four stresses per line, and we get instead a shockingly truncated fourth line throughout the poem: and no birds sing.

Fittingly for a poem itself possessed by, as well as possessing, tradition, Keats gives us a knight haunted by prior vocalizations, from the "faery's song," "sweet moan" and "language strange" of his faery lover to the frightening judgment of the pale kings, princes, and warriors of his dream: "La Belle Dame sans merci/Hath thee in thrall!" Beyond the rich intertextual and critical valences of the poem, we note this internal focus on

---

[20] For an illuminating account of Keats' engagement with "Thomas the Rhymer," and more broadly with the phenomenon of "lyric possession" as a way to understand literary balladry's relation to traditionary ballads (in Hardy as well as Keats), see Susan Stewart, "Voice and Possession," Ch. 3 in *Poetry and the Fate of the Senses* (University of Chicago Press, 2002), 107–43.

the problem of sound, vocalization, speech and song. And yet the narration of this vocalization – its recreation in his story – collapses back into the perpetual present of the knight:

> The sedge is wither'd from the lake
> And no birds sing.

With traditional balladry in mind, we might read "La Belle Dame" as a meditation on an *unmoving poiesis*, one in which songs, sounds, and poems are remembered but never recreated, never made new. The work of *poiesis* is over, or perpetually stalled, into this one story, which the knight seems prepared to repeat "for evermair," in thrall as he is. "And no birds sing." We have here a song beyond song, beyond the living calls of birds, beyond the sound of unenthralled, merely human life.

That birds, and people, sing, not *what* they sing: this is, the knight suggests, the point of a living *poiesis*. (From this as well as the homophonic angle, no birds sing = know birds sing.) And birdsong has continued to resound in our poetries – "the single cry/of the crow," as Jorie Graham puts it, moving "inside the constant repatterning of a thing"[21]: itself a figure for poetic *mouvance*. We might also consider these lines from "Hawthorn," a poem in Tom Pickard's libretto, "The Ballad of Jamie Allan," included in Pickard's recent *The Dark Months of May*. The desperate outlaw hero here beseeches his love, who has bitterly rejected him:

> come with me oh come with me
> come with me my darling
> the berries are red the thorns are sharp
> and the corbies are craawing
> don't send me out don't cut me down
> don't exile me my darling
> let hail lash let snow fall
> let wind rip my body
> the thorns turn red kill the blossom dead
> and the cruel wind is snarling
>
> there is a hawthorn by a wall
> that looks down to the valley
> its berries are red its thorns are sharp
> it's where we'd said we'd marry
> its berries are red its blossom is white
> and the hail makes sharp weather

---

[21] Jorie Graham, "The Dream of the Unified Field," *The Dream of the Unified Field: Selected Poems, 1974–1994* (Hopewell, NJ: Ecco, 1995), sec. 3, 178.

> without her now I'll make my bed
> in the bleeding heather (Tom Pickard, "Hawthorn"[22])

Pickard's "craawing" corbies sing from within a long tradition of black bird song, songs and ballads typically focusing on lost love and death. The corbies' harsh craaw, like the thorns' sharpness, accents the lover's plaint: the roustabout Border renegado Jamie Allen has just been kicked out by his beloved, and this is his plea. Pickard's lines offer a virtuoso orchestration of ballad and song commonplaces: the "come with me" beckoning, the seasonal markers repeated ("the berries are red the thorns are sharp"), the fragments of lines from famous traditional ballads, "I'll make my bed" evoking the fatally poisoned and love-betrayed Lord Randal:

> O I met wi my true-love; mother mak my bed soon,
> For I'm wearied wi huntin, and fain wad lie down.
>   ...
> O yes I am poisoned; mother, mak my bed soon,
> For I'm sick at the heart, and I fain wad lie down.
> (Lord Randal, Child No. 12 A, st. 2, ll. 7–8; st. 6, ll. 24–5)

Jamie Allan, an eighteenth-century horse-thief, outlaw, and famous musician, is a hunted, haunted man; and Pickard (a border-dweller himself, though on the English side) has written a haunted poem – lines marked by the many inflections, innuendos, and formulas of song and story that have preceded and moved through him. We might say too that here Pickard takes the opportunity of singing the song the dead knight might have sung in "The Three Ravens" and "The Twa Corbies": if in those traditional ballads we have birds discussing the situation of the dead, here we have the mortal lover himself, pleading with the beloved, hearing the crows who may soon craaw over his dead body (and perhaps "pike out his bonny blue een"). Like Lord Randal, Pickard's Jamie Allan makes his deathbed testament: "let wind rip my body ... without her now I'll make my bed/in the bleeding heather."

Pickard's reworking of these ballad strains suggests the ongoing vitality of traditional poetry for contemporary poetry; his work, in its delicacy, close listening, utterly contemporary yet deeply grounded tones also exemplifies the richness we may still find in poetries alive to various oral-literate (as well as inter-species) conjunctions. To read, to listen, to encounter such work, is to discover, with Wallace Stevens,

> That the blackbird is involved
> In what I know.

---

[22] Tom Pickard, *The Dark Months of May* (Chicago: Flood Editions, 2004). In 2007 Pickard published his libretto as a book, *The Ballad of Jamie Allan* (Chicago: Flood Editions), which also features the poem "Hawthorn."

Bibliography

PRIMARY SOURCES

Addison, Joseph. *The Spectator*. Nos, 70, 74, 85 [1711]. Vol. I of VI. Ed. Alexander Chalmers. New York: D. Appleton, 1853.

The American Minstrel: Being a Choice Collection of Original and Popular Songs, Glees, Duetts, Choruses, &c. New and rev. edn. With select music. Philadelphia: Henry F. Anners, 1844.

Antin, David. "a private occasion in a public place." *Postmodern American Poetry: A Norton Anthology*. Ed. Paul Hoover. New York and London: W. W. Norton, 1994. 229–46.

Tuning. New York: New Directions, 1984.

Ballads and Songs: Collected by the Missouri Folk-lore Society. Ed. H. M. Belden. Columbia: University of Missouri Press, 1973.

Beattie, James. *The Minstrel; or, The Progress of Genius: A Poem. Book the First*. London and Edinburgh, 1771.

The Minstrel; or, The Progress of Genius: and Other Poems. New York: Barstow, 1821.

Blake, William. *Songs of Innocence and of Experience*. Intro. Geoffrey Keynes. Oxford University Press, 1967.

Border Ballads. Ed., with intro. and notes Graham R. Tomson [pseud. for Rosamund Marriott Watson]. London: Walter Scott, 1888.

Bronson, Bertrand H. *The Traditional Tunes of the Child Ballads*. 4 folio vols. Princeton University Press, 1959–72.

Brooke, Charlotte, *Reliques of Irish Poetry: Consisting of Heroic Poems, Odes, Elegies, and Songs, Translated into English Verse, with Notes Explanatory and Historical; and The Originals in the Irish Character. To which is Subjoined an Irish Tale*. Dublin: J. Christie, 1816; 1st edn. 1789.

Burns, Robert. *The Caledonian Musical Museum, or Complete Vocal Library of the Best Scotch Songs, Ancient and Modern*. The whole edited by his son. 3 vols. London: J. Dick, 1809.

The Canongate Burns. Intro. Andrew Noble. Ed. Andrew Noble and Patrick Scott Hogg. Edinburgh: Canongate Books Limited, 2001.

Byron, George Gordon, Baron. *Childe Harold's Pilgrimage*, in *The Complete Poetical Works*. Ed. Jerome McGann. Vol. II of VII. Oxford University Press, 1980–93.

Child, Francis James, ed. *The English and Scottish Popular Ballads*. 10 vols. Boston: Houghton, Mifflin, 1882–98.
  The English and Scottish Popular Ballads. Corr. 2nd edn. Mark F. Heiman and Laura Saxton Heiman. Vol. I of V. Northfield, MN: Loomis House Press, 2001.
Clare, John. *"I Am": The Selected Poetry of John Clare*. Ed. Jonathan Bate. New York: Farrar, Straus and Giroux, 2003.
A Collection of Old Ballads. Corrected from the Best and Most Ancient Copies Extant. With Introductions Historical, Critical, and Humorous. Illustrated with Copper Plates. London, 1723, 1725.
English and Scottish Popular Ballads. Ed. George Lyman Kittredge and Helen Child Sargent. Boston: Houghton Mifflin, Cambridge edn., 1904, 1932.
The Euing Collection of English Broadside Ballads in the Library of the University of Glasgow. Intro. John Holloway. University of Glasgow, 1971.
Gay, John. *The Shepherd's Week* in *The Poetry and Prose of John Gay*. Ed. Vinton A. Dearing with Charles E. Beckwith. Vol. I of II. Oxford: Clarendon Press, 1974.
Gray, Thomas. "The Bard, A Pindaric Ode." *The Complete English Poems of Thomas Gray*. Ed. James Reeves. London: Heinemann, 1973.
Herd, David. *Ancient and Modern Scotish Songs, Heroic Ballads, Etc.* [Edinburgh, 1769; 2 vols., 1776, rev. 1791] Edinburgh and London: Scottish Academic Press, 1973.
Herder, Johann Gottfried. *Stimmen der völker in liedern*. [Voices of the People in Songs.] Leipzig, 1778–9.
Hogg, James. *Anecdotes of Scott*. Ed. and intro. Jill Rubinstein, with a note by Douglas Mack. Edinburgh University Press, 1999.
  The Collected Letters of James Hogg. Vol. I: 1800–1819. Ed. Gillian Hughes. Edinburgh University Press, 2004.
  The Forest Minstrel: A Selection of Songs Adapted to the Most Favorite Scottish Airs, Few of them ever before Published [1810]. Ed. Peter Garside, Richard Jackson, and Peter Horsfall. New York: Columbia University Press, 2006; 1st edn. Edinburgh: Constable, 1810.
  The Jacobite Relics of Scotland: Being the Songs, Airs, and Legends of the Adherents of the House of Stuart. Collected and Edited by James Hogg. Ed. Murray G. H. Pittock. Edinburgh University Press, 2002–3.
  The Poetic Mirror; or, The Living Bards of Britain. London: Printed for Longman, Hurst, Rees, Orme, and Brown, 1816.
  The Queen's Wake: A Legendary Poem. Ed. Douglas S. Mack. Edinburgh University Press, 2004.
Howe, Susan. "Speeches at the Barriers." *Postmodern American Poetry: A Norton Anthology*. Ed. Paul Hoover. New York and London: W. W. Norton, 1994.
Hughes, Ted. *Crow: From the Life and Songs of the Crow*. London: Faber, 1970.
Hunter, Anne Home. *Poems*. London: T. Payne for T. Bensley, 1802.
The Jacobite Relics of Scotland, being the Songs, Airs, and Legends of the Adherents to the House of Stuart, Collected and Illustrated by James Hogg. Edinburgh: Blackwood; London: Cadell, 1819.

Jamieson, Robert. *Popular Ballads and Songs, from Tradition, Manuscripts, and Scarce Editions, with Translations of Similar Pieces from the Ancient Danish Language, and a Few Originals by the Editor.* 2 vols. Edinburgh: Constable; London: John Murray, 1806.

Johnson, James. *The Scots Musical Museum: Consisting of Upwards of Six Hundred Songs, with Proper Basses for the Pianoforte* [1787–1803]. With illustrations of the lyric poetry and music of Scotland by William Stenhouse. Foreword by Henry George Farmer. Arrangement of most airs by Stephen Clarke. Reprint of the 4-vol. edn. of 1853. Hatboro, PA: Folklore Associates, 1962.

Kinsley, James, ed. *The Oxford Book of Ballads.* Oxford University Press, 1969.

Klancher, Jon P. *The Making of English Reading Audiences, 1790–1832.* Madison, WI: University of Wisconsin Press, 1987.

Letters from Joseph Ritson, Esq. to Mr. George Paton. To Which is Added, A Critique by John Pinkerton, Esq. upon Ritson's Scotish Songs. Edinburgh, 1827.

Marsh's Selection, or, Singing for the Million, Containing the Choicest and Best Collection of Admired Patriotic, Comic, Irish, Negro, Temperance, and Sentimental Songs Ever Embodied in One Work. Three vols. in one. New York: Richard Marsh, 1854.

The Minstrelsy of Britain: or a Glance at our Lyrical Poetry and Poets from the Reign of Queen Elizabeth to the Present Time, Including a Dissertation on the Genius and Lyrics of Burns. By Henry Heavisides. Stockton, 1860.

Minstrelsy of the English Border. Being a Compilation of Ballads, Ancient, Remodelled, and Original, Founded on Well Known Border Legends. With Illustrative Notes. Ed. Frederick Sheldon. London: Longman, 1847.

The Modern Scottish Minstrel; or, the Songs of Scotland of the Past Half Century. Ed. Charles Rogers. 6 vols. Edinburgh: Adam and Charles Black, 1855.

Motherwell, William. *Minstrelsy, Ancient and Modern, with an Historical Introduction and Notes.* Glasgow: John Wylie, 1827.

"Negro Minstrelsy, Ancient and Modern." (J. J. Trux.) *Putnam's Monthly* (January, 1855): 72–9.

The Norton Anthology of Poetry. Ed. Margaret Ferguson, Mary Jo Salter, and John Stallworthy. New York: W. W. Norton, 2005.

Park, Mungo. *Travels in the Interior Districts of Africa.* London: G. and W. Nicol, 1799.

Parry, John. *Antient British Music; or, A Collection of Tunes Never Before Published, which are Retained by the Cambro-Britons, more Particularly in North Wales, and Supposed, by the Learned, to be the Remains of the Music of the Antient Druids, so much Famed in Roman History.* London: J. Parry and Evan Williams, 1742.

The Welsh Harper, being an Extensive Collection of Welsh Music, including Most of the Contents of the Three Volumes Published by the late Edward Jones, called Relics of the Bards, with Numerous Annotations on Historical Subjects. London: D'Almaine, 1848.

Parry, John Douvra. *The Legendary Cabinet: A Collection of British National Ballads, Ancient and Modern, from the Best Authorities, with Notes and Illustrations.* London: W. Joy, 1829.

Peacock, Thomas Love. "The Four Ages of Poetry." *Essays, Memoirs, Letters and Unfinished Novels*, The Halliford Edition of the Collected Works of Thomas Love Peacock. Ed. H. F. B. Brett-Smith and C. E. Jones. Vol. VIII of VIII. New York: AMS Press, 1967.

The Pepys Ballads, 1535–1625. Ed. Hyder Edward Rollins. Vol. I of VIII. Cambridge, MA: Harvard University Press, 1929.

Percy, Thomas, ed. *Reliques of Ancient English Poetry, Consisting of Old Heroic Ballads, Songs, and Other Pieces of our Earlier Poets, Together with Some Few of Later Date*. [Based on the 4th edn, 1794.] Ed. and intro. etc. Henry B. Wheatley. 3 vols. New York: Dover, 1996; London: Swan Sonnenschein, 1886.

Pickard, Tom. *The Ballad of Jamie Allan*. Chicago: Flood Editions, 2007.

The Dark Months of May. Chicago: Flood Editions, 2004.

Pictorial Book of Ancient Ballad Poetry of Great Britain: Historical, Traditional, and Romantic. Ed. J. S. Moore. Vol. I of II. London: Henry Washbourne, 1853.

Pinkerton, John. *Ancient Scotish Poems, Never Before in Print. But now Published from the Ms. Collections of Sir Richard Maitland*. 2 vols. London: Charles Dilly; Edinburgh: William Creech, 1786.

Scotish Tragic Ballads, with A Dissertation on the Oral Tradition in Poetry. London: J. Nichols, 1781.

The Poems of Ossian and Related Works. Ed. Howard Gaskill. Intro. Fiona J. Stafford. Edinburgh University Press, 1996.

Popular British Ballads, Ancient and Modern. Ed. R. Brimley Johnson. London: Dent; Philadelphia: Lippincott, 1894.

The Popular National Songster, and Lucy Neal and Dan Tucker's Delight: A Choice Collection of the most Admired, Patriotic, Comic, Irish, Negro, and Sentimental Songs. Philadelphia: John B. Perry, 1845.

Ramsay, Allan. *The Ever Green, being a Collection of Scots Poems, Wrote by the Ingenious before 1600 [1724]*. Glasgow: James Cameron, 1824.

Tea-Table Miscellany: A Collection of Choice Songs, Scots & English [1724]. 14th edn. Glasgow: Robert Forrester, 1876.

Ravenscroft, Thomas. *Melismata: Musicall Phansies. Fitting the Court, Cittie, and Countrey Humours*. London, 1611.

Reed, James, ed. *Border Ballads: A Selection*. Manchester: Carcanet Press, 1991.

Report of the Committee of the Highland Society of Scotland, Appointed to Inquire into the Nature and Authenticity of the Poems of Ossian. Drawn up, According to the Directions of the Committee, by Henry Mackenzie, Esq. Its Convener or Chairman. With a Copious Appendix, Containing some of the Principal Documents on which the Report is Founded. Edinburgh: University Press for Constable; London: Longman, 1805.

Ritson, Joseph. *Ancient Songs from the Time of King Henry the Third to the Revolution*. London: printed for J. Johnson, 1790. With "Observations on the Ancient English Minstrels" appended.

The Bishopric Garland, in *Northern Garlands*. London: R. Triphook, 1810.

Gammer Gurton's Garland: or, the Nursery Parnassus. A Choice Collection of Pretty Songs and Verses, for the Amusement of All Little Good Children who can Neither Read nor Run. London: R. Triphook, 1810.

Scotish Song in Two Volumes. London: J. Johnson, 1794.

A Select Collection of English Songs. In Three Volumes. With an Historical Essay on the Origin and Progress of National Song. London: J. Johnson, 1783.

Romantic Women Poets, 1770–1838. Ed. Andrew Ashfield. Vol. I of II. Manchester and New York: Manchester University Press, 1997.

Rothenberg, Jerome. "New Models, New Visions: Some Notes toward a Poetics of Performance" [1977]. *Postmodern American Poetry: A Norton Anthology.* Ed. Paul Hoover. New York and London: W. W. Norton, 1994. 640–4.

The Roxburghe Ballads. Ed. William Chapell and J. Woodfall Ebsworth. 8 vols. Hertford: Stephen Austin and Sons, 1895.

[Scott, Walter, ed.] *English Minstrelsy: Being a Selection of Fugitive Poetry from the Best English Authors; with some Original Pieces Hitherto Unpublished.* 2 vols. Edinburgh: John Ballantyne; London: John Murray, 1810.

Scott, Walter. *The Lay of the Last Minstrel.* London: Longman, Hurst; Edinburgh: Constable, 1805.

Minstrelsy of the Scottish Border: Consisting of Historical and Romantic Ballads, Collected in the Southern Counties of Scotland. 2 vols. Kelso: Ballantyne/Cadell; London: Davies, 1802.

The Poetical Works of Walter Scott, Bart. together with the Minstrelsy of the Scottish Border. With the Author's Introductions and Notes [Magnum Opus 1830–3 edn.]. New York: Leavitt and Allen, n.d.

Shelley, Percy Bysshe. "A Defence of Poetry." *Shelley's Poetry and Prose.* Ed. Donald H. Reiman and Sharon Powers. New York: Norton, 1977. 480–508.

Smith, Adam. *The Wealth of Nations.* Intro. Andrew Skinner. 2 vols. Harmondsworth: Penguin, 1997.

Stein, Gertrude. *History or Messages from History.* Copenhagen: Green Integer, 1997.

Stevens, Wallace. *The Collected Poems of Wallace Stevens.* New York: Vintage, 1982.

Tyler, Royall. *The Contrast: A Comedy in Five Acts.* Boston and New York: Houghton Mifflin, 1920; first published Philadelphia: Pritchard and Hall, 1790.

White, Newman I. *American Negro Folk Songs.* Cambridge, MA: Harvard University Press, 1928.

Wolff, Rebecca. *Figment.* New York: Norton, 2004.

Wordsworth, William. *Essay, Supplementary to the Preface. The Prose Works of William Wordsworth.* Ed. W. J. B. Owen and J. W. Smyser. Vol. III of III. London: Oxford University Press, 1974.

Shorter Poems, 1807–1820, by William Wordsworth. Ed. Carl H. Ketcham. Ithaca, NY: Cornell University Press, 1989.

"The Solitary Reaper." *Poems, in Two Volumes, and Other Poems, 1800–1807, by William Wordsworth.* Ed. Jared Curtis. Ithaca: Cornell University Press, 1983. 184–5.

"Song, at the Feast of Brougham Castle, Upon the Restoration of Lord Clifford, the Shepherd, to the Estates and Honours of his Ancestors." *Poems, in Two Volumes and Other Poems, 1800–1807.* Ed. Jared Curtis. Ithaca: Cornell University Press, 1983. 263–4.

Sonnet Series and Itinerary Poems, 1820–1845, by William Wordsworth. Ed. Geoffrey Jackson. Ithaca, NY: Cornell University Press, 2004.

The Thirteen Book Prelude. Ed. Mark L. Reed. Ithaca, NY and London: Cornell University Press, 1991.

Wordsworth, William, and Samuel Taylor Coleridge. *Lyrical Ballads.* Ed. R. L. Brett and A. R. Jones. 2nd edn. London and New York: Routledge, 1991.

HISTORICAL, CRITICAL, AND THEORETICAL WORKS

Anderson, Benedict. *Imagined Communities: Reflections on the Origin and Spread of Nationalism.* Rev. edn. London and New York: Verso, 1991.

Bakhtin, Mikhail. *The Dialogic Imagination: Four Essays by M. M. Bakhtin.* Ed. Michael Holquist. Trans. Caryl Emerson and Michael Holquist. Austin: University of Texas Press, 1981.

Ballads into Books: The Legacies of Francis James Child. Ed. Tom Cheesman and Sigrid Rieuwerts. Bern: Peter Lang, 1997.

Bean, Annemarie, James V. Hatch, and Brooks McNamara, ed. *Inside the Minstrel Mask: Readings in Nineteenth-Century Blackface Minstrelsy.* Foreword Mel Watkins. Wesleyan University Press, 1996.

Benjamin, Walter. "Theses on the Philosophy of History." *Illuminations.* Trans. Harry Zohn. Ed. Hannah Arendt. New York: Schocken Books, 1969.

Benveniste, Emile. "Subjectivity in Language." *Problems in General Linguistics.* Trans. Mary Elizabeth Meek. Miami Linguistics Series No. 8. Coral Gables, FL: University of Miami Press, 1971.

Bernstein, Charles, ed. *Close Listening: Poetry and the Performed Word.* Oxford University Press, 1998.

Bettany, G. T. "Hunter, Anne (1742–1821)." Rev. M. Clare Loughlin-Chow. In *Oxford Dictionary of National Biography.* Ed. H. C. G. Matthew and Brian Harrison. Oxford University Press, 2004. www.oxforddnb.com/view/article/14215 (accessed October 17, 2006).

Bewell, Alan. *Wordsworth and the Enlightenment: Nature, Man, and Society in the Experimental Poetry.* New Haven, CT: Yale University Press, 1989.

Bhabha, Homi. *The Location of Culture.* London and New York: Routledge, 1994.

Bialostosky, Don H. *Making Tales: The Poetics of Wordsworth's Narrative Experiments.* University of Chicago Press, 1984.

Bloom, Harold. "The Internalization of Quest-Romance." *Romanticism and Consciousness: Essays in Criticism.* New York: Norton, 1970. 3–24.

Bohlman, Philip V. "Ontologies of Music." *Rethinking Music.* Ed. Nicholas Cook and Mark Everist. Oxford University Press, 2001. 17–34.

World Music: A Very Short Introduction. Oxford University Press, 2002.

Bourdieu, Pierre. *Distinction: A Social Critique of the Judgment of Taste*. Trans. Richard Nice. London: Routledge & Kegan Paul, 1986.

The Rules of Art: Genesis and Structure of the Literary Field. Trans. Susan Emanuel. Stanford University Press, 1996.

Brady, Erika. *The Spiral Way: How the Phonograph Changed Ethnography*. Jackson: University Press of Mississippi, 1999.

Brickman, Celia. *Aboriginal Populations in the Mind: Race and Primitivity in Psychoanalysis*. Columbia University Press, 2003.

Bromwich, David. *Disowned by Memory: Wordsworth's Poetry of the 1790s*. University of Chicago Press, 1998.

Brown, A. Peter. "Musical Settings of Anne Hunter's Poetry: From National Song to Canzonetta." *Journal of the American Musicological Society* 46.1 (Spring, 1994): 39–89.

Brown, Marshall. "Passion and Love: Anacreontic Song and the Roots of Romantic Lyric." *ELH* 66.2 (1999): 373–404.

Brown, Mary Ellen. *Burns and Tradition*. London: Macmillan, 1984.

"The Mechanism of the Ancient Ballad: William Motherwell's Explanation." *Oral Tradition* 11 (1996): 175–89.

"Placed, Replaced, or Misplaced? The Ballads' Progress." *The Eighteenth Century: Theory and Interpretation* 47.2/3 (Summer/Fall, 2006): 115–29.

William Motherwell's Cultural Politics, 1797–1835. Lexington, KY: Kentucky University Press, 2001.

Buchan, David. *The Ballad and the Folk*. East Linton: Tuckwell Press, 1997; 1st edn. London: Routledge & Kegan Paul, 1972.

Butler, Marilyn. "Antiquarianism (Popular)," Essay 35. *An Oxford Companion to the Romantic Age: British Culture 1776–1832*. Ed. Iain McCalman et al. Oxford University Press, 1999. 328–37.

"Culture's Medium: The Role of the Review." *The Cambridge Companion to British Romanticism*. Ed. Stuart Curran. Cambridge University Press, 1993. 120–47.

"Myth and Mythmaking in the Shelley Circle." *Shelley Revalued: Essays from the Gregynog Conference*. Ed. Kelvin Everest. New York: Barnes and Noble, 1983. 1–19.

Romantics, Rebels, and Reactionaries: English Literature and its Background 1760–1830. Oxford University Press, 1981.

Casanova, Pascale. *The World Republic of Letters*. Trans. M. B. DeBevoise. Cambridge, MA: Harvard University Press, 2004.

Chakrabarty, Dipesh. *Provincializing Europe: Postcolonial Thought and Historical Difference*. Princeton University Press, 2000.

Chandler, David. "Hart-Leap Well: A History of the Site of Wordsworth's Poem." *Notes and Queries* (March, 2002): 19–25.

"The Politics of 'Hart-Leap Well.'" *Charles Lamb Bulletin* NS 111 (July 2000): 109–19.

Chandler, James. *England in 1819: The Politics of Literary Culture and the Case of Romantic Historicism*. University of Chicago Press, 1998.

Clifford, James. *The Predicament of Culture: Twentieth-Century Ethnography, Literature, and Art*. Cambridge, MA: Harvard University Press, 1988.

Colley, Linda. *Britons: Forging the Nation, 1707–1837*. New Haven, CT: Yale University Press, 1992.

Connell, Philip. "British Identities and the Politics of Ancient Poetry in Later Eighteenth-Century England." *The Historical Journal* 49.1 (2006): 161–92.

Craig, Cairns. *Out of History: Narrative Paradigms in Scottish and English Culture*. Edinburgh: Polygon, 1996.

Crawford, Richard. *America's Musical Life: A History*. New York and London: Norton, 2001.

Crawford, Robert. *Devolving English Literature*. Rev. edn. Edinburgh University Press, 2000; 1992.

   The Modern Poet: Poetry, Academia, and Knowledge since the 1750s. Oxford University Press, 2001.

Crawford, Robert, ed. *The Scottish Invention of English Literature*. Cambridge University Press, 1998.

Curran, Stuart. "Women Readers, Women Writers." *The Cambridge Companion to British Romanticism*. Ed. Stuart Curran. Cambridge University Press, 1993. 177–95.

Davis, Leith. *Acts of Union: Scotland and the Literary Negotiation of the British Nation, 1707–1830*. Stanford University Press, 1998.

   Music, Postcolonialism, and Gender: The Construction of Irish National Identity, 1724–1874. Notre Dame, IN: University of Notre Dame Press, 2006.

Davis, Leith, and Maureen N. McLane. "Orality and Public Poetry." *The Edinburgh History of Scottish Literature, Vol. II: Enlightenment, Britain, and Empire (1707–1918)*. Ed. Susan Manning et al. Edinburgh University Press, 2007. 125–32.

De Certeau, Michel. *The Writing of History*. Trans. Tom Conley. New York: Columbia University Press, 1988.

DuBois, Thomas A. *Lyric, Meaning, and Audience in the Oral Tradition of Northern Europe*. University of Notre Dame Press, 2006.

Dugaw, Dianne. "Anglo-American Folksong Reconsidered: The Interface of Oral and Written Forms." *Western Folklore* 43 (1984): 83–103.

   "Deep Play": John Gay and the Invention of Modernity. Newark: University of Delaware Press; London: Associated University Presses, 2001.

   "On the 'Darling Songs' of Poets, Scholars, and Singers: An Introduction." *The Eighteenth Century: Theory and Interpretation*. 47.2/3 (Summer/Fall, 2006): 97–113.

   "The Popular Marketing of 'Old Ballads': The Ballad Revival and Eighteenth-century Antiquarianism Reconsidered." *Eighteenth-Century Studies* 21 (1987): 71–90.

Duncan, Ian. "Authenticity Effects: The Work of Fiction in Romantic Scotland," *The South Atlantic Quarterly* 102.1 (Winter, 2003): 93–116.

Modern Romance and Transformations of the Novel: The Gothic, Scott, Dickens. Cambridge University Press, 1992.

"The Upright Corpse: Hogg, National Literature, and the Uncanny." *Studies in Hogg and his World* 5 (1994): 29–54.

Duncan, Ian, and Douglas Mack. "Hogg, Galt, Scott and their Milieu." *The Edinburgh History of Scottish Literature, Vol. II: Enlightenment, Britain, and Empire (1707–1918).* Ed. Susan Manning et al. Edinburgh University Press, 2007. 211–20.

1800: The New Lyrical Ballads. Ed. Nicola Trott and Seamus Perry. Basingstoke, Hampshire and New York: Palgrave, 2001.

Erickson, Lee. *The Economy of Literary Form: English Literature and the Industrialization of Publishing, 1800–1850.* Baltimore and London: Johns Hopkins University Press, 1996.

Fabian, Johannes. *Time and the Other: How Anthropology Makes its Object.* New York: Columbia University Press, 1983.

Ferris, Ina. *The Achievement of Literary Authority: Gender, History, and the Waverley Novels.* Ithaca, NY: Cornell University Press, 1991.

Fielding, Penny. *Scotland and the Fictions of Geography: North Britain 1760–1840.* Cambridge University Press, 2008.

Writing and Orality: Nationality, Culture, and Nineteenth-Century Scottish Fiction. Oxford and New York: Clarendon Press, 1996.

Finnegan, Ruth. *Oral Poetry: Its Nature, Significance, and Social Context.* Reissued, Bloomington and Indianapolis: Indiana University Press, 1992.

Foley, John Miles. *How to Read an Oral Poem.* Urbana: University of Illinois Press, 2002.

Foucault, Michel. *The Archaeology of Knowledge and the Discourse on Language.* Trans. A. M. Sheridan Smith. New York: Pantheon, 1972.

Fox, Adam. *Oral and Literate Culture in England: 1500–1700.* Oxford University Press, 2000.

Friedman, Albert B. *The Ballad Revival: Studies in the Influence of Popular on Sophisticated Poetry.* University of Chicago Press, 1961.

Fulford, Tim. *Romantic Indians: Native Americans, British Literature, and Transatlantic Culture, 1756–1830.* Oxford University Press, 2006.

Gaskill, Howard, ed. *The Reception of Ossian in Europe.* London and New York: Thoemmes/Continuum, 2004.

Gates, Barbara T. "Wordsworth's Use of Oral History." *Folklore* 85.4 (Winter, 1974): 254–67.

Gerould, Gordon Hall. *The Ballad of Tradition.* Oxford: Clarendon Press, 1932.

Ginzburg, Carlo. "Morelli, Freud and Sherlock Holmes: Clues and Scientific Method." *History Workshop: A Journal of Socialist Historians* 9 (Spring, 1980): 5–36.

Gioia, Dana. *Can Poetry Matter?: Essays on Poetry and American Culture.* 10th anniversary edn. St. Paul, MN: Graywolf Press, 2002.

Disappearing Ink: Poetry at the End of Print Culture. St. Paul, MN: Graywolf Press, 2004.

Gitelman, Lisa. *Always Already New: Media, History, and the Data of Culture.* Cambridge, MA: MIT Press, 2006.

  Scripts, Grooves, and Writing Machines: Representing Technology in the Edison Era. Stanford University Press, 1999.

Gitelman, Lisa and Geoffrey Pingree, eds. *New Media 1740–1915.* Cambridge, MA: MIT Press, 2003.

Goodman, Kevis. *Georgic Modernity and British Romanticism: Poetry and the Mediation of History.* Cambridge University Press, 2004.

Goody, Jack. *The Domestication of the Savage Mind.* Cambridge University Press, 1977.

Goslee, Nancy Moore, *Scott the Rhymer.* Lexington, KY: University Press of Kentucky, 1988.

Grafton, Anthony. *The Footnote: A Curious History.* Cambridge, MA: Harvard University Press; London: Faber and Faber, 1997; paperback edn. 2003.

Groom, Nick. *The Making of Percy's "Reliques."* Oxford University Press, 1999.

Guillory, John. *Cultural Capital: The Problem of Literary Canon Formation.* University of Chicago Press, 1993.

  Poetic Authority: Spenser, Milton, and Literary History. New York: Columbia University Press, 1983.

Harker, Dave. *Fakesong: The Manufacture of British 'Folksong' 1700 to the Present Day.* Milton Keynes and Philadelphia: Open University Press, 1985.

Harris, Joseph, ed. *The Ballad and Oral Literature.* Cambridge, MA: Harvard University Press, 1991.

Hartman, Geoffrey H. *The Unremarkable Wordsworth.* Foreword Donald G. Marshall. London: Methuen, 1987.

Havelock, Eric A. *The Muse Learns to Write: Reflections on Orality and Literacy from Antiquity to the Present.* New Haven, CT: Yale University Press, 1986.

Hayles, N. Katherine. *Writing Machines.* Cambridge, MA: MIT Press, 2002.

Hazlitt, William. "On the Living Poets." *Lectures on the English Poets in The Complete Works of William Hazlitt.* Vol. V of XX. Ed. B. P. Howe. London and Toronto: J. M. Dent, 1930.

Hewitt, David. "Scott, Sir Walter (1771–1832)." The *Oxford Dictionary of National Biography.* Ed. H. C. G. Matthew and Brian Harrison. Oxford University Press, 2004. Online edn., ed. Lawrence Goldman, May 2006. www.oxforddnb.com/view/article/24928 (accessed October 17, 2006).

Hudson, Nicholas. "Constructing Oral Tradition: The Origins of a Concept in Enlightenment Intellectual Culture." *The Spoken Word: Oral Culture in Britain, 1500–1850.* Ed. Adam Fox and Daniel Woolf. Manchester University Press, 2002. 240–55.

  "Oral Tradition: The Evolution of an Eighteenth-Century Concept." *Tradition in Transition: Women Writers, Marginal Texts, and the Eighteenth-Century Canon.* Ed. Alvara Ribeiro, S J and James G. Basker. Oxford: Clarendon Press, 1996. 161–76.

Humphries, Charles, and William C. Smith. *Music Publishing in the British Isles from the Earliest Times to the Middle of the Nineteenth Century.* London: Cassell and Co., 1954.

Hustvedt, Sigrid. *Ballad Criticism in Scandinavia and Great Britain during the Eighteenth Century.* London: Oxford University Press, 1916.

Jakobson, Roman. "Closing Statements: Linguistics and Poetics." *Style In Language.* Ed. Thomas A. Sebeok. Cambridge MA: MIT Press, 1960. 350–77.

Jameson, Fredric. *The Political Unconscious: Narrative as a Socially Symbolic Act.* Ithaca, NY: Cornell University Press, 1981.

Janowitz, Anne F. *Lyric and Labor in the Romantic Tradition.* Cambridge University Press, 1998.

Kidd, Colin. *British Identities before Nationalism: Ethnicity and Nationhood in the Atlantic World, 1600–1800.* Cambridge University Press, 1999.

   Subverting Scotland's Past: Scottish Whig Historians and the Creation of an Anglo-British Identity, 1689–c. 1830. Cambridge University Press, 2003.

Kittler, Friedrich. *Discourse Networks, 1800/1900.* Trans. Michael Metteer and Chris Cullens. Foreword David Wellbery. Stanford University Press, 1990.

   Gramophone, Film, Typewriter. Trans. Geoffrey Winthrop-Young and Michael Wutz. Stanford University Press, 1999.

Koegel, John. "'The Indian Chief' and 'Morality': An Eighteenth-Century British Popular Song Transformed into a Nineteenth-Century American Shape-Note Hymn." In Malcom Cole and John Koegel, eds. *Music in Performance and Society: Essays in Honor of Roland Jackson.* Warren, MI: Harmonie Park Press, 1997. 435–508.

Kucich, Greg. *Keats, Shelley, and Romantic Spenserianism.* University Park, PA: Pennsylvania State University Press, 1991.

Langan, Celeste. "Scotch Drink & Irish Harps: Mediations of the National Air." In *The Figure of Music in Nineteenth-Century British Poetry.* Ed. Phyllis Weliver. Aldershot and Burlington, VT: Ashgate, 2005. 25–49.

   "Understanding Media in 1805: Audiovisual Hallucination in *The Lay of the Last Minstrel.*" *Studies in Romanticism* 40.1 (Spring, 2001): 49–70.

Laughlin, Corinna. "The Lawless Language of Macpherson's *Ossian.*" *Studies in English Literature* 40.3 (Summer, 2000): 511–37.

Leask, Nigel. "Scotland's Literature of Empire and Emigration, 1707–1918." *The Edinburgh History of Scottish Literature, Vol. II: Enlightenment, Britain, and Empire (1707–1918).* Ed. Susan Manning et al. Edinburgh University Press, 2007. 153–68.

Lévi-Strauss, Claude. *The Savage Mind,* University of Chicago Press, 1966.

   "A Writing Lesson." *Tristes Tropiques.* Trans. John and Doreen Weightman. New York: Penguin, 1992.

Lhamon, W. T., Jr. *Raising Cain: Blackface Performance from Jim Crow to Hip Hop.* Cambridge, MA: Harvard University Press, 1998.

Lockhart, J. G. *Narrative of the Life of Sir Walter Scott, Begun by Himself and Continued.* London and Toronto: J. M. Dent; NY: E. P. Dutton, 1915.

Lomax, Alan. *Alan Lomax: Selected Writings, 1934–1997.* Ed. Ronald D. Cohen, with introductory essays by Gage Averill et al. New York: Routledge, 2003.

Lomax, John. *Adventures of a Ballad Hunter.* New York: Macmillan, 1947.

Lord, Albert. *The Singer of Tales.* 2nd edn. Ed. Gregory Nagy and Stephen Mitchell. Cambridge, MA: Harvard University Press, 2000.

Lott, Eric. *Love and Theft: Blackface Minstrelsy and the American Working Class.* Oxford University Press, 1993.

Lyle, Emily, ed. and intro. *Scottish Ballads.* Edinburgh: Canongate Press, 1994.

Manning, Peter. "'Will No One Tell Me What She Sings?': *The Solitary Reaper* and the Contexts of Criticism." *Reading Romantics: Texts and Contexts.* Oxford University Press, 1990. 241–72.

Manning, Susan. "Antiquarianism, Balladry and the Rehabilitation of Romance." *The Cambridge History of English Romantic Literature.* Ed. James Chandler. Cambridge University Press, 2008.

Fragments of Union: Making Connections in Scottish and American Writing. New York: Palgrave, 2002.

"Notes from the Margin: Antiquarianism, the Scottish Science of Man, and the Emergence of Disciplinarity." *Scotland and The Borders of Romanticism,* Eds. Leith Davis, Ian Duncan, and Janet Sorensen. Cambridge University Press, 2004. 57–76.

"Ossianic Testimonies: Mackenzie's Highland Society Report and the Nature of Literary Evidence." Lecture, May 2003 (private communication).

"Post-Union Scotland and the Scottish Idiom of Britishness." *The Edinburgh History of Scottish Literature, Vol. II: Enlightenment, Britain, and Empire (1707–1918).* Ed. Susan Manning et al. Edinburgh University Press, 2007. 45–56.

Marcus, George. "Contemporary Problems of Ethnography in the Modern World System." *Writing Culture: The Poetics and Politics of Ethnography.* Ed. James Clifford and George E. Marcus. A School of American Research Advanced Seminar. University of California Press, 1986.

Marcus, Greil, and Sean Wilentz, eds. *The Rose and The Briar: Death, Love, and Liberty in the American Ballad.* New York: W. W. Norton, 2005.

McDowell, Paula. "'The Art of Printing Was Fatal': Print Culture and the Idea of Oral Tradition in Eighteenth-Century Ballad Discourse." In *Straws in the Wind: Ballads and Broadsides 1500–1800.* Ed. Patricia Fumerton and Anita Guerrini. Aldershot: Ashgate Press, 2008.

"'The Manufacture and Lingua-Franca of *Ballad-Making*': Broadside Ballads in Long Eighteenth-Century Ballad Discourse." *The Eighteenth Century: Theory and Interpretation* 47.2/3 (Summer/Fall 2006): 151–78.

The Women of Grub Street: Press, Politics and Gender in the Literary Marketplace, 1678–1830. Oxford and New York: Clarendon Press, 1998.

"Writing Scotland: Robert Burns." *The Edinburgh History of Scottish Literature, Vol. II: Enlightenment, Britain, and Empire (1707–1918).* Ed. Susan Manning et al. Edinburgh University Press, 2007. 178–82.

McDowell, Paula, ed. *Critical Essays on Robert Burns.* New York: G. K. Hall; London: Prentice Hall International, 1998.

McLane, Maureen N. *Romanticism and the Human Sciences: Poetry, Population, and the Discourse of the Species.* Cambridge University Press, 2000; pbk edn. 2006.

"Romanticism, or, Now: Learning to Read in Postmodern," *Modern Philology* (Special issue on "The Future of Poetry Criticism") 105:1 (August 2007): 118–56.

McLane, Maureen N., and Celeste Langan. "The Medium of Romantic Poetry." In *The Cambridge Companion to British Romantic Poetry*. Ed. James Chandler and Maureen N. McLane. Cambridge University Press, 2008, 239–62.

McLuhan, Marshall. *The Gutenberg Galaxy: The Making of Typographic Man.* Toronto: University of Toronto Press, 1966.

    Understanding Media: The Extensions of Man. Intro. Lewis H. Lapham. Cambridge, MA: MIT Press, 1994.

Mitchell, W. J. T. *Blake's Composite Art: A Study of the Illuminated Poetry.* Princeton, NJ: Princeton University Press, 1978.

Momigliano, A. D. "Ancient History and the Antiquarian." *Studies in Historiography.* London: Weidenfeld and Nicolson, 1966. 1–39.

Orden, Kate van, ed. *Music and the Cultures of Print.* Afterword Roger Chartier. New York and London: Garland, 2000.

Nagy, Gregory. *Poetry as Performance: Homer and Beyond.* Cambridge University Press, 1996.

Newman, Gerald. *The Rise of English Nationalism: A Cultural History, 1740–1830.* Rev. edn. New York: St. Martin's, 1997.

Newman, Steve. *Ballad Collection, Lyric, and the Canon: The Call of the Popular from the Restoration to the New Criticism.* Philadelphia: University of Pennsylvania Press, 2007.

Oliver, Susan. *Scott, Byron, and the Poetics of Cultural Encounter.* New York: Palgrave Macmillan, 2005.

Ong, Walter J. *Orality and Literacy: The Technologizing of the Word.* London and New York: Routledge, 1982.

Paglia, Camille. *Break, Blow, Burn: Camille Paglia Reads Forty-Three of the World's Best Poems.* New York: Pantheon, 2005.

Perkins, David. "How the Romantics Recited Poetry." *Studies in English Literature, 1500–1900* 31.4, The Nineteenth Century (Autumn, 1991): 655–71.

    "Wordsworth and the Polemic Against Hunting: 'Hart-Leap Well.'" *Nineteenth-Century Literature* 52.4 (March, 1998): 421–45.

Perloff, Marjorie. "'No More Margins': John Cage, David Antin, and the Poetry of Performance." *The Poetics of Indeterminacy: Rimbaud to Cage.* Princeton University Press, 1981. 288–340.

Phillips, Mark Salber. "Reconsiderations on History and Antiquarianism: Arnaldo Momigliano and the Historiography of Eighteenth-Century Britain." *Journal of the History of Ideas* 57.2 (1996): 297–316.

    Society and Sentiment: Genres of Historical Writing in Britain, 1740–1820. Princeton University Press, 2000.

Piggott, Stuart. *Ruins in a Landscape: Essays in Antiquarianism.* Edinburgh University Press, 1976.

Pittock, Murray G. H. *Inventing and Resisting Britain: Cultural Identities in Britain and Ireland, 1685–1789.* New York: Houndmills, 1997.

The Invention of Scotland: Stuart Myth and the Scottish Identity, 1638 to the Present. New York: Routledge, 1991.

"Scottish Song and the Jacobite Cause." *The Edinburgh History of Scottish Literature, Vol. II: Enlightenment, Britain, and Empire (1707–1918)*. Ed. Susan Manning et al. Edinburgh University Press, 2007. 105–9.

Poovey, Mary. *A History of the Modern Fact: Problems of Knowledge in the Sciences of Wealth and Society*. University of Chicago Press, 1998.

Porter, Susan L. "'Children in the Wood': The Odyssey of an Anglo-American Ballad." *Vistas of American Music: Essays and Compositions in Honor of William K. Kearns*. Ed. Susan L. Porter and John Graziano. Warren, MI: Harmonie Park Press, 1999. 77–96.

Rajan, Tilottama. "The Eye/I of the Other: Self and Audience in Wordsworth's *Lyrical Ballads*." In *The Supplement of Reading: Figures of Understanding in Romantic Theory and Practice*. Ithaca, NY: Cornell University Press, 1990. 136–66.

Rawson, Claude. "Unparodying and Forgery: The Augustan Chatterton." *Thomas Chatterton and Romantic Culture*. Ed. Nick Groom. London: Macmillan; New York: St. Martin's, 1999. 15–31.

Remediation: Understanding New Media. Ed. Jay David Bolter and Richard Grusin. Cambridge, MA: MIT Press, 1999.

Rethinking Media Change: The Aesthetics of Transition. Ed. David Thorburn and Henry Jenkins, assoc. ed. Brad Seawell. Cambridge, MA: MIT Press, 2003.

Rogin, Michael. *Blackface, White Noise: Jewish Immigrants in the Hollywood Melting Pot*. Berkeley: University of California Press, 1996.

Rothenberg, Jerome. "New Models, New Visions: Some Notes toward a Poetics of Performance" [1977]. *Postmodern American Poetry: A Norton Anthology*. Ed. Paul Hoover. New York and London: W. W. Norton, 1994. 640–4.

Rothenberg, Jerome, ed. *Technicians of the Sacred: A Range of Poetries from Africa, America, Asia, Europe & Oceania*. 2nd edn. Berkeley: University of California Press, 1985.

Rothschild, Emma. *Economic Sentiments: Adam Smith, Condorcet, and the Enlightenment*. Cambridge, MA: Harvard University Press, 2001.

Rowland, Ann Wierda. "'The Fause Nourice Sang': Childhood, Child Murder, and the Formalism of the Scottish Ballad Revival." *Scotland and the Borders of Romanticism*. Ed. Leith Davis, Ian Duncan, and Janet Sorensen. Cambridge University Press, 2004. 225–44.

"Romantic Poetry and the Romantic Novel." *The Cambridge Companion to British Romantic Poetry*. Ed. James Chandler and Maureen N. McLane. Cambridge University Press, 2008, 117–35.

Russett, Margaret. *Fictions and Fakes: Forging Romantic Authenticity, 1760–1845*. Cambridge University Press, 2005.

Schiller, Friedrich. *Naive and Sentimental Poetry, and On the Sublime: Two Essays*. Trans. with intro. and notes Julius A. Elias. New York: F. Ungar Pub. Co., 1966.

Selected Bibliography: James Macpherson and Ossian. Richard B. Sher, with Dafydd Moore. New Jersey Institute of Technology. www.c18.org/biblio/macpherson/html (last revised March 13, 2004, accessed April 2, 2007).

Sher, Richard. *The Enlightenment and the Book: Scottish Authors and their Publishers in Eighteenth-century Britain, Ireland, and America.* University of Chicago Press, 2006.

Simpson, Erik. "Minstrelsy Goes to Market: Prize Poems, Minstrel Contests, and Romantic Poetry." *ELH* 71.3 (2004): 691–718.

Siskin, Clifford. *The Work of Writing: Literature and Social Change in Britain 1700–1830.* Baltimore, MD: Johns Hopkins University Press, 1998.

Smout, T. C. "Scotland as North Britain: The Historical Background, 1707–1918." *The Edinburgh History of Scottish Literature, Vol. II: Enlightenment, Britain, and Empire (1707–1918).* Ed. Susan Manning et al. Edinburgh University Press, 2007. 1–11.

Sorensen, Janet. *The Grammar of Empire in Eighteenth-Century British Writing.* Cambridge University Press, 2000.

St. Clair, William. *The Reading Nation in the Romantic Period.* Cambridge University Press, 2004.

Stafford, Fiona J. *The Last of the Race: The Growth of a Myth from Milton to Darwin.* Oxford: Clarendon Press, 1994.

Stafford, Fiona J., and Howard Gaskill, eds. *From Gaelic to Romantic: Ossianic Translations.* Amsterdam: Rodopi, 1998.

Starr, G. Gabrielle. *Lyric Generations: Poetry and the Novel in the Long Eighteenth Century.* Baltimore, MD: Johns Hopkins University Press, 2004.

Stewart, Susan. *Crimes of Writing: Problems in the Containment of Representation.* Durham and London: Duke University Press, 1994.

Poetry and the Fate of the Senses. University of Chicago Press, 2002.

Sutherland, John. *The Life of Walter Scott: A Critical Biography.* Oxford and Cambridge, MA: Blackwell, 1995.

Sutherland, Kathryn. "The Native Poet: The Influence of Percy's Minstrel from Beattie to Wordsworth." *Review of English Studies* New Series 33 (132) (November, 1982): 414–33.

Sweet, Rosemary. "Antiquaries and Antiquities in Eighteenth-Century England." *Eighteenth-Century Studies* 34.2 (2001): 181–206.

Antiquaries: The Discovery of the Past in Eighteenth-Century Britain. London and New York: Hambledon and London, 2004.

Trevor-Roper, Hugh. "The Invention of Tradition: The Highland Tradition of Scotland." In *The Invention of Tradition.* Ed. Eric Hobsbawm and Terence Ranger. Cambridge University Press, 1984. 15–41.

Trumpener, Katie. *Bardic Nationalism: The Romantic Novel and the British Empire.* Princeton University Press, 1997.

White, Hayden. *Metahistory: The Historical Imagination in Nineteenth-Century Europe.* Baltimore and London: Johns Hopkins University Press, 1973, 1987.

Wickman, Matthew. "The Allure of the Improbable: *Fingal*, Evidence, and the Testimony of the 'Echoing Heath.'" *PMLA* 155.2 (March, 2000): 181–94.

Wilgus, D. K. and Barre Toelken. *The Ballad and the Scholars: Approaches to Ballad Study: Papers Presented at a Clark Library Seminar, October 22, 1983.* Los Angeles, CA: William Andrews Clark Memorial Library, University of California, 1986.

Williams, Raymond. *Marxism and Literature.* Oxford University Press, 1977.

Winthrop-Young, Geoffrey. "Drill and Distraction in the Yellow Submarine: On the Dominance of War in Friedrich Kittler's Media Theory." *Critical Inquiry* 28.4 (Summer, 2002): 825–54.

Writing American Indian Music: Historical Transcriptions, Notations, and Arrangements. Ed. Victoria Lindsay Levine. Published for the American Musicological Society. Middleton, WI: A-R Editions, 2002.

Writing Culture: The Poetics and Politics of Ethnography. Ed. James Clifford and George E. Marcus. A School of American Research Advanced Seminar. University of California Press, 1986.

Index

CAMBRIDGE STUDIES IN ROMANTICISM

General Editors
Marilyn Butler, *University of Oxford*
James Chandler, *University of Chicago*

Lightning Source UK Ltd.
Milton Keynes UK
UKOW030628260112

186096UK00002B/9/P

9 780521 349505